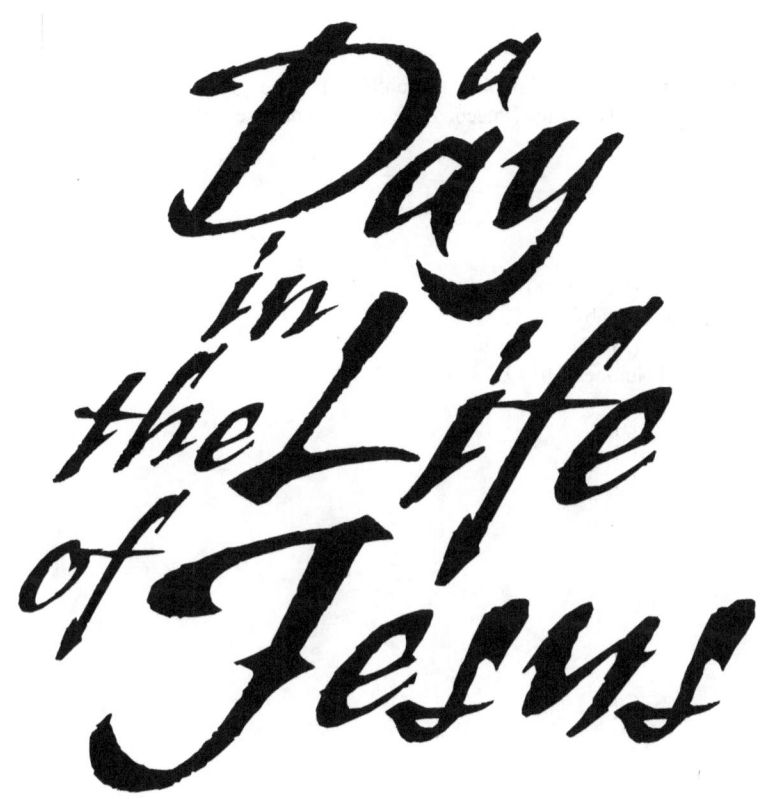

A Day in the Life of Jesus

Dennis Nickel

TEACH Services, Inc.
PUBLISHING
www.TEACHServices.com • (800) 367-1844

World rights reserved. This book or any portion thereof may not be copied or reproduced in any form or manner whatever, except as provided by law, without the written permission of the publisher, except by a reviewer who may quote brief passages in a review.

The author assumes full responsibility for the accuracy of all facts and quotations as cited in this book. The opinions expressed in this book are the author's personal views and interpretations, and do not necessarily reflect those of the publisher.

This book is provided with the understanding that the publisher is not engaged in giving spiritual, legal, medical, or other professional advice. If authoritative advice is needed, the reader should seek the counsel of a competent professional.

Copyright © 2014 Dennis Nickel
Copyright © 2014 TEACH Services, Inc.
ISBN-13: 978-1-4796-0323-7 (Paperback)
ISBN-13: 978-1-4796-0323-7 (ePub)
ISBN-13: 978-1-4796-0325-1 (Mobi)
Library of Congress Control Number: 2014937836

Published by

www.TEACHServices.com • (800) 367-1844

"First-person accounts of incidents in the life of Christ are not common. This book records many first-person insights into the life of Christ. I found it interesting and insightful. It makes the Gospels come alive. The author has thought about these segments of Christ's life and this is the product of a life time of ministry. It is an excellent read."

Ian Hartley
Retired Pastor
Alberta SDA Conference

"Dennis presents the familiar stories of Jesus in a unique first-person narrative that offers a new perspective and fresh look that was enjoyable to read."

Troy McQueen
Communications Director
Alberta SDA Conference

"I thoroughly enjoyed this devotional! It is written almost like a diary from the unique perspective of the people who interacted with Jesus. The book caused me to think about the Gospels in a different light. I would highly recommend this book to anyone who is seeking a deep relationship with Jesus."

Kalie Kelch
Senior Editor
TEACH Services, Inc.

Foreword

Dennis Marvin Nickel was an extraordinary man. He was a devoted pastor with a hippie edge. He was an intellectual without the pretension. He was a walking biblical encyclopedia without ever being stuffy or pharisaical about it. He had a killer sense of humor and unleashed a belly laugh of such mirth and merriment that you found yourself giggling right along with him. When he'd had an especially demanding day of tending his flock, he would pop in a Laurel and Hardy DVD. No matter how many times he watched those two buffoons, their antics never ceased to tickle his funny bone.

He rode a motorbike in the summer and sought out the ugliest, most junkyard-worthy car to buzz between churches in the winter. He lovingly referred to these automotive outcasts as his "beater". He was a favorite with kids because he was a kid at heart. He loved to dazzle a pint-sized audience with his amateur magic tricks and troupe of puppets. During Vacation Bible School craft-making, he devotedly glued popsicle sticks together and painted figurines right along with the kids instead of retreating to his office. The opposite of austere, his office at the church was the most cheerful room in the building, always cluttered with tacky crafts and homemade gifts from kids. He played a mean guitar and belted out gospel songs at the top of his lungs. A self-described rebel, he often felt like he didn't measure up to societal standards. And the truth is, he never did fit into a box. He was a refreshing anomaly.

His compassion for the least-of-these was staggering. You know those people you see headed your way or whose caller ID comes up and you groan inwardly because they are boring or messy or just plain irritating? He always had time for them. Not minutes, hours. He had the rare ability to take abuse from abrasive people without lashing out or retaliating, even though their words cut him deeply. He was generous to a fault, giving money to anyone who asked for it, even telemarketers.

He had a fondness for fast food, especially the Mexican variety. He loved to stroll into Taco Time and call everyone by name, his order memorized by the staff. Bean burrito, nuked for thirty seconds. It was his Cheers. He saw himself as an adventurous foodie and his pride would never allow him to turn down a morsel of food or drink, no matter how alarming its appearance. This culinary bravery almost always landed him in intestinal distress but he was indomitable.

He dabbled in old-school photography and taught dark room techniques to grade-schoolers, never catching the digital wave. He did his shopping at the dollar store and Guitar Center. He always stopped to smell the roses, literally. He liked Rottweilers and Chinese buffets. His drink of choice was a gigantic plastic chalice brimming with ice-cold Mr. Pibb. He showed up with flowers for his wife every Friday night. He despised camping and Tom Cruise movies. An avid reader, his book choices ran the gamut, including everything from classic novels to philosophical tomes to comic books. He was a travel junkie and jetted off to exotic locales to preach Jesus every chance he got.

He scooped up his sweetheart during college and never looked back. She was the yin to his yang and they were very happy together for 34 years. He loved his kids and was fiercely proud of them. He would have been crazy about his grand-daughter, who he missed meeting by 8 months.

This book was written during his early morning meetings with God. He found that Jesus' words and actions came alive for him if he could transport himself into the story, vicariously observing through the eyes of a bystander. He carefully studied the four gospels, weaving together a chronological story of Christ's life. The last story he wrote just happened to be number 365. He would be over the moon to see his name on the cover of this book. If you didn't have the good fortune to know the author personally, we, his family, hope you catch a little glimpse in these pages.

January 1   *John 1:1–5, 14*

The Word of God

This island is a lonely place. Just a few shepherds and fishermen like me live here. Jesus warned us they'd hunt us down and persecute us because of Him. I've always considered myself the least disciple, but I don't mind suffering for Him.

The Romans banned me to this desolate place because they were afraid of me. They must have thought getting rid of me would be easy until they threw me into a vat of boiling oil and were shocked to discover I survived. Upon discovering I had sustained no injuries, they decided I must be some lower god in their pantheon of many gods, and, lest retribution come crashing down on their heads, they decided not to kill me. So they banished me to the isle of Patmos.

I am only one in a multitude of voices—followers who would die in a heartbeat for Jesus if necessary. Many have asked me, "Who is this man, Jesus, that He has such power over people?" All I can do is offer you my witness. I offer you a poor, ignorant fisherman's testimony, and tell you what I found out about Him. But where do I begin? What can I say that might help you know Him?

First of all there was the Word. The spoken, absolute truth, with power to communicate God's thoughts. The magnificent Word was with God. Actually, the Word really is God, too. Not lower, or one of many gods, just simply God. Right from the very beginning, the Word was always God. This Word, who is God, made everything, from fragments of dust to great stars as the sun. There is nothing we can touch or see that He didn't have a hand in making. He is the source of everything. He lights up our lives, shining brilliantly in every dark place. Sometimes the darkness resists the Light, but the darkness can't make it go away.

This Word became flesh and lived on earth among us. He was full of unfailing love and faithfulness. We saw His glory, the glory of the only Son of the Father. In a nutshell, this is who I understand Him to be. I am no wise man, just an old fisherman, but I believe the Spirit of the living God named Jesus, who is the Word, lives in me.

January 2   *Mark 1:4–7; John 1:6–9*

Message of Repentance

There was a friend of ours named John the Baptist. He came to Galilee preaching God's message. With a loud, clear voice he called everyone to repent. "Put away your sins, and submit to God," he admonished the crowds. He spoke with such power and authority that many people responded with heartfelt confession.

My brother James and I believed he was the Messiah. When he spoke, we heard the voice of God. He stirred our souls, igniting fires of spiritual passion deep inside us. We were so sure it was "Him" that we became his disciples. We helped him baptize people, and we encouraged others to believe in him and live godly lives. We gave him a few coins and fish when we could afford to.

John the Baptist liked to be alone in the desert after working with the crowds all day. He said it was his "God-time." He was the kind of guy who liked to pray and fast when he wasn't preaching and baptizing. We respected him, even though he seemed a little strange at times, what with his camel hair clothes and strange diet of locusts and wild honey. But he always preached a good sermon, and his messages were straight from the heart.

We told everybody he was the Messiah, but he insisted that he wasn't. The Jewish leaders sent representatives out to ask him if he was the Messiah. When he told them he wasn't, they wanted to know who he was and what right he had to baptize. "I'm only a witness to the Light," he would say.

I think it was because of John's testimony that people eventually believed in the Messiah. He made it very clear he was not the light, "Only a little light pointing to the Great Light." He told about a Light that was coming very soon that would illuminate everyone who received Him. "He is so much greater than I am that I am not worthy even to be His slave."

"When is He coming, John?" we asked. We wanted to see this Light that was brighter than John.

John the Baptist told us to be patient and wait. He assured us that God would reveal Him soon enough. "Everyone who has a heart for God will know Him," he said quietly.

So we waited, although very impatiently. Every day we would ask John, "Is this the day?"

"Perhaps," he would reply. "Keep your eyes open, and you will know."

January 3   *John 1:10–13*

The Ultimate Gift

Imagine this—the One who was the Word was with God and was Himself God. He made everything in the world in which we live, actually He made everything in the whole universe, yet He chose to come to this world to live among humanity. It gives me shivers to tell you this! In reality, He came here for our sake.

Consider all the billions of stars, the planets, the galaxies in the universe. He could have gone to any of those, but He came here, to this little planet, the earth. This world filled with messed up people. This world filled with pain and misery. This world filled with selfishness and greed.

Most astonishing to me is that intelligent people didn't notice or even pay attention to the One who made this world and all its life forms, from the simplest one-celled amoeba to the complex human being. Those who should have been watching, who had been forewarned of His arrival could have cared less. The people He had created ignored Him and treated Him like a nobody. His own did not welcome Him or accept Him. Yet, there were a few simple folks and a few foreign kings who acknowledged His coming into this world. Later there were others who believed in Him, like myself and my brother James.

To all who believe in Him and accept Him, He bestowed the title of sons and daughters of God, children of the King. They are reborn. This is not a physical birth resulting from human passion but a rebirth that comes from God. I have so often wondered, "Why?" Why would He allow the people of this world, so inferior in comparison to Him, to become children of God? Why would He even want us as His children?

This divinely appointed designation is not because we deserve it. No! It is because we are the work of His hands. We don't have to labor for this title, we can't earn it, and it isn't bestowed on us because we are born into the right family or have an earthly pedigree. No! We have the right to this title because of Him, because of His gift. Jesus came to this earth to save us that through His sacrifice we could stand pure before the Father and be restored to our place as children of God. Out of His unfathomable love for us, we can be reborn of God.

January 4   *John 1:14*

The Unexpected

When John the Baptist pointed out the Messiah to us, we were surprised. And I must admit that we were more than a little disappointed. I guess we had a picture in our minds that He would be something like the religious leaders of Israel—wealthy, wearing nice clothes, accompanied by a host of attendants and priests. We imagined pomp and circumstance like we were familiar with in regards to royalty or other important people.

We had been taught from childhood that the Messiah would come as a mighty conqueror. But the man John the Baptist pointed out to us was just a plain, simple, poor Galilean man. There wasn't anything really attractive about Him, just a regular-looking guy. It was easy to see that there would be no hope of riches or fame by associating with Him.

Yet there was something about Him that irresistibly drew us to Him. He had a spiritual attractiveness that got to us. He looked and acted kingly without all the trappings of royalty. He spoke with authority. He was Spirit-filled.

This Word of God who was with God, who was God, took on human flesh and became like us. He came to earth, moved into our neighborhood, made His home with us, and worked alongside us. He ate the same food, slept in wooden beds or on grassy slopes, cried tears, laughed and played with children, loved, bled, sorrowed, got hurt, had bad body odor on a hot day like the rest of us, bathed, appreciated a woman's beauty, longed for friendship, and grew tired and hungry.

The Messiah was God alive with us in a human form. We witnessed it all. We experienced Him, knew Him, touched Him, talked to Him, and saw Him with our own eyes. This man, God's Son, filled with one-of-a-kind glory, the one and only Son of God, full of grace and truth, came to us direct from God the Father. He was with us, I tell you; we knew Him.

January 5   *John 1:15–18*

Greatness

I still have a vivid recollection of the day John the Baptist stood up and shouted to the crowd, "Hey, all you people! Here He is! He's the One I've been telling you about all along! The One I said would come!"

He pointed toward a man in a peasant's robe walking through the crowd. I craned my neck to get a better look, thinking I must be missing someone that John could see. It certainly couldn't be that plain, ordinary looking guy. Nobody else out of the hundreds of people gathered to listen to John seemed all that impressed either.

John continued. "He is far greater than me because He was around thousands of years before I came on the scene."

Whatever does he mean by that? I wondered.

Some of the people in the crowd laughed. I heard a man close to me say, "I think the desert is getting to John! He is talking nonsense."

John continued. "From the fullness of this man's grace, we have received blessing after blessing after blessing."

At the time, I couldn't help but wonder who he could be talking about that had given us all these blessings. Blessings? What blessings? I hadn't received any blessings. We had been under the Roman curse for years. I looked around again, trying to catch a glimpse of this great benefactor John was going on about. I couldn't see anyone at all who impressed me, certainly not the Galilean John had pointed to.

These thoughts occupied my mind before I knew Him. He may not have been much to look at, but He really did have the truth. In Him were the words of life, as we later discovered. Moses, our Jewish father, gave us the law, but Jesus Christ gave us grace and truth. And not only did He bless us with His ministry while on this earth, but I know He stands at the Father's side in heaven, revealing to anyone who searches for Him the beauty, majesty, magnificence, and grace of salvation. I am God's witness.

January 6   *Luke 1:1–4*

Changed Lives

My dear friend, Theophilus, whose name literally means "god-lover" or "lover of God," asked me many questions one day about my Hebrew God. He wanted to know how I, being a Greek, had gotten mixed up with the people of "the Way." I shared with him that everything changed for me when I accepted Christ as Savior and God of my life.

I was known as Dr. Luke, the loved and well-known physician who never turned anyone away. Even the destitute and the hopeless knew I would do whatever I could to help them. I was convinced that God would never turn His back on me, and consequently, I decided I would not turn my back on anyone else.

Theophilus had taken his wife to every doctor for miles around our city in hopes that someone could help her. Their diagnosis was always the same—her case was terminal and no treatments were available. As they were leaving the office of the doctor who had been their last hope, a stranger suggested Theophilus take his wife to me. He had heard a rumor that I had a special connection with the gods.

When Theophilus came to my office, we talked about Yahweh and His power to heal. Then I told Theophilus, "The power of the Lord Jesus Christ is the only power that can save your wife." He was willing to pray with me. Within a few days she felt much better and soon was perfectly well again!

Theophilus and his wife wanted a full account of this man, Jesus Christ, so I immediately set about writing an account as accurately as I could. I interviewed eyewitnesses and apostles, carefully investigating everything about Him from beginning to end. Then came the difficult task of putting all the information gathered into an orderly chronological account of Christ's life and deeds. I sent it to my friend Theophilus so that he could know beyond a shadow of doubt the reliability of what I had told him. He read my letter, copied it, and sent it to his friends. Praise God, the words of Jesus and His story are being spread to those who need to know Him. And I am hopeful that this is happening even in the Greek Isles.

January 7 *Matthew 1:1-17*

Jesus' Ancestry

Reading a list of names of people you never knew is very boring! If, however, you were to regard the names found in Jesus' ancestry as people with regular lives like you, your family, and your friends, this list takes on new meaning. Pain, joy, courage, success and failure, doubt and faith—the whole gamut of human emotions such as we experience today can be found in the stories of the people on this list.

Checking into their stories, you soon discover those patriarchs were not saints. Tempted and hassled by Satan, they had their flaws. Abraham told some lies and, as a result, got himself and his wife into some tough predicaments. Isaac not only told his share of white lies but caused family conflict by showing favoritism. Then there was Jacob, the deceiver; Judah, the womanizer; and Tamar, the prostitute. Boaz and Ruth seemed like upright people, but I am sure they had their issues even though none are recorded in Scripture.

Then there is David who committed adultery with Bathsheba and then murdered Uriah in an effort to cover it up. Did I mention he was a lousy father? Solomon, the spoiled royal kid, who, although gifted by God with great wisdom, made some really bad decisions. Hezekiah was amazingly healed by God, but instead of bearing witness to God's power to some foreign visitors, he showed them his country's wealth and set the stage for a later invasion.

Manasseh ruled in Israel for fifty-five years but engaged in every imaginable evil, even inventing new wicked schemes that had never been practiced in Israel before. He was captured by the Assyrians.

And there in an Assyrian jail, he repented and God forgave him. Rahab, a prostitute from Jericho, Uzziah, Amnon, and a host of other people who did really bad things are included in the list.

Every person in that list is a sinner, and all of them messed up big time at some point in their life. What a lineage! If they were part of my family, I'd want to disown them all! But then again, that's not Jesus' style. I was a tax collector and cheater and thief, and God forgave me. Jesus even asked me to be a disciple.

If the truth is told, and we admit it, we are all just a bunch of sinners in desperate need of a Savior. Thankfully, most of those ancestors came to their senses, gave their lives to God, and looked for the Messiah.

January 8   *Luke 3:23–38*

Jesus' Ancestry Continued

As a physician, I like details and facts. If I am going to believe in something, I have to find out the how, when, where, and why. If you want me to believe in someone, I have to know everything about them.

That is why, before I became a Christian, I needed to know everything about Jesus that I possibly could. He wasn't the first person to be called the Messiah. There were so many impostors—a constant stream of false christs seemed to parade through the days. Everyone was waiting for the true Messiah to come, so some people took advantage of that fact. I wanted to know for myself if this man from Galilee was the real deal.

Some of my colleagues knew how important this acquisition of facts was to me, so they acquired a list of Jesus' ancestors from the Levites, which I am indebted to them for. The list I have written is the result of the Holy Spirit's leading as I compared information from every source. The only members from Jesus' immediate family that I knew personally were a few of His stepbrothers. James was the one I knew best, but he was killed by Herod. I had the privilege of briefly meeting with Jesus' mother, Mary, who lives with John's family. My interview with her provided much of the information I needed for relating Jesus' birth and early life. She was most helpful, and I might add a lovely woman full of God's Spirit. It was truly a delight to spend time with her and hear her reminisce about Jesus' life and ministry.

Everyone on the list of ancestors besides Mary is unknown to me personally, but the history books and some of the prophets relate their stories. People who struggled with everyday life. Some depended on God, others chose to ignore Him. Some sought forgiveness, others lived their lives in sins and died in them. The list of Jesus' ancestors showcases the ongoing struggle between good and evil—the battle for the mind. I have gladly chosen to turn my will, my power of choice, over to Him because I am totally convinced that He was everything He claimed to be.

January 9   *Luke 1:5–25*

Announcement to Zechariah

My wife and I have always tried to be obedient to God. My work as a priest (I am a member of the priestly division of Abidjan) requires faith and godly living. My wife, Elizabeth, and I, like every Jewish family, have always wanted children. We believed that if we lived godly lives Yahweh would show us His favor by giving us a child. But with each passing year, we grew older, and soon we were beyond the age of childbearing. We were disappointed. We couldn't understand why God hadn't granted our request for a child!

Well, it came my turn to serve as priest and burn incense before the Lord at the temple in Jerusalem. I can still see the worshipers assembled before me, praying to God. I carried the incense cup into the holy place and stood before the altar of incense. Suddenly I saw what appeared to be a tall, winged seraphim standing to the right side of the altar. I was terrified! He quickly assured me that I did not need to be afraid. He proceeded to tell me that Elizabeth and I were to become parents. I couldn't believe what he was saying. He told me we would have a son who would become our joy and delight. The child would grow to do a great work for God in the spirit and power of Elijah. He would turn the hearts of the people to God in preparation for the Lord's coming.

I was astonished because it sounded like Malachi's prophecy. "Why didn't this happen years ago when we were younger?" I asked half aloud. Then, feeling frustrated, I demanded, "And how are two old people supposed to have a baby?"

I heard a slight sigh as the angel said, "I am Gabriel. I have come from God's presence. Because you will not believe me, you will remain silent until all is fulfilled."

I felt something happen in my throat as Gabriel disappeared. I cried out, but no sound came out. Remembering the people outside waiting for me, I hurried out and tried to communicate with them by using hand signals. After my time of service I went home, a mute. Elizabeth did become pregnant, which we were ecstatic about! Yahweh is good, and His words are true.

January 10   *Luke 1:26–38*

The Annunciation

"Why would God chose me? Who am I but a teenager living in Galilee?" I asked myself. My parents are not rich or influential, just poor Galileans. Recently, I became engaged to a man named Joseph. He is a good, honest carpenter with children from an earlier marriage. His wife died several years ago. I'm a little frightened about marriage to an older man with a ready-made family, but he evidently wants me because the dowry has been arranged, and a sizable dowery it is.

One evening when my parents were away visiting neighbors, I was at home cleaning up the kitchen when an angel suddenly appeared before me. He was so tall and beautiful— I had never seen a being like this before! He told me I was highly favored and that the Lord was with me.

Seeing that I was nervous and afraid and perplexed at his greeting, he reassured me. "Don't be afraid, Mary, you have found favor with God."

Then he said that I would become pregnant and have a son who I was to name Jesus. He would be called Son of the Most High, and His kingdom would never end. I couldn't believe what I was hearing. Finally, I blurted out, "How can this be? I am a virgin."

The angel said, "The Holy Spirit will make you pregnant, and God will overshadow you. The Holy Child born to you will be the Son of God."

"Messiah?" I whispered, more as an overwhelmed response than a quest for explanation.

"Your relative Elizabeth, the one who was barren, will soon have a son in her old age. So you see, nothing is impossible for God," he continued.

Why is God choosing me, a plain, poor village girl? I wondered. Then, as a sense of God's inner peace swept over me, I responded, "May it be done to me as you have said." The angel disappeared and left me in wonderment, considering everything he had said. That was more than a month ago, and I am pregnant just as he promised.

January 11 *Luke 1:39–45*

Mary Visits Elizabeth

I'd met Elizabeth many years before when I was just a little girl. My parents and I had taken a trip to the hill country of Judea to visit her and Zechariah. I remembered her being really nice. As I played with the toys she had given me, I overheard her telling my mother how much she wanted a baby. I felt sorry for her. She was old back then with gray hair and wrinkles. I could hardly believe what the angel had said about her being pregnant! I felt the urgent need to visit her and see for myself if it was true.

When I first asked my mom if I could go visit Elizabeth and Zechariah, she immediately said no. But when I told her I might be of some help to Elizabeth in her pregnancy, she consented as long as I could find someone she trusted to take me there. Anticipating her response, I had already spoken to my father's brother, Uncle Ishmael, who reluctantly agreed to take me along on his next trip to Judea.

And so it was that a few days later I threw a bundle of things in the cart and kissed my parents goodbye. Joseph was there, too, but we only embraced. It was a long tiresome trip, and I was weary and very grateful when we finally arrived. Uncle Ishmael grabbed my bag, and we walked to the door. No servants were there to answer my knock, so I pushed open the door and went in, calling to Elizabeth. She gave a glad cry as she came to meet me, talking excitedly about her baby jumping in her womb when he heard my voice. Suddenly, she seemed to be in a vision and literally shouted, "You and your child are blessed and so am I that the mother of my Lord should visit me." I wondered what she meant by "Mother of my Lord." Needless to say, I have never been greeted like that in all my life!

January 12   *Luke 1:46–56*

Mary's Song

No sooner had Elizabeth uttered the words given her by the Holy Spirit than I felt the powerful presence of God course through me. There was a joyfulness and peace that made me laugh and filled me with a great passion for Him, the Almighty. It was like He possessed me, but I was fully aware of everything that was happening around me. I wanted to shout His praises to the whole world! Then the words came, not mine but God's. I had never felt like this or uttered words like these before in my life. I knew I must tell everyone about Him or burst like a wineskin.

"My soul glorifies the Lord, and rejoices in God my Savior. He took notice of me, His humble servant." The words flowed from deep within my being. "Now generation after generation will call me blessed," I continued. "He, the Mighty One, has done great things for me. Holy is His name."

As I spoke, I realized how truly blessed I really was. "He is merciful to all who fear Him, from generation to generation. He has performed mighty deeds with His arm." Then these words, like hammers crashing down on an anvil, poured forth. "He scatters the proud and haughty ones for He knows their thoughts. He brings rulers down from their thrones and exalts the lowly. He lifts the hungry up and fills them with good things, but He sends the rich away empty-handed. They are not hungry for God. He has helped Israel, remembering to be merciful to Abraham and his descendants as He promised."

When I finished speaking, I felt exhausted, but wonderful. For the next three months, I stayed with Zechariah and Elizabeth until young John was born. They were happy to have me with them. Elizabeth often expressed her gratitude, and although Zechariah couldn't speak, I knew from his expressions that he was glad I was there to help Elizabeth. I was glad I was able to be there and help. I loved them.

January 13   *Luke 1:57–66*

The Birth of John the Baptist

Finally the time came for my wife to give birth to our son. Childbearing is never easy, even at the best of times, but when you are an old woman, it is even worse. Thankfully Elizabeth had taken good care of herself through the years and was healthy for her age. When our neighbors and relatives heard Elizabeth was about to deliver, they all came. This was unprecedented, unheard of—an old, old woman giving birth.

On the eighth day, the priest came to circumcise the baby in accordance with Jewish customs. Our kinsmen were expecting us to name him Zechariah Jr., but Elizabeth said emphatically, "His name will be John."

"John, why John?" they all wanted to know. "There is no one in your lineage named John," they contended. I could tell some of them were getting a bit irritated with her when she kept insisting that we call him John, because they said, "Let's ask Zechariah!" They gestured to me and finally wrote the question on a tablet. "What do you want your son's name to be?"

His name is "John," I wrote. Now they were really astonished, and some of the kinsfolk were clearly annoyed. I wasn't about to disobey God or doubt Him a second time! At the instant I wrote his name, I felt my tongue loosen and I could speak, so I began shouting for joy and praising God. Everyone stared at me, thinking I had lost my mind until suddenly it dawned on them that I had been healed. It didn't take long for word to spread throughout the hills of Judea about the miracle of my returned speech, and everyone wondered what kind of person baby John would grow up to be. There was no doubt in anyone's mind that God's hand was in it. Little did they know what great things were about to happen!

January 14   *Luke 1:67-80*

Zechariah's Song

When God loosened my tongue, the Spirit of God overwhelmed me with an intense feeling of peace and great joy. Unless you have experienced this, you have no reference point because it is impossible to describe. I couldn't stop talking! I had to tell the world how much I loved God. The words poured out of me as a flood.

"Praise be to the Lord, the God of Israel. He has come to redeem His people. He has raised up a man of salvation for His people through His servant David as He promised through the prophets."

I remember thinking, *The prophecies are being fulfilled through us—Elizabeth, Mary, and I. Why did God choose us? Why did God chose me? I'm just a faithless old man.*

The words continued to pour forth: "Now will come salvation from our enemies and tormentors. He will show mercy to us and remember His covenant. The One He promised Abraham will save us from our enemies and enable us to serve Him in holiness and righteousness all our lives. My son, you will be the prophet of the Most High. You will go on before the Lord and prepare the way for Him, to help the people understand salvation and forgiveness for sins. God, in His mercy, our God shining as the sun, will come to us from heaven in order to shine on those in darkness and the shadow of death, to guide our feet into the path of peace."

How we loved that boy! We watched him grow; we taught him about God; we prayed over him. When he reached adulthood, he liked living in the desert. He would leave for a week at a time, then come home to be with us and help us around the house. He was the joy of our lives. We often prayed together, and I would tell him about the prophecy and the plan for his life. He always thought it a great honor that God had chosen him to prepare the way for the Messiah.

January 15　　　　　　　　　　　　　　　　　　　　　　　　　　　　　　　　　Matthew 1:18–25

Announcement to Joseph

I must admit, I was not very excited about Mary traveling all the way to Judea to visit some long lost relatives whom she hardly knew. It seemed kind of crazy to me at the time, but she felt strongly about it, so off she went. In the nearly four months she was gone, I only heard from her once. Just a note telling me everything was fine and that she missed me.

I remember the day she came home. She smiled at me, hugged me, and kissed my cheek in greeting. But something was wrong. "Have you gained weight?" I asked. She looked down at her expanding waistline and then back up at me. "Are you pregnant?" I asked in disbelief. She didn't respond, although I didn't give her much opportunity to do so. I wasn't sure I wanted to know the answer.

I carried her bags to her parents place and then went home in a turmoil. This was not the homecoming I expected. *How could she?* I wondered. *She was pledged to me!*

I was stunned. It just didn't seem congruent with the spiritual girl I knew her to be. *Doesn't she realize fornication is punishable by death?* I thought. Then I began to ponder my options. I didn't want to publicly disgrace her or report her to the authorities because I still loved her. I would just break the engagement quietly. Later that day her father came to apologize. I told him that I would annul the pledge. I could tell he was very upset, perhaps even more than I was.

That night as I tossed and turned in a fitful sleep, an angel appeared to me in a dream. He addressed me as "Joseph, son of David." He told me Mary was pregnant by the Holy Spirit and she would have a son who we were to call Jesus, the Savior, because He would save His people from their sins. I remembered the words of the prophet Isaiah: "A virgin will bear a son." Could it be? I awoke perspiring. The Lord told me to make Mary my wife.

The next day we had a long talk, and we compared notes about our dreams and visiting angels. Soon we were married and getting ready to become parents of the Messiah! In the midst of all the whirlwind, I kept wondering, *Why would God chose us?*

January 16　　　　　　　　　　　　　　　　　　　　　　　　　　　　　　　　　　　Luke 2:1–4

Journey to Bethlehem

Shortly after Mary came home from visiting Zechariah and Elizabeth, we married. Over the next five months, the baby grew inside her. With joy we felt Him squirm around. The pregnancy went well, and He was growing fine according to the midwife. We were excited as we anticipated the birth of this special baby! Then came the day near the end of Mary's pregnancy when an announcement was made at the town square. Caesar had ordered a census be taken. The head of every family would need to travel to the city of his origin to register. Mine was Bethlehem in Judah. How in the world were we to make a ninety mile trip with Mary nine months pregnant? I appealed to the Roman authorities, but they were making no exceptions.

I borrowed my uncle's cart, loaded it with what we needed, and Mary and I started out with many prayers. The highways were very busy, and the going was very slow. I tried to make Mary as comfortable as I possibly could by avoiding the potholes as we traveled. By the end of the first day, we were both exhausted. We found a place beside the road and quickly fell asleep.

The rest of the trip was uneventful except that the closer we came to Jerusalem, the more crowded the road became. Seeing the temple and old friends in Zion was magnificent. We spent Sabbath there. On the evening of the eighth day, we arrived in Bethlehem. I hadn't been back in years. It felt good to be in my old hometown, but I didn't know where we would stay. There weren't many family or friends that I had known as a boy who still lived here, most had either died or moved away. To make matters worse, the city was overcrowded with people. I tried inn after inn, but no one had room for us. Then it happened—Mary's water broke and the labor pains began. I panicked. We went back to the last inn from which we had been turned away, and I begged them, "Please, my wife is going to have a baby!"

January 17   *Luke 2:5–7*

The Birth of Jesus

The innkeeper looked at Mary and then back at me. Again, I pleaded, "Please, isn't there something you can do to help us?"

He hurried back inside and returned with a lantern and a blanket. "Come," he said, "all I have is the stable." He motioned around back beneath the inn.

Gratefully I took whatever he could give me. He showed me the hay I could use and promised he would send his wife, who was a midwife, out to the stable to help us. The stable was carved out of the rock foundation upon which the inn rested. I scattered some hay, laid down the blanket, and helped Mary onto it. The labor pains kept increasing in frequency and intensity. Mary was in so much pain. The innkeeper's wife showed up to check on Mary. In an hour she returned with buckets of water and lots of cloth. I held Mary's head in my hands and kissed her while the contractions swept over her. Finally, after intense abdominal pushes, Jesus was born.

We heard Him cry, and the midwife announced we had a son. She cut the cord, washed and salted Him, and handed Him to Mary. "What are you going to call him?" she asked.

"Jesus," Mary answered.

How grateful we were to the midwife. We expressed our thanks as she bade us goodnight. We rejoiced in the safe arrival of our son and took turns holding Him before wrapping Him and laying Him in the manger.

"Who would have ever thought our son would be born in the same village in which I was born!" I spoke softly.

Mary took my hand. "He is really God's Son. We are just caretakers," she said.

"I know," I answered, "but we can be wonderful parents. I want to teach Him to be a good carpenter. He will need a fine chariot if He is to lead armies against Rome."

I looked at Mary, but she was already fast asleep.

January 18   Luke 2:8–14

Angels Appear to Shepherds

It was late. I was tired because my sheep had been as uncooperative as sheep could possibly be. Two of mine had wandered away from my flock, past the watchful eye of my sheepdog, Herod. I spent a good part of the day tracking down those wayward lambs. I finally found them in Jerome's garden, where they had helped themselves to his tasty vegetables. I promised I would compensate him for what my sheep had eaten.

By the time I got my flock to the fold where the other shepherds were gathered, I was beat. We ate supper together and prepared for bed after checking on the sheep. As usual, I was the only one still awake when a light, a very strange light appeared above me. Looking up, I saw a great number of beings, all dazzling bright and some holding trumpets. It was incredible!

Someone shouted from the shepherds hut, "Hey, James, what is going on out there?" It took me awhile to find my voice, but finally I shouted for them to come out and see. They stumbled groggily out of the hut but were soon wide awake as a tall, bright being suddenly appeared right before us.

We fell to the ground, terrified and crying out in fear of what might become of us. "Do not be afraid. I bring you good tidings of great joy for everyone. Today in the city of David a Savior has been born to you. He is Christ the Lord." When we dared look up, we saw a kind smile on his bright face. "This will be a sign to you," he continued, "you will find a baby wrapped in cloths, lying in a manger."

We cowered before him, our mouths open, unable to speak or even scream. Then the sky lit up with thousands of angels singing praises together: "Glory to God in the highest and on earth peace to all people."

As quickly as they had come, they were gone. For a long time, none of us moved. We just stared at each other. Then Philip spoke. "If the Christ is born in Bethlehem, we should go see Him and pay homage." Jesse, the youngest, stayed with the sheep while the rest of us stumbled through the darkness toward Bethlehem.

January 19   Luke 2:15–20

The Shepherds Find Jesus

My legs felt weak as we made our way to Bethlehem. I think we were all in shock. We kept chattering to each other as we ran, asking, "Was that a dream, or was it real?" "Did we imagine that, or could it really be true?" "Are you sure the angel said we would find Him in a manger?" "Has the Messiah come to us?" "Didn't Micah the prophet say that the Messiah would be born in Bethlehem?"

When we got to David's city, we expected there to be a lot of excitement about this baby, but the streets were quiet, and when we asked about the baby, none of the people we spoke with knew anything. "Didn't you see the light and the angels?" I asked some people camped around a fire. They laughed at me as if I was crazy.

Jonas suggested we start checking mangers. At the inn across the street, the manager angrily shouted at us from an open bedroom window when we inquired about the baby. The next inn wasn't far, but instead of waking anyone up, we made our way to the stable to look for ourselves. Down the steps to the back, we walked quietly so as not to disturb anyone.

"I see a light," whispered Othaniel. Soon we stood in front of the stable. The wide entrance carved out of stone made the stable look like a tomb. Inside a man and his wife lay on the straw. On the stone manger lay a baby on a bed of hay wrapped in cloth. The man roused from sleep and sat up, asking who we were and what we wanted. I guess he thought we were travelers bringing our animals to bed.

In our excitement, we all started talking at once. His wife awoke, looking very tired and sleepy. "The angel told us the Messiah is born!" They both smiled and pointed to the baby. We came close to Him, knelt before Him and praised God. Leaving the stable, we couldn't contain ourselves. We excitedly told everyone we met about the angels and the baby. "The Messiah has come!" we rejoiced. They seemed surprised, but no one went to visit the infant King.

January 20   Luke 2:21

The Circumcision

The next day Mary and I talked about the visit of the shepherds during the night. The innkeeper's wife had heard about them coming to the manger after their visit from the angels. She asked us a lot of questions, and with this new knowledge, she treated Jesus as more than just an ordinary baby. For us, she was a lifesaver. She brought us food, water, and another blanket, apologizing that we had to stay in the stable. We assured her that she had made it comfortable for us.

"As soon as a room is vacant, I'm moving you into the inn," she promised. In a few days she had us set up in a very comfortable room in the inn. Having had children from my first marriage, I knew all about the late nights. But Mary was new to the role of being a mother. Poor Mary was up during the night feeding and changing diapers.

Before the eighth day arrived after His birth, we contacted the rabbis and priests to arrange for circumcision. They came with their instruments and performed the ritual, somewhat disgruntled because the eighth day fell on a Sabbath. They recorded His name as Jesus, the name the angel had given Him before He was conceived. Baby Jesus cried and cried as most babes do when they are circumcised. After the ceremony we bundled Him up and rocked Him until He fell asleep.

Later that night Mary and I talked about what to do next. Before we could go to the temple for Jesus' dedication, we needed to wait for Mary's purification time to end. As we talked, we had our first real disagreement. Mary wanted to go back to Nazareth, but I had located a cousin of mine living in Bethlehem, also a carpenter, and asked him about work. He assured me of a place to live and lots of work. I tried to reason with Mary that there was no point in making the long trip home to Nazareth and then having to turn around and travel all the way back to Jerusalem for His dedication.

January 21 *Luke 2:22–24*

Journey to Jerusalem

After shedding a few tears, Mary agreed that it made sense to remain in Bethlehem until the thirty-three remaining days of her purification period were over. According to the Levitical law, this was required before the temple could be entered and sacrifices made. I knew how much she missed her family and wanted them to see the baby, but she also knew how tiring the journey was.

We found a small house in which to live and, thanks to the help of my cousin I had steady carpentry work. I was grateful to be able to earn money to take care of our everyday needs as well as save up for the trip to Jerusalem and then back to Nazareth.

The days passed quickly for me with my work and for Mary and Jesus. In the afternoons they explored the hills of Bethlehem. There in the great outdoors, Mary told Jesus stories—stories of Creation and the flood, stories of Elisha the prophet and David the shepherd, stories of Moses and the children of Israel. Of course, He was too young to understand any of them, but He seemed to love being outside in nature.

Mary's days of purification finally ended, so we packed our few things and bid tearful goodbyes to our new friends. Mary sat on the cart holding Jesus while I led the donkey. The journey from Bethlehem to Jerusalem is only a few miles, seven at most, so we took our time and enjoyed the beautiful day. Early in the afternoon the city came into view with the gilded temple dome shining brightly in the sun. I remembered all the wonderful times I had as a boy traveling to the city with my dad for the festivals. Soon we were at the temple steps. The noise and commotion made by the buyers and sellers was overwhelming. Somewhere in it all was a dove salesman.

January 22   Luke 2:23, 24

Acquiring the Sacrifices

Before I could purchase a sacrificial animal, or bird in my case, I had to exchange common currency into temple coins. Everyone knew this was a scam to steal from the poor and enrich the priests, but no one had the courage to do anything about it. Furthermore, everyone knew it was futile to bring a sacrifice that had not been approved by the priests and sold by the temple merchants. I exchanged my money and found a dove salesman who sold me two doves at an exorbitant price. I knew better than to complain.

We took the doves to the priest who performed the purification ceremony. He went through the motions with a totally bored look on his face. This completed Mary's purification. The next requirement was to have our son dedicated.

As a memorial of God's deliverance of the children of Israel from Egypt, the law of Moses says that if a woman's first child is a boy, he must be dedicated to the Lord. This dedication required the purchase of two more birds. Poor families who were unable to afford a lamb were allowed to sacrifice pigeons or doves. I decided to purchase a pair of pigeons. Again I exchanged more money and found a pigeon salesman. To my chagrin, pigeons were even more expensive than doves. I put the money on the table and glared at the salesman. He was unfazed and glared right back at me.

It wasn't hard to find the line for the dedication of firstborn sons. Some parents had brought lambs but most were like us and could only afford doves or pigeons. I could tell Mary was tiring of all the noise and jostling. I was more emotionally drained than physically tired. There were about twelve families ahead of us. I watched the priests rush through the ceremony without giving much thought to what they were doing. They looked even more bored than the ones who conducted Mary's purification sacrifice.

Where is God in all this? I wondered.

January 23   Luke 2:25–35

Simeon

After waiting for more than an hour, it was finally our turn. Two families ahead of us had their sacrifices deemed unacceptable and uncertified by the priest officiating as sacrifice inspector. They rushed off to purchase temple-certified animals. The priest took Jesus from Mary with an annoyed look on his face because he thought she took too long handing Him over. He mumbled a few words and handed Him back to her.

Without looking up, the scribe asked in a monotoned voice: "What's His name?"

"Jesus," we both answered.

He wrote the name in the registry and shouted, "Next!"

At that moment, an old man, Simeon by name, came up to Mary, smiled at her, and asked if he could hold Jesus. There in front of everyone, once He was in his arms, he declared in a loud voice, "Sovereign Lord, as You have promised, You may now dismiss Your servant in peace, for with my own eyes I have seen Your salvation which You have prepared in the sight of all people, a light for revelation to the Gentiles and for glory to Your people, Israel."

I still remember him holding Jesus up while the people stared. The priests were speechless for a moment, and then they dismissed Simeon as an old man talking nonsense.

"What does this mean?" a man behind us in line asked.

"Whose child is this?" someone else whispered loudly.

Mary and I stood in shock as Simeon spoke, and then he gave Jesus back to Mary. Next he placed his hands on our heads and blessed us. Speaking to Mary, he said, "This child is destined to cause the falling and rising of many in Israel, and to be a sign that will be spoken against, so that the thoughts of many hearts will be revealed. And a sword will pierce your own soul, too." With that he turned and was gone.

I looked around to see people staring at us. As we headed for the temple steps, I asked Mary what she thought it all meant. Bewildered, she just shook her head. The priests were back to business as usual.

January 24   *Luke 2:36–38*

Anna

My life could be measured in degrees of hardship and sorrow. As a young teenager, I was betrothed to a wonderful man in his twenties. He was handsome and kind and godly. We loved each other deeply and those early years of marriage were wonderful. As far as wealth was concerned, we did not have much in the way of this world's goods, but we had each other, and we had God. Then seven years after our betrothal, almost to the day, Josiah became very sick.

Numerous doctors examined him at my request, but they had no recommendations for improving his health. I prayed for him constantly, but the fateful day came when he died in my arms. Losing him was an unimaginable tragedy. I went into seclusion, not wanting to see anyone. I was devastated. How was I ever going to live without my love? I didn't want to go on, and I prayed that I might also die. A widow in her early twenties! I was bitter and angry at God for allowing my Josiah to die.

My father, a very wise man, saw that the bitterness in my soul was destroying me. "Do something good with your life," he said. "Make God your new husband and live for Him." At first I was offended that he would even suggest such a thing, but as I thought about it, I saw the truth of my situation. I started going to the temple every day to pray and do what I could for God.

That was many, many years ago. Just a few days ago at prayer time, Simeon told me that the Messiah was going to be brought to the temple for dedication! The next day I followed him to the courtyard and watched him lift the child and bless His parents. As they made their way to the gate, I approached them and asked to see their baby. He smiled at me! Could it be God, I wondered, looking up at me with a smile? I couldn't help but break into an anthem of praise. I prayed a blessing for the little family and offered encouragement. They thanked me and were gone. How glad I was to be alive and see this day and share the grand news with everyone!

January 25   *Luke 2:39*

Home to Nazareth

As soon as we left the temple, we found a street vender and purchased food to sustain us on the way home. Because of the census, there were still many travelers on the road from numerous locations. Upon reaching the brow of the first hill, we stopped to look back at the city and the magnificent temple with its dome glistening in the afternoon sun. We were relieved to have completed our ritual requirements and leave the city behind.

Both Mary and I were excited about heading home. It had been a very eventful day, and we talked about everything as we traveled. Foremost in our thoughts and conversations was our encounter with Simeon. The things he had said puzzled us. There was his statement that Jesus would be a light to bring revelation to the Gentiles. Neither of us had any inkling as to what that meant. And Mary wondered what "a sword piercing her soul" referred to. "Am I going to die by the Romans?" she asked. I had no answer for her. We did agree that it sounded to both of us as if God had promised Simeon he wouldn't die until he saw Jesus. Everything about it was confusing. Added to our excitement was the encounter with the old prophetess named Anna.

In a few hours the sun began to set, so we looked for a place to camp. We found a nice spot near some trees where I unhitched the donkey, and Mary made a bed in the back of the cart with blankets the innkeeper's wife had given us. After breakfast the next morning, we were on our way again. A few more days of travel, and Nazareth came into view. As soon as we entered the city gates, Mary was off the cart and heading toward her mother's place. I'm sure their shouts of greeting could be heard on the other side of town! My kids ran out to greet me. What a reunion! It was so good to see everyone. Of course, everyone really wanted to see Jesus—like most babies, He stole the show! I unhitched the donkey, gave it some grain, and went in to join the celebration.

January 26   *Luke 2:40*

Back to Bethlehem

After being home for only a few weeks, I realized things had changed in our community, or perhaps it was us. Nazareth was a fine Galilean town, but in Bethlehem I had earned twice as much for my work. I quickly realized that there was far more opportunity for a carpenter in Bethlehem than here. Some of my best clients in Nazareth had found other carpenters while I was gone.

To make matters worse, Mary still had to deal with the stigma of having an illegitimate child. In fact, most of her former friends refused to associate with her. Neither one of us really had any friends, and I hated listening to some of my relatives constantly criticize me for marrying "that woman." I hadn't always been able to keep my older boys from hearing their comments, so they had mixed feelings about Mary and showed jealousy toward Jesus. Many times I came in from the shop to find Mary crying. She tried to escape as much as she could with little Jesus to the hills surrounding Nazareth where they observed the wonders of nature, but she had responsibilities at home.

Life was less than ideal, so, after a particularly bad day, I said to Mary, "Let's go back to Bethlehem for a visit." At first she was excited about the idea of seeing our friends, but she gradually realized that I meant more than just a visit.

Even though it would be tough to live far from her parents, Mary was willing to make the move. She said, "You are my husband. Where you go, I will go."

Thankfully, during the time we had been back in Nazareth, I had saved enough out of my meager earnings to purchase a donkey, and I had built a good sturdy cart. I made arrangements with my youngest brother and his wife to care for my kids until we were settled. I knew that they would be loved and well cared for in their home. Selling the belongings we couldn't take with us and packing the rest into the cart, we made all the final preparations. After tearful goodbyes, we were off. The trip was uneventful, and we found Bethlehem had not changed at all while we'd been gone. The house we had lived in previously stood empty, and I was able to start work immediately. The friends we had made when Jesus was born welcomed us joyfully. We praised God for His providence!

January 27 *Matthew 2:1*

The Magi

For us, my colleagues and I, this whole trip to Jerusalem began with a strange celestial phenomena. We are part of an elite Persian group called Magi, whose goal is to acquire knowledge of everything and anything. Of course, this included the study of astronomy and the writings of the ancients. When a brilliant new "star" appeared in the night sky, we thought it was a comet. In many ways it resembled one, but in other ways we found that it was totally different. We finally concluded that it must be a displaced star.

With great care we explored the writings of various cultures to see if there was a heavenly sign or portent predicted. One of my brothers found an obscure passage in a Hebrew text written by a prophet named Balaam stating, "Out of Jacob a star will arise and a scepter (King) out of Israel." Upon further exploration and inquiry, we learned of a prophecy foretelling the coming of a powerful leader. This royal personage would arise to govern Israel and many other nations with an iron rod. All our research involved a great deal of time and effort, but a number of us discussed the possibility of journeying to Jerusalem to pay homage to this King of kings. It would involve a huge commitment because of the great distance. Every night for more than a year the star shone brightly as though beckoning us to follow.

After making a decision to go, it took us a month to complete arrangements for the grueling trip. Our king and countrymen sent us off with great fanfare and blessing. More than forty Magi started out initially, but the days were hot and the nights were cold so many turned back after a few weeks of travel. Even though we knew how to get to Jerusalem, we decided to make the star our guide. The journey was long, slow, and difficult, but we felt compelled by an unexplainable force or power to press on. Finally, after many days, Jerusalem came into view.

January 28   Matthew 2:2

The Magi Arrive in Jerusalem

As we passed through Jerusalem's gates all the people stopped and stared at us. Being a crossroads city, we thought the residents would be used to strangers, so we were puzzled at their reaction to our arrival. We were also surprised there were no celebrations happening. There didn't seem to be any indication of the coming of a great King. "Where is the King of kings?" we asked several passersby.

"You mean Herod?" they questioned in response.

We were well aware of Herod. His vile character and cruel reputation were known in far away Persia. "No, no," we answered, "the great King predicted by Balaam and the ancient prophets Isaiah and Micah."

No one seemed to know what we were talking about. Messengers wasted no time in telling Herod of our arrival and query. "There is no king here but Herod," the people kept saying. Many asked us who we were.

"I am Baltasar, a member of the Magi of Persia, and these are my friends," I said. "Where can we find food for our animals and us? We also need a place to stay for the night."

Someone offered to guide us to the marketplace and show us an inn. We made a few purchases, and then secured a room at a fine inn. The proprietor was most gracious, especially when he realized we were wealthy. The food at dinner was wonderful, the first regular meal we'd had for months. And how good it felt to clean up and rest on a real bed after nights of sleeping under the stars.

"What do you make of this?" I asked my friends.

"Could we have been wrong?" one of the Magi questioned. "No one seems to know anything. Either they are keeping it secret or they honestly don't know anything."

"Don't they read their own writings and prophets?" I asked. I walked to the window and looked up. There it hovered, directly above us, far up in the evening sky. "The star is proof that we were not wrong and that we have not failed," I said. "We will find the King!"

January 29   *Matthew 2:3–6*

King Herod and the Priests

I was at the temple carrying out my responsibilities on behalf of the people when a messenger from Herod's court arrived, insisting I come at once. *Me? Why me?* I wondered. *I'm just a regular priest doing my work.* At times the high priest and council had been summoned before Herod regarding important religious matters, but he had never called the regular priests before. *This must be of very great importance*, I surmised.

As we assembled in the throne room, Herod's counselors were gathered around him, carrying on an animated discussion. I heard something about visitors from the East. Magi, they called them. I wondered what that had to do with us. Momentarily, Herod turned toward us, a very agitated look on his face. It was easy to see that he was more than a little upset about something. Assembled in front of us regular priests were members of the council, Sadducees, Pharisees, the chief priest, and teachers of the law.

"I have called you here," he bellowed, "to hear your answer to my question about the Christ, and I expect honesty and clarity. Do I make myself clear?"

Everyone nodded submissively. "Yes, your majesty," we answered in unison.

"Where is the Christ to be born?" he asked, stepping down in front of the high priest, his eyes darting from one of us to the other.

Without conferring with anyone else, a teacher of the law spoke up. "According to the prophet Micah, your majesty, He is to be born in Bethlehem." Then he quoted: "'But you, Bethlehem, in the land of Judah, are by no means least among the rulers of Judah, for out of you will come a ruler, who will be shepherd of my people, Israel.'"

"Is this true?" Herod shouted at the high priest.

"Yes, your majesty."

"You had better be telling me the truth or there will be trouble," he growled. He then ordered us to get out. Little did we know at the time that it was a death sentence for the children of Bethlehem.

January 30   *Matthew 2:7, 8*

Herod and the Magi

We could not understand why the people in Jerusalem, "God's City," seemed totally ignorant of the arrival of their King! The people knew that someday the Messiah would come in might to conquer the Romans and free them. They were also certain that when the Messiah appeared the religious leaders would alert them to the fact.

"But there is a star foretelling His coming. He must be here now, somewhere," we argued. Late that night, there was a loud banging on our apartment door. "Who is it?" I asked.

"The king's messenger. King Herod wishes to see all of you, now."

We dressed and followed him to the palace and were ushered in before the king who was seated at a council table with men from his court. He welcomed us graciously. Then he asked, "Tell me, what was the exact time the star appeared?"

"Nearly two years ago," we answered.

"Then this great king must be somewhere between one and two years old?" the king queried.

"Your majesty, if I may speak," I said, bowing low.

"Of course, Magi. What is on your heart?" King Herod said.

"Why doesn't anyone know anything about this King whose birth is predicted in your own writings? It is a marvel to us that you and the priests know nothing. It just seems strange that Zoroastrian Magi from a foreign land travel all the way to remind the Jews that their great King has come."

Herod stared at me as if not sure how to respond. Then a smile came to his face. "Thank you for coming here," he finally responded. Walking over to me, he placed his hand on my shoulder and said, "The ancient prophecies foretell that the birthplace of this King is Bethlehem. Please go there, make a careful search for the Child, and as soon as you find Him, report to me so I may come and worship Him, too." Then he turned and left while we were ushered out.

January 31   Matthew 2:9–12

The Magi Go to Bethlehem

On the way back to the inn, I asked my friends why Herod would not want to go to Bethlehem and see for himself. Things did not add up. "One thing I am certain of," I said as we entered our room, "I do not trust Herod."

We went back to bed, but we couldn't sleep. Finally, we arose, packed our things, paid the innkeeper, and left Jerusalem for Bethlehem. There, ahead of us, was the same star we had seen in the East. Much larger and brighter now than before, we rejoiced as we followed it the seven miles to Bethlehem. It positioned itself directly over a commoner's home. The streets were empty and it was dark. We knew we took a chance of awakening the residents, but this was an urgent matter—the whole purpose of our trip hinged on the Child King we hoped to find inside.

I knocked on the door. A man opened it and asked in surprise, "Who are you?"

"I am Baltasar and these are my friends. We have traveled from the East, a great distance. We saw the star of the Great King and have followed it here to worship Him."

Opening the door, he gestured for us to come in. Inside the humble cottage, we were greeted by his wife who had obviously been asleep. In her arms, she held the little Child. As soon as we saw Him, we fell to our knees, prostrating ourselves before Him. "Long live the Great King," we lauded. Then we gave Him the gifts we had brought—gold, frankincense, and myrrh.

The couple told us of the shepherds who had been visited by angels the night He was born and came to the stable to worship Him. Inquiring about an inn where we might freshen up, they directed us to the very inn where the Child had been born. The innkeeper and his wife were very gracious to us, inquiring as to what brought us to Bethlehem. For some reason, we felt impressed not to reveal our purpose. Exhausted from our journey and the troubling experience in Jerusalem, we went to bed. During the night each of us had the same identical dream of an angel warning us not to return to Herod. We didn't want to see him again, anyway, so after replenishing our supplies, we headed home another way, rejoicing that we had found the King of kings.

February 1 *Matthew 2:13, 14*

The Angel Appears to Joseph

After the Magi left, the three of us tried to go back to sleep. Baby Jesus was soon peacefully dreaming, but Mary and I were wide awake. How could we sleep with a small fortune in our possession? I went to work early. During the day there was much excitement in the village about the visitors from the East who had stayed at the inn and were now purchasing supplies. I tried to act as surprised and curious as everyone else as to the reason they were in Bethlehem.

That evening Mary and I talked about how we could safeguard the valuable gifts the Magi had given Jesus. Tired from the excitement and lack of sleep the previous night, we turned in early. About midnight I had a vivid dream, just like the one in which I was told to take Mary as my wife because she was pregnant by the power of the Holy Spirit. In the dream the angel told me to get up and leave Bethlehem immediately with Mary and Jesus because Herod wanted to kill Him. I awoke with a jolt. The urgency of the message was just as vivid and real as if someone had shaken me awake.

I awoke Mary and told her what I had dreamed. She immediately started packing what few possessions we owned. I loaded the cart, tied the donkey to it, and headed down the road toward Egypt, which is where the angel had directed us to go. I wondered what the people of Bethlehem would think when they found out we had left in the middle of the night without a goodbye. Who in their right mind would do what we had just done based on a dream? It didn't make sense, but we had learned to take God at His word. Our confidence was entirely in Him. Furthermore, He had placed His Son in our care, and His safety and well-being were of paramount importance to us. The moon was bright as I led the donkey down the lonely road. I thought about the future as Mary and Jesus slept in the cart.

February 2 *Matthew 2:16–18*

Herod Kills the Children of Bethlehem

Herod sent out spies to keep an eye on the Magi. I, Jeoram, was one of them. Herod seemed obsessed about finding this child the Magi had spoken of. It was our duty to keep track of them and report back to him our findings. We saw them go into a house near the city gate then later to an inn. We assumed they would be there for awhile, so we went to a local tavern for refreshments. It was early afternoon by the time we arrived back at the inn. Inquiring of the innkeeper about the Magi, he told us they had left through the east gate two hours before. We knew there was no road back to Jerusalem via the east gate, so we rode back to Jerusalem as fast as our horses would take us. All the way back, the other spies and I worried that Herod might punish us for allowing the Magi to slip away.

Upon reaching the palace, we found him brooding in the throne room. When we reported what had happened, he flew into a rage, swearing at us and cursing us. He was furious because the men from the East had outwitted him. Immediately he summoned the captain of the palace guard and told him to round up a troop of soldiers. "Go to Bethlehem and kill every male child two years old and under," he ordered.

I couldn't believe what I was hearing. The man was mad! The captain tried to reason with him, but Herod accused the captain and all the soldiers of insubordination. It was the death penalty if they refused. It took some time to round up a troop in preparation for carrying out Herod's orders. We figured we would leave at first light, but Herod, in a great rage, dispatched us immediately.

Words cannot begin to describe the horror of that night. The screams and cries of parents filled the night, and the piles of small bodies lying in the street was more than enough to cause me to have nightmares and great remorse. May God forgive me.

After we carried out our dastardly deed and were on the road back to Jerusalem, one of the men quoted the words penned by Jeremiah: "A voice is heard in Ramah, weeping and great mourning, Rachel weeping for her children, refusing to be comforted because they are no more."

February 3 *Matthew 2:15*

Joseph, Mary, and Jesus in Egypt

We passed through Tekoa, about six miles south of Bethlehem, in the early predawn hours. I was anxious to put as much distance as possible between us and Herod and was thankful for the progress we had made in the darkness. I kept looking back to see if soldiers were approaching, but I wondered what I would do if they did come.

Dawn finally came, and we pushed on faster. Fortunately, we had a good supply of bread, cheese, and dried fruits that we could eat as we traveled, because we did not dare stop. We paused only to relieve ourselves as nature called. My goal was to get to Beersheba by nightfall, some fifty miles distant. When the road was smooth, I climbed on the cart and tried to get our donkey to jog. That was a challenge at the best of times! The day was long, and we were tired as the sun set behind the hills. I kept wondering what was happening in Bethlehem. People must be worried about our disappearance.

Around nine o'clock, the third hour of the night watch, the lights of Beersheba came into view. There we found an inn with a comfortable room. I fed and bedded our tired donkey. Then Mary and I slept the sleep of the exhausted. At six in the morning, the beginning of day, I paid the innkeeper and questioned him about the road to Gaza. Although he hadn't had many travelers from that direction, he hadn't heard of any problems. Hitching the donkey to the cart, we got on the road again. Through it all, Mary and Jesus did surprisingly well.

Traveling west, we arrived in Gaza by evening where we stayed overnight. Morning found us following the coast highway to Memphis. The Nile, with all its tributaries, was beautiful. Upon arriving in Egypt, I moved my family into a cozy house. Having brought my carpentry tools, I soon found work. Surprisingly, we discovered a large and very helpful Jewish community complete with a synagogue. God was caring for us.

February 4   *Matthew 2:19–23*

In Egypt and Return to Nazareth

We had not been in Egypt long when we heard the terrible news of the great tragedy in Bethlehem. Shocked and saddened, we mourned for our friends who would have lost children in the massacre. A vigil was held at our synagogue, and many prayers were offered for those affected by Herold's cruelty.

Life in Egypt was good, and we soon made many friends. Jesus was growing into a fine young boy. He was very observant and took everything in. We taught Him to make good choices. From a very young age, He was thoughtful and cheerful. Even though He was serious about life, He had a wonderful sense of humor. His father and I taught Him all we could about the Scriptures, and we often took Him into the quietness of the country. Because of the generous gifts of the Magi, Joseph did not have to work as much, so the three of us enjoyed many picnics and country outings. Then one day we heard that Herod had died. We breathed a sigh of relief.

Soon after that Joseph had another dream in which an angel told him to move back to Israel. It was hard to say goodbye to all the new friends we had made even though we had known all along this day would come. The journey from Memphis to Gaza was uneventful. We took our time and stopped often. It felt good to be going home. We stayed at the same inn we had stayed at on the way to Egypt. While there, Joseph heard that Archilaus had taken Herod's place on the throne. Archilaus was of the same character as his father, so Joseph was worried about going back to Bethlehem. God warned him in a dream to go to Galilee, so we headed back to Nazareth.

I prayed that things would be better for us this time around. I still remember the look of surprise on my mother's face as I stood in the doorway. What a homecoming! Jesus had changed so much in the years that we had been gone. It was good to be back in the company of family. We celebrated and told everyone of the events we had experienced while we had been gone. Yes, it was good to be back.

February 5   *Luke 2:40*

Growing Up in Nazareth

Life in Nazareth was a mixed bag. Joseph was able to start up his carpentry shop again, and he soon built up a business that provided for our basic needs. Many of his former customers returned because they appreciated his craftsmanship and honesty. As for me, life wasn't always easy. There were still people who remembered that I had gotten pregnant out of wedlock. Some still whispered about me and cast sideways glances when we met at the well, the village gathering place. It hurt, but there was nothing I could do about it. I was grateful that at least my family believed the truth of Jesus' birth.

Similarly, childhood was not easy for Jesus. Between the ages of four and eleven, He faced many challenges. The kids in the neighborhood liked Him a lot as He was cheerful, athletic, and a good sport. But they often wanted Him to do things that were not right and contrary to what we had taught Him. They were quick to ridicule Him when He refused to participate in things He conscientiously could not do. They also teased Him for helping those who were different or those whom they had played pranks on.

Jesus loved spending time with His dad in the carpenter shop. He was very clever and insightful, and He picked up concepts quickly. Both at home and in the shop, He was always helpful and cooperative.

Jesus and I took many excursions into nature where we could watch the animals and study the plant life. Usually we studied the Scriptures in the great out-of-doors. He asked lots of questions, and I answered as many as I could. Those were great years and not so great years. It was during those years that the rabbi from the synagogue often asked why Jesus was not in school. Joseph and I encouraged Jesus to go, but our son politely, but firmly, refused. He told them that I was His teacher. I felt inadequate, but God gave me wisdom and knowledge. When people asked me about His schooling, I told them that Jesus was in God's school.

February 6   *Luke 2:41, 42*

First Passover Visit

The Passover was the greatest feast of the year. Every young boy looked forward to the time when he would be old enough to celebrate the Passover, and Jesus was no different. Finally the year came that he was of age. We loaded our things in the same old cart we had used to go to Jerusalem and Bethlehem.

The only difference was that we now had a horse, since our donkey had retired after many years of faithful service.

At the appointed time, we met up with friends and began the journey. The roads were full of travelers headed for Jerusalem, singing psalms and hymns. It was wonderful. This Passover was even more special than usual because Jesus was twelve and was, according to Jewish custom, entering adulthood.

The next few days and miles went by quickly, and soon the beautiful temple dome came into view. After finding a place to camp, we joined the festivities. What a reunion, meeting old friends we hadn't seen in years! Joseph saw some relatives from Bethlehem. I saw the innkeeper's wife and some of the ladies I had known there. They were surprised to see us and wanted to know the story behind our secret departure, where we had gone, and what had become of our baby. With tears they spoke of that terrible night when the children were slain. I didn't know what to say. I didn't know how to ease their grief. I still had my son, they did not.

The Passover festivities flew by, and before we knew it the week had come to an end and we were packing up to return home. As we loaded the cart, Joseph told me his cousin was still upset over us leaving Bethlehem without any word. Our hearts ached for our friends and family in Bethlehem who were still grieving, but sadly there was nothing we could do to ease their pain. We had followed the command of God. We didn't understand why He had allowed so many innocent children to die, but we realized that God's ways are not our ways.

As we joined our group of friends heading toward Nazareth, I asked Joseph if he had seen Jesus. "Yes. He was with friends."

February 7　　*Luke 2:43–46*

The Missing Son

We traveled a good distance that first day. By evening we were tired and ready for bed. "Have you seen Jesus?" I asked Joseph.

"No," he answered. "In fact, I haven't seen Him all day. I assumed He was with His friend Josiah."

I began to worry. He always helped us set up camp. Memories of what Herod had done to try and destroy Him began to haunt us. Frantically we looked all around the camp, asking everyone if they had seen Jesus. No one had. Then we began to blame each other.

"Why didn't you look for Him at dinner when I asked you if He was eating with friends?" I lamented.

Joseph responded angrily, "You are His mother; it is your job to keep track of the children."

There was only one thing to do—go back to Jerusalem. The going was slow as we made our way back toward Jerusalem through the steady flow of travelers leaving the city. Later the traffic thinned out as people stopped to camp beside the road. We didn't get back to the city until about nine o'clock, the third hour.

"Where would He go?" we wondered. "He doesn't know anyone, and no one knows Him." We stopped everyone we saw and asked, "Have you seen a young boy of twelve wearing a white jalavah and blue cap?" No one had seen Him or had any suggestions as to where He might be.

For three long days we searched, looking in every conceivable place, constantly calling His name. Our fears and concern heightened with each passing day until we began to wonder if we'd ever find Him again.

Finally, in desperation, I said, "Joseph, He is God's Son. Let's ask Him to help us find Him." Right there on the temple steps we poured out our despair to God. After asking for divine guidance, I felt impressed to go to the classrooms in the temple courtyard where the rabbis taught students. As we walked, I heard a familiar voice. Forgetting my manners, I ran to the room and burst through the doorway. There I saw Him sitting at the feet of the rabbi asking questions. Relief flooded through me and tears sprang to my eyes—He was okay!

February 8 *Luke 2:47-49*

Jesus and the Rabbis

I remember Jesus of Nazareth. At age twelve, He was brilliant, far brighter than any of the students attending the Rabbinical School of which I am master. I am Jeremiah, head master of the Temple School. This Jesus was remarkable! For three days He sat in on our classes. He respectfully listened to what we were teaching, but He also asked questions, questions that left my colleagues and I fumbling for answers.

I asked Him where He had been educated. "From the Scriptures" was all He said. I couldn't think of a school in Nazareth or all of Galilee for that matter. I asked the other rabbis if they knew of any schools. "Well, somebody must have taught Him," I exclaimed. When I asked who taught Him, He said His mother and heavenly Father had been His teachers.

The first day He was with us, He made friends with another student who invited Him to stay at his home. I went to that home at the end of the first day to ask more questions and encourage Him to become a student at our school. He politely refused, saying He needed to return to Nazareth with His parents. I plied Him with questions regarding the Messiah because He had memorized all the Messianic prophecies, especially from the book of Daniel. I asked the family if He could board with them, providing His parents were in agreement. I even offered to pay for His board. They readily agreed. When I asked Him where His parents were, He didn't know.

On the third day of His attendance at our class, His mother showed up in the doorway. We were in the middle of a lively discussion regarding the time of the Messiah's arrival. Evidently the parents had been searching for Him the entire three days He'd been with us. They were greatly relieved, but His mother reprimanded Him. "Where have you been?" she demanded. "Your Father and I have been looking for you!"

He looked at her and replied gently, "Why were you searching? Don't you know that I must be about My Father's work?" He pointed heavenward, said goodbye to us, and slipped out with His parents.

February 9   *Luke 2:50*

Journey Back to Nazareth

As we headed back to Nazareth, it was evident that Jesus had changed in the three days He had been apart from us. It was as though He'd suddenly grown-up and wasn't just a kid anymore. Along the way we met up with a few of His friends and their families from Nazareth, but He didn't hang out with His friends as He had on the way to the Passover. I began to wonder if something bad had happened to Him in Jerusalem. He seemed contemplative, withdrawn, reflective, introspective.

Mary felt that she had been too harsh with Him in front of everyone else at the temple school and that that was why He was so quiet. "I really must have hurt Him," she said to me as I walked beside the donkey.

"I don't think He's upset at you," I told her. "It's something else." I turned around to look for Jesus; I didn't want to lose Him again. About fifty feet behind us, He was walking with His head down as if He was deep in thought or something was bothering Him.

"What did He mean when He said He needed to be about His Father's work in His Father's house?" Mary asked.

I shrugged. "I'm not sure. Perhaps this is all about His relationship with God, His Father."

At Mary's urging I went back to walk with Him while she guided the donkey. "Son," I began, "Your mother and I are concerned about You. Is everything okay?"

He looked at me and smiled. "Everything is fine, Dad," He answered. "This Passover had a big effect on me. I've come to some realizations and gained a clearer picture of who I am and why I've come into this world. Talking with the priests at the temple school affirmed Scriptures that refer to the Messiah. At the temple service when the priest took the life of the lamb, I realized that that lamb represented Me. Now I understand what Isaiah meant when he wrote, 'He was led like a lamb to the slaughter.'"

We stopped in the road. I pulled Him close, and we embraced.

February 10   *Luke 2:51*

The Young Teenager

Growing up in Nazareth was not easy at any age, but especially not as a teenager. There were a lot of temptations and people ready to take advantage of the youth. Jesus was very popular, and most everyone liked Him because of His positive attitude. No matter how bad a situation was, you could be sure that Jesus would be able to find something good about it. People had a great deal of respect for Him because of His honest heart and compassionate spirit. He was always ready to help the underdog, the poor people, and the disadvantaged—He even invited poor kids to His house for lunch and took bread to the beggars by the city gate. All were grateful for His concern for them and in turn were His loyal friends. It seemed to me that He consistently put others before Himself.

Life was good for Jesus, but yet life was hard for Him. Sometimes He'd say, "Aaron, you're my best friend, and I appreciate your friendship, but don't you get hassled because of me?" I did get teased when Jesus refused to do stuff the other kids wanted to do, but everyone knew in their hearts it was wrong and that Jesus was right. He'd memorized the whole Scripture it seemed. He always gave a reason from the Scriptures, usually Proverbs, as to why He couldn't or wouldn't do something. The kids called Him every possible name when He refused to get involved in wrong activities or play a joke on someone that would cause that person pain or embarrassment.

Lots of the girls in Nazareth liked Him, and He was always nice to them. One very bold girl named Hannah was dared by her friends to kiss him. I asked Him later what it was like. He smiled and simply answered, "Nice."

He wasn't your normal teen, but He was a great friend.

February 11   *Luke 2:52*

Young Adulthood

The carpenter's shop was always a busy place. People needed this made or that repaired. We didn't just work with wood, sometimes we had to work with stone or metal. We tackled whatever job needed to be done.

Matthan, my grandfather, started the business in Nazareth and trained Jacob, my father, to continue it. My father taught me, and as much as I wished Jesus would take over the business, I knew He had other plans. One of my other sons would manage the family shop. It wasn't that my other sons weren't good carpenters, but Jesus exhibited qualities that made Him excel. He was an excellent and skilled worker.

It is safe to say that Jesus was a perfectionist—He was never satisfied unless His finished project was perfect. He would spend hours making sure yokes and harnesses were a perfect fit. The customers loved Him and always asked for Him. I must admit, He frustrated me more than once because He was so meticulous, but the people were willing to pay extra for His work.

When He was young, His mother and I had tried and tried to talk Him into attending the synagogue school. But He politely refused, citing Scripture as justification for not attending. Even the rabbis begged Him to come, but He wouldn't go. The main reason He gave was that men's ideas were taught there instead of what God said. I didn't really care for the rabbis myself, finding them rather arrogant, but I still thought it would be in Jesus' best interest to gain their respect and support. We weren't able to convince Jesus of that, and eventually we gave up.

The years passed and He grew into a wonderful young man. News of political events reached our shop on a daily basis. It had become "the meeting place" in town. One day we received news of a preacher named John who was speaking by the Jordan River. We heard that he was calling for people to repent and baptizing them. Upon hearing this news, Jesus stopped working and looked at me. I knew His time had come. He had just turned thirty. Two days later He hung up His tools, kissed us goodbye, and was gone.

February 12   *Matthew 3:3, 4; Mark 1:6*

John the Baptist

John always loved the desert. From the time he was a little lad, his parents would take him out into nature, and when they visited the desert, he always wanted to stay longer. "Someday I am going to live here," he would say.

When John became a teenager, his father, Zechariah, passed away. In his teens, Elizabeth, his mother, was laid to rest. Years before they had made arrangements with me, Sarah, Elizabeth's younger sister, to take good care of him when they were gone. They believed God had a very special work for him to do, and I promised them I would do my best to raise him should they pass away before he was a man.

John was always very spiritually minded, and he loved the Scriptures. An excellent student, he was also a keen observer of people. Other boys his age invited him to do things with them, but he was more interested in going to the desert, searching the Scriptures, or sometimes traveling to the temple in Jerusalem to listen to the rabbis.

I spent as much time with him as I could, but I had children of my own and many times I ended up being a referee between my boys and John. They thought of him as a religious freak and far too straight-laced. Although I tried to encourage them to be a little more like their cousin, they had no interest. John was always a great help to me when he was home, but with each passing year he became more and more distant, disappearing into the desert for two or three weeks at a time.

The last straw for my kids was when John started wearing hermit's clothing—a camel hair robe and a leather belt. Finally, after he celebrated his twenty-eighth birthday, he told me he needed to leave. He felt like he was to stay in the desert in order to be fully prepared for the work God had called him to do. I was worried about him, yet I knew about his miraculous birth and that God had brought him into the world for a specific reason. He thanked me for everything, gathered up his few belongings, and was gone. I never saw him again. However, later I heard reports that he was preaching at the Jordan River.

February 13   *Matthew 3:5; Mark 1:4-6; Luke 3:1-3, 10-14*

John's Call, Ministry and Message

I was at my desert hideaway when the call came, clear and distinct. "John, now is the time to call my people to repentance. You must prepare the way for the Messiah." This is what I had been preparing for my whole life. Finally, God was going to do something about freeing His people from Roman rule!

The Holy Spirit guided me to the Jordan River near Aenon. This was a perfect location because many would hear God's message as they crossed the bridge over the river. There was also plenty of water here for baptizing.

I began to preach from a large rock near the water's edge. God gave me power to speak above the flow of the river so people could easily hear my words. My message was simple but direct: Repent of sin, give yourself to God, and get ready for the coming Messiah. Many of the people, honest at heart, confessed their sins and were baptized. They were hungry for truth from God and not the dry recitation of traditions that they got from the religious leaders.

The word of my preaching spread quickly to the whole area, and people came from Jerusalem, Judea, and the region around the Jordan to hear me speak. As they listened the Holy Spirit convicted them of their sins, and they cried out, "What shall we do?"

I told them, "The man who has two coats should give to the man who has none. Those with extra food should share what they have."

Tax collectors came, too. "What should we do?" they asked.

"Be honest," I told them. "Collect no more than required."

"What about us?" a soldier in the Roman army asked. His friends laughed, but he was sincere.

"Don't exhort money or accuse falsely, and be satisfied with your pay," I responded. Later, he came alone and thanked me for my honest message and asked me to pray for him.

Day after day the people came. A few offered to help me and became my disciples. I could see God's spirit at work—lives were being changed and hearts were being drawn to God.

February 14   *Matthew 3:7-10; Luke 3:7-9*

John and the Pharisees

One day as I was helping John prepare some people for baptism, he said, "Andrew, we have guests." He nodded toward a large number of Pharisees and members of the council coming toward us. Everyone watched as John strode fearlessly toward them, his arm extended and forefinger directed at the delegation.

"You brood of vipers," he shouted. "Who has warned you to flee from the wrath to come?" They stopped dead in their tracks, mouths agape, afraid to come any further. They'd never been spoken to like this before. Filled with the Holy Spirit, John continued, "Produce fruit in keeping with repentance and do not think you can say to yourselves, 'We have Abraham for our Father,' for I tell you, God could raise up children for Abraham out of these stones. Being a descendant of Abraham is neither here nor there. What counts in your life is the fruit you are producing."

I watched them. They appeared very uncomfortable, but also very unrepentant as they pulled their robes about them in defiance. I watched John; his arm appeared as a flaming sword as he pointed at them. "The ax," he cried, "is already at the root of the trees, and every tree that does not produce good fruit will be cut down and thrown into the fire."

I looked at the crowd. There was complete silence as they watched the exchange. Most everyone in the crowd knew about the scandals, the abuses, and the injustices perpetrated by these men. They needed to repent! John stood his ground, waiting for a response. Finally, they began to mutter to each other, "Who does this wild man think he is trying to teach us?" Then every one of them turned and walked away. John looked over at me. I was surprised to see tears streaming down his face. "God wants to save them, too," he said.

February 15   *Luke 3:15–18; Mark 1:1–3, 7, 8; Matthew 3:3, 11, 12*

Is John the Messiah?

We watched the religious leaders stomp off. "What do you think, Andrew?" my friend and fishing partner, John, asked. "Is John the Messiah?"

My answer wasn't very definite, "I don't know, but I guess he could be."

At that exact moment, someone in the crowd shouted, "John, are you the Messiah, the Christ?"

The words seemed to catch John the Baptist by surprise. But in an instant, he responded, "Come near," he called to them. "I must tell you the truth." The people came forward, expecting John to make the long awaited announcement. "I baptize you with water," he began, "but One more powerful than I is coming, whose sandals I am not worthy to untie." He pulled off his sandal and held it up for emphasis. "I am not even worthy to be His slave. He will baptize you with the Holy Spirit and with fire," he continued. "His winnowing fork is in His hand to clear His threshing floor and to gather His wheat into His barn," he gestured with a wide sweep of his hand, "but He will burn up the chaff with unquenchable fire. He will place everything true in its proper place before God and everything false He'll put out with the trash to be burned."

We all listened carefully as John made it clear to us he was not the Messiah but only the one preparing the way for Him. He shared with us the prophecy of Isaiah that explained his purpose. "I am the 'voice of one calling in the wilderness, prepare the way for the Lord. Straighten out the path before Him. Every valley shall be filled and every mountain brought low. The crooked places shall be made straight and the rough places made smooth. All mankind will see God's salvation.' We are looking for the mighty One," John cried, emphasizing every word.

"But when will He come?" someone asked.

"Soon," John declared. "Yes, very, very soon the Messiah will come. He will restore to us all we have lost."

I looked at my friend John and said, "The sooner the better!"

February 16   *Matthew 3:13–17; Mark 1:9–11; Luke 3:21, 22*

Jesus Is Baptized

Andrew and I were at the Jordan helping John prepare people for baptism. We came as often as we could, even though some family members were beginning to complain that we weren't pulling our weight with the net repairs and preparation of the fish for market. When we tried to get our brothers to come, they maintained they were too busy "keeping things going" and just couldn't afford the time away. My brother James was beginning to show his resentment at all the time I was spending with John the Baptist, but for some reason I felt irresistibly drawn there.

I watched as a young man about our age joined the line of people wanting to be baptized. When He spoke, I could tell from His accent that He was a Galilean. John turned and, seeing who it was, literally stopped dead in his tracks and stared at Him. The young man approached John and asked to be baptized. John shook his head and said, "No! I need to be baptized by You, and yet You come to me?"

John's words from a previous day flashed into my mind: "One is coming whose sandals I am not worthy to loosen." Could this be the One he spoke of?

I listened as the young man responded, "Let it be so now; it is proper for us to do this to fulfill all righteousness." John seemed to understand, smiled and consented. They waded out to the deeper place and John laid Him under the water.

As soon as He was standing again, a most amazing thing happened. When He bowed His head in prayer, it appeared as though heaven opened and a bright form like a dove descended and lit on Him. Then a loud voice from the heavens, almost like thunder, declared, "This is My Son whom I love, with Him I am well pleased."

All of us there saw the dove and heard the voice. In amazement we watched as He exited the water and was suddenly gone. I turned to look at Andrew. He smiled and nodded at me. I couldn't wait to go home and tell James that we had seen the Messiah!

February 17   *Mark 1:12; Matthew 4:1*

Preparation for Ministry

I am Gabriel, the one who stands in the presence of God, always ready to do His will. I am the angel who took the place of Lucifer as covering cherubim after he chose to rebel against God. In that time long ago, I pled earnestly with him to return to God, but he was adamant that he would never again declare allegiance to the second Person of the Godhead. Finally his rebellion turned to open conflict and he, my brother, and millions of our fellow angels with him were cast out into this world.

Now, here we are again, in a face to face battle for the human race. None of us in heaven believed our Commander would give up everything that pertained to deity and become a human being, lower even than us angels! We were dumbfounded to see Him, the One who created the universe, transformed into a helpless baby in the care of unpredictable, sinful humans. Now, in this barren wilderness, He has come to prepare for ministry and the work of salvation. God sent me to be His invisible companion, giving only a sense of the presence of heaven as He fasted and prayed.

Lucifer was there, too, watching His every move. I shuddered to imagine what Lucifer, because of his hatred for Jesus, might be planning to do. During the day Jesus found a place of shade that gave Him some protection from the heat of the desert. During the long hours He meditated upon His mission and work. I often heard Him in prayer, calling out for strength to accomplish the work before Him. Without food, His human body became emaciated and gaunt. At night He frequently awoke from sleep to pray as prompted by the Spirit. My work was to protect Him from the wild animals, the creatures He Himself had created. His sole objective was to be as close as He possibly could to the Father. I watched Him grow weaker and weaker, and wondered how He could survive.

February 18   *Matthew 4:1-10; Luke 4:1-12; Mark 1:13, 14*

The Temptation

I couldn't believe He would actually stoop to a human form! You can't comprehend the transition from divinity to humanity unless you have actually lived with divinity. It really cannot be explained in human terms; no language can describe it. I told my followers it would never happen, but, shockingly, it did. When I stared down at Him, God, as a baby in a cradle, I knew that the threat to my kingdom was very real. I resolved then, as I do now, that He would never succeed. He has to be stopped at all costs. That is why I am here in this wilderness, paying very close attention to Him, my eternal nemesis, the Son of God.

For thirty years I have tried everything to cause Him to sin, but to no avail. He safeguards Himself with prayer and meets my temptations with Scripture. I have succeeded with every other human but not Him. Not yet. I cannot entice Him to let His guard down. But in the forsaken wilderness, I watched Him grow weaker with each passing day. Still, He spent His time praying, which worried me.

I knew why He was there. He was accomplishing what the Israelites failed to do—forty years and forty days. On the last day I was sure I could make Him fail as did they. I approached Him as an angel messenger from God.

"Son of God, if this is who You are, God declares You successful. Your fast is over. Change these stones into bread and eat," I said.

"It is written, man does not live on bread alone," He quoted.

Then I took Him to the temple dome and told Him to prove His divinity by jumping off. "Hasn't God promised to send angels to protect You?"

Again He responded with Scripture. "Do not put the Lord your God to the test."

Since that tactic didn't work, I took Him to a mountaintop and showed Him the world's kingdoms.

"Worship me and all this is Yours," I offered.

In His response He called me by name. "Get away from me, Satan! We are to worship the Lord God and Him only," He responded.

I was forced to leave Him. I had failed. I vowed to catch Him at a more opportune time. But if I must be honest, I am worried.

February 19   *Matthew 4:11; Luke 4:13*

The Temptation Aftermath

I was given explicit instructions not to intervene unless directed by the Father. I, and the angels with me, watched with keen interest as Lucifer attacked our beloved Commander at His weakest moment. It all seemed so unfair and unjust. We struggled not to step in. He was so weak and emaciated, and there was so much at stake. What if He failed because of sheer exhaustion?

Satan's first deception was so subtle. The devil came to Him as an angel from God, as one of us, declaring His fast was over because God had accepted His sacrifice and all was well. I watched Jesus struggle. He was desperate for food. For just a moment I thought He might succumb to the temptation. Then it was as though His senses and mind realized something was wrong. Turning stones to bread would break His dependence on His Father by working a miracle on His own behalf. When He refused and quoted Scripture, we breathed a collective sigh of relief. Satan had been uncovered.

But unfortunately, Satan wasn't done. He had another test and this time he misquoted Scripture, suggesting that we angels would protect Him if He threw Himself off the temple. Again Jesus countered by quoting Scripture correctly. We were amazed that, in His condition, He could think clearly. Satan had one more attack prepared, but once again Jesus stood on the true Word of God.

After this final temptation, a messenger from God's throne told us the Father wanted us to intervene on behalf of His Son. Satan was driven away, and we rejoiced in Jesus' victories as we tenderly cared for our beloved Friend, feeding Him with bread from heaven. After He had eaten and rested, I asked Him why He was so determined to save a world of people who did not seem to care. "Because of love," He answered. "When you really love, you will do whatever it takes to save them at whatever cost to yourself." That was the answer I knew He would give, and it was the answer I really wanted to hear.

February 20   *John 1:19–28*

The Pharisees and Council Return

My fishing buddy, John, and I continued to assist John the Baptist. We were encouraged by His daily message and the commitment of those who were baptized. But John and I could not get that young Galilean off our minds. We repeatedly asked John the Baptist about Him, but all he would say was, "Be patient; you will know Him soon enough."

However, when we asked him today, his answer surprised us. "He is here in the crowd." We searched all the faces but saw no one who looked like Him. However, as we scanned the crowd, we saw the Levites and priests coming with their grand entourage. "Here they are back again. I wonder what they want now," John the Baptist mused aloud.

We watched as they made their way to the front of the crowd. One of them demanded, "Baptist, who are you? We have been sent by the Sanhedrin to find out who you really are."

John answered, "If you are asking if I am the Christ, the Messiah, no, I am not."

"Well then, are you a prophet?" they asked.

"No, I am not."

"So tell us who you are that we may give an answer to those who sent us. What do you say about yourself?" they queried.

"I am the one spoken of by Isaiah the prophet," John said. "I am the voice of one calling in the desert, make straight the way of the Lord."

One of the Pharisees in the delegation called out, "Why do you baptize if you are not the Christ or Elijah or the prophet?"

"I baptize with water," John responded, "but among you stands One you do not know. He is the One who comes after me, whose sandals I am not worthy to untie. He will baptize you with the Spirit."

Everyone immediately looked around to see who John was talking about. "Who is he talking about?" they all began to ask each other.

"John," I asked, "you are speaking of the Galilean, the one you baptized, right? I don't see Him anywhere."

"Keep watching," was all John would say.

February 21 *John 1:29-34*

Jesus, the Lamb of God

The next day Andrew and I went back to the Jordan hoping to find the One whom John the Baptist had spoken of. We had stayed up late into the night discussing John's statement that day about Him being in the crowd. The coming of the Messiah, which was prophesied by Daniel, had been talked about by everyone for years, and many false prophets had come and gone. How could we know for sure that it was Him? We had prayed together until the early morning, asking God to show us the truth.

It was about the fourth hour, or 10 in the morning, when John the Baptist saw us coming and waved us over to him. "He is here," he said, "coming now!" Then he climbed up on a large rock and spoke to the crowd. "Look!" he cried. "The Lamb of God who takes away the sin of the world is coming!"

We strained to see where he was pointing. John continued, "This is the One I meant when I said, 'A man who comes after me has surpassed me because He was before me.'"

We looked for the young man John had baptized, but all we saw was a rather frail looking, emaciated soul who did not fit our description of the Messiah. "Him? That skinny guy?" we exclaimed to each other. We looked at each other and then at John, wondering if we had all been deceived. "How can you be sure that He is the one?" we asked John.

"I saw the Spirit come down from heaven as a dove and remain on Him. You saw it, too," he reminded us. We nodded. "I would not have known for sure, either, except the One who sent me to baptize with water told me 'the man on whom you see the Spirit come down and remain, He is the One who will baptize with the Holy Spirit.' I have seen, so I testify this man is indeed the Son of God."

We had every reason to believe John; his testimony was good enough for us. Without delay, we knew we had to meet Him.

February 22   *John 1:35–39*

The First Disciples Meet Jesus

The day John pointed to Him and declared Him to be the Lamb of God we immediately went to meet Him, but we were disappointed to discover that somehow He'd disappeared into the crowd.

That night we prayed and asked God to send Him back so we could meet Him. Early the next morning we headed back to the Jordan River. "John, have you seen Him?" I asked.

"Not yet, Andrew," he replied with a smile, "but I am sure He will come."

At about the third hour, nine o'clock, John the Baptist looked up and cried out, "Look, here He comes, the Lamb of God!"

Yes, there He was, but no one except my fishing buddy, John, and I seemed very interested. I have to admit that He didn't look like royalty in His ordinary peasant clothes, but we followed Him as He passed through the people and headed away from the crowd. Suddenly He stopped, turned around, and asked, "What do you want?" Not sure what to say, I asked where He was staying. "Come," He smiled, "and you will see." We went with Him to His place. It was a simple rented upper room on the roof of someone's home not far from the Jordan where John the Baptist was preaching. He invited us in and made us feel very welcome. We felt a little awed to be in the presence of the Messiah. "What would you like to know?" He asked.

I answered, "John gave his testimony that You are the Messiah, the Son of God. Is it true?"

He paused a moment and then smiled, putting us at ease. "Let me tell you about Myself," he began. Then He took us on an amazing journey through the law and prophets from Genesis onward, quoting one passage of Scripture after another, bringing it all together like no rabbi had ever done before. We were amazed at His knowledge of Scripture and the wisdom He possessed. Our hearts burned within us as we listened. We spent the entire day there listening to Him and asking questions. We had found the Messiah, and we didn't want to leave!

February 23   *John 1:40–42*

Telling My Brother

After spending a day and night with Jesus, we finally tore ourselves away, knowing that we had to get back home. All the way we talked excitedly about the things Jesus had said. Passages the rabbis had interpreted in their own way now took on new meaning as Jesus had explained them in light of John's work and the coming of the Messiah. The time had passed so quickly. We had been so totally engrossed in His words that we didn't even notice it was getting dark. When He invited us to stay the night, we could hardly believe it was so late.

It took us about a day and a half to walk home to Bethsaida, which is on the shores of the Sea of Galilee. The first thing I did when I got home was track down my brother Simon. I was so excited! I told him he had to come and meet the Messiah. However, Simon did not match my enthusiasm. "There has been such a proliferation of false prophets. How do you know He is the Messiah?" he asked me.

"John's testimony and Jesus' knowledge of the Scriptures confirm that He is the Messiah. I am certain of it."

Simon had a great deal of respect for John the Baptist. "Well, if John testified that He was the Son of God, that is significant," Simon said.

"This truly is the Christ. Please come meet Him," I begged.

Simon finally agreed after I promised to help him mend nets on our return to Bethsaida. We traveled the long road back to the Jordan where Jesus was staying. Before I even had a chance to introduce my brother, Jesus said, "You are Simon, son of John. You will be called Cephas or Peter."

"How do you know me and my father?" Simon asked. "Did my brother tell you?"

Jesus simply smiled and said, "Let me introduce Myself to you." So Simon Peter listened as Jesus opened the Scriptures.

February 24   *John 1:43, 44*

Jesus Calls Philip

My brother Simon, now named Peter by Jesus, was completely taken away by Jesus' explanation of the Scriptures. Late into the night He shared passages of Scripture with us, all from memory. Never had we heard anything like this before (or since, for that matter)! Peter was convinced. We stayed overnight with Jesus in His rooftop apartment. The next morning as we ate breakfast He asked us about our family and friends. Then He said, "I think we should go to Galilee."

Gathering up our coats, we excitedly headed north toward our home. Time passed quickly in the company of our new Friend, and the next day we were home at Bethsaida. We introduced Jesus to everyone. He showed a genuine interest in each person. Later, we took Him to the Sea of Galilee and showed Him our fishing boats. He asked a lot of questions about fishing, which we were happy to answer.

Then, all of a sudden, He turned to me and said, "Andrew, where can we find your friend Philip?" He caught my look of surprise.

"How do you know about Philip?" I asked.

Ignoring my question, He continued, "I need to speak with him."

"Come, I will show you," I replied. Peter stayed by the boats to mend some nets. It didn't take us long to walk to Philip's home. Soon we were entering the courtyard. Philip's family had moved to Bethsaida because his father had something to do with the Roman army. Although the family was Greek, they were interested in the God of the Jews and had been studying with a local rabbi.

When we found Philip, I introduced him to Jesus who greeted him and then gazed at him for a long time, as though looking into his soul. Finally Jesus said, "Let me tell you about Myself." And Jesus opened the Scriptures to Philip as He had done with John, Peter, and me. After talking for some time, Jesus said to Philip, "I would like you to be my disciple. Come, follow Me."

Philip's response was, "Yes, Lord!"

February 25 *John 1:45, 45*

Philip Calls Nathanael

After meeting Jesus and hearing Him explain the Scriptures, I was as convinced as Andrew and Peter were that Jesus was indeed the true Messiah. When Jesus and Andrew headed back to where Peter was working on the nets, I could not keep the good news to myself. I had to tell someone! Naturally the first person I thought of was Nathanael, my best friend. We had grown up together in Bethsaida. It was because of the influence of Nathanael's family that my parents had become interested in Judaism and had arranged for my studies with the rabbi.

It didn't take long to find him in the backyard of their home reading the Scriptures under a huge fig tree. "What are you reading?" I asked.

"Jacob's vision of God when He was in the wilderness," he answered.

I could hardly let him finish what he was saying because I was so anxious to tell him about Jesus. "Listen to me!" I exclaimed. "We have found the One Moses wrote about in the law! The One you were just reading about! The One the prophets predicted would come! The One we have waited for so long! He is here! I know, because He opened the Scriptures and showed me how they all point to Him. His name is Jesus of Nazareth, the son of Joseph."

"Nazareth?" Nathanael wrinkled his brow. "I don't remember reading about a good prophet or Messiah coming from there. Nazareth is small and hardly even mentioned in the Scriptures. In fact, I can't imagine any good thing coming out of that place."

I didn't know how to answer him except to simply say, "You must come meet Him. You have to see for yourself and listen as He opens the Scriptures to you. I am certain you will be convinced. He asked me to be His disciple, and I came right away to tell you about Him. I know where He is. Please come meet Him!"

February 26   *John 1:47–51*

Jesus Calls Nathanael

I must admit, I was skeptical and not at all convinced. There were so many claiming to be the Christ, but because Philip was so insistent, I agreed to go with him. As we walked along the shore to where Andrew and Peter's boat was docked, I asked Philip what had convinced him that this man was the Messiah.

"Oh, there's a number of things. His understanding of Scripture is unsurpassed, and conviction gripped my heart as He explained the Word of God to me. Then there is John the Baptist's own testimony that Andrew shared with me. John said plainly, 'This man is the Son of God.'"

"The Son of God?" I asked incredulously. I thought He was to be a great prophet or king.

"I'm only telling you what Andrew told me," Philip replied.

We saw the three of them near the boat working together on the fishing nets. As we come near, the one they called Jesus looked at me and said, "Here is a true Israelite in whom there is nothing false."

I was taken aback in surprise by His statement. "How do you know me?" I asked.

He answered, "I saw you while you were under the fig tree, before Philip called you."

I was stunned. How could He know I had been reading under a fig tree? Only God could know that. Then I remembered Andrew's comment about what John the Baptist had said, "This man is God's Son!" A powerful conviction came over me that this man was truly the Son of God. I looked at Him and declared, "Rabbi, You are the Son of God. You are the King of Israel."

He smiled and said, "Nathanael, you believe in Me because I told you I saw you under a fig tree. You will see greater things than that. I tell you the truth, you will see heaven open and angels ascending and descending on the Son of man."

I looked around at the others. We all nodded in amazed agreement. Truly, we had found the Christ.

February 27   *John 2:1*

Invitation to the Wedding in Cana

I hadn't seen Jesus in more than a month. Every day I prayed for Him and asked God to take care of Him. I also told God how much I missed Him and how wonderful it would be to have Him come home, even if only for a little visit. Life was not easy after Jesus left and Joseph died. The older children were busy with their own families. I was grateful that they came by when they could and made sure my needs were met, but life had changed so much for me. I often found myself feeling very lonely.

One day when I was feeling particularly blue, He showed up. "Son, you've come home!" I cried. We embraced for a long time. Then, like a typical mother, I looked at Him carefully and noticed that He had lost weight. I also sensed a new depth of confident strength about Him.

"Mother, I have missed you, but I prayed that God would take good care of you." He told me all about where He had been and what He had done. I didn't understand why He had spent so long in the wilderness fasting, except as He said, to prepare for His ministry. That explained why He was thinner. When He told me He had been baptized in the Jordan River by John the Baptist, my mind flashed back to my visit years before with Elizabeth and Zechariah. Jesus said He had met several godly young men whom He had asked to become His disciples.

He was very anxious to know all about life at home, especially His brothers and sisters. I told Him we would plan a big family reunion for the next night. Then I remembered the big wedding being planned in Cana for His cousin and asked if He would come and bring His new disciples. He assured me He would come with His friends so we could meet them. The next night we celebrated together as a family, and everyone caught up on all the news. I told Him about a young woman here in Nazareth that would make a wonderful wife. He just smiled and said, "Caring for a wife and family does not fit in with God's plans."

The following day He left with a promise to meet us in Cana.

February 28 *John 2:3*

A Wine Shortage

At first I was a bit reluctant to attend the wedding at Cana, partly because we didn't know the people, but mainly because we had lots of work to do. But Jesus was insistent, mostly because He wanted us to meet His family. He said He really needed to be there and felt it was important we come too. So off we went—Jesus, my brother Andrew, Philip, Nathanael, and myself, Peter.

It took us a day to get to Cana from Bethsaida. The festival was in full swing when we arrived that evening. We met the happy couple and Mary and Jesus' stepbrothers and stepsisters. After the introductions were done, we sat down to enjoy the food and festivities. And I have to say, the food was fantastic. We stayed with relatives of the groom that night. The next day we were back at the wedding banquet. There were events planned and lots of dancing and feasting. It was definitely a great wedding.

On the third day of the festivities, the steward in charge of provisions ran out of wine, the fresh grape juice we had all been enjoying. A wine shortage at a wedding feast was a major problem. The steward was frantic. There was no place to get the quantity of wine needed for so large a crowd. This was a disaster of major proportions. They couldn't just call the celebration off, but no one seemed to have a solution to the problem either. Thankfully, the guests were oblivious to the situation.

I would have known nothing about it, either, except I happened to overhear one of the servants telling the steward that there was a shortage of wine. It was then that Mary went to Jesus and told Him there was no more wine. That was all she said. I couldn't wait to see what He would do about resolving this problem.

March 1   *John 2:4–8*

Jesus Turns Water to Wine

I must admit, I was surprised at Jesus' response to His mother, but afterward it all made sense. Jesus leaned over and said, "Peter, come with me." We walked back to where the food was being prepared. His mother was already there, nodding at Jesus and telling the servants to do whatever He instructed them to do. Looking back, it is easy to see how a mother's pride in her son drove Mary to act as she did.

Near the door to the kitchen were six huge ceremonial washing jars used in Jewish cleansing rituals. Each jar held about twenty gallons of water. They were extras, ready to be filled if needed. Some Jews wouldn't eat unless their hands had been ceremonially cleansed. Jesus told the servants to fill the jars with water. This meant loading a donkey cart with ten two-gallon jars, taking them a quarter mile to the town well, filling them, and hauling them back to the banquet. It took seven trips to fill the jars because some of the water was lost in transport. At two miles an hour, including loading and unloading the jars, it took them more than two hours to fill six large jars. Finally, the servant in charge of the kitchen staff came and told Him the mission was accomplished—the jars were filled.

Jesus told him to pour a cup and give it to the steward of the feast. He objected, "Sir, we cannot serve the guests water!"

I told the servant to just do as he was told. I will never forget the look of shock and bewilderment on that servant's face. As he lifted the jar and poured its contents into a cup, we were all amazed to see pure juice flow out of the jar instead of water! We all tasted it. It was the best I'd ever had! The servant took a cup to the steward after he had checked all of the ceremonial jars—they were all full of the best grape juice ever. I looked at Jesus. He just smiled and asked if I liked it. "Like it," I answered, "I love it!"

March 2   *John 2:9–11*

The Wedding Feast Saved

The steward came back to the kitchen as giddy as a teenage boy. "This is superb!" he cried. "Where did you get fresh juice this time of year?" Before the servant had a chance to answer, the steward had swung around and headed back to the banquet room and straight to the bridegroom. He privately asked the groom where he'd been hiding the best juice he had ever tasted. The bridegroom sampled the juice from the cup held by the steward and shook his head.

"This is delicious! I have no idea where it came from. Where would I get juice like this at this time of the year?" In all the excitement, the servants began pouring the juice into cups to be served to the guests. Only the head servant came to Jesus and asked Him who He was, "Who are you? Are you a prophet?" Before Jesus could answer, one of the servers called him away.

Jesus turned to me and said, "Let's go."

At that moment, Mary approached Jesus. "Come," she said, "I want to tell everyone about the miracle! The people are asking who provided the best juice they have ever tasted."

Jesus simply said, "No, Mother, this is not the time." I went to find my brother Andrew and the other two disciples. Jesus had already begun to walk back to the place where we were staying.

Remembering the disappointed look on Mary's face, I asked Jesus why He hadn't at least gone to the bridegroom. He said to me, putting His hand on my shoulder, "Peter, My time has not yet come, but someday it will."

This miracle of changing water to wine was the first miracle Jesus performed, and we were witness to it. The next day we said our goodbyes to the bride and groom. No one mentioned the miracle, but the groom gave Jesus a hug and said, "Thank you."

March 3 *John 2:12, 13*

To Capernaum

After the wedding Mary and her stepchildren joined us for breakfast at the house the bridegroom had arranged for us to stay at. The home was large and comfortable, and our gracious host provided a lovely meal for us. Everyone was in good spirits. Of course, the talk around the table included much discussion about the fresh wine that had suddenly appeared at the end of the feast. Someone suggested the groom had imported it from the South, Egypt perhaps. I looked at Mary, and she flashed a knowing smile my direction. Everyone concluded it was a mystery and that God had provided just as He always does when there is a need.

As soon as He could, Jesus changed the subject, "Where shall we go from here?" Some of Joseph's sons said they needed to get home soon because of work-related responsibilities. "Why don't we go to Capernaum for a few days?" Jesus suggested. "I don't know when I will be back to Nazareth again, and that way we can enjoy each others company for a few more days."

Everyone thought it was a good idea. One of the boys said he needed to pick up supplies there anyway. We thanked our host and offered to pay him for his kindness, but he refused, saying only that it was his pleasure. We gathered up our things and headed off to Capernaum. Jesus, the four of us, Mary, and her family made up our group.

On the way James, Jesus' stepbrother, came to me and asked, "Simon Peter, you were there in the kitchen with Jesus when this fresh wine appeared. Can you tell me what really happened? I need to know."

I looked at him, smiled, and said, "It was a miracle. Jesus turned water to wine."

We all had a great time at Capernaum getting better acquainted with Mary and the family. Then they left for Nazareth while we headed back to our fishing business. Jesus decided to go to Jerusalem about a week before the Passover, and we made plans to meet Him there.

March 4   *John 2:14–22*

The First Passover and Cleansing the Temple

Let me introduce myself. I am Nicodemus, a Pharisee and member of the Sanhedrin. I was near the temple gate, feeling disgusted with all the noise of merchants, when I overheard arguing on the temple steps over the sale of sacrificial animals. It was deplorable! I wished someone would do something about it. Every time I mentioned it at the meeting of the Sanhedrin the subject was ignored.

Suddenly, this young rabbi appeared and literally turned the place upside down! He tipped over the money changers' tables, released the animals, and chased them away from the temple. Buyers and sellers in His path scattered. In His hand He wielded a whip of leather cords used for driving cattle. It appeared like a flaming sword. The rest of us stood in shocked silence.

A money changer ran up to me shouting, "Stop this madman!"

I laughed at him and said in return, "You stop Him!"

There were coins, tables, and cages scattered everywhere. Then the rabbi stood at the top of the steps like God Himself and shouted to the sellers hurrying away, "Get these out of here! How dare you turn My Father's house into a marketplace?"

I remembered the words of the psalmist: "Zeal for your house will consume me."

Suddenly a delegation of religious leaders appeared. "What miraculous sign can You perform to prove to us You have the authority to do what You just did?"

"Destroy this temple and in three days I will raise it again," He answered.

Much later I shared His words with the disciples, but it wasn't until after the resurrection that we realized what temple He was referring to. His words were used against Him at His trial and were a great perplexity to all of us until much later when the meaning came clear.

The Pharisees laughed at Him. "It took forty-six years to build this temple, and You are going to raise it in three days!" they cried.

By now a large crowd had gathered around Jesus. He healed the sick and spoke words of encouragement to the downhearted. Everyone was in awe. Some began to say, "He must be a prophet." I was sure of one thing—I had to meet Him privately.

March 5   *John 3:1*

Nicodemus Searches for Jesus

I knew it would be impossible to meet this rabbi during the day. It would not be wise for me to be seen in public with such a controversial figure. But who would know where to locate Him at night? After checking at a few of the local inns and not finding Him registered, I realized that He would, of course, be with the Galileans. As I made my way through the streets, I overheard many of the townsfolk discussing the incident at the temple, and I heard someone say, "I saw Him and a few friends leave the city by way of the Kidron Valley and the Mount of Olives."

At dusk I headed off in that direction. It was dark by the time I reached the Mount of Olives. I tried to ask individuals rather than groups for the Galilean so not too many people would wonder why I was asking for Him and start rumors. It was a little embarrassing, but I led them to believe that I was on official business for the Sanhedrin and needed to ask Him some questions.

Inwardly, I admired Him for doing what He did. It took a lot of guts. Even though no one would openly admit it for fear of recrimination, the people agreed that it needed to be done and should have been done a long time ago. Unfortunately, the sellers and money changers were back on the temple steps the very next day with their noise and animals—still someone had dared to confront the establishment. I'll never forget the power that attended Him that day.

March 6   *John 3:2–7*

Nicodemus Finds Jesus

After making a few inquiries at some of the camps, I found His friends sitting around the fire. "Where is the rabbi?" I asked.

Very surprised to see a Pharisee standing there at night, one of them asked, "Why? Do you want to question His authority too?"

"No," I answered, "I just want to find out who He is."

Seemingly pleased with my answer, they pointed to where a man was praying, about fifty feet away. I thanked them and walked over to Him. He looked up at me as though He'd been expecting me. When I introduced myself, it seemed as if He already knew me. So I began, "Rabbi, we know You are a teacher from God because no one could perform the miraculous signs You are performing were He not from God."

He completely ignored my comment, which I meant as a compliment, and said, "Unless a person is born again he cannot see God's kingdom. I'm telling you an absolute certainly."

His statement took me by surprise. I wanted to say, "But I am a son of Abraham and a Pharisee, that qualifies me for God's Kingdom," but I was curious as to what He meant by being "born again," so

I said, "How can a man be born when he is old? Surely he cannot enter into his mother's womb and be born when he is old." It was a dumb question. He knew it and I knew it.

He gave me an incredulous look, but He patiently began to explain. "No one, absolutely no one, can enter heaven unless he is first born of water and the spirit. Flesh is born of flesh and spirit of spirit. You shouldn't be surprised," Jesus continued, "that I am telling you that you must be born again."

I was aware that new converts to the faith needed baptism. But me? I had always been a righteous man, not to mention all my other credentials. Now He was telling me I was unfit without this rebirth. I wondered, *If I'm not qualified, who is?*

March 7   John 3:8–12

The Discussion Continues

I was a little upset that this young, unknown rabbi would presume to teach me, a Pharisee. He made things worse by implying I was not savable in my present condition. Although I was shaken, a little voice inside me said, *Why don't you just keep your mouth shut and listen because He is telling you what you need to hear.*

He continued, "The wind blows wherever it wants to. You can hear its sound, but no one knows where it came from or where it is going. So it is with everyone born of the Spirit."

Was He suggesting that some invisible power sweeps across a person and makes him fit for God's kingdom? I'd been told salvation, that is, earning God's favor and a place in His kingdom, required a lifetime of ceremony and ritual. But this rabbi was telling me nothing I had done counted with God, unless the Spirit was working through me.

Shaking my head in amazement, the words tumbled out, "How can this be?" My thoughts were going a mile a minute. *All I have been told is untrue. I am sure this man is from God—He must know the truth.*

He saw my bewildered look so with compassion, He continued to explain. "You are one who teaches the people of Israel, and you do not know these things? The prophets and John the Baptist and now I are telling you the truth. We simply speak about the things we know and testify to what we have seen, but still you teachers of Israel will not accept our testimony."

Somehow He'd known all along I'd come here to test Him, check Him out, find out who He was and if He was sent of God, and learn what His plans for the nation were. But here He was teaching me amazing things. He made it clear He knew I had come with an agenda by what He said next. "I've spoken to you about earthly things, and you do not believe. How will you believe when I speak to you of heavenly things?" He was right. What I was being told was the essence of eternal realities, the stuff of God's kingdom.

March 8   *John 3:13–18*

Jesus Tells Nicodemus of Kingdom Realities

I kept my mouth shut and let Him do the talking because what He was saying spoke to my heart. Conviction griped me. He continued, "No one has ever gone into heaven except the One who came from heaven, the Son of man." I knew He was referring to Himself. "Just as Moses lifted up the snake in the wilderness, the Son of man must also be lifted up that everyone who believes in Him might have eternal life."

I knew the story of Moses and the bronze snake from the Pentateuch. I knew that the people had been healed when they looked up at the serpent. It wasn't until He was crucified that this statement came home full force and my mind went back to our evening talk. That evening I just listened and tried to take it all in.

"For God so loved the world," He continued, "that He gave His one-of-a-kind Son, that whosoever believes in Him will not perish but have eternal life." Again conviction swept over me that this man in front of me was the Son of God. He must have seen the look of astonishment and bewilderment on my face as He explained, "God did not send His Son into the world to condemn it, but to save it through Him."

The world? I asked myself. *I thought the Messiah was to save Israel from the Romans and restore her to her rightful place.*

Jesus continued, "Whoever believes in God's Son is not condemned, but whoever does not believe stands condemned already because he has not believed in God's unique Son."

He was basically telling me if I did not believe in Him, God's Son sent to save the world and give eternal life, I would be condemned and not see God's kingdom. I had come here to find out who He really was and He had told me He was God's Son. How could this be? This was much more than I had bargained for. *How does the saving of Israel from the Romans fit into all of this?* I wondered. *He hasn't even mentioned that. He is upsetting everything I have been taught and believed.*

March 9   *John 3:19–21*

Interview With Nicodemus Concludes

He could tell I was agitated because of all He had said. He knew I needed time to think these things through. "Let me summarize what I have just told you," He said. "A Great Light has come into the world, but men love darkness more than the light because their deeds are evil. All who do evil hate the light and will not come into the light for fear their deeds will be exposed."

But I have lived a godly life, I thought. *I'm not an evil person.*

He concluded His remarks by saying, "Whoever lives by the truth…" He paused and looked at me as though He were searching my very soul. "Whoever lives by the truth comes into the light so that it may be plainly seen that what he has done has been done through God."

He summarized it all very well. It was clear. He was the Light through whom the truth of God would be revealed. Those who would not come to Him would remain in darkness. Again conviction took hold of me. *This man is the truth. What He has said is eternal life*, I thought. Never in my life had I heard anything like this. Never in my life had I met anyone like this. He had single-handedly, in one short interview, turned all that I had ever believed upside down. I thanked Him and told Him I needed to be going.

He put His hand on my shoulder, "You came to find out who I am and now you know." I smiled and nodded. All the way home and every day to come, I thought about what He had told me. As I watched Him and heard the reports of His work, my faith grew stronger, and I became convicted that He was all He claimed to be, the very Son of God. How could we have been so shortsighted to think He'd only come to save the Jews from the Romans?

March 10 *John 3:22–24*

Baptizing at Salim

I will admit that I, Andrew, was under strong conviction that Jesus was indeed the Messiah, the Son of God, as John the Baptist had testified. There were, however, some things about Him I simply did not understand. After the miracle at Cana, we had a nice time together in Capernaum. Then He went to the Passover and drove away the money changers in the temple, upsetting the leading Jews in Jerusalem, the very ones whom He needs to be on good terms with to organize our army to drive out the Romans.

One night He had a private interview with a Pharisee who came looking for Him among a bunch of Galileans. Were it not for John the Baptist's testimony and the miracles I have witnessed, I might have doubts as to who He is. But when I am with Him, I feel at peace. When the Passover ended, He invited us (Philip, Nathanael, James, John, Peter, and me) to go into the Judean countryside with Him.

We were near the spot where John the Baptist was baptizing the many people who were still coming to him. We were at a place called Tenon, near Salim, just across the river from where John was preaching. Some of the people at the Passover recognized Jesus as the one who confronted the Jews and healed sick people near the steps where the money changers had been. They came to us and wanted Jesus to baptize them. Jesus told us to baptize them.

I said to Jesus, "Rabbi, aren't we cutting in on and interfering with John's work?"

He simply said, "John has plenty of work to do."

We baptized many and soon others came. It wasn't long before there were more with us than with

John. I knew most of John's disciples, so I felt awkward. Why hadn't Jesus taken us someplace else? While we baptized, Jesus spoke to the people and healed some. I kept looking across the river at John and his disciples, wondering what they were feeling as more and more people came to us and less to them.

March 11   *John 3:25–36*

John Testifies of Jesus Again

By the ninth hour or three o'clock in the afternoon, our crowd was three times the size of John the Baptist's. I felt sorry for him. We had stolen all his "customers," but Jesus didn't seem to care. I knew John's disciples were becoming more and more frustrated. One of them, Samuel, even shook his fist at us. John immediately rebuked him. It wasn't long before some of John's disciples got into a big argument with one of the prominent Jews from Jerusalem over ceremonial washing. Their voices were raised, and some harsh things were said.

John stepped in and put an end to it. Then he asked, "What is the matter? Getting into arguments is not like you."

They pointed across the river to us. "Rabbi," one of them said in an angry tone of voice, "that man over there on the other side of the Jordan, the One you testified about, well He is baptizing, and everyone is going to Him. Don't you care?"

I couldn't hear everything John said to them, but I did hear a few things. He told them he was only able to receive what was given him from heaven. I clearly heard him say, "I already told you that I am not the Christ. I am just here to prepare the way for Him. He is the bridegroom; I'm only the bridegroom's friend. He must become greater," John pointed to Jesus, "and I," pointing to himself, "must become lesser."

I didn't catch much else because just then someone wanted to be baptized. Although I didn't hear every word, I admired John all the more for giving testimony to Jesus and meekly and humbly taking the role God had given him.

March 12   *John 4:1–3*

Jesus' Popular Support

We had been in Aenon about a week while Jesus taught and we baptized the people. His message was a call to repent because God's kingdom was very near. He healed the sick and comforted the discouraged. Even the children caught His attention. It did not matter who needed help, He took the time to attend to them.

I headed across the Jordon to speak with John the Baptist's disciples. They were still pretty upset even after John's little talk. One of them, Daniel, told me the Pharisees were sending Levite spies to listen to Jesus on a daily basis. They were reporting to the Jews that Jesus was gaining more support than John and that the people were flocking to Him. Rumor had it that Jesus was about to organize an army and a popular front to defeat the Romans. I told Daniel he should become one of Jesus' disciples, but he laughed and declined. When I rejoined Jesus and the others, it was getting late and the crowds had pretty much dissipated.

Jesus seemed interested in my visit across the Jordon and said, "John, I'd like to talk to you." He asked about the visit, and I told Him everything, even about the spies and the rumors. I watched as His disposition changed and His brow furrowed. I thought He would be happy, but instead He seemed upset.

I told the others about what Daniel had said. Peter rejoiced, "Finally we are going to beat the Romans!"

We were sound asleep when Jesus awoke us about the tenth hour of the night watch (4:00 a.m.) and informed us we were going to Galilee. Bewildered, we shook ourselves awake and splashed cold water on our faces.

Peter protested, "Lord, what about all the people who will come to us? This is where we need to be."

Jesus simply said, "John the Baptist will take good care of them."

Why should we leave when everything is going so well, I wondered. *It doesn't make any sense, but I want to be with Him wherever He is, so I will follow.* In His presence I felt secure.

March 13   *John 4:4–10*

To Galilee Through Samaria?

Before the people began to arrive the next morning, Jesus had us up and ready to go. It seemed so counterproductive to leave behind a blossoming ministry. We ate a hurried breakfast of fruit, bread, and cheese. Instead of going east across the Jordan and then north on the main highway on the east side of the Jordan where all self-respecting Jews traveled, Jesus headed west back toward Jerusalem.

I said, "Rabbi, I thought You said we were going to Galilee?"

He answered, "We are, Andrew, we are."

"We just missed the road, didn't we?" I asked.

He smiled at me as He said, "There is more than one way to Galilee."

Suddenly, it dawned on us that He was planning to take the Samaritan route! No Jew ever traveled through Samaria if he could possibly help it. As we turned north onto the road that went right through Samaria to Galilee, both Jews and Samaritans gave us strange looks. Samaritans had always been shunned by the Jews not only because they were a mixture of Jews and other races but also because they practiced an irregular form of Judaism.

My brother John and I had some issues with Samaritans because of the fishing industry and the fact that they insisted on fishing traditionally. We stayed in Ephraim overnight at the campsite for travelers. Early the next morning, we finished our fruit, bread, and cheese and made good time traveling the sixteen miles which brought us to Sychar close to noon. The road had been at a steady incline, so we were tired when we came to Jacob's well. We were glad we could stop to catch our breath. After resting awhile, we realized how hungry we were. It had been a long time since morning when we ate the last of our food. All of us disciples decided to go into Sychar and buy some food for dinner, but Jesus chose to wait at the well.

March 14   John 4:7–15

The Woman of Samaria (Part 1)

My life was a nightmare. Much of what I had to deal with on a day-to-day basis was because of my own choices or, as the people of Samaria would quickly tell you, "bad habits and a bad attitude." I am kind of a rebel. I don't like rules much, so I live life the way I want to. However, this comes with a price, for nobody has much to do with me. Then one day my life changed.

These Galilean guys showed up in town. You hardly ever see Jews in a Samaritan village, so they made a lot of heads turn as they headed toward the marketplace. I was on my way to the well to get water when I saw them. I was going when it was least populated so that I didn't have to deal with the wagging tongues of the townswomen. I was tired of the whispering, pointing, and dirty looks from those self-righteous women who had nothing better to do than kick someone when they were down!

When I arrived at the well, there was another Galilean guy sitting there. I figured He must be traveling with the other ones I'd seen in town. He was decent looking, but He was a Galilean and I a Samaritan. *Probably better than the jerk I'm living with now*, I mused. I stole a quick look at Him when I lowered my bucket. He smiled and spoke to me, asking for a drink. I was shocked. Talk about breaking the rules! Jews don't talk to Samaritans; men don't talk to women in public; and we were complete strangers. Maybe He was a rebel, too!

I looked at Him with surprise and the words tumbled out, "You are a Jew, and I am a Samaritan woman. Why are You asking a favor of me?"

"If you knew who was asking you for a drink, you'd be asking for living water."

I was confused, but I was also a bit amused, so I asked, "Well, where do you get living water? If it's in the well, how are you going to get it when you don't have a bucket? Are you going to get better water than Jacob, our ancestor?"

"Anyone who drinks water from this well will get thirsty, but whoever drinks the living water I give will never thirst again. In fact, it will become an everlasting spring of water welling up to eternal life."

It dawned on me He was talking about spiritual water, but I played along. "Okay, Sir, give me this living water so I don't need to come to the well anymore."

March 15   *John 4:16–26*

The Woman of Samaria (Part 2)

I couldn't believe I was at Jacob's well talking with a friendly Jewish guy! I was curious about this living water because I hated coming to this well. "When can I have this water that will make me thirst no more?"

Then He touched a raw nerve. "Go get your husband," He said, "and bring him here." My jaw tightened. I looked down at the well and told Him that I had no husband. "You are right when you say you have no husband. The fact is that you have had five husbands and the man you are living with now is not your husband."

I couldn't believe what I was hearing—how did He know all about my sordid life? Shocked, my eyes opened wide and my mouth dropped open as I stared at Him. "Sir, you must be a prophet!" He had my undivided attention, but I had to divert the conversation. Maybe I'd ask Him about the age old issues that separated Jews and Samaritans. I'd overheard a heated discussion about worship in the village the other day so I said, "Our fathers worshiped on this mountain," pointing to Mt. Garizim, "but you Jews claim the place we must worship is Jerusalem."

He answered, "Believe me, the time is coming when you will worship the Father in neither place. You Samaritans aren't even sure about what and why you worship. We Jews know what we worship because salvation comes from the Jews." I knew He was referring to the Christ who would come. "The time has come when all true worshipers will worship the Father in spirit and truth, regardless of ethnic, cultural, or religious boundaries. These are the kinds of worshipers the Father wants. God is spirit, so His worshipers must worship Him in spirit and truth."

I sensed this man before me was much greater than even a prophet. "I know the Messiah is coming, and He will explain all these things to us."

He looked at me with those piercing dark brown eyes as He said, "I who speak to you am He."

March 16   *John 4:27–42*

The Woman of Samaria (Part 3)

I couldn't believe my ears. The Messiah, in front of me? Again my eyes widened and my mouth dropped open. Just then His friends returned, grumbling about the high prices they'd had to pay for food. When they saw Him talking to me, they stopped dead in their tracks. A few of them raised their eyebrows but said nothing. I heard one of His friends offer Him some food and encourage Him to eat as I ran back to Sychar, leaving my water jug at the well. I had to tell everyone in the village that the Messiah had come!

"Come out to the well and meet a man who uncovered my past. Could this be the Christ?" They all wanted to meet Him. Later on one of His disciples, Philip, told me what happened at the well after I left. He wouldn't eat the food they offered Him. "I have food to eat you know nothing about," He said. The disciples thought maybe I had given Him food, but He explained, "My food is to do the will of the One who sent me and finish the work. You say, 'there is four months until the harvest.' I tell you, open your eyes and look—the fields are ripe for harvest." He held His hand out toward Sychar. People were beginning to arrive from the town, so the disciples understood that He was talking about harvesting souls. He went on to tell His disciples that the reaper and sower work together to produce a rich harvest. In the end, when the grain is harvested, they all rejoice. That was Philip's testimony.

When we got to the well, the village elders encouraged Jesus to stay for a few days. He spoke to our people and many people believed on Him, including myself. He healed the sick and encouraged the down and out during His visit in Sychar. The people's attitude toward me changed. They told me, "We no longer base our belief in Him on what you said but on what He told us. We heard for ourselves and now we believe. He is the Savior of the world." Those were the best two days of our lives. There wasn't a sick person in Sychar. The best part for me was feeling loved and accepted by God. That is my real love story.

March 17   John 4:43, 44

Leaving Sychar

I had always been told Samaritans were heretics and never to have anything to do with them. My parents and the rabbis at the synagogue school had taught me that God Himself disapproved of them because they were a mix of pagan and Jewish. This visit to Sychar helped me realize how wrong I'd been to believe these things. While we were there, my friend Philip called me aside and said, "You know, Nathanael, these people have all been very kind to us. We have been judging them wrongly." I nodded in agreement.

After two days of wonderful Samaritan hospitality, Jesus said it was time to go. They packed us a lunch and made us promise to come visit them again soon. Those two days in Samaria were two of the best in my life. Traveling on toward Scythopolis, about thirty miles to the northeast, we discussed the events of the past two days. It gave us a chance to be alone with Jesus and ask questions. Jesus made it clear that the Father was as much God to the Samaritans as He was to the Jews, for in His sight all people were equal. It was a beautiful day. We ate the delicious meal packed by the Samaritans and rested awhile before continuing our journey.

By the time we got to Scythopolis, it was the twelfth hour or six in the evening so we rented a room at one of the many inns. Scythopolis was a crossroads city, so there were lots of inexpensive places to stay. We all slept well. The following day the fishermen said they needed to go back to Bethsaida and their fishing. Philip and I felt that we should go home, too, since we had not been home since before the Passover. Jesus had plans to go back to Cana and visit the newly married couple. We said our goodbyes and were on our way, filled with a greater appreciation and love for our friend Jesus. However, we worried about Him going alone because He had once said, "A prophet has no honor in His own country." We prayed that God would protect and care for Him.

March 18 John 4:45

With Friends in Cana

It was wonderful to see my friend Jesus again! We hadn't seen Him since the wedding, and He graciously accepted our invitation to stay at our home. I thanked Him again for the provision of wine. I told Him we had heard all kinds of rumors about Jerusalem and the Passover from people who attended. "Did you really drive the money changers out of the temple with a sword?" I asked.

He smiled, "No, I upended their tables and released their animals and told them to get out because they were a bunch of thieves."

"Tell us about the miracles," I said.

He told of healing the sick and ministering to the poor and needy. I told Him He'd earned quite a reputation around here. We talked late into the night about spiritual values. Finally, I told Him about a rich nobleman who had called at our home asking if we knew where he could find Him. "His son was very sick. The doctors have given the boy up to die. He'd heard how You had healed people in Jerusalem. Having traveled all the way from Capernaum to find You, he was very distraught that You were not here."

Jesus nodded and said He was very tired and would like to go to bed. The next morning my lovely bride made us breakfast while we visited some more. He told us about Sychar and all that happened in that town. There were some repairs to our house that Jesus, being a seasoned carpenter, was very happy to make. He put on His apron, gathered up the tools and lumber, and went to work. It didn't take long for the word to get out that Jesus was in town. In just one day we had more visitors than we'll probably ever have in the next five years! Some brought their sick friends, and He healed them. He also took time to teach the people wonderful spiritual truths they had never heard in the synagogue. He spent a busy couple of days with us. What a blessing to have Jesus in our home!

March 19 John 4:46–54

The Nobleman

My son suffered from a strange disease that drained him of strength. Then a high fever nearly killed him, and we didn't know how much longer he would live. I'm a government official, so I had access to the very best of doctors, but none of them knew what to do. A friend said he'd heard of a miracle-working prophet who had healed people at the Passover and also turned water into wine at a wedding in Cana. A coworker mentioned that his son, Philip, was a friend of this prophet. Philip told me the prophet had gone to Cana, so I headed there early the next morning.

I'll admit, I had plenty of doubts. I knew people who had been swindled by so-called healers who preyed on the sick and vulnerable. I wasn't about to believe He was a prophet of God until He actually healed my son. Cana was only twenty miles to the west of Capernaum, so I was there shortly after the sixth hour.

Upon entering the town, I inquired about His whereabouts. When I arrived at the house where He was staying, there was a large crowd of people. They made way for me when they saw my uniform. My doubts increased when I saw that He was just an ordinary peasant, but I was desperate—anything was worth a shot for my son. I told Him I was an official at Capernaum and asked Him to come heal my son. I turned to leave and expected He would follow, but He just stood there looking at me. I felt like He was reading my very soul. I was compelled to turn back and beg Him to come heal my son.

Looking around at the crowd, He said, "Unless you people see signs and wonders you will not believe."

His eyes came back to mine, and suddenly I realized my son might die because of my unbelief. I fell on my knees before Him. "Please, Sir," I cried, tears streaming down my face, "please come with me before my son dies."

He put His hand on my shoulder, "You may go; your son will live."

I instantly felt a peace sweep over me, and I knew my son was going to live. I took my time going home, thanking God all the way. As I reached Capernaum, my servants hurried to meet me with the good news. I asked them when the boy improved. "Yesterday at the seventh hour." The very moment Jesus spoke the words. My family and I are faithful believers in Jesus.

March 20 *Matthew 14:3–5; Luke 3:19, 20*

John the Baptist Imprisoned

I suppose we all knew something like this would happen sooner or later because of his boldness in pointing out sin and calling it by its right name. We had cautioned him to be careful, but he insisted he was God's messenger, a chosen vessel and must be God's spokesman regardless of who was offended. Well, Herod was the wrong person to offend. Herod and his "so-called wife," Herodias, had heard all the reports circulating about John, so they came to hear him preach. Herod had taken his brother Philip's wife as his own, which was immoral and a scandal among the Jews.

Everyone knew Herod was a tyrant and a despot, but no one was brave enough to confront him—until John the Baptist spoke up. Herod and Herodias stopped their chariot by the road that led to the east side of the Jordan. John leaned over to me and asked, "Jonas, isn't that Antipas and his entourage?"

"Yes, sir, it is," I answered.

He moved closer to them to make sure he'd be heard. He shouted, "Herod Antipas, what are you doing with your brother Philip's wife? This is immoral, sinful, and wrong in God's sight."

Herodias exploded! "Who do you think you are speaking to, you Samaritan peasant? How dare you accuse him of immorality! Are you God?" She was furious. "Arrest this wretch," she shouted at Herod. "He has just insulted you in front of your people."

Herod tried to calm her down but to no avail, so he finally instructed the driver to take them back to Jerusalem. As a parting shot, she shouted at John, "I'll have your head!"

Herod would have arrested John on the spot were it not for the popularity John held with the people. However, within the week, after the crowds had dispersed one day, soldiers arrived, charged John with insubordination, and arrested him. John went quietly. Even the arresting soldiers were sympathetic and did not put him in shackles. We were devastated. Nothing was the same without John. We tried to continue his ministry, but the crowds soon stopped coming. I went to the prison to visit him as often as I could. *Why is God letting this happen?* I wondered. If only John hadn't spoken against Herod.

March 21 *John 5:1–9*

Healing of the Paralyzed Man at the Pool

I just wanted to die and get it over with. For thirty-eight years my life had been a nightmare. When they could spare the time, family or friends brought me to the Pool of Bethesda because rumor has it that from time to time angels stir the water and the first one to jump in is healed. I think I saw the water stir a few times, but I've never honestly seen a real substantial healing. Of course, it really didn't matter, because I couldn't move even if I saw the water stir, and no one was able to sit with me to help me in the water.

I was sick of my life, sick of laying by the pool, sick of everything. It was the Passover, which meant that there were more sick people at the pool than usual. I was laying about five feet from the edge of the pool praying for the miracle of angels when, out of the corner of my eye, I saw a stranger approaching. He seemed like He knew where He was going, and then, all of a sudden, He bent down, smiled at me, and said, "Do you want to get well?"

I told Him there was no one to help me get to the pool, and even when there was someone, I never got there in time. I told Him if He wanted to stay and help me, I could give him the few coins my son had given me. He got down, His face close to mine, and said, "Get up, pick up your mat and walk."

At first, I thought He was going to help lift me up and together we'd stumble closer to the edge of the pool. My brain told my limbs to respond. When I tried to move, a jolt of power, healing power, erupted inside of me. My arms and legs, before withered and atrophied, now strong and healthy, responded to my brain's command. I couldn't believe it! I stood and looked around. Everyone nearby sat in stunned silence as they watched the miracle unfold. I felt my legs and arms—they were like new! I picked up my mat and shouted, "Hallelujah! Thanks be to God!" I looked for my benefactor, but He was gone. I walked away as if in a dream.

March 22   John 5:9–15

The Healed Paralytic Confronted

I had heard rumors of a prophet who healed people, but who would have believed He would help a broken-down, sick sinner like me! But now I felt better than I ever had in my whole life.

"Thank you, God," I whispered. I looked down at my limbs—they were strong and healthy. I slapped my face to make sure I wasn't dreaming. I couldn't wait to tell my family, but first I needed to go to the temple to give a thank offering to God. Walking up the steps, I was accosted by some of the Jewish leaders, zealous for strict Sabbath observance. They were rude and indignant.

"It is the Sabbath. The law forbids you to carry your mat."

I suppose I could have just put the mat down, but I didn't like their attitude. "The One who made me well told me to carry it," I answered coolly.

"Who was it?" they shot back.

"I don't know," I said with an air of incredulity that they didn't know about a prophet who had power to heal.

They glared at me with disdain. It was true; I really didn't know who my benefactor was because He had quietly slipped into the crowd before I had a chance to thank Him. Since I didn't put down my mat, they stormed off, muttering under their breath that I was a Samaritan and unbeliever. Purchasing a sacrificial offering with the money my son had given me to pay someone to help me into the pool, I took it to the priest. Then, still carrying my mat, I left the temple courtyard down the same steps the Jews had confronted me on.

Suddenly He, the prophet, appeared before me. "Stop sinning," He said gently, "or something worse may happen to you."

"Oh, yes, Sir," I said gratefully. "Thank You for healing me."

Then He was gone. I asked those nearby, "Who was that?"

"Jesus of Nazareth," they told me. I soon met the Jews who had confronted me about carrying my mat and told them it was Jesus who had healed me. Then I headed home. What a joyous homecoming! When I walked through the door, my family showered me with hugs and tears of joy! We are all followers of Jesus now, for He gave me back my life.

March 23   John 5:16–18

Rejection by the Sanhedrin

    It had been a year since Jesus had upended the money changers' tables and created such a stir. Ever since then His relationship with the Sanhedrin had been strained. Many times during council meetings His name would come up in some negative context, such as healing people on the Sabbath, stealing the masses away from the Sanhedrin, befriending sinners, associating with Galileans and Samaritans. The list went on and on. The biggest offense was breaking the Sabbath. When I spoke in His defense, my friends would ask, "Nicodemus, why do you support this Sabbath breaker?" My standard answer was, "Who do you think gives Him power to heal on the Sabbath?" It was a question no one would answer although they knew the answer.

    After the incident with the man at the pool, things progressed to the point where some of my colleagues wanted to kill Him. A few had cornered Him and asked why He insisted on breaking the Sabbath and encouraging others to do the same. His reply was, "My Father is always at His work, and I, too, am working." According to the Jews of the Sanhedrin, He was calling God, Yahweh, His Father, and thereby making Himself an equal. This, of course, was blasphemous, intolerable, and called for the death sentence. Some Sanhedrin members began to push hard for His arrest and execution.

    I came to Jesus' aid whenever I could, citing the good He was doing and all the people He had helped. Then there was another big confrontation near the temple. Those most zealous in seeking His death began questioning Him about His Father, Yahweh, hoping to discredit Him in front of the people. The real reason for their antagonism was a fear of losing control over the people. Jesus was stripping away their man-made rules and freeing the people to enjoy the Sabbath. I was there that day and heard what Jesus said.

March 24   John 5:19–30

Jesus' Response to the Pharisees

    A large delegation of the Sanhedrin found Jesus teaching near the temple a few days after the "Sabbath healing and mat-carrying" incident. Based on my interview with Him a year earlier and everything I had seen and heard since, I was convinced He was more than just a man. Some began to ply Him with questions about breaking the Sabbath and implying He was equal with God.

    "What do you have to say for yourself?" one of the priests shouted angrily.

    Jesus stood His ground with calm dignity and composure. "I do nothing without the help of my Father, Yahweh. As Father and Son, we work together. So whoever does not honor the Son, does not honor the Father."

    I watched the faces of the delegation grow cold and hard. I thought to myself, *He is uttering His own death sentence.* I looked at the crowd who listened to Him in rapt attention. He went on to say that those who believed His words and the One who sent Him possessed eternal life and had passed from death to life. Both Father and Son have eternal life to give, but He had been given authority to judge because He is the Son of man. He spoke of a time coming when all in the graves would hear His voice and rise either to life or to death. He said His judgment was just and He came only to please the One who sent Him.

The Pharisees believed in a resurrection of the dead, but the Sadducees did not, so His words caused arguments among the council members. There were members so full of hatred for Jesus that had it not been for the crowd, they would have stoned Him right then. I overheard one Pharisee say, "This Nazarene carpenter is no Son of God. He needs to die for committing blasphemy against God!"

In my own heart, I knew what Jesus was saying was true. I believed in Him.

March 25   John 5:31–46

Testimonies About Jesus

The crowd was becoming frustrated with the arguing. They wanted to hear more and began to shout for Jesus to continue. When the noise quieted down, Jesus spoke again. He told about His testimony not being valid if He testified of Himself. If others did, then this testimony of Him was valid. He cited John the Baptist's testimony about Him as valid and true, but still only from a human source. More important than John the Baptist's testimony was God's testimony.

"I am doing the work and performing the miracles He sent me to do. But you don't get it because you don't know Him." Some of the Sanhedrin were infuriated over that statement and plugged their ears. "You search the Scriptures," Jesus continued, "because in them you think you have life, but the Scriptures are all about Me. You refuse to come to Me for life."

"Come to you?" a Pharisee shouted. "You are not Yahweh!"

Jesus boldly continued, "You have no love for God in your hearts. I come in the Father's name, but you do not accept Me. If some impostor comes in his own name, you accept him. What good is it going to do to accept praise from each other and do nothing to obtain praise from God?" Then He said something that really upset them. "I won't accuse you to the Father, but Moses will, the one upon whom your hopes are set. If you believe Moses, you would believe Me because he wrote about Me. You don't believe what he wrote so you won't believe Me."

There was silence as they thought about what He had just said. They were at a crossroads, and they chose to reject Him. Some called Him a liar, others a false prophet, others a deluded Samaritan. They all gathered their robes about them and turned their backs on Him. I studied Him as He watched them walk away. There were tears streaming down His cheeks. That marked the end of His Judean ministry and the Sanhedrin's rejection of Him.

March 26   Matthew 4:12; Mark 1:14

Jesus Hears John Is in Prison

After his arrest, we, John the Baptist's disciples, were devastated. If only he hadn't criticized Herod, he would still be free. It was so hard to see him chained up, wasting away in that dungeon. At least Herod allowed us to visit him as often as we pleased and bring him some of the things he liked to eat. John always questioned us about Jesus' ministry. He wanted to know what He was doing and where He went.

However, after the Jordan River incident, we hadn't paid much attention to Jesus, for we weren't sure how we felt about Him. We heard bits and pieces now and then, but we didn't pay close attention. Then one day I saw Him at the temple in Jerusalem speaking to some of the Sanhedrin. They looked pretty upset about the things He'd said.

I approached Jesus after the members of the Sanhedrin had left and told Him how hard it was on John to be in prison. "He always asks us how 'the Son of God' is doing. John hopes that he might be soon released when the Messiah organizes His army to deal with the Romans." I paused to allow Him time to respond. All He did was look at me in a strange sort of way and tell me to be sure to give John His regards. Then He was gone. I thought perhaps He would have said something more encouraging than that. He didn't even tell me to give John some hope regarding being released.

I made my way to the prison where my master was being held. I was definitely a little angry at Jesus' response to my statement. When I told John what had happened, he didn't say much, but I could tell he was even more discouraged. I asked him, "If this man is the Messiah, when is He going to meet with the Jewish leaders to plan a strategy? If anything, it seems to me He is pushing them away. It has been a whole year now and all He has to show for His work is a few fishermen and a handful of followers."

John put his hand on my shoulder. "Patience," he said, "it's all in God's time."

March 27   Mark 1:15; Luke 4:14, 15

Jesus Begins His Galilean Ministry

During that first year in Judea, we had not been able to keep in touch with Jesus as we would have liked. We had to work and take care of our families. Occasionally our work would take us to Jerusalem, and we would make contact with Him, and He would tell us about His ministry and the good things God was doing. He spoke of the antagonism of the Jewish leaders, but He encouraged us to pray for them and Himself that He might reach their hearts. It was always difficult to say goodbye. We encouraged Him to come to Galilee where the people were more receptive. He simply said His Father had work for Him to do in Judea.

Shortly after receiving the news that John the Baptist had been imprisoned by Herod, Jesus returned to Galilee. Just as we suspected, the people were very happy to see Him. Huge crowds gathered to hear Him speak. Many who were sick came to Him and were healed. He taught in the synagogues, and everyone rejoiced at His messages. He spoke with conviction and power—His message was full of hope and gave us great encouragement. "The time has come, the kingdom of God is near, repent and believe the good news."

The people began to say, "Here is someone who will restore Israel."

What we had hoped for all our lives was about to be fulfilled. There was only one thing that we did not understand, and my brother Peter and I discussed it often as we fished with James and John. If He was about to set up a kingdom, wouldn't He need the help and support of the Sanhedrin? We had heard they were trying to kill Him. We wondered if He might just build an army of those in Galilee, but would that be enough to overthrow the Romans? Nevertheless, we were glad He was back in Galilee where His ministry was appreciated.

March 28 *Luke 4:16–30*

Rejection at Nazareth

My stepbrother, Jesus, was making quite a name for Himself. He was very popular with the people, especially in Galilee. Since He was speaking in all the synagogues, we extended an invitation for Him to come speak in His hometown. One Friday afternoon He showed up. We had a family get-together to bring in the Sabbath.

The next day we went to the synagogue to worship, and the scroll was handed to Jesus. He stood up to read, choosing the Messianic passage in Isaiah. "The Spirit of the Lord is upon Me because He has anointed Me to preach the good news to the poor. He has sent Me to proclaim freedom for the prisoners and recovery of sight to the blind, to release the oppressed, to proclaim the year of the Lord's favor."

This was the very work the great Messiah would do—we clung to these promises. He rolled up the scroll and gave it back to the attendant. Then He sat down. All eyes were fastened on Him. What He said next put everyone into a state of shock. Even Mary looked surprised. He said, "Today this Scripture is fulfilled in your hearing." He might as well have shouted, "I'm the Messiah."

Some people said, "We know He has done great things, and His sermons are wonderful, but the fact remains that He is just the son of Joseph the carpenter. We watched Him grow up. Now He claims to be the Messiah!"

Jesus knew what they were saying about Him, so He responded, "You will quote this proverb to Me 'Physician, heal yourself.' In other words, do for us here in Your hometown what You did for those in Capernaum. The truth of the matter is no prophet is accepted in his own country."

He had everyone's attention. "There were lots of starving widows in Israel, but Elijah was sent to a Gentile widow in Sidon. There were lots of lepers in Israel, but the only one healed was a Gentile named Naaman."

They got the message. Furious, they jumped up, grabbed Him, and dragged Him out of the synagogue to the edge of a cliff. My brothers and I tried to intervene to save Him. Suddenly the crowd stopped at the edge and let go of Him. Without a word, He looked at the crowd for a moment, then sadly walked away.

March 29   *Matthew 4:13-17; Luke 4:31*

To Capernaum

We were very glad that, after returning from Nazareth, Jesus decided to make His home in Capernaum, which was located not far from Bethsaida. My brother Peter and his wife had moved to Capernaum. They had found a house where they could take in his wife's mother and care for her because she was a widow. Jesus was staying with a middle-aged couple who had a spare room on the roof above the living quarters. It was a comfortable place, and the woman of the house prepared meals for her husband and Jesus.

We came into Capernaum as often as we could. Sometimes we docked there and sold fish at the marketplace. Then we would invite Jesus to Peter's place for a fish dinner. Those were good days; we had some great times together. One day I asked Jesus why, of all the cities He could have lived in that would have gladly welcomed Him, He had chosen Capernaum. He paused, then looked at me and said, "To fulfill what the prophet Isaiah wrote about me: 'Land of Zebulen and land of Naphtali, the way to the sea along the Jordon, Galilee of the Gentiles, the people living in darkness have seen a great light. On those living in the land of the shadow of death a light has dawned.' I came here, Andrew, because this is where the greatest need is and the greatest opportunity to reach people traveling through."

Capernaum was indeed a crossroads city that connected main trade routes from north to south. There was a large Gentile population here as well. The prophecy made by Isaiah was being fulfilled as we watched Jesus teach the people wherever they gathered. Nathanael, Philip, Peter, and I helped out when we could. The theme of His preaching was a call for the people to repent because the kingdom of God was near. Many listened to Him and believed in Him. Within a few weeks of having returned from Nazareth, He had quite a following.

March 30   *Matthew 4:18-22; Mark 1:16-20;*
                                                                                                                         Luke 5:1-11

The Call by the Sea

One day we were down by the sea washing our nets and doing some mending when I saw Jesus coming toward us with a crowd of people. Jesus came near our boats and began to teach them. As the crowd grew larger, He was pressed into the water. My boat was closest to Him, so He climbed in and sat down and taught the people from there. It was a beautiful day. Many of the people sat down on the sand and listened while He spoke words of life. I held the rope attached to the bow so the boat would not drift.

When He'd finished speaking, He said to me, "Simon, put out into deep water and let down the nets for a catch."

I knew that daytime was not the time to catch fish, so I told Him we had worked the whole area all night and had caught nothing, not even one fish. I knew it was of no use, but the thought came to me that He just might know something that I didn't. After all, He did turn water to wine. So I said, "Lord, because it is You who is asking, I will let down the nets."

So the three of us, Jesus, Andrew, and I, went to our usual fishing location and let down the nets. Suddenly I felt the boat lurch to the side. All three of us grabbed the net and pulled. I could not believe my eyes—the net was so full it began to tear. I signaled for James and John to come out and help us. Both boats were filled with so many fish they began to sink. We pulled the boats up on shore with the help of Zebedee and his hired men. No one had ever seen a catch like this, let alone in the daytime!

I knew, we all knew, it was a miracle. I ran to the Lord and fell on my knees at His feet, looking up into His face. "Depart from me, Lord," I cried, "for I am a sinful man."

The sale of this catch would take care of our families for many days. Then Jesus gathered the four of us—Andrew, James, John, and me. "Come with me," He said, "and I will make you fishers of men." We did. We left everything behind to the hired workers and followed Jesus. It was the best decision I ever made in my life.

March 31 *Mark 1:21-28; Luke 4:31-37*

The Demoniac in the Synagogue

The following Sabbath we all went to the synagogue in Capernaum where Jesus had been invited to speak. When the time came, Jesus was handed the scroll and began to teach, presenting fresh new ideas from the text. When others spoke, it was usually a rehash of the same things spoken of a hundred times before. I looked around at the people. They were completely focused on what Jesus was saying. He spoke about salvation and the Father's love.

He then read from the prophet Jeremiah: "I have loved you with an everlasting love; therefore, with lovingkindness I have drawn you." Then He turned to the prophet Isaiah: "Though your sins be as scarlet, they shall be white as snow; though they be red like crimson, they shall be as wool."

He presented the Father as One who loves us as His own children, just as we love our kids. Suddenly a man near the front jumped to his feet, took a few steps toward Jesus, and shouted loudly, "What do You want with us, Jesus of Nazareth? Have You come to destroy us? I know who You are—the holy One of God!" The man's arm and forefinger were stretched out, pointing at Jesus. He began to shake violently and froth at the mouth.

Someone cried, "He's demon possessed." The synagogue leaders couldn't restrain him.

Jesus stepped off the platform to stand in front of the possessed man. With authority He said, "Come out of him!" The demon shook the man violently and came out with a shriek. The man collapsed on the floor as the people stared at Jesus in amazement.

They began to ask each other, "What is this, a new teaching? It has such authority that even the evil spirits obey Him!"

Jesus bent over the formerly possessed man and helped him to his feet. The man thanked Jesus again and again, apologizing for disturbing the service. The news spread quickly: "Evil spirits obey the Nazarene Teacher!" Even my skeptical Greek father asked questions about Him after the healing.

April 1   *Matthew 8:14–17; Mark 1:29–34; Luke 4:38–41*

Peter's Mother-in-law Healed

After leaving the synagogue we made our way to Peter's house. His mother-in-law was very sick, and Peter's wife felt that she was dying. We found Peter's wife kneeling beside the elderly woman, tears streaming down her cheeks. Her mother's features were drawn and pale, and her breathing was shallow. Peter's wife gently bathed her mother's fevered brow with cool water. She looked up at Jesus through tear-stained eyes. "Please, can You help us?"

Without hesitation, Jesus stepped forward, bent over the sick woman, looked into her eyes, and rebuked the fever. Instantly, her eyes opened, and she sat up—the fever was gone. She looked vibrant and healthy! "Why, I feel better than I have in many years!" she said.

Jesus smiled, took her by the hand, and helped her up. She thanked Him and praised God for restoring her health. After washing her face and freshening up, she prepared us a wonderful meal while we told the women about the healing at the synagogue. That afternoon Jesus shared truths from the Scriptures. As the sun was setting, there was a great commotion outside Peter's house.

When we looked out, it seemed as if the whole town of Capernaum was standing there. Seeing us, the people shouted, "We want to see Jesus!" Peter opened the door, and the people crowded into the house. Jesus healed everyone who was sick or demon possessed—each one was touched by His gentle hands. The demons tried to speak, but He rebuked them. It was the most amazing day the people of the city had ever experienced! There were shouts of joy and praises to God. I am certain there was not one sick person left in town. Late that night, I remembered a passage Jesus had shared with us earlier that afternoon from the prophet Isaiah: "He took up our infirmities and carried our diseases." No truer words were ever spoken that day in Capernaum.

April 2   *Matthew 4:23–25; Mark 1:35–39; Luke 4:42–44*

Ministry in Galilee

The following morning everyone slept in—everyone except Jesus. Unlike my brother Andrew, I am a light sleeper, so I awakened when Jesus got up and left the house around 4:00 a.m. I fell back to sleep until Mom got up and started making breakfast. I asked her how she felt. She smiled and said,

"Wonderful!" James and John were awake.

Some people were already gathering at the front door. "Where is Jesus?" they asked.

I told Mom we were going to look for Jesus. "Hurry back; breakfast is almost ready," she said.

As we were leaving the house, more people arrived looking for Him. I knew where Jesus had gone, or at least I thought I did. There was a quiet spot just out of town where He and I had gone before to pray. We made our way to the spot, and sure enough, there He was in prayer. When He looked around to see who was coming, I said, "There are people at the house looking for You."

He answered, "Let's go to some of the other villages and towns so I can preach there too. That is why I have come." A few people had followed us from the house and begged Him to come help their loved ones. I told Him Mom had breakfast ready, so we went back to my place to eat. Jesus then ministered to the needs of those who had come. Finally, Jesus said, "We must go now." But before we got away, more people arrived and begged Him for help. He could not let the people suffer, so He helped them too. He then thanked Mom for her hospitality, and we left.

Those were wonderful days, traveling to different places with Jesus and preaching the good news of the kingdom of God. He healed people of every disease imaginable until whole towns were disease free. Even the demon possessed were made whole. People came to Him from Galilee, Decapolis, and Jerusalem. People came from Syria and beyond Jordan. Large crowds followed Him, listening to His words of life and hope. Never before had the world ever seen anything like this, nor since. Thank you, Father, for sending us Your Son.

April 3   *Mark 1:40–45; Luke 5:12–16*

First Leper Healed

According to the law, I was not permitted to go into a town, but I could beg beside the road. The priests had told me that leprosy was God's curse for some terrible sin I had committed. I was no saint, but I had never raped or murdered anyone. Nevertheless, I was banished from friends and family to a life of unbelievable misery. Acting as if I was already dead, my wife remarried and my kids never came to see me. Always hungry and lonely, I just wanted to die.

One day while begging by the road, someone told me about a healer named Jesus who was said to be the Messiah. I asked the stranger if Jesus had ever healed a leper. He said he didn't know, but probably not since lepers were cursed of God. I decided to find out. As I stood by the road leading into Sepphoris, a town not far from Nazareth, I heard people talking about the miracles Jesus performed. I knew this might be my only chance. Then doubts flooded over me as I wondered if someone as pure and undefiled as the Messiah would tolerate me in His presence.

I waited by the road all night, and in the morning I saw Him. I knew I had to get to Him. There were people all around Him, but I didn't care. Someone saw me coming and swore at me to get away. The closer I got, the farther back the crowd fell. The only one who didn't move was Jesus. I knelt before

Him and begged for help. "Please, Lord," I cried, "if You are willing, You can make me clean."

I looked up into His face, which was full of compassion, and marveled when He said, "I will!" Then He touched me. No one had touched me in years! Instantly I was at peace. Then my body was transformed. My fingers and toes grew back, the oozing sores disappeared. Everyone watched in stunned silence.

I jumped to my feet and shouted, "Praise be to Yahweh! Thank You, thank You!"

Then Jesus said in a loud voice, "Don't tell anyone. Show yourself to the priest and offer the sacrifice Moses required."

I headed for Jerusalem but couldn't contain myself; I told everyone. My former business acquaintances were amazed. My friends couldn't believe it. My family was shocked. But even better than the healing was the peace of knowing I was loved and accepted of God.

April 4   *Matthew 12:1–8; Mark 2:23–28; Luke 6:1–5*

Picking Grain on Sabbath

On the way back to Capernaum, we stopped at Jotaparta for a few days. The people were very receptive. From there we went down through the valley to Magdala near the Sea of Galilee.

After we arrived in town, Jesus was asked to speak in the synagogue on Sabbath. It was a good service, and the people were blessed. Afterwards we were invited to dinner at the home of the man in charge of the synagogue. His wife had prepared a wonderful meal on Friday, the day of preparation. We ate dried figs, soup, nuts, cheese, bread, and greens from her garden. After dinner, we relaxed and visited with the family. We accepted their gracious offer to stay with them until Sunday.

Toward evening, about the tenth hour, Jesus asked our host if we could be excused to walk in the field near his home. He said, "Of course, go ahead." The fields were ripe and loaded with grain. Walking along discussing future plans, we watched as Jesus picked some of the heads of grain, threshed them in His hands, blew away the chaff, and ate the kernels. The rest of us decided to do the same. It wasn't long before we saw two of the local Pharisees coming toward us on the road. When they saw us picking and eating the grain, they made a beeline toward us. They went up to Jesus and asked why we were harvesting grain on Sabbath. In response, He reminded them that David ate the bread that only the priests were allowed to eat because he was hungry. Then He mentioned the priests that desecrate the Sabbath when a circumcision falls on that day. His next comment really made them angry.

"One greater than the temple is standing here before you. If you had any idea what God meant when He said: 'I prefer mercy before sacrifice,' you would not have condemned the innocent. The Son of man is Lord of the Sabbath." They glared at Him, then continued down the road.

I asked my brother James what Jesus meant by the words "One greater than the temple is here." He simply stated, "I guess He meant that He is equal to God."

April 5   *Matthew 12:9-14; Mark 3:1-6; Luke 6:6-11*

Man With the Withered Hand

After spending the night with the governor of the synagogue and eating a wonderful breakfast, we thanked them and were on our way back to Capernaum. It was good to be home and with family again. The week went by quickly. Jesus spent time in the marketplace teaching and healing people, and we had work to do on the fishing boats. It was kind of nice to get back out on the lake. We did pretty well considering the time of year—Andrew and I made enough from fish sales to keep food on our families' tables for awhile.

When Sabbath came, we all went to the synagogue together. Jesus was asked to speak to the people. As usual His message was from the heart. There were a large number of priests and Pharisees from Jerusalem in attendance. Nathanael and I wondered what they were doing here. We noticed that they watched Jesus carefully throughout the service, whispering to each other. Finally one of them stood up and asked, "Rabbi, is it lawful to heal on the Sabbath?"

Jesus sighed heavily and looked at them for a moment. In the midst of the well dressed group of Pharisees was a poor man dressed in simple clothes with his hand tucked in his vest. Jesus invited the poor man to come forward and stand in front of everyone. He looked very nervous. "I ask you," Jesus said, "which is lawful to do on the Sabbath, good or evil, to save life or destroy it? Which of you having a sheep that falls in a ditch on Sabbath would not lift it out? How much more valuable is a man than a sheep? Therefore, it is lawful to do good on the Sabbath."

He said the final words with strong emphasis. Then He turned to the man. "Stretch out your hand." The man glanced at the Pharisees, then stretched out his hand to Jesus. It was completely restored! Everyone in the synagogue had seen this fellow begging at the marketplace. Now he stood with tears streaming down his face for his hand was normal once again. Jesus stepped down and placed His arm around his shoulder. The Pharisees were furious. Jesus had blatantly disregarded one of their Sabbath regulations. I saw the murderous look on their faces.

April 6   *Matthew 12:15-21; Mark 3:7-12*

Jesus' Popularity

The number of people wanting to see Jesus increased with each passing day. News of His power to heal traveled quickly. One beautiful day we walked to the shore of the lake, close to where my brother Andrew and I kept our fishing boats. More than a thousand, maybe even two thousand people followed us. Many of the people were foreigners. They came from Galilee, Judea, Jerusalem, Idumea, and the cities east of the Jordan River. Some were from as far north as Tyre and Sidon. It was easy to figure out where they came from by their clothing and language. I thought to myself, "Here is the army we need to overthrow Rome!"

Most people were there because of His miracles. Often evil spirits would throw their victim to the ground and start shouting, "You are the Son of God." Jesus would command them to be quiet and leave the possessed person alone. As Jesus healed the sick, they pressed closer and closer to touch Him. He kept backing up until His feet were at the water's edge. Trying to control the crowd was impossible; there were just too many people.

Finally, Jesus called to me, "Peter, get the boat ready." I quickly untied my boat and brought it to where Jesus was standing in twelve inches of water. He stepped into the boat. Still the people pressed forward like sheep without a shepherd. I thought I knew why Jesus had come to the lake. He needed a reprieve from the animosity of the Pharisees. As I reflected on the day, I thought about the words of Isaiah, "Look at My servant whom I have chosen. He is my Beloved who pleases me. I will put My Spirit upon Him, and He will bring justice to the nations. He will not fight or shout or raise His voice in public. He will not crush the weakest reed or put out a flickering candle. Finally, He will cause justice to be victorious, and His name shall be the hope of all the world." He was most certainly the hope of all those who saw Him today.

April 7   Matthew 9:9; Mark 2:13, 14; Luke 5:27, 28

Call of Levi Matthew

We disliked tax collectors with a passion. The Romans used them to collect money from local citizens, and most of them were Jewish opportunists looking for a chance to make a fast buck. Rome demanded a certain amount, but the tax collector could add a percentage on top of that for himself. Charging far more than the suggested amount set by the Romans was the usual practice.

Levi Matthew was the appointed officer just to the west of Capernaum. We knew him well. Whenever we brought a load of fish to market, he would inspect the catch and charge the rate set by the Roman government. Then he'd charge us his share. Levi was very careful, however, about his finances, never charging more than what was recommended. This may sound like an oxymoron, but you could say he was an honest publican. Even though he was friendly, it bothered me that a Jew would stoop to do Rome's dirty work.

Whenever Matthew saw us, he would ask about Jesus and His work. I wondered why he should care since he was a lost man like the prostitutes and criminals. One day my brother Peter, the Zebedee boys, Philip and Nathanael, and I were walking along the road by the sea with Jesus. Matthew watched as we approached his tax station. What happened next shocked all of us.

Jesus walked right up to Matthew and said, "Follow Me, and be My disciple." The rest of us couldn't believe what we had just heard.

"What?" I asked in dismay. "A publican for a disciple?" How could Jesus compromise our reputations like this? What was He thinking? I was too dumbfounded for words. Matthew sat there speechless.

Then I saw a tear in his eye as though this is what he'd wanted all along. Jesus just smiled.

Matthew stood up, turned his books over to his assistant, stepped out of the booth, and simply said, "Yes, Lord." He became one of us just like that—he went from being a lowlife sinner to a disciple in a matter of minutes!

As I got to know Matthew, my perception changed. He proved to be one of my best friends and a true man of God.

April 8   *Mark 3:13-19; Luke 6:12-16*

Appointment of the Twelve

Jesus was unlike any other teacher or rabbi I had ever met. Many people chose to follow Him and become His disciples. Some of the followers had formerly been disciples of John the Baptist. Jesus even had female disciples, which was unheard of! Consequently, His enemies tried to discredit Him because of it.

Late one afternoon Jesus made His way up a mountain. Most of the crowd had dispersed, leaving Him and His devoted disciples to make their way up the hill. We had been with Jesus before when He went to a quiet place for prayer. On this occasion something seemed to be weighing heavily upon Him. I commented about it to my brother John who agreed. As I expected, Jesus told us He was going a short distance away to pray. Within an hour we were all asleep.

I awoke just as the sun peeked over the horizon. As my eyes adjusted to the early morning light, I saw Jesus walking toward us. I gathered that He must have been praying all night. He seemed calm and at peace. Waking everyone up, He asked us to come close. "Last night I prayed to my Father and asked Him to provide Me with faithful apostles to do the work of soul-winning, and He has answered my prayer." Then He walked through the crowd of about thirty disciples and chose twelve of us.

He called brothers Simon and Andrew, my brother John and me, James, then Philip, and Nathanael, also known as Bartholomew. I remembered the day by the sea when He promised to make us "fishers of men." We made up the original six. Then there was Matthew, sometimes called Levi; Thomas; James the son of Alpheaus; Thaddeus, also known as Judas the son of James; Simon the Zealot, who hated Rome; and Judas Iscariot, a tall, handsome, educated man.

I wondered at the mix as I thought about each of the twelve men He had chosen. After He had chosen the twelve, He prayed for us that we would be faithful servants of the most High God. Then He blessed and ordained us. Later He sent us out to work for the lost. I made the best choice of my life when I chose to follow Him, but I was honored when He chose me.

April 9   *Matthew 5:1–32; Luke 6:17–19*

Sermon on the Mount (Part 1)

After Jesus had chosen twelve of us to serve as apostles to advance the kingdom of God, we made our way down to a large open area on the hillside where a huge crowd of people had already gathered. As soon as they saw Jesus approaching, the entire crowd surged toward Him, like "sheep without a shepherd," as Jesus often described them. They were anxious to hear Him and be healed of their diseases.

All morning and into the early afternoon Jesus healed the people—men, women, and children with every possible malady. Soon every person who needed healing was made well and the demon-possessed were set free. It was an amazing day! I wished I had not wasted my life collecting taxes but had spent more time helping the poor. I thank God that Jesus saw something in me and called me to follow Him.

Wanting to hear Jesus speak, the crowd sat on the grass and listened. He knew how to project His voice so the people could hear. He spoke with authority, often quoting Scripture, to reinforce His point. Let me share a brief summary of what He said. He blessed the poor, the mournful, the hungry, and the persecuted. He told us we were the salt of the earth and the light of the world. He elaborated on the law, confirming it is valid and here to stay. He said being angry at someone is like murder, and he encouraged us to be reconciled to one another. Furthermore, lust is more than sexual desire in God's eyes; it is adultery. Divorce and remarriage without just cause such as infidelity is considered adultery. As I watched the crowd, I saw some people squirm. Jesus was calling them to a higher standard, and some clearly weren't sure how to respond.

April 10   *Matthew 5:33–6:15*

Sermon on the Mount (Part 2)

The people listened carefully as Jesus spoke—they hung on every word. They were not used to hearing such a message. He spoke with compassion and not criticism. Those doing wrong felt convicted to change. He counseled us not to make rash vows. A simple "Yes, I will" or "No, I won't" will suffice. He spoke about revenge, getting even. I often felt angry and revengeful when someone took our fishing spot or cheated us out of a fair price for our fish. Andrew and I often got into verbal fights, and once in awhile, we even got into fist fights. Jesus suggested turning the other cheek. If someone sues you for your coat, give him your shirt, too. If a Roman forces you to carry his pack one mile, take it two. I hated being forced to carry anything for a Roman, but Jesus was teaching us to look at the world in a different way.

"Love your enemies and pray for those who persecute you," He said. Was that possible? Even the Pharisees didn't do that. Someone shouted, "Are we to love the Romans?" Jesus simply repeated what He'd said and added, "Even sinners love those who love them. Be like your Father in heaven who sends rain on the good and evil alike." He went on, "Give from the heart privately, without a big show." Everyone knew the Pharisees liked to make a big production of their giving.

He continued, "Pray sincerely from your heart." We'd all heard the showy, hypocritical prayers of the Pharisees. At these statements, the Pharisees in the crowd became noticeably agitated! Jesus asked us to forgive others so that God would forgive us. Then He taught us a simple prayer: "Our Father in heaven, may Your name be kept holy. May Your will be done on earth as it is in heaven. Give us today the food we need, and forgive us our debts and sins as we have forgiven those who sin against us. Don't let us yield to temptation, but rescue us from the evil one." I memorized the prayer He shared with us that day and repeated it often.

April 11   Matthew 6:16–7:6

Sermon on the Mount (Part 3)

Jesus continued His sermon. As He spoke I saw a group of Pharisees talking among themselves and pointing at Him. They were obviously upset because what He had said exposed them as hypocrites regarding giving and praying. Now He spoke about fasting, which the Pharisees were famous for.

"Don't be a hypocrite and promote your piety to others by looking gaunt and disheveled," He said. "Don't become a public spectacle. Instead, with a pure heart fast quietly at home. That way it will be between you and God."

Then He addressed money, again implicating the Pharisees who dressed in beautiful clothes and lived in nice houses. "Store up treasure in heaven, not in this world. You can't serve God and money."

Jesus then spoke about something that affects everyone—worry. "Don't worry about the things of everyday life. God will take care of you. Birds don't worry, and God cares for them. Flowers are dressed beautifully and don't spin or sew. If God cares about them, how much more for you?"

I worry all the time about my fishing business. Are the hired workers doing it right? Will we catch enough fish? Will the price of fish go down? Jesus put it all into perspective.

"Don't worry about things that your heavenly Father knows you need. If you seek the kingdom and a relationship with Him, all these things will be taken care of. Don't worry about tomorrow. Tomorrow has enough problems of its own."

He continued. "Do not judge other people, or you will be judged. Hypocrites look for a speck in someone else's eye and fail to see the log in their own."

I must admit, when Jesus invited Matthew to be a disciple, I was not very happy, and I judged Jesus as having made a big mistake. Time has proved me wrong, and I have asked Jesus and Matthew for forgiveness. At first I thought this sermon was just what the Pharisees needed to hear, but now I realize I needed to hear it too and apply the principles He taught to my own life. I don't want to be a hypocrite. I want to become more and more like Jesus.

April 12   *Matthew 7:7*

Sermon on the Mount (Part 4)

As Jesus spoke on the mountain that day, we began to realize that we were not as righteous as we thought we were. But He gave us encouragement in what He shared next. "Don't give up! Keep on asking, keep on seeking, and you will find. If you ask, you will receive; if you seek, you will find; if you knock, the door will be opened to you. If parents know how to give good things to their children, then how much more will your heavenly Father give good things to you when you ask." Jesus portrayed God as someone who really cares about people.

"Do to others what you would like them to do for you." I needed to apply that principle. Andrew complains because I give him all the dirty jobs; maybe I needed to handle some of those jobs myself.

Jesus talked about the road to heaven. "The road to hell is wide, but the road to heaven is narrow, and few people find or even look for it. You can tell people by the fruit they produce just like plants and trees," He continued. "You can't get grapes from thorn bushes or figs from thistles. Trees that produce no fruit or bad fruit are cut down and thrown into the fire. In the end the same thing will happen to people who produce bad fruit."

Then He said something that caught everyone's attention, especially the Pharisees. "Not everyone who says 'Lord, Lord' will enter the kingdom. Only those who do the will of My Father. They will argue, 'But we did wonders in Your name.' I will tell them, 'Get away from Me, I never knew you.' In the final judgment, they will be lost because they break God's laws."

He ended His sermon with a story. "Those who listen to My words and apply them are like a man who built a house on solid rock. When the floods came, the house stood firm. But those who ignore My teachings are like a man who built his house on sand, and when the floods came, it came crashing down."

The people were amazed at His teachings because they were unlike anything they had heard before. Jesus touched their hearts. But the religious leaders kept saying, "He doesn't decide who goes to heaven! It is the sons of Abraham, like us, who will be saved."

April 13   *Matthew 8:1–4*

Leper by the Mountain

I watched Him go up into the mountain with about thirty of His followers. I knew I had to keep my distance until the time was right. I was a victim of leprosy. The disease had disfigured me terribly—my nose was missing, as were both of my ears. My fingers and toes were only stubs, making walking or holding anything very difficult. I hadn't spoken to anyone except other lepers for a very long time. My life was pretty much over; all I had to look forward to was dying.

But one day I heard about this young teacher named Jesus. Begging by the road, I kept hearing people talk about Him healing the sick. One man said he was taking his son with a deformed leg for healing. I shouted at him, "Has Jesus ever healed a leper?" Keeping his distance, he responded that he'd heard Jesus had healed a leper near Capernaum. That was all I needed to know. I spent the night at the base of the mountain near some trees so as not to be seen.

The next morning the crowds gathered quickly as Jesus and the others came down from the peak. I watched Him heal people and heard Him speak words of hope to the crowd. I heard about love and forgiveness. I desperately needed both. After the sermon the crowds began to disperse. Jesus and His disciples headed my direction, so I slipped out of my hiding place, hobbling toward Him. The crowd gasped and moved backward. Only Jesus moved toward me. One of His companions lifted his staff as if to hit me. Jesus held up His hand.

I knelt at His feet, tears streaming down my face. All the years of pain and rejection came pouring out. "Lord," I cried, "if You are willing, You can heal me!"

Jesus said, "I will." He touched me and said, "Be healed." I felt a jolt of power shake my entire body. I was instantly healed! No scars, no pain—I had a new nose, ears, and digits. Everyone stood and stared at me in shocked silence. Someone handed me a coat.

"Thank you, Lord!" I repeated again and again. Jesus instructed me to show myself to the priest and offer the sacrifice required by the law. I thanked Him again, then I ran off shouting and rejoicing.

April 14   Matthew 8:5–13; Luke 7:1–10

The Centurion's Servant

I am a Roman soldier in charge of a hundred other soldiers. My duties include keeping the peace and making sure orders are carried out. One of my young servants had grown very dear to me, but he became deathly ill. The doctors could do nothing. Having a good relationship with the elders of the synagogue, I begged them for help. One of the elders mentioned a Nazarene rabbi living in Capernaum who reportedly had power to heal. I asked them to present to Him my request for healing of my servant. I felt unworthy to be in the presence of such a man myself.

The condition of my servant worsened, and I thought I would lose him. I was so anxious I decided to go see if the elders had found the rabbi. Yes, they reported, Jesus was coming. They said they had told Him I was very deserving because I had helped build their synagogue. Returning home, I checked on my poor servant and believed that he was surely near death. I sent my close friends to ask Jesus to just speak the word. "Tell Him I'm a Gentile and unworthy to come before Him."

Kneeling by my servant, I cried out, "Oh, God of the Jews, please save my servant!" Then I felt compelled to go meet the Healer myself. When I saw Him, I dismounted and knelt before Him, "Lord, I am unworthy to have You come into my house. Just speak the word and my servant will be healed. I know this because my soldiers obey my orders, and this disease will obey You."

There was silence. I was afraid I had offended Him, so I looked up. He smiled down at me. Then He turned to the crowd. "I haven't seen faith like this in all of Israel. Gentiles from all over the world will come and sit down with Abraham, Isaac, and Jacob in the kingdom of heaven, but many Israelites will be cast out." Turning His attention back to me, He said, "Because you believed, it has happened. You can go home."

Back at home I found my servant completely recovered! His healing was also my healing. My servant and my family and I are devout followers of Jesus Christ.

April 15 *Matthew 9:35*

Second Galilean Tour

Jesus seemed anxious to be on the move again. He had a great burden for souls. Wherever the people were was where He wanted to be. We, the newly appointed twelve disciples, accompanied Him on a tour around Galilee. The people were always glad to see Him, and huge crowds flocked to Him. I had no idea so many people were sick, but Jesus healed each person who came to Him. He was invited to speak in the synagogues. Thankfully the prejudice He had encountered with the Pharisees at Jerusalem hadn't spread to the villages of Galilee. Most of the people saw Him as Israel's Redeemer.

The Galileans were surprised to see that I, a former tax collector, was now a disciple of Jesus. Some made smart remarks like, "How much of our hard earned money did you have to pay to become His disciple?"

"Nothing," I would reply with a smile. "He invited me." I had tried to be fair with people and not take more than Rome allowed, but I had made sure I was paid well for my work. Everyone was glad I no longer worked for Rome. I was glad to be working alongside Jesus. I experienced such peace and joy being with Him! Never in my life had I experienced such happiness.

At each place we visited, I watched as Jesus took a special interest in every soul. Some brought children to be blessed, others came for healing, others just needed some encouragement and prayer. He had compassion on the people. With large crowds surrounding Him, He would turn to us and say, "The harvest is ready, but the workers are few. Pray to the Lord in charge of the harvest that He might send more workers into His fields."

It was true, we were only a handful, and the need was great. Where would we find more workers? The religious leaders didn't seem to care about the people. I prayed that the laborers would increase. Little did I know then that I would be part of the answer to my own prayer.

April 16   Luke 7:11–17

Jesus Raises the Widow's Son

   I couldn't believe my bad fortune. First my husband died and, as if that was not terrible enough, shortly afterwards my only son became ill. In spite of many trips to visit doctors who might help him, he grew progressively worse. No one was even able to diagnose his illness. I did everything I could think of to save him, but it was to no avail. He died. I knew he was ill, but I had no idea the end was so near. It almost seemed that he died without warning. I woke up in the middle of the night because I heard him struggling to breathe. I prayed for God to help him as I had prayed many times before. He made a few desperate gasps for air, stiffened, and cried out, "Help me!" Then he was gone. All I could do was put my arms around him and sob. I don't know how long I stayed there before it dawned on me that I needed to let my brother know that he was gone.

   We were devastated. How could God let this happen after all our prayers? We were good people and tried to follow all the instructions of our rabbi. Somehow we managed to make the funeral arrangements and secure a burial plot. When the time for the funeral came, I walked numbly beside the coffin of my beloved son. In the distance I saw a large crowd approaching the city. That seemed unusual, but I was too grief-stricken to really care.

   All at once I realized a young man from the crowd was right beside me. I felt His arm around me and heard Him say gently, "Don't cry." There was such comfort in His touch and compassion in His face. He moved to the coffin and touched it. The procession came to a stop. *What is He doing?* I wondered. Then He touched my son's arm and said, "Young man, I tell you, get up."

   My son moved, sat up, looked at me, and smiled. There was stunned silence. Was this a dream? But no, Jesus helped my son up and presented him to me. You can't imagine my joy! I threw my arms around him and hugged him with all my might. Thanks be to God for turning my unbelievable sadness into incredible happiness!

April 17   Matthew 12:22; Mark 3

Healing of the Blind, Dumb Demoniac

   We worked with people on a daily basis, morning to night. They came in droves. Everyone wanted to see Jesus. Some days we didn't have time to eat, and we often went to sleep late. Lack of food and lack of sleep were taking their toll. Word was getting around that we were becoming fanatics and not taking care of ourselves. It is true, we were overextended, but we were certainly not fanatics. It was just that Jesus could not turn away a hurting soul.

   On one particularly busy day in Capernaum, some people from Judea brought a man who was blind, dumb, and possessed by an evil spirit before Jesus. When He commanded the evil spirit to leave, it did so with such an intense show of power that it was as if Satan himself was being forced out of the man. This grand display of satanic power was a very emotional experience for the family of the man. Especially moving for them was when Jesus restored him to his right mind.

People who witnessed the healing began to talk with the man's family. "Could this be the Son of David, the Messiah?" they asked. Several family members tried to pay Jesus for healing their loved one, but He refused and told them it was a gift from God. He encouraged them to give an offering and sacrifice to the Lord God and show their appreciation by helping the poor and underprivileged. Full of gratitude, they readily agreed to do this.

As they left Jesus said to me, "Peter, there could be trouble."

When the formerly demon possessed man and his family arrived back in Jerusalem, they boldly declared to everyone that Jesus must be the promised Messiah because of His power over Satan and his evil spirits.

The Pharisees were infuriated! "Jesus' power comes from Satan himself! He is no friend of God!" They angrily told the people to be quiet. But many were convinced that the Messiah had come just as the prophets promised, and they proclaimed that His name was Jesus.

April 18 *Matthew 12:25-37; Mark 3:20-30*

The Unpardonable Sin

Soon after the healing of the blind and dumb demoniac, we were inundated with people seeking Jesus. It seemed like the whole world was looking for Him. He was teaching and healing the people at my place in Capernaum when two of His stepbrothers showed up. When I met them outside, they insisted that Jesus needed to come home with them because rumor had it He was losing His mind from overwork. His mother was very concerned also. I assured them He was very busy but He hadn't lost His mind. They stayed and watched from a window for awhile but left, promising to return with the rest of the family. I got the feeling they were more concerned about their reputation than they were about Jesus.

No sooner had they left than a delegation of the Sanhedrin in their fancy clothes and with an air of superiority arrived. The people made way for them to sit on benches near the wall. After listening for a while, one of them stood up, positioned himself near the doorway so both those outside and inside could hear, and said, "This man is possessed by the prince of demons and that is where He gets power to cast them out," he shouted.

The people waited to hear how Jesus would respond. "How can Satan cast out Satan?" He asked. "A divided nation or family will fall apart. Who could enter the house of someone as strong as Satan? Only someone stronger. Even your own exorcist will condemn you," He chided. "But if I am casting out demons by the Spirit of God, then the kingdom of God has arrived."

The religious men squirmed uncomfortably. Jesus stood and walked over toward the benches. "Every sin and blasphemy can be forgiven except blasphemy against the Holy Spirit. It will not be forgiven in this world or in the world to come." With guilt written all over their faces, they hurriedly stood and tried to escape.

Jesus continued to speak to the people. "A tree is identified by the fruit it produces. Everyone must give an account for the words they speak in the day of judgment."

April 19 *Matthew 12:38-45, 46-50; Mark 3:31-35;*
Luke 8:19-21

Pharisees Ask for a Sign and the Visit of Jesus' Mother and Brothers

Jesus had been teaching at my place in Capernaum for several days now. Once again a group of religious leaders and Pharisees joined the crowd and asked Him where His authority came from. "Give us a sign," they demanded. "Perform a miracle to prove yourself."

"Only an evil and adulterous generation would ask for a sign. The only sign you will get from Me is the sign of Jonah," He replied. "As he was in the belly of the whale three days and nights, the Son of man will be in the heart of the earth three days and nights. Nineveh will judge you on judgment day. They repented; you will not. One greater than Solomon is here, but you refuse to repent or even listen. Beware, because an evil spirit leaves a person and goes to look for rest in the desert. Finding none, it returns, and since the house is empty, it invites seven other evil spirits, worse than he, to live there too. That person is worse off than he was initially. These words apply to you."

Extremely angry with Jesus, the religious leaders hustled away. Word was then passed to Jesus that His family was outside and wanted to see Him immediately. I was close to the window and saw the people crowded tightly around the house in hopes of hearing Jesus' words. Mary was on the edge of the crowd while Joseph's sons and daughters were pacing back and forth, looking frustrated because the crowd wouldn't let them through. One of the brothers had a rope in his hand. Jesus and I exchanged glances. We knew they had come to take Him away by force.

Someone standing at the door again announced, "Your family wants to see You right now."

Jesus responded, "Who are My brothers and My mother?" Then He pointed to us, His disciples. "Look, these are My mother and brothers. Anyone who does the will of My Father is My mother, brother, and sister." Then He continued with His message. His family eventually got tired of waiting and left. Later that night I asked Him if He planned go see them in Nazareth. He simply said, "When they understand I am about My Father's business."

April 20 *Matthew 13:1-53; Mark 4:1-34; Luke 8:4-18; 13:18-21*

Parables and Stories

In the afternoon when the crowd dispersed to their homes to eat, Jesus headed to the lake where our fishing boats were docked. I knew the situation with His family had gotten to Him. He loved them all so much, but He could not let them interfere with His ministry. He had gone to the lake to be alone, but that was nearly impossible. Somehow people always seemed to find out where He was, and soon there was a crowd gathered to hear Him speak the words of life. He was a shepherd to them.

I watched Him climb into my boat and begin to tell them stories about the kingdom. The crowd grew as He shared stories from real life that the people could relate to. There was one about a farmer who sowed seeds. Some fell on bad soil, some on good. The soil represented people's hearts—rocky, thorny, shallow, or good. Only the good soil produced fruit. Every time I look at a field I think of that story.

He told another one about a farmer who planted good seed but enemies sowed weeds in the field. They all grew together, but at harvest the weeds were separated from the grain and burned.

He told the story of the kingdom of heaven being like a mustard seed, which is so very tiny but grows very large. Comparing the kingdom to leaven and how a little pinch of yeast affects the whole loaf brought smiles from the women. The gospel affects the whole person. There were stories about hidden treasure, the pearl merchant, and the fishing net, all designed to help people realize the great value of the gospel and the great value God places on us.

Because it was getting late, He dismissed the people to their homes. Some followed Him back to my house, but we left them outside so we could talk to Jesus. My brother Andrew asked what the parable of the weeds meant. Jesus explained that at the end of the world the good people will be saved while the wicked are destroyed. Evil doers, like the weeds, will be destroyed, but the righteous, like the wheat, will shine like the sun. Jesus looked dead tired, so I spread the mats out on the floor, and we went to bed.

April 21 *Matthew 13:54-58; Mark 6:1-6*

Back to Nazareth

After the family altercation at my house in Capernaum, I expected Jesus would return to Nazareth to visit His family. But I was really concerned about Him going because of what had happened the last time when the town was ready to kill Him. Nazareth wasn't that far from Capernaum, but we took our time getting there. It was nice to rest a little after the crowds and late nights. Mary was overjoyed to see Him and His stepbrothers and sisters also seemed glad. He tried to explain to them He was very busy, but He assured them that He was not insane as rumor had it.

The ruler of the synagogue stopped in and asked Jesus if He would speak on Sabbath. Jesus agreed. On Sabbath the synagogue was packed. Seemingly the whole town had come to hear Jesus. They listened as He shared more parables to describe the kingdom of heaven. The common everyday objects and events He drew His illustrations from were things they could relate to. When He finished speaking, the people were amazed at His message. Folks near me asked each other where He'd gone to school because He hadn't attended the synagogue school.

Suddenly someone said, "He's no prophet or Messiah. He's just the son of Joseph the carpenter. We know His family—Mary, James, Joseph, Simon, and Judah. In fact, His stepsister is married to my brother. He's no different than us," the man scoffed.

Someone else blurted out, "Maybe His miracles are just magic."

When people laughed at that comment, anger surged through me, and I was about to speak in His defense, but Jesus firmly said, "Peter, no."

The townspeople refused to believe and were offended that anyone should call Him Lord and Messiah. When Jesus stated that a prophet is honored everywhere except in His own town and among His own family, the crowd dispersed. There were many people in Nazareth who needed healing, but only a few sought Him out. Some were full of unbelief, and others were afraid of being ridiculed by friends and neighbors. We stayed only a few days then moved on.

April 22 *Matthew 8:18–22*

Cost of Discipleship

Arriving back in Capernaum, we found the people waiting for us. Jesus was right—they were like sheep with no shepherd. People who needed healing, those who wanted to hear Jesus' words or needed encouragement, as well as the curious and those who wanted Him dead made up the massive crowd.

One of Jesus' favorite places was by the lake near the spot where we docked our fishing boats. My brother James and I had a berth beside Peter and Andrew so we could work together fishing and mending nets. After He had spoken to the crowd one morning, He climbed into our boat and asked us to take Him to the other side of the lake. I knew it wasn't a good time of year to be on the lake because of unpredictable weather, but nevertheless, I prepared the boat. We were about to shove off when a teacher of the law hurried up to the boat and said to Jesus, "I will follow You anywhere."

Well, this sounds promising, I thought to myself. *Here is a perfect opportunity to get a religious leader on our side!* He looked very sincere, but for some reason, Jesus seemed to be putting him off.

"Foxes have holes to live in," He replied, "and birds have nests, but the Son of man has no place to lay His head." We watched in surprise as the man turned and walked away.

I remembered another occasion when a man asked Jesus to make him a disciple and said that he would follow Him. "I will follow You as soon as I take care of my personal affairs and when my father dies." It sounded like he was basically saying that when he was free and had the time he would be Jesus' disciple. Jesus, in a loving but earnest tone, had said, "Let the spiritually dead bury their own dead. Come and follow Me right now." That man, too, had turned and walked away.

Maybe this teacher of the law thought there might be some monetary gain in discipleship. Jesus knew his heart and responded accordingly. I'm glad He knew my heart, and I'm glad I made the decision to follow Him.

April 23 *Matthew 8:23-27; Mark 4:35-41; Luke 8:22-25*

The Storm on the Lake

It was early evening when we finally set sail. I was tempted to suggest we wait until morning, but Jesus seemed anxious to go. Galilee is a small lake fed by surrounding mountain streams. It is mostly calm, but it can flare into a stormy conflagration of wind and waves without notice. This evening was quiet with a light breeze.

Five or six other small boats filled with people who wanted to be close to Jesus followed us. We discussed the day's events for a short time. Then Jesus, wiped out, lay down at the back of the boat where it was partially sheltered. The rest of us talked while the breeze caught the mast and pushed us along toward Decapolis.

At the second hour of the night watch, Matthew and I were the only ones still awake. "Peter, I think I'm going to get some sleep too." That left me to keep us on course. I was used to being up all night fishing, so it didn't bother me. About an hour later, the wind began to gust, so I pulled the mast down. Before long the wind was blowing furiously. The others awakened as the storm gained strength. Waves sloshed into the boat as it rocked crazily from side to side. I shouted orders to bail out the water and evenly distribute the weight.

As the storm increased in fury, I began to fear for our survival. The waves, now four feet high, were swamping the boat, and we could not keep up with the bailing. I had never seen anything like this, and I had encountered plenty of storms in my years of fishing. It was all I could do to turn the boat into the waves—I was afraid the tiller would break.

When the lightning flashed, I glanced in Jesus' direction and found that He was still sleeping! I was astonished! How could He sleep in this? I shook Him awake. "Teacher, don't You care that we are about to drown?" I shouted.

He reached for the mast, pulled Himself up, stretched out His arm, and cried, "Peace, be still." The wind instantly stopped; the clouds disappeared; the moon was bright; and the lake became dead calm. We looked at each other, mouths agape. He said to us, "Why were you afraid? Do you have no faith?" Then He lay down and went back to sleep. The rest of us sat in stunned silence.

Finally finding my voice, I said, "Who is this man that even the winds and waves obey Him?"

April 24   *Matthew 8:28, 29; Mark 5:1–10; Luke 8:26–31*

The Demoniacs at Gadera

The storm had pushed us westward toward Capernaum, but now it was so calm we weren't going anywhere with the sail. Since we couldn't sleep, we decided to row to Gergesa on the eastern shore. We talked about the amazing events of the night as we rowed, changing off occasionally to give one another a break.

Another smaller boat drew up next to ours. "What happened last night?" the owner asked. "We were about to go under when the storm stopped. My wife told me she saw Jesus raise His hand and all of a sudden everything became calm. Is that true?"

I nodded my head. "It is true," I replied.

He shook his head. "Peter, in all the years we have fished, have you ever seen anything like that?"

"No, never," I said.

"It was a miracle; He saved our lives."

"We're going back to Capernaum. Everything is wet, and my wife is sick." With that he pushed away and headed home.

We arrived at Gergesa just as the sun rose over the hills. Steep cliffs marked much of the eastern shoreline, so we looked for a place to land. Jesus awoke and stretched as though nothing unusual had happened the night before. We pulled the boat up on a rocky shore. While I secured it, Jesus and the others headed up the trail. The stillness of the morning was shattered by a piercing scream. I looked up in time to see the disciples racing back to the boat.

"Crazy people—demons!" Andrew said, pointing at the trail.

"Where's Jesus?" I asked.

"Back there!"

Although scared, I raced in His direction, foolishly thinking I could protect Him. When I reached Him, two demon possessed men faced Him. Bruised and bleeding, broken chains hung from their arms and legs. They foamed at the mouth and swung the chains at Jesus. I'd brought an oar from the boat and was about to attack them when Jesus raised His hand.

"It's okay, Peter."

"Why are You tormenting us, Son of God? Have You come to torture us before God's appointed time?" one of them shrieked.

Jesus commanded the demon to leave them. "What is your name?" He demanded.

"Legion," they shouted in unison, "because many of us possess these men. Please don't send us to the abyss." They pointed at a large herd of swine and pleaded, "Please send us to that herd of pigs."

"Go," Jesus answered.

April 25   *Matthew 8:30–9:1; Mark 5:11–20; Luke 8:32–39*

Demon Possessed Pigs

We stared at the two men foaming at the mouth. Jesus stood His ground, but I kept the oar ready. All of a sudden they both screamed and fell to the ground in convulsions—writhing and shrieking. "Leave us alone, Son of God!" they shouted. Then, just as suddenly, they lay unmoving like dead men. The air was deathly quiet.

So caught up in the drama with the wild men, we had barely noticed that herders were tending an enormous herd of pigs on a nearby hill. But in an instant the pigs captured our full attention as two thousand or more pigs began squealing and racing crazily down the hill toward a precipice that dropped into the Sea of Galilee. The herders frantically tried to stop them, but to no avail. The noise was deafening! Over the brow of the cliff, the pigs plunged to their death in the sea. Carcasses floated everywhere in the water. I could hardly believe what I had just seen. The herders were beside themselves. They shouted accusations at us as they raced into the town to tell the owners.

The two previously demon possessed men now knelt at Jesus' feet, thanking Him for their freedom. Jesus asked us to provide them with clothing. Andrew and I had a change of clothes stashed in the boat, so we ran back to the boat and retrieved the clothes. People from the village hurried to the scene. They were angry about the pigs, but when they saw the demoniacs sitting sane and normal, they were afraid. The elders asked us to leave because they were afraid worse things might happen. Jesus did not resist. He simply said, "Let's go."

The healed men followed Him. "Please take us with you," they implored.

"No," He said, "go back to your families and town of Decapolis and tell them what God has done for you."

We pushed the boat out into the carcass-laden water and through the bloated swine. We waved goodbye and made our way back to Capernaum. No one spoke. Lost in thought, we pondered all that had happened in the past twenty-four hours. We were convinced that Jesus was indeed the Son of God.

April 26   *Matthew 9:18–26; Mark 5:21–24; Luke 8:40–48*

Jarius and the Bleeding Woman

The trip back across the lake was uneventful, which was a relief. Nearing the western shore of Galilee, we quickly saw that a large crowd had gathered awaiting Jesus' return. The people had heard all about the storm and how Jesus had calmed it by rebuking the wind and waves. No sooner had we stepped out of the boat onto shore than Jarius, the leader of the synagogue in Capernaum with whom we were all acquainted, ran up to Jesus, knelt at His feet, and, with a flood of tears, begged Him to come quickly and heal his dying daughter. "Please come and lay Your hands on her so she will live," he pleaded.

We knew the little girl. Jarius' only child, she was so sweet to everyone. Jarius had not been supportive of Jesus but that did not bother the Lord. He at once agreed to go to his house. So many people crowded around Jesus that progress was slow. We could see how anxious Jarius was for Jesus to hurry, but we could only go so fast with so many people pressing around us.

Suddenly Jesus stopped and asked a very odd question. "Who just touched Me?"

The crowd had been bumping against Him ever since we got out of the boat, so I thought it was a strange thing to ask. The people grew quiet, and no one spoke. "Lord," I said, confused, "this whole crowd has been touching You!"

Jesus responded, "No, someone deliberately touched Me because I felt healing power go out of Me."

For a long moment there was silence. Finally a woman came forward. Sobbing, she knelt at His feet and blurted out her story. She had suffered from a bleeding disorder for twelve years. She had spent all her money on doctors but had found no relief. "Then I heard about Your healing power. 'If I can only touch the hem of His garment, I will be healed,' I told myself. And I was!"

Jesus reached down and took her hand, helping her to her feet. He looked into her eyes and smiled. "Daughter, your faith has made you well. Go in peace." She wiped her tears, thanked Him, and disappeared into the crowd.

As the procession continued to Jarius' home, some of his servants pushed through the crowd and spoke to him. He fell to his knees, buried his face in his hands, and broke down in sobs. "No, no! Not my little girl!"

April 27 *Matthew 9:23-26; Mark 5:35-43; Luke 8:49-56*

Jarius' Daughter Healed

Jesus had taken time to speak to the woman who was healed by touching His garment. I must admit, I was impatient to keep moving. All I could think about was how my little girl needed help before it was too late. I was so relieved when we started moving again toward my house. But we hadn't gone far when my head household servant and my daughter's governess pushed through the crowd to me. "She's gone, sir. There is no use troubling the teacher now." I burst into tears and fell to the ground, crying bitterly. Head in my hands, I sobbed. If only the crowd hadn't slowed our progress. If only there had been no delays.

Having overheard what my servant said, Jesus knelt beside me on one knee. He put His arm on my shoulder and said, "Don't be afraid. Just have faith."

Through tear-filled eyes I looked into His face and saw divinity, which I cannot define. And in His touch, I felt strength to heal and even raise the dead. I stood to my feet and said, "Let's go."

When we arrived, the mourners were already there. Jesus stopped, turned to the crowd, and instructed them to wait there. Then He called to Peter, James, and John, "Come with me." The five of us walked into the courtyard. The noise from the mourners was deafening. My wife ran to meet me, crying uncontrollably. Jesus addressed the mourners. "Why all this commotion and weeping? The girl isn't dead; she is just asleep."

They laughed at Him. "You don't know anything! The girl is dead! We've seen her with our own eyes."

In a loud voice, Jesus ordered them to get out. He spoke with such authority they obeyed immediately and left the house. My little girl was lying lifeless on her bed. She did look asleep, except her skin was white and mottled where the blood had pooled. Jesus went to her side, looked down at her, took her hand, and said, "Little girl, get up."

We watched a miracle happen! She opened her eyes and got out of bed. Too shocked to speak, completely overwhelmed and astounded, we stood frozen in place. Then my beautiful twelve-year-old daughter said, "I'm very hungry!"

Jesus smiled and said, "Give her some food." What a reunion! We danced, we laughed, we cried, we hugged. He warned us to keep what had happened to ourselves. I took His hand and thanked Him, and then He was gone.

April 28 *Matthew 9:27–31*

Healing Two Blind Men

We knew Him. We had both seen Him before. He was Jesus, the Great Healer. Jarus, my blind friend, and I knew what He looked like because we had seen Him a thousand times in the darkness that was our world. His kind, benevolent face and eyes. We had followed Him all the way from the shore of Galilee. We heard with our own ears everything that had happened that day. I knew He had the power to restore our sight if He could raise up a dead girl. There was no doubt in my mind. He was the Messiah, the Son of David.

When we left Jarius' house, I sensed the crowd was headed toward Capernaum. We could not lose Him now. "Jonas, hurry!" my friend urged.

I knew He was not far from us. I shouted, "Son of David, have mercy on us."

Someone nearby said, "Watch what you are saying."

I was using the Messianic designation, and he was offended. *Too bad*, I thought. "Son of David," I shouted again, and Jarus echoed my call. "Please have mercy on us."

"Be quiet. He's not the Messiah," someone yelled.

We paid no attention. I held tightly to Jarus' hand. The crowd slowed and stopped. I pushed forward. My stick found the wall of a house. I searched for the door, and we boldly walked inside. "Where is Jesus?" I asked.

Then I heard His voice. "Do you believe I can make you see?"

We both fell to our knees. "Yes, Lord, we do."

He touched our eyes with His fingers and said, "Because of your faith, it will happen."

I cannot begin to describe what it was like to actually see for the first time. He didn't look as I had imagined, except for the kind eyes and smile, but I could see! I put my head down and sobbed for joy. Jesus warned us not to tell anyone. How does a former blind man keep his mouth shut? We thought He was just being modest, so we told everyone we met. Sadly, all we did was hasten His death, but we know in our hearts He is risen and alive.

April 29 *Matthew 9:32–34*

Demon Possessed Mute

My brother Thomas was always curious about everything. He wanted to know how things worked. He drove everyone crazy, always asking questions. As he grew older, he became fascinated with the magic arts. This involved conjuring and communicating with the dead. My parents and I and others warned him that the Scriptures spoke against these things, but Thomas would not listen. He had to know how the magicians performed their magic—he just laughed at me when I told him it was the devil behind it all.

He began working as an apprentice to a traveling magician. Some of what he did was slight of hand, but parts of the show were clearly based on the occult. Then it happened. A demon entered my brother and turned him into a mute. He could not speak. His eyes often rolled back in his head, and sometimes he would foam at the mouth. Some days he would lay on the floor all day and tremble as though he were shivering. Doctors were at a loss, and the Pharisees told us God had abandoned him.

One day while in the marketplace in Capernaum I overheard two women talking about a demon possessed man whom Jesus had healed. I knew about Jesus, but I assumed that since the Pharisees believed God had abandoned Thomas Jesus would have nothing to do with him either.

I was present in the house the day the blind men were healed. When I witnessed the miracle, hope surged through me, and I ran to fetch my brother. Reaching our house, I raced inside, grabbed him by the hand, and half dragged him back to Jesus. Together we pushed past the crowd and through the door. I begged Jesus to heal Thomas. He looked at my brother and commanded the spirit to come out. The spirit threw Thomas against the wall. I thought he was dead, but Jesus raised him to his feet, and for the first time in two years, he began to speak. The crowd was amazed at what they had just seen! We praised and thanked Jesus. When Thomas went to the temple to offer a sacrifice, the same Pharisees who told us God had abandoned him said that Jesus was casting out demons through the power of the devil! Our family all became followers of Jesus.

April 30   *Matthew 9:2–8; Mark 2:1–12; Luke 5:17–26*

The Paralyzed Man (Part 1)

My life was a mess because of the way I had lived. For years I had problems with immorality. My work took me to places like Rome and Athens where prostitutes and liquor were readily available. I knew it was wrong, and my conscience bothered me, but I did nothing until my health failed. I acquired a degenerative disease no doctor could do anything about, and I was gradually left paralyzed. Needless to say, I lost my job because I could no longer move about under my own willpower. My family tolerated me, but worse than all was the sting of a compromised conscience. I'd brought all this trouble on myself by my own stupid choices. I was sure God despised me because of my past.

The religious teachers confirmed my feelings. They said I was under God's judgment because of the sins I'd committed. That is exactly how I felt—condemned, forsaken, forgotten, hopeless. I knew I was dying, and I felt sure that God was getting even with me for my sins. I could just hear Him say "good riddance" as I breathed my last.

One day my loyal friend and ex-business partner came to my house to tell me I should go see a man named Jesus. He believed that Jesus had power from God to heal people. He told me stories of lepers and paralytics who were healed, demon possessed individuals who were restored to a sound mind, and even dead people who were raised to life again. It sounded wonderful, but I reminded him that I was suffering all this because of my own sins. "Why would God do anything for the likes of me?" I asked.

"Lepers are under the curse of God according to the Pharisees, so why would Jesus heal them?" my friend countered.

I paused and thought about what he had just said. If this man Jesus would heal a leper, perhaps there was hope for me. He told me Jesus was at Peter's house, which was not far away. I knew Peter. We'd been friends when I was young. My friend went to find stretcher bearers. Lying on my mat, I thought that if this man of God could give me some assurance of sins forgiven, I would be happy to live or die. I really only wanted peace.

May 1   *Matthew 9:2–8; Mark 2:1–12; Luke 5:17–26*

The Paralytic (Part 2)

Soon my friend returned with three other men. They hoisted me up, and we made our way to where Jesus was teaching. When we arrived, the crowd completely surrounded the house. My friends tried repeatedly to break through the wall of people. They said, "Make way for a dying man." No one budged.

I was so close to possible peace that I felt panic rising. "God, please help us," I prayed. As I lay on the cot looking up in the clear blue sky, I saw it! The roof. I knew that roof. I had helped Peter build it. It was tile with thatching. I asked my friend if he could get some rope and let me down through the roof.

He grinned, "I think so. Let me go get some rope." In a few minutes, he was back with the rope. Thankfully no one was blocking the steps to the roof. Up we went. Everyone watched as my friends pulled me up the steps and then began taking off the thatching and tile.

Jesus stopped speaking and looked up at us when we broke through the roof and sunlight peeked into the house. At first Peter was upset about his roof being dismantled, but when he saw it was me, he understood. Soon the hole was large enough to let me through. My friends lowered me down until I rested at Jesus' feet. He looked at me and smiled. I relaxed. He seemed to see into my soul and understand the greatest need of my heart—forgiveness. He said in a bold voice, "Son, your sins are forgiven."

I sighed heavily. At that moment, I had peace of mind and spirit like I had never known. I didn't care if I lived or died—I was forgiven! Then they started. The Pharisees whispered something about blasphemy. Jesus' demeanor changed as He asked them, "I know what you are thinking: Who does He think He is—God? Forgiving sins. What is easier to say, 'Your sins are forgiven' or 'Get up and walk'? I will prove to you I have authority to forgive sins." He turned to me and said, "Pick up your mat and go home."

A surge of healing power electrified my dead muscles. I jumped to my feet, bowed before the Lord in thanks, grabbed my mat, and walked out. This time the crowd moved aside to let me pass—amazed to see me walking. My friends met me outside where we danced and shouted praises to God! It was the best day of my life.

May 2 *Matthew 9:10–13; Mark 2:15–17; Luke 5:29–32*

Matthew's Feast

The day Jesus called me to follow Him was the best day of my life! To show my appreciation for the peace and purpose that He had given me, I invited Him to be the guest of honor at a great feast at my home. He was pleased and thanked me.

Because I had been a tax collector, most of my friends and acquaintances were tax collectors, so I invited every tax collector in Judea to come to my feast and meet Jesus. On the evening of the feast, more than fifty tax collectors showed up. Jesus sat in the best seat, enjoying the company of my invited guests. They asked questions about His work and why He, a rabbi, had a tax collector as a disciple. Jesus was happy to answer all of their questions.

As the guests were leaving after the banquet, we learned that a group of Pharisees who had been invited were still standing outside the gate. They had refused to come in for fear of defilement. Peter, John, and a few others went with me to speak to them. As soon as they saw Peter, whom they knew, and John, who was related to one of them, they said, "Why do you eat and drink with these scumbags?"

Peter was visibly angry, and I figured he was about ready to spout off something he most likely would regret later when Jesus appeared. "Healthy people don't need a doctor—sick people do," He said.

"I haven't come to call the righteous but those who know they are sinners and need to repent." Then He put His hand on my shoulder and added, "Go learn the meaning of this scripture: I want you to show mercy, not sacrifice." He gave my shoulder a squeeze and we turned and walked back into the house.

May 3   *Matthew 9:14-17; Mark 2:18-22; Luke 5:33-39*

The Question Regarding Fasting

One day not long after the banquet I gave in Jesus' honor, some of the religious people came to Jesus accompanied by a few of John's disciples and asked Him, "John's disciples and the Pharisees' disciples fast and pray regularly, but You and Your disciples are always eating and drinking. We never see You fasting."

I knew they were trying to get at Jesus for attending my banquet. *Why don't they leave Him alone*, I mused. *Why don't they throw a feast in His honor for all the people He has helped?*

Jesus didn't answer their question right away. He allowed it to linger in the air while He walked slowly around the room. Finally He turned to them and said, "Do wedding guests fast while celebrating with the groom?" Before they had a chance to speak, He answered His own question. "Of course not." Then He came face to face with the group's spokesman and asked him, "If your son or daughter was getting married, would you fast and refuse to celebrate?" The poor man shook his head no. "Well, someday the groom will be taken away from these," He said, pointing to us. "Then they will fast."

What did He mean by that? I wondered. Then He illustrated His point. I saw a smile around His lips. He was about to go deeper. "Who in this crowd would patch an old garment with new cloth?" He asked. "No one, of course. The new garment would be ruined and the patch wouldn't match the old garment. Who would put new wine in old skins?" Now He was smiling broadly. "The new wine would burst the old skins," He continued, bringing His arms in sharply to simulate an explosion. He paused, then spoke again. "The wine would be wasted, and the old skin ruined. New wine must be stored in new skins," He said, emphasizing each word.

When He finished, everyone was smiling too. The point was clear. Everyone understood. New teaching could not mix with old ideas. Even the questioners had to agree.

May 4   *Matthew 10:1-15; Mark 6:7-13; Luke 9:1-6*

Jesus Instructs and Sends Out the Twelve

My brother John and I had been with Jesus since the early days. We had witnessed His ministry to the people. Wherever there was a need, He met it. He'd been a good teacher for us, and now it was our turn to go out and do the work of advancing the kingdom. He called us together one day and gave instructions regarding the work we were about to do. At this point in time, He wanted us to go just to the lost sheep of the house of Israel, not to the Gentiles. We were to announce the nearness of the kingdom, heal the sick, cure leprosy, cast out demons, even raise the dead. We were not to take money, a change of clothes, or even a walking stick.

He continued instructing us, saying, "Don't hesitate to accept hospitality, for those who work deserve to be fed. When you go to a town, find a good person to stay with, and remain there until you are ready to leave. If the home is worthy, give it your blessing. If not, take the blessing back. If any town refuses to welcome you or listen to your message, shake its dust from your feet as you leave. Evil cities like Sodom and Gomorrah will be better off than such a town in the day of judgment."

Then He divided us into teams of two. Brothers Peter and Andrew were a team as were my brother John and I. Philip and Bartholemew went together; Jesus put Thomas and Matthew together as a team; James and Thaddeus served together; and finally Judas Iscariot went with Simon the Zealot. Everyone seemed happy with their partner. Jesus then placed His hands on the heads of each team and vested them with power, authority, and courage to do the work. Jesus divided up the surrounding region and systematically sent each team to cover all the towns and villages in the area assigned. I was excited and ready to go, but He had few more things to tell us.

May 5   Matthew 10:1–5

Jesus Warns His Disciples of Persecution

Before sending us out, Jesus wanted us to know some of the issues we'd face doing mission work. "You are going out as sheep among wolves so be shrewd as snakes but harmless as doves." He told us we would be witnesses before kings and rulers and could face arrest and trials before governors. "God will give you the words to speak when these things happen. The Holy Spirit will bring you words from the Father. People will hate you and persecute you because you are My followers. If you are persecuted in one place, go to the next."

He continued, "You know, students are never greater than their master. So if they call Me, your Master, the prince of demons, what will they say of you?" I remembered when the Pharisees had accused Him of being demon possessed.

"Don't forget," He reminded us, "that the time will come when all the secret things will be revealed. What is said in darkness will be revealed in broad daylight. What I whisper to you, shout from the housetops. Whatever you do, do not be afraid of those who kill the body, for they cannot touch the soul. Fear God who can destroy both body and soul at the end of the world. God truly cares for you," He told us. "He sees when a seemingly insignificant sparrow falls, and you are worth more than many sparrows. God cares about every detail of your life—even numbering the hairs on your head, so don't be afraid. If you acknowledge Me before men, I will acknowledge you before God. If you deny Me, I will deny you."

I thought to myself, I will never deny You, Lord. Little did I know then how wrong I was and how very weak I was.

Jesus concluded with these words: "I did not come to bring peace but a sword. My teachings will turn families against each other. If you love anyone more than Me or even your life more than Me, you are not worthy of Me. If you lose your life for Me, you will gain it. Those who receive you receive Me. If a cup of cold water is given to My follower, the giver will be rewarded." He completed His instructions, blessed us, and sent us out. What an experience—one I will never forget!

May 6 *Matthew 11:1*

Jesus' Third Galilean Tour

After sending the twelve out to the towns and villages of Israel, I searched for a quiet place to rest. Keeping My body and mind in good mental and physical condition was very important to Me. I always encouraged the men to eat properly and get plenty of water and sleep. We didn't need to worry about getting enough exercise; that came naturally considering the distances we had to travel by foot! Sleep and rest were often very difficult to achieve, however, because everywhere we went the people followed like sheep without a shepherd. I knew the disciples would have a difficult time on their first mission, but I also knew there would be rewards and blessings.

Over the few years we had been together, I had tried to teach them truths about the Father and the kingdom of heaven, and now I had sent them to share those truths with others. While they are gone, I will pray for them and ask the Father to send angels to give them wisdom and courage as well as protection. Of course, I do this for *every* disciple who goes out in My name. Anyone who shares the gospel receives My blessing and can be assured of My support. While the disciples are on their mission to the places I have assigned them, I will continue working.

But tonight I will spend time in prayer for My disciples. I know Satan will tempt them and throw barriers in their path—they have much to learn. The thing that bothers Me the most is their misunderstanding of the kingdom. They are convinced it is of this world. All they can think about is defeating the Romans, but it is so much bigger than that. Then there are their personal ambitions, each one wanting to be the greatest. It really hurts that they don't understand that humble service makes one great in the kingdom. Judas is a constant concern. I love him, but I fear for him. I see the direction he is taking, but I will continue to pray for him.

A full night in the presence of My Father can be as refreshing as a night of sleep. Now I must pray.

May 7   Matthew 11:2-6; Luke 7:18-23

Inquiry of John's Disciples

I can't understand why Jesus isn't doing something for John. It seems like He doesn't care. John languishes in Herod's prison, and Jesus hasn't even come for a visit to bring him some encouragement. As one of John's disciples, I asked Peter why Jesus hasn't done anything. All Peter would say was, "Jesse, I don't know. Perhaps He is waiting for the right time."

Well, the time is now because John is prepared to do whatever God's will is. I know John has been feeling discouraged because he is hearing reports of all the things Jesus is doing for others while He is doing nothing to release him. We often talk about what will happen when the Messiah comes to restore Israel, but Jesus has not done anything to accomplish the goal of restoring Israel. He hasn't solicited the help of the leaders or raised an army. All He does is heal and teach.

Yesterday morning, John sent us to find Jesus and ask Him if He really is the true Messiah or if we should look for someone else. We found Jesus near the temple healing people. I asked Him the question, "Are You the Messiah? John wants to know." He told us to observe. What we saw was people with every kind of disease being healed and Jesus speaking to each one about faith and trust in God. He spoke of heaven and how this world would pass away. As I listened and watched, I began to realize that the kingdom far surpassed anything this world had to offer. Jesus was preparing people for heaven.

At the end of the day, Jesus called us to Himself. "Go tell John what you have seen and heard. The blind see, the lame walk, lepers are cured, the deaf hear, and the dead are raised. The good news about heaven is preached to the poor and needy. Tell him God blesses those who are not offended by Me."

We went to John and told him what Jesus had said. He seemed to be at peace. He assured us God had revealed to him that Jesus was doing just what the Scriptures said He would do. We are all encouraged.

May 8   Matthew 14:3-12; Mark 6:17-29

Martyrdom of John the Baptist

John was always bold. He was not afraid to point out sin even when the sinners were King Herod and Herodias, his brother Philip's wife. John told them both they were living in sin and displeasing God. Herod's conscience was pricked, but Herodias was furious. She held a murderous grudge and badgered Herod until he sent soldiers to arrest John. No one was clear on the charges against John, but he was kept in prison. Surprisingly, Herod visited John in prison even though what John said to Herod disturbed him.

Herodias' opportunity for revenge came the night of Herod's birthday party at which all the official guests were there. Government and army officials, statesmen and others of importance indulged to great excess on fine foods and drinks. As one of Herod's stewards, I tried to caution him to be careful with the wine.

Before the banquet I saw Herodias conspiring with her daughter, also named Herodias. A beautiful young woman, she danced seductively before the guests. Dazed with alcohol, everyone was overwhelmed with her beauty and body. Herod, in a drunken stupor, offered her anything she wanted. She asked to speak with her mother, but I figured it was already planned. She came back to a standing ovation and asked for John's head on a silver platter. Silence descended on the banquet hall. Everyone sobered up instantly. Herod looked around, as if hoping that someone would object. No one spoke. He motioned for me to come over.

"Chuza, what shall I do?"

"Don't do it, go back on your vow," I urged.

"I cannot," he stammered. "I will look foolish." He gave the order. In a few minutes the soldiers returned with John's bloody head on the platter and gave it to his stepdaughter. After that, the party ended, and Herod fell into a terrible depression, filled with remorse and spite for his wife. John's disciples came, gathered his things and his body, and buried him. Then they went to tell Jesus.

May 9 *Matthew 14:1, 2; Mark 6:14-16; Luke 9:7-9*

Herod Believes Jesus Is John Resurrected

Everyone was talking about Jesus and the miracles He was performing. Rumors were flying. Some people claimed He was Elijah. Others said he was John the Baptist risen from the dead. Speculation abounded as to whom Jesus could be. Joanna, my wife, was sure of who He was. He had healed her when the doctors had given up on her. She believed He was, without a doubt, the Son of God. I still had some doubts.

After executing John the Baptist, Herod lived in terror. Harassed constantly by a guilty conscience, he was unable to sleep at night. Believing Jesus was John resurrected, Herod was afraid that he would appear and exact revenge on him in the middle of the night. I saw how he suffered. Often he would call me and ask for some words of encouragement. Some nights he would sit on his bed and weep, repeating again and again how much he missed talking with John. "What will become of me?" He cried.

Herodias finally told him that if he didn't shake it off and stop being so depressed she would leave him. That seemed to get his attention, and within a few days he was back to himself around her and in public. However, at night he still wept and called for me. "I beheaded John. What am I going to do?"

I really felt sorry for him. Although I wanted to help him, I didn't know what to say. There were times I thought he was losing his mind. Thinking Joanna might be able to help, I asked her if she would come to the palace and speak with him. She refused, saying simply that he was reaping the whirlwind he'd sown. I spoke with John the Baptist's disciples whenever I saw them. They reminded me of lost sheep. Eventually some became followers of Jesus while others resented Him for not rescuing John from Herod. Little by little, as I heard more and more about Jesus, I realized I was being drawn to Him. One day Herod asked me to arrange a meeting with Jesus, but it never happened.

May 10   *Matthew 11:7-19; Luke 7:24-35*

Jesus' Testimony to John

We were devastated when John was executed. We knew the longer he remained in Herod's prison the lower his chances were for survival. I had been so certain that Jesus would intervene to save him, so I admit, I did harbor resentment. But I decided that since John had sent me to ask Jesus if He was the Messiah, I should be the one to give Him the news. I heard that Jesus was in Capernaum, so I headed there. When I arrived, the crowds were so heavy that it would have been a fight to get near Him.

I decided to just watch awhile and wait for the crowds to disperse. As usual, He was healing and teaching. Someone would ask a question and He would answer it. Then He would heal again. As I watched, I remembered the day my friend Jacob and I went to Him to ask John's question. He had spoken to the crowd about John as we were leaving that day. We had turned and listened before heading back to John. Jesus had asked the people, "When you went to see John by the Jordan, what did you expect? Someone swaying like a reed in the wind, a fancy dressed prince in a palace? No. Were you looking for a prophet? John was more than a prophet. He was the one spoken of in Scripture. 'Look, I am sending My messenger before You. He will make the path straight.' There is no one greater than John. He advanced the kingdom more than anyone because all the prophets before him looked forward to the present time. He is the Elijah of whom Malachi spoke." Then He paused and looked at the Pharisees standing to the side. "Wisdom is shown to be right by its results," He concluded.

I felt very convicted that Jesus was everything He claimed He was. Now with tears streaming down my face, I worked my way forward and told Him about John. He put his head in His hands and wept. His disciples had just returned from their mission. They were shocked when I told them the news. We all mourned together the passing of a great man of God.

May 11   *Matthew 11:20-30*

Jesus Promises Rest for the Soul

I loved listening to Jesus speak. I believed that He was indeed the Messiah. Nicodemus and I talked often of the work He was doing and spent much time reading the books of the prophets, searching and comparing texts. Our colleagues had a murderous contempt for Him. It was really jealousy—they wanted the crowd's attention for themselves.

Then one day as I listened to Him speak, His words solidified my belief in Him. He denounced some of the towns where He had taught and healed. He compared Chorazin and Bethsaida to the wicked port cities of Tyre and Sidon, declaring that if the same miracles had been performed there, they would have repented in sackcloth and ashes. Then He hit the people of Capernaum hard. "You people think you are honored in heaven. You are dead. If these miracles had been done in Sodom, it would still be around. I assure you it will be better for Sodom in the judgment than you."

You can imagine the people of Capernaum were not happy about being compared with Sodom! Then Jesus prayed a simple prayer. "Father, thank You for hiding these truths from the wise and arrogant but revealing them to those with childlike faith." As He spoke He looked right at our friends, not with vindictiveness but compassion. It was as a father would look at a wayward son. He added, "Yes, Father, it pleased You to do it this way."

He then raised His voice, "My Father has entrusted all to Me. No one knows the Son except the Father, and no one knows the Father except the Son and to whomsoever the Son reveals Him." Then softly and entreatingly, He spoke to the crowd. "Come to Me all of you who are weary and carry heavy burdens, and I will give you rest. Take My yoke upon you. Let Me teach you because I am humble and gentle at heart and you will find rest for your souls because My yoke is easy to bear and the burden I give you is light."

My fellow Pharisees turned and walked away but I pressed closer to Him along with the crowd, vowing to wear His yoke and carry His burden forever.

May 12   *Matthew 14:13, 14; Mark 6:30–34; Luke 9:10, 11; John 6:1, 2*

Jesus Seeks a Quiet Place With His Disciples

At the appointed time, we arrived in Capernaum to met with Jesus at my house. What a wonderful reunion! Everyone had stories to tell. My brother Andrew and I were thrilled that we had led some people to Jesus. Others shared similar experiences. There were exciting reports of healing the sick and casting out demons. We were inspired by our missionary trip, but we were also exhausted. Jesus looked really tired too, so I found Him a blanket and told everyone it was time to go to sleep; we could talk more tomorrow. As we settled down, I told Jesus this mission He had sent us on was the best thing I had ever done. He smiled.

When we awoke the next morning, Jesus was already gone. My mother-in-law told me He'd gotten up early and headed out to pray before going to the marketplace. After breakfast we walked into town to join Him. A large crowd was gathered around Him as usual, and He was healing and answering questions. Suddenly we saw Jesus put His head in His hands. A moment later Jesse, one of John's disciples, approached us and told us the sad news of John's execution. We were shocked. "How could God let this happen to him?" we asked each other.

Seeing that Jesus was distraught, we told the crowds we needed to go. I suggested we go to my boat.

A little larger than the Zebedee's boat, there was lots of room for all of us and John's disciple who joined us. The crowd followed us to the shore, and after we shoved off, they continued to follow us along the shoreline as we headed to Bethsaida.

The news about John put a damper on our excitement, but we still shared our stories with Jesus. Hearing about the miracles performed and the people helped put a smile on His face. We had lots to share and many questions to ask. Jesus kept looking to shore. "Look at all those people in need, like sheep without a shepherd. We must help them."

I guided the boat to a natural inlet where there was sand. We disembarked and headed up into the hills to rest. It seemed as if it wasn't long before the huge crowd was climbing the hill. Jesus welcomed them compassionately, and we got back to work. Our rest didn't last long!

May 13   *John 6:3, 4*

Jesus Meets on Hilltop With His Disciples

Once on top of the hill, we relaxed. The view of the lake and surrounding area was magnificent. It was nice to do as Jesus suggested to get away and rest awhile. We talked some more about our mission experience. The best story came from Judas Iscariot. As he and Simon entered a small village, the news spread quickly that Jesus' disciples had come. Feelings among the villagers were mixed; some were opposed while others were grateful. The two disciples found a home that welcomed them. As they were eating the evening meal with their hosts, one of the most vocal opponents of Jesus and His ministry came to the house where they were staying and begged them to ask Jesus to heal his wife who had suddenly become very ill. Judas stood and asked the man to please take them to her.

Upon arriving at the home, they found several doctors at her bedside. However, they could do nothing. Mourners had even begun to gather. Judas, Simon, and the husband entered the room. Blood was pouring from her mouth and nose as she lay shaking with a seizure. She looked almost dead. Judas went to her side, bowed his head in a moment of silent prayer, and then he placed his hand on her forehead and said, "In the name of Jesus Christ be healed." Suddenly the bleeding stopped, as did the seizure. Her eyes, which had been rolled back in her head a moment before, were now focused, and she sat up. She looked at Simon and Judas and whispered, "Thank you." The husband embraced her, overjoyed at her recovery. The man announced that he was going to follow Jesus, and he encouraged those gathered in his home to do the same. Most of the people in that village came to believe in Jesus.

All the disciples excitedly shared their stories. It was good to be together again! Soon the first of the crowd arrived and sat down nearby. Since it was the time of Passover, the crowd continued to grow. We estimated there were about 20,000 people present. They just kept coming. It was like Jesus said, "The people are like sheep in need of a shepherd."

May 14   *Matthew 14:15-21; Mark 6:35-44; Luke 9:12-17; John 6:5-13*

Jesus Feeds 5,000 Men and Their Families

It had been a wonderful day. Hundreds of people had been healed. Jesus had spoken to the huge crowd that had gathered. The people did not want to leave. As late afternoon drew on, some of us became concerned about the people's welfare. They hadn't eaten anything all day. I asked Peter, Andrew, James, and John what we should do. "Send them home," Peter offered.

We went to Jesus and told Him we should send the people out to the surrounding towns and villages to buy food. Jesus paused for a moment then looked at us with a slight smile on His face and suggested, "Why don't you feed them?"

"Us?" we asked in unison.

He turned to me and asked, "Philip, where do you suppose we could find enough bread to feed all these people?"

"I don't know. Even if we worked for months, we wouldn't have enough money to purchase food to feed them all."

Andrew spoke up. "There is a young boy here with a basket containing five barley loaves and two fish. But what is that compared to this huge crowd?"

Jesus said, "Bring the boy to Me and seat the people in groups of a hundred and fifties." Andrew brought the boy to Jesus, and he gladly gave his lunch to Him. The other disciples seated the people. I watched as Jesus took the bread and the fish, held them heavenward, and prayed, "Father, bless this good food and nourish the people with it." Then He began to break it into pieces.

Jesus had told Thaddeus to find some large baskets, which he had done. The loaf of bread Jesus broke filled ten baskets. The fish in His hand filled another ten baskets. He then instructed us to distribute the food among the people.

We were exhausted after delivering food to everyone—about 20,000 people. It was unbelievable. To top it off, there were twelve baskets of leftovers brought back to Jesus—nothing was wasted. After a closing prayer and benediction, Jesus dismissed the people to their homes. However, they did not want to leave; everyone excitedly discussed the miracle.

May 15   *John 6:14, 15*

The People Want to Make Jesus King

Some of the people left when Jesus dismissed them, but most of the crowd remained. There was such an air of enthusiasm everywhere. I mingled with the crowd and heard some things that stirred me.

People were saying, "Surely this is the prophet we have been waiting for." I heard excited suggestions. "We should make Him our king!" "We could become an army and beat those Romans!" "Jesus could heal the wounded and provide us with food!"

A group of men signaled me over and said, "You are one of His disciples; come with us, and we'll make Him king!" It sounded great to me. I hadn't seen Jesus make any effort to secure honor for Himself. Perhaps this was God's plan for restoring Israel. Apparently others had the same idea, and soon a large portion of the remaining crowd had rallied with us.

We approached Jesus as He was handing out the leftovers. Several of the men in the group spoke boldly to Him. "Sir, we are making You our king. We want You to lead us against Rome so that we may overthrow the Romans."

Jesus looked disappointed in me when our eyes connected. "I will not become your king. I do not have any plans to overthrow Rome," He said with great authority. "Gather up your things and your families and go home!" His command made it clear that He had no intention of allowing them to make Him king.

I stepped forward, "But, Lord…"

Jesus interrupted me. "Peter, I said 'No' and I mean 'No.' You and the others go down to the boat now and cross back over the lake. I'll meet up with you later."

The crowd dissipated quickly. Jesus had never spoken to me like that before, and I knew better than to argue. I headed toward the shore with the others. Jesus strode farther up the hill. I will admit I felt a bit angry and upset about the way things had ended. Wasn't this what we had hoped would happen? The people would rally around Jesus and honor Him as He deserved and Israel would be restored? We didn't set sail right away as Jesus had told us to, deciding to wait and see if He might come down and join us. None of us said much while we waited because disappointment absorbed our thoughts.

May 16   Matthew 14:22, 23; Mark 6:45, 46; John 6:16, 17

Heading for Capernaum

A few determined stragglers followed Jesus, insisting He be their king. He turned around and said firmly, "I dismissed you to your homes. Now, please, go home. You will not crown Me king." The finality in His voice was unmistakable. "I must pray alone now. Good night." With that He turned and continued up the hill.

The people, muttering under their breath, turned toward the direction of their homes. It was beginning to get dark. We waited on the boat awhile but finally decided to leave. Matthew objected. "How will He get back to Capernaum?"

"I don't know," I said. "He told me that we were to cross the lake and He would join us later."

"He told me to get in the boat and leave," John added.

I pushed the boat into deeper water with the help of my brother Andrew and the Zebedee brothers.

We took turns at the oars, setting a course for Capernaum. The lake was calm. A gentle breeze blew against us, but it wasn't strong enough to impede our progress. I asked the others how they felt about the events of the day.

"Disappointed," Thaddeus mumbled.

"I thought Jesus would at the very least accept the support of the people even if He did not want to become king," Judas said in frustration.

Andrew spoke next. "I was amazed at what He did with that boy's lunch!"

"I watched it all while the rest of you were seating the people," Philip said. "After Jesus blessed the food, it kept multiplying! I watched one loaf fill one basket after another!"

"What about you, Peter?" John asked.

"I don't know what to think," I responded. "I thought it was perfect, all those people supporting Him. And He refused. When is He going to establish His kingdom?"

"Perhaps the time is not right," James said thoughtfully. "God's ways are not always our ways. What we want is not always what is best in God's eyes."

Soon everyone fell silent again. The only sound was the oars dipping into the water. There were so many thoughts racing through my mind. *Maybe James is right, but don't the prophets tell us that the Messiah is going to overthrow our enemies and establish His kingdom?*

May 17　　　　　　　　　　　　　　　　　　　*Matthew 24:14; Luke 6:47, 48a; John 6:18, 19a*

Storm on the Lake

Thomas broke the silence awhile later by asking, "Jesus is always talking about the kingdom—the kingdom is like this or that, but what is it really? Is it the nation of Israel restored, another kingdom He will establish, a spiritual kingdom, or heaven? What is it?"

None of us were sure. Oh, we had opinions. Most of us thought it would be a kingdom of people who believed in Jesus and He would be king. We believed most of the Jews would be in that kingdom and Israel would become a great nation as in the days of Solomon.

I surprised myself by saying, "What if the kingdom is nothing like we have ever imagined?"

"What do you mean, Peter?" John asked.

I continued my radical thought, "What if there is no glory, wealth, or position attached to it? What if it is only a spiritual kingdom? What if the kingdom is in us?"

"Every kingdom has a king and subjects," John replied irritably.

I didn't have a chance to respond. A sudden gust of wind nearly knocked me into the water. Those of us who had spent our lives on the Sea of Galilee knew what was coming. Within minutes, a gale force wind pushed the boat almost sideways. We were three or four miles from shore, so we were totally at the mercy of the wind. Soon waves four and five feet high crashed over the bow, filling the boat with water. Those who were not at the oars trying to steer the craft into the waves were bailing out water.

Lightning, thunder, and driving rain accompanied the squall.

A veteran fisherman, I had weathered many a storm, but this was worse than any of them. The sea was wild, and I knew we were in trouble. Judas, who had no stomach for the sea, was hanging over the side throwing up. Even I, a seasoned seaman, was feeling a bit queasy, but maybe it was from fear. I thought of the terrible storm that Jesus had calmed. Where was He now? Holding onto the tiller with both hands, I shouted, "Pray for God's deliverance! Pray!"

May 18   *Matthew 14:25–27; Mark 6:47b–50; John 6:19b, 20*

Jesus Walks on the Water

Some time later Jesus talked with us about the events of that night on the lake. All of us had been terrified—even the life-long fishermen. The storm had been as bad as the one in which we were about to go under while Jesus slept in the boat. Our cries had awakened Him, and He had amazingly calmed the storm.

Battling this storm without Him, we had cried out for God's mercy and deliverance. We felt alone and scared, but what we didn't realize is that Jesus was with us. He had kept us in His watchful eye from the time we left shore until the storm was about to overtake us. While we were struggling to survive, He was praying for us. He came to us in our hour of greatest need.

I remember bailing water and retching from sea sickness. Peter yelled at me, "Simon, take the oar from Thaddeus—he's worn out!"

As I maneuvered to where Thaddeus was seated, a glance at the horizon from where we had come gave me a fright. A flash of lightning revealed a ghostlike figure coming toward us. I pointed toward the apparition with one arm while clinging to the mast with the other. "There's a ghost!" Sure enough, closer now, all the others saw the ghastly specter approaching us. Suddenly we were even more afraid. "What does this mean? Are we going to die?" I cried.

Judas shouted, "It is an omen of death!"

Fear gripping our hearts, it felt like we stared at the figure for an eternity, but it was only a matter of minutes before we heard the reassuring voice of our Master: "Don't be afraid, take courage, it is I!" We all breathed a collective sigh of relief. Never in my life was I so glad to see someone than I was to see Jesus that night. He came closer to the boat. "Don't be afraid," He called again, "I am here." What great relief to see Him. As our fears dissipated, we realized He was standing on the water. His miraculous acts never ceased to amaze us.

May 19   Matthew 14:28–32

Peter Walks on Water

I am always ready for a new adventure, so when I saw Jesus standing on top of the water, I spontaneously cried out, "Lord, if it is really You, tell me to come to You." I knew it was Jesus, but sometimes I say things without thinking.

"Yes, come!" He said.

I stepped over the side of the boat, carefully planting my feet on the water. Waves lapped at my ankles, but my feet felt solid as if I was on land. I glanced down to see if I was standing on a shoal, but there was nothing beneath me but water. I fixed my eyes on Jesus and started walking toward Him. I began to feel confident and comfortable, so I turned to make sure the others were watching me. Suddenly the wind picked up again and the waves began to churn and lash at my legs. I glanced at Jesus and looked back at the boat, wondering if I should make a dash for it. I was afraid. My feet were no longer on solid ground, and I sank like a stone. Memories of a time I had fallen into a rough sea and nearly drowned flashed into my mind. "Jesus, save me!" I yelled.

In an instant, He was beside me, pulling me to my feet. As we stood there on the water in the midst of the sea, He said to me, "You have so little faith. Why did you doubt Me?" We walked back to the boat together. I was glad Jesus said what He did to me privately and not in front of the others. I deserved the rebuke and knew it. As soon as we stepped into the boat, the storm stopped. It was dead calm. We worshiped Him and declared Him the Son of God. Only God could have power over nature, so He had to be God. Awestruck, we sat and stared at Jesus and each other. Jesus had saved us again!

May 20   Matthew 14:34–36; Mark 6:53–56

Arrival at Capernaum

Streaks of gray lined the eastern horizon, announcing the dawn of a new day, as we stepped from the boat and pulled it up on shore. My brother Peter and I pulled it into the docking berth our father had built. Even though it was still semi-dark, people had already gathered in hopes of seeing Jesus. When they saw Him step from the boat, they hurried to Him with their sick loved ones. I tried to interfere, but Jesus stopped me.

"Lord, You have been up all night. You need to rest. Come to Peter's house and get some sleep."

He smiled an appreciative smile—I knew He was grateful for my concern about His well being—then He pointed to the people and said, "They need a shepherd."

Years later when I set out to spread the gospel, I remembered those words wherever I felt tired but saw people in need. I set to work with my fellow disciples organizing the people into orderly lines so each one could take their turn with Him.

"Please," people begged us, "we know that if we are just able to touch even the hem of His garment, we will be healed."

"Do you have that much faith?" I asked, incredulous.

"Yes, we do," they affirmed. One very sick little girl lay in her father's arms, yet she reached out her hand to Jesus. The minute His fingertips touched hers she was instantly made well. A deaf mute touched His garment and began to speak. I watched with joy as the people came to Jesus. I watched as He touched young and old and made them whole. I watched as others with great faith simply brushed His robe and found healing.

"Truly, this man is God's Son," I said, more to myself than to anyone else. It hadn't taken long for the word to spread that Jesus had returned. There were people from all over the Roman world, even Africa and India, seeking an audience with Jesus. Everyone who came to Him for healing that day was restored.

May 21 *John 6:22–29*

Questions About Jesus' Arrival in Capernaum

After Jesus fed the multitude with five loaves of bread and two fish, we were anxious to hear Him speak again. We knew He had to be a prophet. I am Jacob, a fisherman from Tiberias. My family and some friends boarded my boat early the next day and headed back to the hillside. I was certain Jesus would be there because I had been one of the last to leave the mount the night before.

It was only four miles from Tiberias to the mount where Jesus had taught, so we were soon there. We searched the entire area but found no one. We all had seen Him go up the mount. Where could He be? We climbed back in the boat and headed for Capernaum, another five miles, to ask His disciples where He was. Arriving at about ten o'clock in the morning, we were surprised to discover Jesus was there, surrounded by a large crowd of people. I docked my boat next to Peter's, and we pushed our way through the crowd toward Jesus.

"Rabbi, when did You get here? How did You get here? You went up the mountain last night. When did You descend and come to Capernaum?"

Jesus seemed to look straight through me and said, "You truthfully only want to be with Me because of the miracles I perform and because I fed you."

It was true. If there had been no miracles, I would not have wasted time searching for Him.

He continued, "It isn't because you want to understand why the miracle was performed or about Me and My mission here. Don't be concerned with perishable, transient things. Be concerned about eternal life. Spend your energy seeking eternal life that only I can give you. God has approved of the work I am doing."

It dawned on me that here was someone much greater than I ever imagined. My friends and I fell to our knees. "Lord, we want to do the things of God. What should we do?"

He took my arm and stood me up until I was eyeball to eyeball with Him. "This is the work God wants from you. Believe in the One He has sent." At that moment, I knew He was the Son of God.

May 22   *John 6:30–40*

Dialogue About the Bread From Heaven

Some of the people from Tiberius were still kneeling before Jesus when a group of Pharisees and lawyers standing nearby began directing scornful comments toward Jesus.

"Show us a miraculous sign if You want us to believe in You."

"What miracles can You do?" another one said.

"What makes You so great? Moses provided our ancestors with bread from heaven."

Jesus responded, "First of all, Moses didn't give them bread, my Father did. Secondly, now He offers you the true bread from heaven. The true bread from heaven is the One who comes down and gives life to the world."

What He said never registered with them because they were still dwelling on the idea of physical bread. "Give us this bread every day," they said.

Jesus paused and sighed heavily. Then He said plainly, "I am the Bread of Life. Whoever comes to Me will never be hungry again, and whoever believes in Me will never be thirsty again." I saw frowns on many faces. "You have seen Me but still do not believe in Me. However, those who the Father has given Me will come to Me, and I will never reject them. I came down here to do My Father's will, not Mine. It is My Father's will that not one of these be lost but be raised up in the last day."

My brother John looked at me with concern. It was clear that some of the people were not happy with what Jesus was saying. I nodded as a few people close to me began to murmur.

"Who is He telling us He is?" one asked. "The Messiah?"

"What an impostor," another said.

"My Father's will is that everyone who sees Me, His Son, and believes in Me will have eternal life," Jesus continued. "I will raise them up at the last day."

Now the complaining began in earnest. Some people were upset because He claimed to be God's Son. Others didn't like that He claimed to be greater than Moses. Still others were upset because He claimed to be the Bread of Life from heaven.

May 23   John 6:41–52

The People Disagree That Jesus Is From Heaven

The religious leaders had done what they had come to do, that is, turn the people against Jesus. Some Jews from Nazareth, His hometown, complained bitterly. "Isn't this Jesus, the son of Joseph? We know His father and mother. How can He say He came down from heaven?" Many of the people sided with them and started to murmur against Him as well.

I said to my brother Peter, "We need to stay close to Him in case things get out of hand." He looked at me and nodded.

Jesus raised His hands to quell the noise. "Please, let Me speak," He said with authority. All eyes were upon Him. "Stop complaining about what I said. This you must know because it is true. No one comes to Me unless the Father draws him to Me, and at the last day I will raise him up. Read the Scriptures; everyone who is taught by God will come to Me. No one has ever seen the Father except Me, because I was sent by God to come here." This statement stirred things up again.

Someone said, "He really is crazy." I had to wonder why He was saying these things. All He was doing was making the people angry.

He raised His voice and continued. "Truthfully, anyone who believes in Me has eternal life. I am the Bread of Life. Your ancestors ate manna in the desert, yet they all died. All who eat the bread from heaven will never die." He pointed to Himself as He spoke. "I am that living bread who came down from heaven." He opened His arms. "Anyone who eats this bread will live forever. The bread I offer so the world will live is My flesh."

That was the last straw. "How can this man give us His flesh to eat?" they shouted. "He is crazy!"

Others who had been led by God to Jesus argued in His defense. "He is talking about sacrificing Himself for the sins of the world."

Some of the people waved a hand at Him and said, "You are mad!" and turned and walked away.

May 24   John 6:53–59

Jesus Offers the People His Flesh and Blood

I was among the Pharisees sent to spy on Jesus. The council had heard rumors of many miracles and huge crowds. People were flocking to Him not only in Galilee but also in Judea. Nicodemus had planned to come with me, but something had come up. In my heart I knew Jesus was all He claimed to be. My colleagues, on the other hand, scoffed at Him, called Him a lunatic, and did everything they could to turn the crowds against Him.

Today everyone had been invited to the synagogue where the people could be seated and listen to Jesus speak. I can still remember Him at the front; simple, without pretense, sincere, speaking passionately as a man might with little time left to live. Then He said, "Unless you eat the flesh and drink the blood of the Son of man, you cannot have eternal life within you."

That sounded repulsive. Some people jumped to their feet. A few shook their fists at Him. But He continued. "All who eat of Me I will raise up in the last day. My flesh is true food, My blood true drink."

Many shook their heads. Others left. "I feed on the Father, so you must feed on Me," He continued. "In this way you will live because of Me."

My friend from the council looked at me suspiciously and asked, "Do you believe in this mad man?"

"Well, go and eat His flesh and blood—here take my knife," one of them mocked.

I answered, "He doesn't mean literal flesh and blood. It's His teachings He is referring to." They knew I was right, but they hated Him and refused to believe.

"I am the true bread from heaven," He repeated. "Anyone who eats this bread will never die. Your ancestors died in the wilderness, but whoever eats this bread will live forever." I watched the people. A few stamped their feet, blocking their ears and shaking their heads. Insults were hurled at Him. My friends joined in the fray. I stood apart from them. Why had He been so blunt and offensive—especially to Jews who were repulsed at the thought of eating blood? Perhaps it was to root out the unbelievers. I knew there was a reason for what He did, and I knew He was the Bread of Life from heaven.

May 25 *John 6:60–66*

Many Disciples Desert Jesus

We heard all the reports people were bringing back to Nazareth about the work Jesus was doing. It was also reported that He worked long hours, rising early and retiring late. Mary worried about Him. One day she said, "James, please go see how your stepbrother is doing. I am concerned." Mary had always been good to us, so this was the least I could do for her.

I packed a lunch and set out for Capernaum, where I arrived the next day. I heard Jesus was at the synagogue. As I was preparing to enter the synagogue, a man emerged from the building and said sarcastically, "This Jesus wants us to eat His flesh and drink His blood."

"Are you sure that's what He said?" I asked.

"Go listen to Him if you want; I'm leaving," he said. There were others leaving also. Things didn't seem to be going well. I stepped inside to hear for myself.

Someone shouted, "This is very hard to understand. How can anyone accept it?"

Jesus' disciples were close by Him, along with some people from Nazareth who seemed to be ridiculing Him. "Do My words offend you?" He asked. "What will you think when you see the Son of man ascend back to heaven?" I moved closer as He spoke. "The spirit alone gives eternal life, human effort cannot accomplish this. Eating flesh means nothing. It is the very words I have spoken to you that are spirit and life, but some of you do not believe Me."

By this time the majority of the crowd had left, shaking their heads and muttering as they exited the synagogue. I watched as Judas slipped away from the other disciples and joined a group of Pharisees. Only a few people seemed to be listening now as Jesus spoke, "That is why I told you, people cannot come to Me unless the Father gives them to Me."

The Pharisees made a big show of leaving and motioned for those remaining to follow. Only a handful of people remained—Jesus, His disciples, and I. Jesus saw me and smiled, obviously glad to see me. I lifted my hand and smiled in response. I was closer to Him than my siblings, but I believed He was more than just a man, more than just an ordinary common person.

May 26 *John 6:67–71*

The Twelve Remain

Jesus turned to us and asked, "Everyone else has deserted Me. Are you going to leave Me too?" I couldn't understand it. Why, when Jesus had so much popular support and a packed to overflowing synagogue of people prepared to do His bidding, would He drive them all away with this discourse on eating His flesh and blood?

It seemed to me that every time the people were ready and willing to make Him king, He sabotaged their support and did something or said something to turn them off. They were prepared to make Him their leader at the lake, and He sent them home. They were prepared to do whatever He asked here at the synagogue, and He chased them away by what He said. *What kind of kingdom is He establishing anyway? How are we ever going to get rid of the Romans at this rate?* I wondered. And, yet, I was committed to following Him.

I turned to Him and said, "Lord, where should we go? Or whom should we follow? You have the words of eternal life. Even though we do not completely understand, we know You are the holy One of God."

The others all voiced their agreement. I watched as Jesus' eyes left mine and looked at Judas standing beside me. That was when I saw something I had not seen before. I don't know if any of the others noticed, but I clearly saw Jesus' countenance change to one of sadness, as though He read something that broke His heart. He looked at Judas for a long time. I heard Judas mumble his affirmation. Jesus stepped down from the podium, reached out, and gave my shoulder a squeeze. Then He went to James, embraced him, and inquired about Mary and His siblings. The rest of us were buried in our own thoughts regarding the events of the day.

After speaking with His stepbrother, He returned to us and dropped a bombshell. "I chose the twelve of you, but one is a devil." This threw everyone into a turmoil. "Who, Lord?" we all asked in shock. I saw Him glance for a brief second at Judas, but He did not answer us.

May 27 *Matthew 15:1, 2; Mark 7:1-7*

Pharisees From Jerusalem

After the episode at the synagogue in Capernaum, people in the town were cool and distant. Some were even downright hostile. One poor wretch cried mockingly, "Is it time to drink Your blood and eat Your flesh? I'm hungry!" Everyone within hearing had a good laugh, but Jesus ignored their snide remarks. Of course, I wanted to slug the guy!

It was later that week that some Pharisees from Jerusalem arrived in Capernuam. Very seldom would Jews from the Sanhedrin come to Galilee. In their opinion, we were nothing but a bunch of ignorant low-class peasants. They followed us everywhere, whispering to each other like mischievous and secretive children. It was confirmed that they were spies sent to trap Jesus when they asked Him a ceremonial question. "Why don't Your disciples wash their hands ceremonially before they eat?" All good, law-abiding Jews were to dip their cupped hands in water stored in large jars for this purpose. "They are not following our Jewish customs and traditions. They are not supposed to eat anything from the marketplace until they have ritually washed. These are our traditions. They are ignoring them along with the cleansing and purification of cups, pitchers, and kettle," they proclaimed loudly so all could hear. "Why don't Your disciples follow our age-old traditions? We have not seen them perform a ceremonial washing since we arrived here."

I wanted to blast them, but Jesus gave me a look that reminded me that He would handle it. Every eye was on Him. He looked at them for a moment before speaking. "You hypocrites! Isaiah was right about you when he said, 'these people honor Me with their lips but their hearts are far from Me. Their worship is a farce, for they teach man-made laws as commands from God.'"

If they were upset because He had called them hypocrites, they did not show it. They just stood there in front of Him frowning, faces showing little emotion other than disgust. Such a stark contrast to Jesus' countenance which was full of compassion and love for these people He was rebuking.

May 28 *Matthew 15:3-6; Mark 7:8-13*

Disregarding God's Commandments

I came into company with Jesus and the disciples by invitation. My friend Simon thought I could be an asset to the group because of my business acumen. At the time, I believed connecting with Jesus could be to my advantage. If there was to be a kingdom established, I wanted to be part of the inner circle. Of course, to set up a kingdom, one would need the support of the Jewish leadership. Calling them hypocrites was not endearing them to Him. Such statements are causing me to wonder if being a part of this group is a worthwhile enterprise. Most of the men are just simple, uneducated fishermen. Lucky for them, I hold the purse, and I am a shrewd money manger.

In my heart I believe Jesus is empowered by God, because I experienced that power when He sent us out as missionaries. However, I doubt that He is really the Son of God.

In addition to calling the Pharisees hypocrites, Jesus had other harsh criticisms that He threw at them. "By your traditions you sidestep the commandments of God. For instance, God's command is to respect your parents or you will be put to death. You say people can tell their parents 'I refuse to support you because I vowed to support the temple.' You disregard God's direct command with your traditions. People give the money they should be giving to their parents, and yet you squander it on whatever you please. I'll say it again, you Pharisees are nothing but hypocrites. You like to act religious and pretend to love God, but your hearts are far, far away from Him."

I must admit that everything He accused them of was true. My brother did it to our parents. He was pressured into it by his father-in-law who was one of the Pharisees on the Sanhedrin. At the time, I was furious because my parents' money was going into that Pharisee's pocket. It's a fact, they are a bunch of hypocrites. But He doesn't need to tell them that. He needs to use them to set up His kingdom and then get rid of them. Unless He has them on His side, He will never win the support of the people.

May 29 *Mark 7:14, 15; Matthew 15:10, 11*

Jesus Speaks to the Crowd About Defilement (Part 1)

I had been in the synagogue the day Jesus spoke of eating His flesh and drinking His blood. I knew He was simply offering Himself as the source of eternal life. It was just the way it came across, the visual imagery, that turned most people off. I walked out along with everyone else, somewhat disgusted. However, it occurred to me afterwards that Jesus may have been offering an out to those who were insincere, those disciples who really weren't committed. I had seen Him perform miracles, healing the lame, blind, and deaf. I had eaten of the fish and loaves on the mountain. I had watched Him walk up into the mountain afterwards to pray and then somehow show up the next morning in Capernaum with His disciples.

I am convinced He is the Son of God. I just don't understand exactly where He is going with this ministry He started. As a part-time disciple/follower of Jesus, I want to see Him do something to deal with the Romans and establish Israel to its former glory. I have been told ever since I was five years old at my mother's knee that the Messiah would come and restore Israel. If He is the Messiah, why isn't He doing something about the Romans?

I'm confused! I know He's from God, but I don't know what He is trying to accomplish. He is alienating the Pharisees, the very people He needs to secure the popular support. He calls us together and speaks to the people apart from the Jewish leaders. He looks at me, "Listen and try to understand," He pleads. "It is not what goes into your mouth that defiles you. You are defiled by the words that come out of your mouth and from within your heart."

Suddenly it clicked! The kingdom was within me and all believers. He wanted us to purge our hearts of sin, not the nation of the Romans. Why hadn't I seen it before? No wonder He refused kingship on the mount. His kingdom is in the hearts of believers—that is where He wants to reign. As He left with the twelve, I cried out, "Lord, reign in my heart!" He stopped, turned, and smiled at me. I finally understand!

May 30   *Matthew 15:12-20; Mark 7:17-23*

Jesus Speaks to the Disciples About Defilement (Part 2)

It wasn't the first time that a crowd of people had argued over what He had said, but what concerned me was the angry gestures and loud voices of the Pharisees who had posed the question about ceremonial defilement. They were furious! They didn't like being exposed in front of the people as hypocrites. I looked at Jesus. He was looking in the direction of the Pharisees. "I think You really offended them by what You said," I commented.

He looked at me and nodded. There must have been a bit of frustration in my voice, so He said, "Every plant not planted by My heavenly Father will be uprooted, so ignore them. They are blind guides leading the blind. If one blind person leads another, both will fall into the ditch."

"Explain to us the parable that says people are not defiled by what they eat," I asked.

Jesus looked at the Pharisees who were pointing at us and trying to stir up the crowd against us, and then said to me, "Peter, I think we should go to your house." We called the others and left.

After settling in at my place, Jesus asked, "Don't you understand yet? Whatever food you eat passes through the body and out into the sewer. What you say comes from the heart—that is what defiles you. Out of the heart come evil thoughts, murder, adultery, immorality, lying, slander, theft. This is what defiles a person. Eating with unwashed hands will never defile a person."

What He said made a lot more sense than the traditions of the Jewish leaders. But breaking with tradition had its own consequences. The Pharisees were seeing to that. I agreed with His point of view, but I still wished He wouldn't alienate the religious leaders. We spent most of the day relaxing at my place. It was nice to get away from the crowd and the Pharisees.

May 31   *Matthew 15:21; Mark 7:24*

Ministry in Tyre and Sidon

Things were heating up in Galilee. The Pharisees Jesus had rebuked tried to inflame the people against Jesus every chance they got. They accused Him of disregarding the traditions of the Jewish people. Some of the strong supporters of tradition showed open hostility toward us, accusing us of corrupting the nation by not following tradition. When we attended the synagogue on Sabbath, there were people who called us names and would not come near us. Finally, the ruler of the synagogue, under pressure from the Pharisees, refused to allow us entrance. Capernaum was turning its back on the very source of life.

The rejection spread to other areas of our lives. When my wife and her mother started finding it difficult to locate vendors willing to serve them in the marketplace, we knew it was time to go elsewhere. We had been kicked out of Judea, and now Galilee. Instead of building support, we were fast losing it. One day Jesus announced we were going to leave Galilee. "Where will we go?" I asked.

"Tyre and Sidon," He replied.

"To the Gentiles?" Matthew questioned.

"Yes," Jesus answered. "We are going to the Gentiles. Our people have rejected us."

"What hope is there for the Gentiles?" I asked my brother Andrew.

He shrugged, "I don't know."

The following morning we headed out, south to Tiberius, following the road west across Samaria, then north to Ptolmais and Tyre. At twenty miles a day, it took us three days to get there. Jesus knew some people in Tyre, so upon arriving in town, we went directly to their place. What a relief to be somewhere besides Galilee, at least until things calmed down.

June 1   *Matthew 15:22-28; Mark 7:25-30*

Phoenician Woman's Daughter Healed

When my daughter was a baby, family members told me to dedicate her to the gods of Tyre and Phonecia for her own protection and safety. Wanting the best for my little girl, I took her to the temple where the spirits were invoked in a special dedication ceremony.

During the early years of her life, she was a normal, happy child, but when she turned eight, I noticed a big change in her personality. Then, by the time of her ninth birthday, I knew that the spirit which had been invoked was evil. She and I suffered a great deal. I consulted doctors and tried to get the priests to exorcise her, but to no avail. Then someone told me about a teacher in Galilee who could cast out demons. Dissatisfied with my own religion, I began to talk to my Jewish neighbors about theirs. They talked about the Messiah, the Son of David, who would come and restore Israel. They told me the Messiah would heal the sick and help people. I decided I had to go find this man they called Jesus.

Imagine my surprise when one afternoon a friend who knew what I was planning rushed in and excitedly told me that He had come to our town. My daughter was being tormented by the demon, so I asked my neighbor to stay with her while I went to find Him. When I saw Him, I burst into tears and fell at His feet. "Have mercy on me, Lord, Son of David. My daughter is severely possessed of a demon."

He looked at me with such compassion, but He did not speak. I was born in Phonecia and was, therefore, a Gentile; most Jews wanted nothing to do with me. I pleaded again. Still no word. His disciples told Him to send me away. They were bothered by my begging. I ignored them.

"I was sent only to Israel," He replied.

"Lord, help me!" I pleaded, not willing to give up. "It isn't right to take the children's food and throw it to the dogs." The love in His eyes spoke louder than His words. "Even the little dogs eat scraps under the table," I responded. "Give this little dog a morsel."

He put His hand on my shoulder. "Woman, your faith is great, and your request is granted. Your daughter is healed." I thanked Him profusely and hurried home to find my daughter free of the demon. We are now followers of Jesus.

June 2 *Mark 7:31a*

Ministry in Sidon

The woman had just left the house when others started coming. Jesus spent the rest of the day and half the night healing people and listening to their troubles. We tried to help by organizing the people into a waiting area so He wasn't overwhelmed with everyone at once. We stayed in a large room on the flat roof. The hosts put down mats for us so it was very comfortable. In the predawn light, I awoke to see Jesus in a corner of the roof looking heavenward, talking with His Father.

Once everyone was awake, our friends fed us a wonderful breakfast of fruit, bread, dried figs, goat's milk, and cheese. We thanked them and headed for the great market square. It didn't take long for the people to find Jesus. We spent the rest of the day there while Jesus spoke and healed people. Everyone believed He had been given the power of the gods.

That night we stayed at the same house. The man of the house was a fisherman, and he showed James, John, Andrew, and me his boat and nets, which were much bigger than our small craft.

Early the next morning, before the city was awake, we left Tyre and walked thirty miles to Sidon, a large Phoenician city. Most of us had never traveled far from Galilee. Everywhere we looked we saw strange temples and statues to the pantheon of Phoenician gods. By the time we reached the city, my feet hurt. We were all very tired after walking all day, so we found an inn where Judas paid for us to stay the night. Thaddeus found a street vendor and bought some bread and fish. We ate and went to sleep. In the morning we made our way to the market square. The place was so noisy and busy it was hard to do very much.

On Sabbath we went to the synagogue. Jesus accepted the invitation of the ruler to speak. However, there were a few Jews who had been in Capernaum when Jesus spoke about eating His flesh and blood who made a lot of trouble for us. So we spent only one more day in Sidon before heading out to Caesarea Philippi. Here Jesus was so well accepted that we spent two weeks ministering to the people. The Holy Spirit touched the hearts of the people, and they begged us to stay. Jesus promised to return.

June 3   *Mark 7:31b*

To Decapolis

After leaving Caesarea we traveled south to Galilee where Jesus told us to take some time with our families. I told Him He should go see His mother and siblings. He smiled and nodded. I was glad to be home. James and I went to see how Dad was doing with the fishing business. Almost immediately he told us to come back and work as fishermen. I told him that we were fishing.

"Who are you working for?" he demanded.

I looked at James and we started to laugh. "Jesus," I replied. "We are fishers of men now, Dad, getting people ready for the kingdom." We told him about all the people we had helped in Tyre and Sidon.

For the rest of the week, we fished with him, which made him happy. He could never accept that we had left a good business to wander about with an itinerant preacher. When we originally told him we were going with Jesus to become disciples because we believed He was sent from God, he responded, "What about the commandment to honor your parents?"

As usual, the time off went quickly. When Jesus arrived back in town, we all met at Simon's house for a meal and fellowship with our families and Jesus. Matthew brought his wife and kids, so did Thaddeus and Simon the Zealot. Our parents came, as well as my sister and her husband with their new baby. It was a wonderful day! Jesus spent time with our spouses and parents and played with the children. For over an hour, He talked with Dad.

In the evening when family members were leaving for their homes, my dad came to me and said, "I had no idea He knew so much about fishing." I smiled and nodded. "He is a good man, John," Dad said. Then he turned and left with my mom. We spent the night at Peter's place. Early the next morning we were on our way to Decapolis.

"Why are we going there?" Peter asked.

"I want to see how our missionaries have done," Jesus answered.

"Missionaries? What missionaries?" we asked.

"The two healed demon possessed men," He answered with a wink.

June 4   Mark 7:31c

Decapolis

We traveled from Capernaum to Bethsaida that morning. The going was slow because people along the way wanted to see Jesus, and He never passed by anyone in need. By noon we reached Gergessa and the caves where the demoniacs had lived. The people welcomed Jesus now. We were invited to stay with some prominent residents and apologies were made regarding our being asked to depart their shores. After being healed, the demon possessed men had visited Gergessa first. Seeing how completely changed these men were, they wanted to know more about the Miracle Worker who had healed them. And here He was now in the flesh! There was a rush to bring sick loved ones to Jesus. We spent two days there while Jesus taught and healed everyone in town.

Traveling on to Hippus, then Abila and Gadera, the people welcomed us warmly. Everywhere we went people had heard about the healing of the demoniacs. We spent a few days in each town before traveling on to Pella, Dion, and then Geresa. This last city was on the King's Highway and the home of the demoniacs. When they learned Jesus was in town, they quickly found us and insisted we stay with them. Again and again they expressed their love and appreciation for what Jesus had done for them. Since their healing, they had spent all their time traveling around the area sharing their testimony until most everyone east of Jordan knew about them. Many had witnessed what they were like while demon possessed and to see them healed made a strong impression.

We spent a week in Geresa. Jesus spoke in synagogues and marketplaces and healed everyone who came to Him. The people urged us to stay longer, but He wanted to go on to Philadelphia, Eobns, and Madeba. Each of these towns welcomed us, too.

"Why aren't the Jews as accepting of us?" I commented.

"Remember what I told you, Matthew," Jesus said. "A prophet is not accepted in His own country."

June 5   Mark 7:32-37

Deaf Man With Speech Impediment Healed

On our last day in Madeba, the people brought a deaf man with a speech impediment to Jesus. It was impossible to understand what he was trying to say. All he could do was point to his mouth and ears. He must have been an important person in town because many people came with him. They knelt down along with the deaf man and begged Jesus to heal him. All their pleading and crying out for help made it nearly impossible to hear anything. Jesus tried to silence them but to no avail.

Finally Jesus bent down, took the man by the hand, and led him away from the noisy crowd. Peter, James, and I followed Him while the other disciples stayed with the group. Jesus healed the man in a totally different way than I had seen Him heal anyone before. He put His fingers into the man's ears. Then He removed His fingers, spit on them, and touched the man's tongue with them. He looked up to heaven, sighed deeply, and said, "*Ephphatha*," which means, "Be opened."

I will never forget the look on that man's face as suddenly he could hear! When he tried to speak, intelligible words came out. As Jesus led him back to the group, he shouted praises to God. He was so happy. He kept taking Jesus' hand and thanking Him. When the people realized the man had been healed, their rejoicing was as noisy as their pleading had been. Overwhelmed, they kept saying to each other, "Everything this man does is wonderful. He makes the deaf hear and gives speech to the speechless."

Jesus directed them not to spread the news of this man's healing, but they praised God all the more and told everyone who passed by about the miraculous healing, completely disregarding Jesus' instructions. I assumed the reason Jesus requested this was because we were so near Judea and Jesus did not want to stir up more trouble. We later learned the man was father to the governor of Decapolis. Early that afternoon we headed north to Hippus on the main highway.

June 6 *Matthew 15:29–31*

Ministry by the Sea

The journey back to Hippus was hot and tiring. It took us three days from Madaba, but for the most part the trip was uneventful. We passed through the same towns going north as we had traversed going south. The people shouted their welcomes. In Geresa the missionary demoniacs asked Jesus if they could travel with Him. They expressed their desire to become full-time disciples along with us and never be separated from Him. Jesus told them there was still a very important work for them to do in this area. Reluctantly they agreed to stay.

It was early afternoon when we reached Hippus. We bought some food in the marketplace and headed west out of town toward the Sea of Galilee. Many people in town recognized us and followed us. We climbed a grassy slope near the sea to eat our lunch. The crowd grew larger and larger. I recognized people from Pella and Dion and even Geresa. Many from neighboring provinces we had not visited brought their loved ones for Jesus to heal. People from Batania, Tracconitus, and Aranitis came. There were cripples, blind people, demon possessed individuals, and disfigured souls. Those who couldn't come on their own were brought by family and friends. What a sight! Sick people with family or friends sitting, kneeling, stretching toward Jesus—hundreds of them begging for healing.

All the rest of the day Jesus healed those in need. It was something to see. Where sickness and death had once reigned, now joy and praises rang out. The lame ran and jumped. The blind looked at everything and described what they saw. The dumb shouted praises to God. Everyone was amazed at all the miracles Jesus performed. Well into the night, Jesus healed until there was not another sick person in the crowd. About 11:00 p.m. Jesus and the other disciples fell asleep. My brother Peter and I talked about what an amazing day it had been until finally we nodded off too.

June 7   *Matthew 15:32–39a; Mark 8:1–10*

Jesus Feeds Four Thousand

The following day more people joined the crowd. Those who had been healed wanted to stay and listen to what Jesus had to say about the kingdom. Somehow word had spread, and people came from Iturea and other towns in the east. Jesus taught and healed all that day and the next. Some people left, but it seemed they were quickly replaced by newcomers.

Toward afternoon of the third day Jesus called us together and said, "I feel sorry for all these people. Many of them have been here for three days, and they have nothing left to eat. What are we going to do? Thaddeus, what do you recommend?"

I didn't know what to say. I remembered when He had fed the 5,000 men and their families in Galilee with just a few loaves and fish, but that miracle had been for Jews. This was a mixed crowd of mostly non-Jews. I didn't think He would waste a big miracle on Gentiles.

"I don't want to send them away hungry, or they may faint on the way home," Jesus said compassionately.

"I don't know," I replied. "Where would we find enough food for this big crowd?"

Jesus seemed disappointed with my answer. Actually, He looked sad. "How much food do you have?" He asked Peter.

"A few loaves and fish," Peter answered as he pulled them out of our food basket.

Jesus told the people to sit on the grass. He took the seven loaves and fish, thanked God for them, and broke them into pieces. We remembered the miracle in Galilee, so we borrowed baskets from people nearby. He gave us the full baskets, and we took them around to the people. Nearly 12,000 men, women, and children were fed that day. Everyone ate their fill and still there were seven baskets filled with bread and fish. Jesus asked us to give the leftovers to the poorest families. He dismissed the people and sent them to their homes. While we were gathering up our things and getting ready to cross the lake, Jesus came near to me and said quietly, in almost a whisper so that just He and I knew, "Every single person matters to God, Thaddeus." I understood.

June 8 *Matthew 16:1-4; Mark 8:11-13*

In Dalmanutha and Magadan

As soon as the leftover food had been distributed to the poor families, we followed Jesus to the lake shore where a boat waited to take us to Magdala and Dalmanutha on the southwestern shore of the lake. Apparently Jesus had made arrangements earlier with the man who owned the boat. Many of the people followed us to the shore, asking us to come back as soon as possible.

It was good to be back on the sea again and away from the crowds. By the time we landed at Dalmanutha, it was dark. There hadn't been much wind, so we had all helped with rowing and were quite tired. The boat owner invited us to his home, telling us we were welcome to stay as long as we wanted. As it turned out, his boat was one of those that came from Tiberius when Jesus preached on the mount and fed 5,000 men and their families. Having heard Jesus was in Decapolis, he had made his way to Hippus to find us. Also a fisherman, we had lots to talk about. He was convinced Jesus was the Messiah.

For three days Jesus taught and healed people in Dalmanutha. As usual, as soon as the word spread that Jesus was in town, the crowds arrived. Along with the common people came the Pharisees and Sadducees. On the third day, Jesus was teaching in the synagogue when the delegation of Pharisees and Sadducees stood up in the middle of the service and demanded that Jesus show them a sign from heaven to prove His authority. He sighed deeply and replied, "You know how to read the weather; a red sky at night will bring fair weather tomorrow and a red sky in the morning means watch for stormy weather, but you can't read the signs of the times." Looking steadily at them He continued, "Only an evil and adulterous generation would demand a miraculous sign. But the only sign I will give them is that of Jonah the prophet."

He stepped down from the platform, spoke to our friend with the boat, and motioned for us to follow them to the dock. The crowd followed us. We stepped into the boat, and without another word we began to cross the lake.

June 9 *Matthew 16:5-11; Mark 8:14-21*

Boat Ride to Bethsaida and Leaven of the Pharisees

The weather was pleasant with a slight breeze as we made our way across the Sea of Galilee. It was about noon when I started feeling hungry. "Anyone have something to eat?" I asked.

Peter responded, "Judas, tell me, how were we supposed to buy food when we left in such a hurry? Besides, you have the money bag. Why didn't you get something on the way to the dock?"

I didn't like the way Peter always seemed to make me look stupid in front of the others. Who did he think he was anyway? I had been a business man and a financier and what was he? A fisherman! Furthermore, I didn't like the way Jesus played favorites with him, James, and John. Jesus looked at me as though He was reading my thoughts, then He simply said, "Beware of the yeast of the Pharisees and Sadducees." Accusations flew from one to another for forgetting to get food for the trip. Although we all tried to keep Jesus from hearing our arguing, He knew. Finally Thomas reached into his bag and pulled out a loaf he had been saving for later. "Here," he shouted, "eat this and quit arguing." He threw it to Peter.

Peter began to divide it up and hand it out. Jesus shook His head sadly and said, "You have such little faith. Why are you arguing with each other about having no bread? You have eyes and ears—you saw Me distribute bread to 5,000 men and their families from five loaves and 4,000 men and their families from seven loaves. Don't you remember all the leftovers? When are you going to learn there are much larger issues at stake here than a loaf of bread? I am talking about the deceptive teachings of the religious leaders."

Everyone became quiet and ate their piece of bread in silence. *Why is He always putting down the Pharisees?* I wondered. *How does He ever plan to establish a kingdom? He needs to win these people over and not distance them.* It was late afternoon when we arrived in Bethsaida.

June 10   Mark 8:22–26

Healing of a Blind Man in Bethsaida

I've always been a skeptic. I never believed in much of anything except myself and God, and now I wasn't sure about Him. I have always been a good person, but here I am, blind. I faithfully attended synagogue services, prayed daily, attended the annual feasts, paid a faithful tithe, but misfortune has befallen me. It just isn't fair. I used to keep financial records for a business man, but now I've been reduced to begging because I cannot see to work. I figure I have no one to blame but God! The Pharisees told me that either I had done something wrong or my parents had offended God. I couldn't think of any law I had disobeyed. And to be cursed because of something my parents did? Where is the justice in that?

I was in my usual begging spot when the few friends I had left told me the Nazarene healer was in town. "If God won't help me, why should He?" I told them cynically. I'd heard of Jesus. He'd been in Bethsaida before, but I had never bothered going to see Him.

"Please," my friends begged, "we believe He can help you."

I finally agreed. "Alright," I said, "I'll go."

My friends led me to Him. "Please heal this man," I heard them plead. There was a pause. Then I felt a strong hand take my right arm and lead me away.

"Where are we going?" I asked.

"To a quiet place," was all He said. The noise of the crowd faded, and I could sense it was just the two of us somewhere outside the town. He put His arm around my shoulder and said gently, "God is not angry with you, and neither am I, but Satan is." I had never considered my situation in those terms. Then He gently spit on each eye and touched the lids. "Can you see now?" He asked.

"Yes, I think I see people over there, but they look like trees walking around." He placed His fingers on my eyes again and suddenly I could see clearly. I fell on my knees before Him and thanked and worshiped Him. My sight had been restored, but even more important, my faith in God had been made whole.

Then He said something I did not understand. "Don't go back into town. Go home another way." Although it didn't make sense, I was glad to do anything my Healer asked.

June 11 *Matthew 16:13–17; Mark 8:27–30; Luke 9:18–20*

Journey to Caesarea Philippi and Peter's Confession

We spent the night in Bethsaida. The friends who had brought the blind man to Jesus had been searching for us, anxious to know what had happened to their friend since they hadn't seen him since Jesus led him out of town. Jesus simply told them He had sent him home a different way. They seemed relieved, thanked Him, and left.

Early the next morning, Jesus awakened us long before anyone was up. Philip's parents owned a large home and had graciously invited us to stay there. Andrew and I had offered our parent's place, but Philip insisted we stay with his family. Jesus wrote thank you on a small slate used for leaving messages, and then we left.

It was a beautiful morning. The sun cast a red glow on the clouds in the eastern sky. Merchants were setting up their shops and kiosks for the day. We headed north on the highway to Caesarea Philippi. Jesus had told us the night before that He wanted to spend some time alone in prayer as well as visit some of the small villages along the thirty mile route to Caesarea from Bethsaida.

It was the middle of the afternoon, and we were five miles from town when Jesus stopped alongside the road near an ancient well believed to have been dug by Abraham. Whether the story was true or not, the water was very refreshing. After everyone had finished drinking, Jesus turned to us and asked, "Who do people say I am?"

Philip replied, "Some people say You are John the Baptist resurrected." Matthew said he'd overheard someone say Jesus was Elijah. James had heard Him called other Old Testament prophets, like Jeremiah and Isaiah.

Then Jesus gazed earnestly at each of us and asked, "But who do *you* say I am?"

Without hesitation I said, "You are the Messiah, the Son of God, sent from the Father." I really believed that to be true.

He smiled at me as He said, "You are blessed, Simon, son of John, because My Father in heaven has revealed this to you. You did not learn this from a human being." Then He looked at all of us and said, "Please do not tell this to anyone else."

Why not? I wondered, confused. *Shouldn't people know that Jesus is the Messiah?*

June 12   *Matthew 16:18-20*

The Rock on Which the Church Is Built

I really could not understand why Jesus wanted to keep the fact that He was the Messiah to Himself. Many people already believed Him to be the Messiah. It wouldn't take much to start a revolution and get Israel on track if everyone *knew* He was the Messiah. I was sure that even the religious leaders could be brought into line. I saw Jesus watching me out of the corner of my eye. I was standing on the opposite side of the well.

Suddenly He called out loudly so everyone could hear. "Now, I say to you," pointing at me, "you are Peter, which means 'rock.'" Everyone stopped what they were doing and looked at Jesus. He paused and looked at each one.

I nodded; it was true that my name meant stone or pebble. When I was young, my friends teased me. "Let's pick up this pebble and see how far we can throw him." Inwardly, I felt glad when Jesus changed my name to Simon.

Jesus then pointed to Himself. "But on this Rock I will build My church." The word He used to describe Himself portrayed a giant fortress-like rock, one that is impossible to overcome. He walked over to me as He continued speaking, "All the power of hell shall not prevail against it."

It was then I began to realize that His idea of a kingdom was not the same as mine or any of the other disciples. His vision was far greater than Roman conquest; He was out to conquer Satan. Looking at me and then around at the group, He said, "I will give you the keys to the kingdom, though. Whatever you forbid on earth will be forbidden in heaven. Whatever you permit on earth will be permitted in heaven."

It wasn't until a later time that I understood He was speaking of the church. Once again He warned us not to share this with anyone. Reflecting back, I can say that Jesus is not only the rock on which the church was built, but He is also the rock of my life, the rock upon which I stand.

June 13 *Matthew 16:21–23; Mark 8:31–33; Luke 9:21, 22*

Jesus Predicts His Death for the First Time and Rebukes Peter

---

Leaving the well, we traveled the rest of the way to Caesarea. After ministering a few days in the city, Jesus headed to the villages outside of town. Quite a number of people from Caesarea followed along as we traveled. Jesus wasn't the same. Something had changed Him. I mentioned Jesus' different demeanor to my brother Andrew. He agreed that he had noticed it too. He seemed different, very different. It was as though He had something on His mind that was causing great distress.

"Are You okay?" I finally asked Him when we paused for a rest. It was then He opened up and began to talk about what was going to happen to Him. He said He must go to Jerusalem and suffer many terrible things at the hands of the religious leaders, the priests, and teachers of the law. He continued by saying that He would be killed but would rise again on the third day. We stood there in stunned silence. The crowd was shocked too.

"It is impossible for the priests to kill the Messiah. The people will never allow it," I said. I couldn't believe He was saying these things. Afraid of what the people might think, I took Him by the arm and led Him away from the people. "The people will lose confidence in You if You talk like this. Heaven forbid, this can never happen to You!" I reprimanded Him for speaking so disparagingly.

He shook His arm free of my grasp. Then He looked at me with a look I will never forget, like I was the epitome of evil. "Get away from Me, Satan," He shouted. "You are a dangerous trap to Me. You are seeing things merely from a human viewpoint, not from God's viewpoint."

Shock upon shock! I stood in disbelief. For a few minutes Jesus kept staring at me as though looking through me at something I could not see. Then He turned and walked back to the other disciples and the crowd. *This is not the way the script reads. The Messiah is not supposed to die by the hands of His own people,* I thought. *He is to lead them to victory.*

June 14 *Matthew 16:24–28; Mark 8:34–38; Luke 9:23–27*

Jesus Speaks Encouragement to the Crowd and Disciples

Jesus called us to Him and then asked the people to come close. Everyone crowded near Him, anticipating what He had to say. "This is very important," He said. "If any of you want to become My disciple, you must turn from your selfish ways, take up your cross daily, and follow Me." As a zealot for the Jewish cause, I was familiar with the cross. Many of my friends had died hanging on one of those Roman death machines.

Jesus continued, "If you try to hang unto your life, you will lose it. If you give up your life for My sake, you will save it." Jesus paused, looked at each of us, and then spoke again. "What benefit is there if you gain the whole world but lose your own soul and are lost and destroyed in the end? Is anything worth more than your own soul?"

I knew we were all guilty. Believing He was about to establish His kingdom and reign as the Messiah, we often argued about the pecking order. Who would occupy the top spot next to Jesus? I had my own selfish ideas about the new kingdom. Because I was so zealous about restoring our Jewish independence, I was sure I would occupy a top position.

Jesus was speaking again, so I snapped back to attention. I felt as if He was talking directly to me, but I didn't like the message about loving one's enemies and turning the other cheek. Why should we bow to Roman authority? "If anyone is ashamed of Me and My message, the Son of man will be ashamed of that person when He returns in the glory of the Father and holy angels," He continued. "Each individual will be judged and rewarded according to their deeds."

I felt convicted I needed an attitude change. I prayed that God would help me to see things as Jesus did. His next statement really surprised me. "Some who are standing right now will not die before they see the kingdom of God."

Is He talking about a kingdom with all heaven included? I wondered. No earthly kingdom could ever compare with that.

June 15 *Matthew 17:22, 23; Mark 9:30–32; Luke 9:44, 45*

Journey Back to Galilee and Jesus Predicts His Death a Second Time

For a few more days we traveled to the villages of Caesarea. Jesus was as gracious to the people as ever, healing the sick and comforting the sorrowful. But there was something different about Him; He seemed preoccupied in private thoughts. Although we all noticed the change and discussed it amongst ourselves, none of us could put our finger on just what it was.

One morning Jesus announced it was time to go back to Galilee. Our previous trips had been full of conversation, but this journey was marked by silence. Jesus walked ahead by Himself, and we followed behind, not sure what to say to Him. We stopped for the night at Peter's house in Capernaum. In the morning his mother-in-law, whom we all called Mother, made us a wonderful meal. When breakfast was finished and we'd helped clean-up, Jesus called us into the courtyard.

"The Son of man is going to be betrayed into the hands of His enemies. He will be killed, but on the third day He will rise again."

I had heard Him say the same words just days before, but I had dismissed them because I just couldn't wrap my mind around the thought of Jesus being killed. This time the words seemed to strike home. "How can this be?" I asked Thaddeus who was seated next to me. "I have no idea, Thomas," he responded, shaking his head. Questions whirled through my head. *Why would anyone want to kill Him? He never hurt anyone. Perhaps His remarks have a symbolic meaning. What will we do without Him if He is killed? What will happen to all the work we have accomplished over the past three years?*

I looked around at the others. Shock and grief marked each face. Peter held his peace and did not try to reprimand the Lord as he had done previously. I just couldn't believe it. It was not logical. It just could not be true. I didn't want to think about it. What was to become of the kingdom Jesus had been telling us about? What was to become of our beloved nation? All our hopes were fixed on Him. I refused to believe what I was hearing.

June 16   *Matthew 17:24–27*

The Temple Half Shekel and Peter and the Fish

I was totally overwhelmed by Jesus' apparent obsession with His impending death. I did not want to hear about it. It scared me and depressed me at the same time. *Why is He telling us He is going to die?* Not once, but twice now He had indicated that He was to be killed in Jerusalem. I had to get out of the house. I didn't tell anyone where I was going—I just left. When stressed, I liked to walk the beach or go to the dock and sit in my fishing boat and listen to the waves.

After a couple of hours of quiet, I headed back to Capernaum. On the way home, the temple tax collectors stopped me and asked if Jesus paid the required annual temple tax. According to the law of Moses, every male twenty years old and above had to pay this tax. Only the king and his sons were exempt. "Yes, of course, He does," I declared in Jesus' defense. They followed me to the house.

The moment I walked through the door, before I had a chance to say a word, Jesus said, "What do you think, Peter? Do kings tax their own people or the people they have conquered?"

How did He know about the tax people? I wondered. "The people they have conquered," I replied.

"Well, then," Jesus said, "the people are free." I couldn't miss the smile that played around His mouth. The tax collectors stood behind me. Jesus continued, "We do not want to offend these men so go to the lake and throw in a line. Open the mouth of the first fish you catch. In it you will find a large silver coin. Use it to pay the tax for both you and me."

"Yes, Lord," I said quietly as I turned and headed toward the lake with the tax collectors in tow. I rigged a line and threw it in the water. In no time at all, I had caught a large trout. I opened its mouth, and sure enough, there was the coin. I handed it to the collectors. They stood there with their mouths open.

"Who is this man?" they asked in amazement.

"Jesus, the Son of God," I responded. As they turned and walked away, I saw them shaking their heads. I sat on the shore a long time, thinking about what had just happened and what Jesus had said. I was more convinced than ever He was all He claimed to be.

June 17   *Matthew 17:1-8; Mark 9:1-8; Luke 9:28-36*

The Transfiguration

It had been six days since Jesus first told us about His impending death. Since then a gloom had permeated our company. No one wanted to think about it or talk about it. It made me angry to think anyone would conspire to murder someone who only loved and helped people. Jesus invited us all to ascend a mountain near Capernaum and pray with Him. Upon reaching the base, Jesus invited me, my brother John, and Peter to accompany Him to the summit. He told the others to remain at the base and pray until we returned. I saw the look on Judas' face as we headed out—he was not happy.

Within a few hours, we reached the top. We knelt to pray while Jesus moved about sixty feet from us. We heard Him, with loud cries, pouring out His heart to God. Soon the three of us were fast asleep. Suddenly we awakened to a bright light and voices. Jesus' face was transformed and shining as the sun. His clothes were dazzling white, brighter than anything we had ever seen. Two men, we assumed to be Moses and Elijah, were speaking to Him.

Peter, clearly overwhelmed by the sight before us and not thinking before he spoke, cried out, "Lord, it is wonderful to be here. Let's make three shelters or memorials, one for You, one for Moses, and one for Elijah." Moses and Elijah looked at us as they turned to leave. Then suddenly a bright cloud enveloped us. We were terror stricken, and fell on our faces.

A voice from the cloud resounded loud and clear. "This is my Beloved Son, my Chosen One, listen to Him." When the cloud lifted and disappeared, Jesus was standing there alone, looking very normal. Had we seen a vision, or were we dreaming? No, we had experienced something very wonderful. We had seen Jesus glorified! We were the ones He had spoken about just days before who would witness His coming in miniature. Moses represented the dead resurrected and Elijah the translated. We didn't share this with anyone else.

June 18   *Matthew 17:9-13; Mark 9:9-13*

Descent and Elijah

We remained on the mountain overnight. Jesus told us what Moses and Elijah had spoken to Him about. He wanted us to know what was coming. We asked a lot of questions, but we did not fully understand His answers. Early in the morning we made our way down the mountain. Along the way, He stopped and made a request of us. "Please do not say anything to anyone about what you saw on the mountain until the Son of man has risen from the dead." We promised.

Continuing down the trail, I whispered to my brother James, "What does He mean, 'risen from the dead'?"

"I guess it must have something to do with what He told us about dying at the hands of wicked men and then rising again," James replied.

I held up my hand. "I don't want to think about anyone dying," I said, "especially Him," nodding toward Jesus.

James changed the subject. "Do you remember what the teachers of the law taught us about Elijah coming before the Messiah." I nodded. "Well, we just saw Elijah, but we believe Jesus is the Messiah, and He has already come."

"That is an interesting thought, James," I said. "Let's ask Jesus." I called out to Him, "Rabbi, why do the teachers of the law insist Elijah must return before the Messiah comes?"

He stopped and turned toward us. "Elijah is indeed coming first to get everything ready for the Messiah," He replied. "Yet why do the Scriptures say the Son of man must suffer greatly and be treated with utter contempt?" He paused. None of us responded, so He continued, "I tell you the truth, Elijah has already come, but they did not recognize him. They chose to abuse him, and in the same way they will also make the Son of man suffer."

It dawned on us that He was speaking about John the Baptist. So it was John who paved the way for Jesus in the spirit and power of Elijah. He is most certainly the Messiah, but was He telling us He would suffer the same fate as John?

June 19 *Matthew 17:14–17; Mark 9:14–19; Luke 9:37–41*

The Demon Possessed Boy (Part 1)

My son, my only son, Misha, was demon possessed. Every day was a trial. He suffered from convulsions, spasms, and self-mutilation. The demon would choke him and throw him against walls, knocking him unconscious. We consulted doctors and tried exorcism. Nothing worked.

I know exactly how it happened. My son and his friends played a game that invoked spirits of dead conquerors and wizards. When I learned of it, I strictly forbade him from associating with those boys, but he disobeyed and kept playing. During the course of one of the games, a demon entered him, and now the spirit tortured him.

I had heard there was a man named Jesus who healed the demon possessed, but the priest at my synagogue forbade me to go to Him. "He casts out demons by the power of the devil," he had said. However, three days ago a rabbi leader in Jerusalem told me to find Jesus because He was sure He could help Misha. When we arrived in Capernaum, we followed the crowds, for everyone was in search of Jesus. We finally reached the base of the mountain, where we found His disciples. They stated that Jesus had gone up the mountain to pray, and they were waiting for Him to return. I asked them if Jesus could heal my boy. One of the disciples assured me He could.

A group of Pharisees standing nearby shouted, "You are His disciples, why don't you heal the boy?"

"We have healed the demon possessed before," retorted the disciple.

"Well, prove it," taunted the Pharisee.

The disciple placed his hand on Misha's head and cried, "Come out of him in the name of Jesus." The demon threw my son to the ground in a fit of rage and ridiculed the disciple. Another disciple tried, but to no avail. The Pharisees mocked the disciples, telling everyone that this proved Jesus was a fake. Just then Jesus appeared.

I ran to Him in tears, "Lord, my son is possessed with an evil spirit that makes him deaf and dumb. The demon throws him into the fire, makes him foam at the mouth, and throws him on the ground into a seizure. I asked your disciples to heal him, but they could not."

Sensing the conflict in the crowd, Jesus sorrowfully said, "You faithless people! How long must I be with you? How long must I put up with you? Bring the boy to me." I ran to bring my son to Jesus.

June 20 *Matthew 17:18; Mark 9:20–27; Luke 9:42, 43*

The Demon Possessed Boy (Part 2)

I brought my son to Jesus. It was like the demon recognized Jesus and went into a horrible rage. Helplessly I watched as the demon threw Misha to the ground in violent convulsions. He writhed uncontrollably, limbs bent in all sorts of contortions. Foam covered most of his face. The crowd moved back in a mix of fear and disgust. Jesus looked at me. "How long has he been like this?" He asked.

In anguish, I replied, "This has been going on for more than two years. At home the spirit will throw him into water to drown him or fire to kill him." As I looked at my tormented son and realized the power of this spirit, I began to feel hopeless. I blurted out, "Have mercy on us and help us if You can!"

The look Jesus gave me seemed to lay bare my very soul. "What do you mean, 'if I can'?" He asked. "Anything is possible if a person believes."

A conviction welled up in me that in Jesus there was hope. "I do believe, but please help me overcome my unbelief," I cried out, falling to my knees in tears. The crowd had grown silent, anticipating what would happen next.

With an authority I had never heard in any other human voice, Jesus ordered the demon to leave. "Listen, you spirit that makes this boy unable to hear or speak, I command you to come out of this child and never enter him again." Using my son's voice, the demon screamed as though in agony and gripped Misha in another horrible convulsion. Then all was still.

My son lay on the ground; to all appearances, he seemed dead. People gasped and say, "Look, the demon killed him!"

Jesus bent down, gently took Misha by his hand, and helped him to his feet. I saw and felt a peace about Misha. Jesus brought him to where I was kneeling, tears streaming down my face. My wife joined us, and we embraced and held each other for a long time. I couldn't stop thanking the Lord for bringing our son back from the death grip of the demon. He simply smiled. I am a doubter by nature, but one thing I am certain of, Jesus is the Son of God.

June 21   Matthew 17:19–21; Mark 9:28

The Disciples Question

The healing of the boy possessed with a demon made a huge impression on the people. Everyone present was in awe and talked about the event for days afterward. Jesus spent the rest of the day with the people at the base of the mount. He performed many more miracles of healing and shared kingdom truths with those gathered. Mothers brought their babies to Him to bless. About midday I watched as the boy and his parents left the crowd and headed toward Capernaum.

Why couldn't I cast the demon out of that kid? I wondered. *I cast out demons in the name of Jesus while traveling from village to village with Thomas on our missionary journey. Why not now?* I thought about this all day, but I just couldn't figure out what the difference was. As evening drew near, the crowd began to disperse, and we made our way back to Capernaum to Peter's house. Maybe it was the tax collector in me, needing to make sure things added up at the end of the day, but I had to find out why I couldn't cast out that demon. As soon as I could, I asked the question all of us wanted answered. "Lord, why couldn't we cast out the demon from that boy?"

"You don't have enough faith," He replied. "In fact, truthfully, if you had faith even as a grain of mustard seed, you could say to this mountain, 'move from here to there' and it would move. Nothing would be impossible." Then He said something that really caught my attention. "This kind of demon won't leave except by prayer and fasting."

I thought back on the time spent waiting at the foot of the mount for Jesus to return. The nine of us had passed most of the time away arguing about who was best qualified to be Jesus' second in command in the new kingdom. A few voiced their displeasure at being left behind and the favoritism Jesus was showing toward Peter, James, and John. I didn't remember spending any time in prayer or seeing any of the others praying. Now I understood.

June 22   Matthew 17:22, 23; Mark 9:30–32; Luke 9:44, 45

Jesus Again Predicts His Death

The excitement generated among the people about the healing of a demon possessed boy made it impossible for Jesus to have even a minute alone. As the word spread, the sick came from everywhere. I had no idea there were so many suffering from so many maladies, but I did know that Jesus was feeling the stress. About a week later, Jesus awakened us very early one morning and announced we were leaving. We quickly dressed while Peter, his wife, and her mother fixed us breakfast. It was still dark outside as we began our walk. Jesus explained that He needed to get away from the crowds and spend time with just us. He hoped we could find a retreat where we wouldn't be found.

This day we traveled south to Tiberius, then west toward Mount Tabor, finally stopping in a village near the mountain. Everyone was able to relax. Over the next few days, Jesus spent hours sharing truths with us from the Old Testament. He explained unfamiliar passages that we had seldom heard spoken about. He quoted from Isaiah about the suffering servant who was despised and rejected by men. He mentioned a passage from the psalms about hands and feet being pierced but bones not being broken. We tried to take everything in, but so much didn't make sense.

Then He said, "All these passages I have quoted to you are about Me. The Son of man is going to be betrayed into the hands of His enemies." He paused to let what He'd just said sink in. "I want you to listen to what I am telling you," He said with authority. "He will be killed, but three days later He will rise from the dead."

I shook my head! I did not want to hear about Him dying. James, the son of Alpheus, leaned over and asked, "Thaddeus, what is He talking about?"

"I don't know, James. I do not understand all this talk about death and suffering. Furthermore, I don't want to know," I retorted. I glanced up to find Jesus looking at me. All I could do was shake my head, no.

June 23   *Matthew 18:1-6; Mark 9:33-37; Luke 9:46-48*

Who Will be the Greatest?

Toward the end of a relaxing week in the country listening to Jesus, we headed back to Capernaum. Jesus had talked extensively about the kingdom of grace. He told parables to describe it, but I didn't completely understand the meaning of the stories. Judas and I had become good friends ever since Jesus had sent us out by twos. He called me "the Zealot" for short. I hated Rome and all it stood for. However, watching Jesus and how He treated even the Romans had made an impression on me. I'd come to realize that they were people whom God loved too.

This is where Judas and I began to disagree. I was slowly changing my thinking and becoming more like Jesus, but Judas just seemed stuck in his old ways and thoughts. Judas thought Jesus should compromise and make amends with the Pharisees so the kingdom could be established. I disagreed. This set us on edge toward one another.

I guess I started the argument, but Judas pushed it. The issue was who should be second in command in the kingdom Jesus was going to establish. Judas declared that not only was he the most educated and best qualified, he also knew many of the Pharisees and could broker a deal with them, bringing them on board to our cause. Before long, every one of us was arguing about who was the greatest.

After reaching Peter's house and sitting down for the evening meal, Jesus said, "What were you talking about on the road?" No one said a word. We were all too embarrassed. Jesus called one of the servant's little boy over to Him. Taking him in His arms, Jesus said, "Truthfully, unless you turn from sin and become as meek as a child, you will never enter the kingdom of heaven. Whoever becomes as humble as this little boy is greatest in the kingdom of heaven. He who is least among you will be great. And whoever welcomes a little one like this welcomes Me and Him who sent Me. But whoever causes an innocent little one like this to sin, it would be better to tie a millstone around his neck and be drowned in the sea."

Everyone got the message—heaven values humility, not greatness.

June 24 *Mark 9:38–41; Luke 9:49, 50*

The Disciples Forbid a Man to Use Jesus' Name

As Jesus spoke of being as humble and innocent as the little boy He was holding, I did a spiritual inventory. I was quiet, non-aggressive, and pretty unassuming, but underneath all of the calm spiritual exterior burned a desire to be first. I felt good knowing I was chosen as one of the inner circle of three—Peter, my brother James, and myself. I had always believed if there was to be a second in command, it would be one of us. Now Jesus was telling us if we wanted to be greatest in the kingdom, we must be willing to be servant of all. Well, servanthood did not appeal to me.

I reached up and touched my throat as I thought about having a millstone tied around my neck. Suddenly I recalled an encounter with a man whom we met on our mission tour who was casting out demons in Jesus' name. James and I told him to stop using Jesus' name. When he asked why, I told him it was because he was not part of our group. He replied, "But if God is working through me in Jesus' name, why must I stop?"

I told him he must speak with Jesus first, which he was agreeable to do. Now, I related the incident to Jesus. He said, "No, don't stop him. Anyone who performs a miracle in My name will not speak evil of Me. Anyone who is not against us is for us. In fact, if anyone gives you a cup of water because you belong to the Messiah, that person will most certainly be rewarded."

I honestly thought I had done the right thing by forbidding that man from using Jesus' name. I needed to ponder Jesus' teachings about humility and servanthood and examine my feelings about being first.

June 25   *Matthew 18:7–9; Mark 9:42–50*

Jesus Warns Against Temptation

As Jesus spoke, a sadness came over Him. He bowed His head and slowly shook it from side to side. "What sorrow awaits the world," He entoned, His voice heavy with grief. "Temptations are inevitable," He continued, "but what sorrow awaits the person who does the tempting." Suddenly, He looked at each of us with great seriousness. "If your hand causes you to sin, cut it off and throw it away. It is better to enter eternal life with one hand than to be thrown into the fires of hell with both hands. And if your foot causes you to sin, cut it off and throw it away. It is better to enter eternal life lame than be thrown into the fires of hell with both feet."

I looked at my brother John and whispered, "Is He encouraging self-mutilation?"

"No," John whispered back, "I think He is trying to impress us with the seriousness of temptation and sin."

Jesus continued, "And if your eye causes you to sin, gouge it out and throw it away. It is better to enter eternal life half-blind than to have two eyes and be thrown into the fires of hell." Jesus paused. We sat silently, deep in thought. He continued, "For in hell, destruction continues until there is nothing left to destroy." Jesus stood to His feet. "Everyone will be tested by fire." He walked over to the salt dish on the table. Pinching a few grains between His thumb and forefinger, He dropped them on His tongue. I could almost taste the salt as He licked His fingers. He looked at us, smiled and spoke, "Salt is good for seasoning, but if it loses its flavor, how does it get salty again? You must have the qualities of salt in and among yourselves and live in peace with each other." I hung my head, feeling very guilty. I think we all did, for just a few hours earlier we had all felt angry and resentful toward each other. I turned to Simon the Zealot and asked forgiveness for the angry words I had spoken.

June 26   *Matthew 18:10–14*

Jesus Warns Against Looking Down on Others

Jesus sat down again and drew little Tamar to Himself. She liked to be near Him. He played with her for a few minutes before continuing to speak to us. "Beware that you don't look down on any of these little ones. I tell you with assurance that their guardian angels are always in the presence of My heavenly Father."

It was time for Hannah, Peter's sister, to leave, but her little girl snuggled in closer to Jesus. Peter and his wife agreed to babysit for a few hours while Tamar's mother did her shopping. We waved goodbye to Hannah as she left.

Jesus continued, "The Son of man came to save those who are lost. If a man has a hundred sheep and one wanders away, what will he do?"

I looked at Thaddeus; his father was a shepherd. I remembered visiting his home on our mission tour. We arrived just as the shearing was being completed. Jesus' words brought back a lot of fond memories of that visit. I remember his father telling us how difficult it was to find lost sheep. More often than not, they were found dead or never seen again.

"Won't he leave the ninety and nine in the hills and go in search of that one lost sheep? And when he finds it, I assure you he will rejoice more for that one sheep than the others that did not wander away. In the same way, My heavenly Father does not want even one of these little ones to perish."

We nodded in agreement. As I watched Tamar, I was reminded of my own children, now grown up and gone from home. I thought of my father, Alpheus, who had raised my brothers and sisters well, making it possible for us to go to school and earn a living for ourselves. I thought of other children. What about those we saw begging on the street corners? Did I have a responsibility to help them? Jesus always made a point of giving a coin to each of the street kids. In fact, Judas often complained that Jesus gave to everyone who begged.

June 27   *Matthew 18:15–20*

Jesus Teaches on How to Treat a Believer Who Sins

All the while Jesus had been speaking, I was paying attention to what was being said. Just because I am only eight years old doesn't mean I don't know what is going on. My father had been a strict Jew all his life. He attended the festivals, sacrificed, and prayed often. He was beginning to show an interest in Jesus after having been at Uncle Peter's house when Jesus healed a paralyzed man. Then, everything fell apart when a man who professed to be a follower of Jesus cheated him out of a large sum of money. Dad not only lost interest in Jesus' teachings, but he stopped attending the synagogue. I turned to Jesus. "What can be done to help my father," I asked, tears forming in my eyes. Everyone knew about the situation.

Jesus pulled me close and gave me a hug. "If someone who is a believer sins against you, go to that person privately and point out the offense. If the person listens and confesses, you have won that person back. If you are unsuccessful, take one or two other people with you and go back to that person so that everything you say may be confirmed by witnesses. If the person still refuses to listen, take your case to the church."

I know my uncle and some of the others, I think Matthew and Nathanael, had gone to this person and confronted him, but it hadn't done any good. The ruler of the synagogue in Capernaum had spoken with him too. I even asked my dad if he would take me to the man so I could speak with him. Dad refused. I am worried about my dad—he just gets angrier and angrier every day.

All these thoughts were swirling around in my head as Jesus continued, "If he or she won't accept what the church says, treat that person like a pagan or a corrupt tax collector. Truthfully, what you forbid on earth will be forbidden in heaven. If a few of you agree on anything here on earth, my Father will do it. Where a few of my followers are gathered, I am there among them."

Then He whispered to me, "I'll speak with the man and your dad."

I looked up, and He smiled at me.

June 28   *Matthew 18:21–35*

Parable of the Unforgiving Debtor

Since we were all together and Jesus was teaching us, including my young niece, I decided to ask a question of my own. "Lord, how often should I forgive someone who sins against me? Seven times?" I knew that was the number prescribed by the religious establishment. James and John had borrowed my nets many times and brought them back tangled and torn. They apologized and helped mend them, but it was frustrating. I always forgave them, but I was feeling a bit resentful.

Jesus answered, "No, not seven times but seventy times seven."

I did a quick mental calculation. "Four hundred and ninety times!" I whispered out loud.

Then Jesus told a parable and compared it to His kingdom. "There was a king who decided to bring his accounts up to date. One man owed an enormous sum that he could not repay. The master ordered that he, along with his family and all his possessions, be sold to pay the debt. The man fell on his knees and wept, begging the king for mercy. The master, filled with pity, released him and forgave his debt.

"The man thanked the king but immediately went out, grabbed a fellow servant who owed him a small amount, and demanded repayment. The poor servant begged for mercy. 'A little more time. Be patient with me,' he cried. Refusing to wait, the creditor had the man arrested and thrown into prison until the debt should be paid.

"Other servants saw what happened and told the king. The king called in the man he had forgiven. 'I forgave your huge debt. Why couldn't you have done the same for your fellow servant?' Filled with anger, the king sent the unforgiving creditor to prison to be tortured until the debt was paid. This is what My heavenly Father will do to you unless you forgive others from the heart."

I got the point. Always, under every circumstance, be patient and forgiving of others. The last thing I wanted to do was jeopardize my place in God's kingdom. Since it was almost time for the Feast of Booths, Jesus sent us to be with our families. He was stopping at a few places before going on to His home in Nazareth. Would He go to Judea? Rumor had it that the Jews wanted to kill Him.

June 29   John 7:1–9

Jesus' Brothers Ridicule Him

Jesus came home late one afternoon when the rest of us were preparing for the Feast of Booths in Jerusalem. When Simon, Joseph, and Judas saw Him coming, they yelled at me, "James, your brother is home." They were still upset over the episode at the synagogue when Jesus claimed to be the fulfillment of Isaiah's Messianic prophecies. I was the youngest of Joseph's sons, and although a number of years older than Jesus, He and I spent a lot of time together. There was something very different about Him. He wasn't like anyone else I knew. He had experienced a lot of abuse from the neighborhood kids and His own stepbrothers while growing up, yet He had always treated them with kindness and love.

Regardless of what my other brothers thought of Him, I believed in Jesus. The miracles He performed had to be from God. Judas asked Jesus if He was planning to go to Jerusalem for the feast. Before He could answer, Joseph interjected, "You'd better go to Judea where Your followers can see Your miracles. How do You expect to become famous if You keep hiding like this?"

Simon had a smart comment to make, too. "If You can really do all these wonderful things, show Yourself to the world," he said.

I kept my mouth shut. I wished my brothers would quit mocking Him. Jesus simply replied, "Now is not the right time for Me to go, but you can go anytime. The world can't hate you, but it hates Me because I accuse it of doing evil. You go ahead and go," He said to them. "I'm not going to this festival yet because My time hasn't come."

What does He mean by that? I wondered

Joseph muttered under his breath, "Fine, stay home. We don't care what You do." They had finished their preparations and were ready to go early the following morning. Mary had been away visiting a friend. I was glad she didn't hear the exchange. When she saw Jesus, her face lit up. She was so happy to see Him. She fixed Him His favorite foods, and we talked late into the night.

June 30   John 7:10–15

Jesus Goes to the Festival of Shelters

Early the next morning my brothers and sisters and their families headed out for the Feast of Booths. Mary said, "James, aren't you going with the others?"

"No," I answered.

"When are you going, Mother?" I asked.

"Tomorrow with some friends," she replied.

I knew something had changed with Jesus, but I wasn't sure what it was. He seemed distant, as though He was deep in thought over some mystery. Later that morning He announced His plans to take a different route to the festival. I asked Him if I could go with Him. He hesitated briefly, then smiled, and agreed to have me as a traveling companion. We packed up a few things and headed out. On the way we talked about lots of things: family, Jesus' work, and the disciples. Suddenly He said to me, "James, please don't say anything about Me to anyone." I promised.

When we arrived in Jerusalem, a few friends met with Jesus. "The Jews are asking about You. They want to know if anyone has seen You."

We constructed a booth in the Garden of Gethsemane and stayed there. Jesus wore a hooded robe, which He kept close to His face to prevent being recognized. We overheard people talking about Him. Some believed He was a good man and miracle-worker, but others claimed He was a fraud who was out to deceive the people. A lot of people who believed in Him didn't have the courage to stand up and speak publicly in His favor because they didn't want to get in trouble with the Jewish leaders. It seemed that everyone was wondering if He was coming to the festival.

Jesus remained unnoticed until midway through the festival. On the third day of the feast, Jesus removed the hood, went up to the temple, and began teaching the people. Everyone was shocked, including me. He showed how the parts of the feast pointed to the Messiah and were partially fulfilled in Him. The ultimate fulfillment of the feast would be when God's people were permanently settled in the new earth. It made so much sense. The people kept asking each other, "How does this man know so much when He hasn't been trained in our schools?"

July 1 *John 7:16–24*

Jesus' Message Is From God

I hadn't seen Jesus for what seemed a very long time. Since He had moved to Galilee, no one in Jerusalem had seen Him, but it appeared that He hadn't changed. Watching Him now on the temple steps brought back a flood of good memories of my midnight visit with Him in the garden and the day He had chased away the money changers.

Jesus began to speak. "My message is not My own. It comes from God who sent Me. All who want to do the will of God will know if My teaching is from God or merely My own."

I was standing with some members of the Sanhedrin. "He has come back," they whispered.

Jesus continued, "Those who speak for themselves only want self glory, but One who seeks the glory of the One who sent Him speaks truth, not lies." He looked at a group of Pharisees standing near Him. "Moses gave you the law, but none of you obey it. In fact, you are trying to kill Me."

"You must be demon possessed! Who is trying to kill You?" one of them shouted angrily. What Jesus said was true. I knew how much they hated Him.

Jesus responded, "I did one miracle on the Sabbath, and you were amazed, but you were also angry. However, you work on the Sabbath, too, when you perform Moses' law of circumcision."

That's right, I thought to myself, *circumcision goes way back to Abraham.*

Jesus spoke again, "If the correct time for circumcision falls on the Sabbath, you do it so you don't break the law of Moses. So why should you be angry with Me and plan to kill Me for healing a man on the Sabbath?" He paused and stared at them. They were furious.

The people began to ask questions. "Why would they be so angry that Jesus healed someone? Are they trying to kill Him just because He healed on the Sabbath?"

The Pharisees to whom Jesus had spoken were the most vocal about putting an end to His ministry. They constantly tried to make Him look foolish before the people. Instead, He exposed them. Haughtily, they gathered their robes about them and stomped off. Jesus called after them, "Look beneath the surface so you can judge correctly." They kept walking.

July 2   *John 7:25–31*

People Argue About Whom Jesus Is

My friend Nicodemus and I decided to walk through the crowd to get a feel of what they were thinking. I had come to the city to have a new tomb hewn out of the rock near Golgotha, and I met Nicodemus on the way to the temple. I was surprised to see that Jesus was in town, considering the rumors going about. Apparently the Jews wanted Him arrested. I overheard a group of people who lived in the city asking each other, "Isn't this the man they are trying to kill?"

Kill Him! I thought to myself in surprise. *I thought they only wanted to arrest Him.* Weaving my way through the crowd, I heard all sorts of contrasting thoughts and opinions. On my way to rejoin Nicodemus, I was distracted by the conversation of two elderly men.

The one asked his friend, "Why are the leaders allowing Him to speak in public? They aren't even saying anything to Him."

The other answered, "Could the leaders possibly believe He is the Messiah?"

The first countered, "How could He be? For we know where this man comes from. When the Messiah comes, He will just appear and no one will know where He is from."

I couldn't keep quiet at this comment. "Whose teaching is that?" I asked them. "What does the Scripture say about the Messiah?"

They both looked at me with surprise that I would interrupt their discussion. Before they could respond, Jesus began to speak again. "It is true, you do know Me and where I am from, but I'm not here on My own. The One who sent Me is true, and you do not know Him." Everyone listened. "I know Him," He continued, "because I have come from Him, and He sent Me to you."

Suddenly, a member of the Sanhedrin jumped up on the steps. "Where are the temple guards? Arrest this man," he shouted. I looked for Nicodemus to see if he knew what was going on. The guards stood still. The Pharisee kept calling for an arrest, but no one paid any attention to him. Jesus pulled His hood over His head and walked away.

Many people in the crowd believed on Him. Their argument was simple: "After all, would you expect the Messiah to do more miracles than this man has done?" I agreed with them.

July 3 *John 7:32–36*

Temple Guards Sent to Arrest Jesus

Word had gotten to the Sanhedrin that Jesus was openly speaking with the people near the temple steps. A report was also given to them regarding what Jesus was saying. They promptly sent temple guards to arrest Him. I had been at the temple, listening to Jesus, when I was called to meet with the Sanhedrin. I was there with the high priest when the order was given. I was about to say something in Jesus' defense, but at the last minute, I decided to follow the guards because I was very interested in what might happen. I watched as the guards approached Jesus. Joseph of Armathea was still in the crowd. He came up to me and asked what was happening.

"They have been sent to arrest Him," I said, nodding toward the guards.

"Nicodemus," he whispered, "we must do something. How can we help Him?"

I could only shake my head and shrug my shoulders because I really didn't know what we could do. We watched closely and listened to what Jesus answered when they told Him they had come to arrest Him. "I will be with you only a little longer. Then I will return to the One who sent Me. You will search for Me but not find Me. You cannot go where I am going."

The guards looked at each other and asked, "What has He done wrong?" Leaving Him there, they went back to the Sanhedrin. I followed them back to the council. The priests were upset at the guards, wanting to know why they hadn't brought Jesus with them. "He has done nothing wrong," they reported.

Then they told those present what Jesus had said about going away. Very puzzled, the leaders asked, "Where is He planning to go? Is He planning to visit Jews of other lands?"

"Maybe He will teach the Greeks," someone suggested.

I kept my mouth shut. The other members were perplexed by His words and kept asking each other again and again what He could mean by "you will search but not find Me for you cannot go where I am going." I left the council chambers relieved that Jesus had not been arrested.

July 4 *John 7:37–44*

Jesus, the Water of Life

It was very early the last day of the festival when Jesus got up and crawled out of our makeshift booth. I was still half asleep. I stuck my head out of the doorway and watched as He walked twenty feet away to a large bolder where He liked to pray. He poured out His heart to God, asking for clarity of thought and requesting that the Holy Spirit might touch the hearts of the people. I crawled back inside and slept.

Sometime later He returned and prepared breakfast for us. While we ate I asked Him where He planned to go today. "The temple," He answered. After finishing breakfast I followed Him to the temple steps. Just as the water and wine libation was being poured out as part of the climax of the festival, Jesus shouted, "Anyone who is thirsty may come to Me. Anyone who believes in Me may come and drink!"

Everyone stopped what they were doing and turned toward Him to listen to His words. He continued, "For the Scriptures say that he who believes in Me, out of his heart will flow rivers of living water." (Later we understood the Living Water to be the Holy Spirit, which would not be given until Jesus entered into glory.)

The crowd responded very favorably, and I heard people saying, "Surely this is the prophet we have been expecting." Still others said, "He is the Messiah."

Jesus' prayer in the garden is being answered, I thought.

But then I heard other voices saying, "He can't be the Messiah because the Messiah is not to come from Galilee. Don't the Scriptures clearly state the Messiah will be born of the royal line of David?" The person right beside me said, "Yes, in Bethlehem the village where King David was born."

The crowd was evidently divided about my stepbrother. Some of the people even wanted Him arrested, but no one moved to do their bidding. As evening came, the crowd dispersed. It was getting dark and time to go back to our booth. I told my brother I was worried about Him because some of the crowd wanted Him arrested. He just smiled, "Don't worry; My Father in heaven will take care of Me until that time comes."

July 5 *John 7:45–53*

The Temple Guards Testimony

When the guards were sent to arrest Jesus the second time and returned without Him, the priests were furious. "Why didn't you bring Him in?" they demanded.

The guards looked at each other, and finally one of them spoke. "We spent most of the day there listening to His words. We have never heard anyone speak like this," he said.

The Jews just stood and stared at them for a moment, unable to believe the temple guards were so completely drawn to Jesus. Finally one of the Pharisees found his voice, "Have you been led astray, too?" The other religious leaders began mocking them as followers of the poor, deluded Nazarene. The rancor and hatred in their voices was evident. "What makes you believe Him? Do you know any religious leader who believes in Him?" Jabesh, the Pharisee who had done most of the talking, stuck his face inches from the face of the captain of the guard and snarled, "Answer me!"

"I can't explain why we believed in Him. His words just spoke to our hearts. But to answer your question, 'No,' none of you believe in Him or are His followers." I admired the guard's courage.

Jabesh turned to the other Pharisees. "Only this foolish crowd follows Him, but they are ignorant of the law. Furthermore, God's curse is upon them," he said with bitterness. The rest nodded in agreement.

I knew I must say something. I could not remain silent. Asking God for courage, I boldly stood up, announcing I had something to say. "Is it legal to convict a man before He has gone to trial?" I asked. "Surely He deserves a hearing," I added.

They all looked at me with surprised expressions, amazed that I would speak up for the Galilean. Then Jabesh spoke with anger and annoyance, "Are you from Galilee, too? A part of the ignorant crowd?" he asked with mock sarcasm. He walked toward me with a scroll in his hand. "Read the Scripture," he sneered, throwing it down on the table in front of me, "and see for yourself if any prophet comes from Galilee." The meeting broke up, and they all walked out of the assembly room.

July 6   *John 8:1–3*

The Adulterous Woman (Part 1)

I had been secretly flirting with a member of the Sanhedrin for a while. Of course, my husband knew nothing of our relationship. Yes, it was wrong, but I loved the attention this high ranking Pharisee showered upon me, constantly giving me compliments and little gifts. It had only progressed to a kiss or a hug when my husband was away. I rationalized that I deserved to enjoy some love and affection since I didn't get any from my husband, who treated me no better than a servant.

This morning, as usual, I arose, bathed, dressed, and went to the market to buy food for the day. Walking past the temple, I noticed a crowd. I saw the rabbi everyone had been talking about and listened for awhile. He looked directly at me as He spoke of His Father in heaven. I hurried home, feeling convicted that I needed to end this secret affair. My husband had left for work when I arrived back at the house. Hearing a sharp knock on the door, I opened it to find my secret paramour standing there. He had a strange look on his face, drawn and nervous. Pushing his way inside, he said, "I need you now." He pulled me to the bed, tearing at my clothes. I tried to resist but was soon overpowered—there was no doubt in my mind that I was being raped.

As if on cue once the deed was done, members of the Sanhedrin burst through the door and charged me with adultery. I pleaded with my lover, but he turned his back. I cried and begged all of them to remove the charge against me because my husband would divorce me and throw me out in the street. None of them listened. Instead, they dragged me out of the house, half naked, down the dusty streets to where the Galilean taught at the temple steps. The people cleared a path for them, watching as they threw me down in a heap at His feet. Too ashamed to look up at Him, I just lay there on the temple steps. I know now that all they wanted was to use me against Him. I was guilty, but He was innocent. I heard the murmurings of contempt from the crowd. I felt their looks of disdain boring through me. It seemed like an eternity passed as I lay there, trembling and weeping quietly. I knew what was coming. I had seen the hatred in their eyes.

July 7   John 8:4–11

The Adulterous Woman (Part 2)

"Teacher, this woman was caught in the act of adultery." Without looking, I knew every eye was upon me—the adulteress. The Pharisee continued, "The law of Moses commands us to stone someone like her. What do You say?" It was obvious they were trying to trap Him. No matter what He said they would condemn Him. I was the expendable pawn in this charade.

I waited for His answer, trembling. The only sound was my weeping. Strangely, I began to feel worse for Him than for myself. I knew He was a good man. I had listened to His words. He had spoken to my heart. The silence seemed to last forever. I felt His presence near me; then I saw Him kneel on the steps. He spread the dust evenly with the flat of His hand. With His finger, He began to write. My accusers kept on insisting He give them an answer. He remained silent. They pressed in close, loudly demanding that He answer them. Still He kept silently writing in the dust. I looked and saw them peering over His shoulder, trying to read what He was writing.

He finally stood, looked at them, and spoke. "In time I will answer you, but for now, let the one who has never sinned throw the first stone." Then He stooped down and began to write again. Now every one of the priests was curious. They gathered close to look at what He had written. As soon as the accusers saw what was written, they quickly exited, beginning with the eldest down to the youngest.

How did He know the secret sins they were guilty of? I wondered.

In a matter of minutes, Jesus and I were alone on the steps. Jesus stood up, reached down, and helped me to my feet. He asked, "Where are your accusers?" I looked around, and sure enough, they were all gone! "Isn't there anyone here to condemn you?" He asked.

"No, Lord," I said, "no one."

Then He looked into my eyes. "Neither do I condemn you—go and sin no more." Tears burst from my eyes and ran down my cheeks. I fell to my knees, thanking Him. I knew word would get to my husband, but in that moment my life was forever changed because I became a follower of Jesus.

July 8   John 8:12–18

The Light of the World (Part 1)

The Feast of Booths was over, and some of the people had packed up and were heading home. My brother was not in the booth when I awoke. The morning was still cool as the sun had not yet risen. I splashed water on my face to wake up, then headed down the hill from the Mount of Olives, and into the city. I knew where to find Him. Sure enough, He was at the temple steps teaching the people. I watched as He spoke.

The rising sun dimmed the light provided by the great pillars at the temple entrance, which had been lit like giant candles when the feast began. Jesus climbed to the top step and stood silhouetted in the sun. He cried out, "I am the Light of the world." Everyone turned to look at Him. "If you follow Me, you won't have to walk in darkness because you will have the light that leads to life." He looked out at the crowd as the people reflected on what He had just said.

A group of Pharisees came closer to the steps. One called out, "You are making those claims about Yourself; therefore, Your testimony is not valid."

Jesus walked down the steps toward the group. Looking at His antagonist, He said, "These claims are valid even though I make them about Myself. For I know where I came from and where I am going, but you don't know this about Me. You judge Me by human standards, but I do not judge anyone." The crowd was listening intently, but I could tell that the Pharisees were agitated. They knew they could not afford to lose ground with the people. Jesus continued, "And if I did judge, my judgement would be correct in every respect because I am not alone. My Father, who sent Me, is with Me. Your own law says that if two people agree on something, their witness is accepted as fact." He pointed to Himself. "I am one witness, and My Father, who sent Me, is the other." Then He pointed heavenward. This infuriated the priests because He called God His Father. In my heart, I knew this was the beginning of the end for Him.

July 9   *John 8:19, 20*

Light of the World (Part 2)

The crowd had grown considerably larger. There were the curious. There were those interested in hearing the exchange between the religious leaders and Jesus. But there were still others who were there because they genuinely wanted to know the truth. This was the first time I had heard my brother really speak about His heavenly Father. I wanted to know the truth, and I could not understand why the jealousy and the hatred of the Pharisees blinded them to the truths He was teaching.

One of the Pharisees, an older man, who was obviously very angry and fighting to control his hostility in front of the people, asked Him. "Where is Your Father?"

If He had said 'in heaven,' they would have seized and probably killed Him on the spot. Wisely, His answer put the onus on them. "Since you do not know who I am, you don't know who My Father is." Jesus had moved from the steps into the temple area near the treasury. The people followed, as did the Pharisees. "If you knew Me, you would have known who My Father is also."

The people began to discuss among themselves the words Jesus had spoken. Some were not sure what He meant by "His Father." I knew He was not referring to my dad, Joseph. The majority of the people had figured out that He was talking about God in heaven as His Father. The Pharisees were becoming very animated as they pointed and gestured at Jesus. I could almost imagine what they were saying. "This man is a blasphemer, calling God His Father."

As I watched, the thought came to me that the crowds of people were like sheep in need of a shepherd. There was no one to teach them the truth. I moved closer to the members of the religious establishment and listened. They were discussing how they might arrest Him, but no one had any answers. I made my way to where my brother stood alone. "We need to talk," I said. I suggested we go get lunch. He smiled and nodded.

July 10 *John 8:21–25*

Jesus Claims to be God

During lunch I asked Jesus about His comments concerning His Father. He spent a long time explaining who He was and how important it was that He maintain a close relationship with His Father. Early morning prayer reinforced that connection. I asked if He was concerned about being arrested. "As long as I am doing My Father's will, nothing can happen to Me that is not part of His plan. Up until now, the Pharisees have not been able to do anything because My time has not yet come, but it soon will."

We finished our lunch and headed back to the temple where a crowd was gathered in hopes of seeing and hearing Him again. Jesus climbed the steps and looked at the people. "Where are You going?" someone shouted.

"I am going away. You will search for Me but will die in your sin. You cannot come where I am going."

A gentleman near me turned and asked his friend, "Do you understand what He is talking about?"

I heard another man ask, "Is He planning to kill Himself?"

"Why can't we go where He is going?" people around me kept asking each other.

Jesus spoke again, "You are from below. I am from above. You belong to this world; I do not." The people listened intently. They really wanted to grasp the meaning of His words. He continued, "That is why I said you will die in your sins, for unless you believe that 'I AM' who I claim to be, you will die in your sins."

Everyone within earshot stood still and stared at Him. They could not believe their ears. Finally the silence was broken by a voice filled with awe, "Who did He say He was?"

"Just what I have been saying to you from the beginning. I AM the One standing beside," He said.

People stared at each other in disbelief. "Is He claiming to be the One who spoke to Moses at the burning bush?" All of a sudden many voices were heard demanding, "Who are You?"

Jesus calmly answered, "The very One I have always claimed to be." He had once again announced to the crowd that He was God.

July 11   John 8:26–30

Jesus Claims to be I AM

I looked around at the people as it dawned on them who He was claiming to be. Some accused Him of blasphemy. Others, as if trying to comprehend, kept asking, "How can He be God if He's a Nazarene carpenter from Galilee?"

There were a few who recognized me as His companion. "Who is this man?" they demanded of me.

"My stepbrother, the son of Joseph and Mary of Nazareth."

"Ah ha," they cried. "He is no more God than I am," one man shouted. "Here is His stepbrother."

As everyone looked at me, I said, "I believe He is from God and that God is His Father."

Then Jesus spoke again. "I have much to say about all of you and much to condemn, but I won't. For I say only what I have heard from the One who sent Me, and He is completely truthful."

I was glad He had taken the spotlight off of me but I was happy that I was able to give testimony about Him. I could tell they still did not understand the One He was referring to as having sent Him was His heavenly Father. Then He said something that shocked everyone, including me. "When you have lifted the Son of man up on the cross, then you will understand that I AM He."

"Put God, Yahweh, on a cross! This man is crazy!" I heard someone say.

What does He mean? I asked myself. *Is He predicting His death?*

Jesus spoke again, "I do nothing on My own except what the Father has taught Me. The One who sent Me is with Me. He has not deserted me, for I always do what pleases Him."

I noticed a number of people shaking their heads in disbelief. I overheard the comment, "I could accept His claim to be Messiah or a prophet, but not God. Not the I AM!" But I could tell there were many who were convinced He was everything He claimed to be, including the I AM. Over to my right, a group of Pharisees scoffed at Him, calling Him a liar, a deceiver, and a blasphemer. In my heart, I believed He was God. I found it hard to comprehend that God would become a man—and to think He was my brother—but what disturbed me most was His reference to the cross.

July 12   John 8:31–38

"I Will Set You Free"

Many of the attendees of the Feast of Booths had gone home. Jesus and I continued to stay in the booth we had constructed and others still camped out in their booths. This lodging was definitely a lot cheaper than an inn. I asked Jesus about the cross and what He meant by it. He became serious and responded simply, "When the time comes, you will know." I didn't say any more.

After breakfast, we headed back to the city. Many of the people who had been there the day before were back. A lot of these were local residents, but some travelers lingered after the feast to hear Jesus speak. There were those who came for healing and, as always, the curiosity seekers. But I guessed the majority were believers and supporters of Jesus. Near the edge of the crowd were the ever present Pharisees.

Jesus spoke, "You are My disciples if you remain faithful to My teachings, and you will know the truth and the truth will set you free." I could tell the people were having a hard time accepting that idea.

Someone said, "We are children of Abraham. We have never been slaves to anyone. What do You mean, 'We will be set free'?" They didn't understand that He was addressing freedom from sin and guilt.

Jesus replied, "I tell you the truth, everyone who sins is a slave to sin. You know a slave is not permanently part of the family, but a son is part of the family forever. If the Son sets you free, you are truly free." God spoke to my heart that day. If I held to the Son's teaching, that is, to Jesus who was a permanent Son of the Father in heaven, then I was a permanent member, too, and completely free. The people were stuck on Abraham. Jesus continued, "Yes, I know you are descendants of Abraham. But true children of Abraham will do the works of Abraham."

At the mention of Abraham, the Pharisees moved in closer to Jesus. "Some of you are trying to kill Me because there is no room in your hearts for My message. I'm telling you what I saw with My Father. You are following the advice of your father." He paused and looked directly at the Pharisees. They glared back as they struggled to formulate a response.

July 13   *John 8: 39–47*

Confrontation

A heavy tension permeated the crowd. Now the Pharisees were in the fray. Satan knew these people must not know the truth and be set free. Diversion was the only way to interrupt their train of thought. "Our father IS Abraham," one of the Pharisees shouted at Him.

Jesus paused. "No, because if you were children of Abraham, you would follow his example. Instead, you are trying to kill Me because I told you the truth which I heard from God." This statement upset everyone. To tell a Jew that he was not a descendant of Abraham was asking for a fight. "Abraham never did such a thing," Jesus continued. "No, you are imitating your real father."

The Pharisees cried out, "We are not illegitimate children! God, Himself, is our true Father."

Jesus replied, "If God were your Father," He paused and sighed heavily, "you would love Me because I have come to you from God." Pointing to Himself, He said, "I am not here on My own, but He sent Me." These words stirred up the leading Jews. Jesus continued, "Why can't you understand what I am saying?" He raised His arms to quiet them. His voice was filled with pathos. "It's because you can't even hear Me." He waited until they quieted down. "You are children of your father, the devil, and you do the evil things he does. He was a murderer from the beginning. He always hated the truth because there is no truth in him."

I looked around at the crowd. Some were plugging their ears with their fingers. Others were talking in small groups. "When he lies, it is consistent with his character, for he is a liar and the father of lies. When I tell you the truth, you won't believe Me."

He raised His voice, "Which of you can truthfully accuse Me of sin?" He paused, but no one spoke. "Well, since I am telling the truth, why can't you believe Me? Anyone who belongs to God gladly listens to His words, but you don't listen because you do not belong to God." Now the people were furious.

July 14   *John 8:48–59*

Jesus Claims to be Eternal

The Pharisees were stirring the people up against Jesus—things were going from bad to worse. A man shouted, "You Samaritan devil!"

The Pharisees added their sentiment to this cry, accusing Him, "Didn't we say all along You were possessed by a demon?" The people cheered.

It was getting more difficult for Him to say anything because the people no longer wanted to listen. They were turning against Him. I was worried for His safety. "No," Jesus said, "I have no demon in me because I honor My Father. I do not wish to glorify Myself. God is going to glorify Me. He is the true Judge. I tell you the truth, anyone who obeys My teaching will never die."

The same man who called Him a Samaritan devil shouted to the people, "He is a devil!" Turning to Jesus, he denounced Him, saying, "Now we know You are demon possessed because Abraham and the prophets died. Who do You think You are?"

The Pharisees then took up the cause, "You say if we obey Your teachings we will not die. Are You greater than Abraham and the prophets? They died. Who do You think You are?"

I was amazed. People who had believed in Him just hours before were now turning against Him. Jesus spoke, "If I was seeking glory for Myself, what good would that do? My Father plans to glorify Me anyway. You say Yahweh is your God, but you don't even know Him. I know Him. If I said I didn't, I'd be a liar like you." He paused and looked at the Pharisees. They were incensed. "I know and obey God. Incidentally, your father Abraham looked forward to My coming and rejoiced. He saw it and was very glad."

He keeps adding fuel to the fire, I thought.

Someone shouted, "You aren't even fifty years old. How can You say You have seen Abraham?"

Jesus replied, "I tell you the truth—before Abraham was even born, I AM."

Those words sealed His fate. The people started to wail and shake their heads and their fists at Him. Some picked up stones. The Pharisees shouted, "Blasphemy!"

I hurried forward to rescue Him, but He was gone. No one could find Him.

July 15   *John 9:1–12*

Jesus Heals the Man Born Blind

Together Jesus and I dismantled our booth. I had to get back to Nazareth. The disciples had returned to be with Jesus after time with their families. As we walked in Jerusalem, I was glad Jesus avoided the temple area. The hostilities He had encountered there were vivid in my memory. I told my stepbrother to be careful. He smiled and said, "My Father is with Me. He will care for Me." We embraced.

As I journeyed, I reflected on everything I had seen Jesus do. Yesterday, which was the Sabbath, we came across a blind man on one of the main streets. Everyone knew him, and everyone knew that he had been born blind. He'd been begging at the same place since he was young.

Peter asked, "Rabbi, why was this man born blind? Because of his own sin or his parents' sins?"

What a strange question, I thought. *If it was because of his own sins, he would have had to sin in the womb.*

Jesus replied, "It is neither his sin or his parents but so the power of God could be seen in him. We must quickly do the work of the One who sent us. The night is coming when no one can work. While I am here in the world, I am the Light of the world." He bent down, spit on the ground, and made some mud. Rubbing it on the man's eyes, He told him to go wash in the pool of Siloam, which means "sent."

In no time the man came running back, rejoicing and praising God. With unabashed amazement, he looked at everyone and everything. Jesus and the disciples had slipped away, but I couldn't stop watching the man's delight in being able to see.

The people were surprised. "He's the blind beggar!" some said. Others said, "No, he just looks like him."

The man kept saying, "I am the beggar."

The people asked, "Who healed you?"

The beggar replied, "The man they call Jesus made mud, put it on my eyes, and sent me to wash in the pool of Siloam. Now I can see!"

Some scribes and lawyers arrived and demanded, "Where is He?"

"I don't know," he replied. I rejoined Jesus and the disciples. I couldn't help but wonder if there would be repercussions since Jesus had healed the man on the Sabbath. It was the most memorable Feast of Booths I had ever attended. I had lots to share with the family.

July 16   *John 9:13–17*

The Beggar Is Taken to the Synagogue

I had always dreamed of being able to see. I had no idea what it was like, but I figured it must be amazing. I could feel things, and friends would describe them to me, but how I longed to see them. When Jesus opened my eyes, it was like starting life all over again. It was marvelous!

But my excitement turned to fear when I was led before the religious leaders like a criminal. The people around me were angry because I had been healed on the Sabbath. In some strange, unbelievable way, it appeared that Jesus and I were accomplices in breaking the Sabbath. I vowed to tell the simple truth.

The religious leaders began firing questions at me. They wanted to know how everything had happened, so I told them, "He put mud on my eyes and told me to go to the pool of Siloam. There I washed the mud away, and suddenly I could see." Under my breath, I added, "Thanks be to God!"

With an air of superiority, several of the Pharisees declared, "This man is not from God because He breaks the Sabbath. He is actually working on the Sabbath."

Nicodemus, with whom my family was acquainted, spoke up, "How could an ordinary sinner do such miraculous signs?" A few of the others agreed with him. This led to arguing and division among them.

I decided to keep my mouth shut unless questioned. It seemed strange to me that someone able to perform a miracle like restoring sight to the blind would be considered not from God! I was shocked when they turned to me and asked, "What is your opinion about this man who healed you?" That they would ask my opinion about anything was truly surprising. I was just a poor beggar!

It took me a few minutes to recover and find my voice. Finally I said, "I think this man is a prophet." Everyone stared at me, not believing that I would be so bold as to contradict any of these important men. Then the stares turned to ice cold glares. But strangely, I didn't care what they thought. I believed in Him. Once I was blind, but now I could see.

July 17   John 9:18–23

The Blind Man's Parents

When our oldest son came home with his vision restored, we were filled with amazement. He had been blind from birth—we knew it had to be God who had healed him. What a celebration we had! He was thrilled to be able to see our faces; He kept staring at us and everything in the house.

"Who healed you?" I asked.

"A man named Jesus," he replied.

"Ah, the Nazarene," I said.

"He put mud on my eyes. I washed, and now I can see. He must be a great prophet."

"Don't say that," I reprimanded, "or you could be banned from the synagogue."

After awhile he headed out the door saying, "I'm going to look at everything. I want to see the world!"

The next thing we knew, there were temple guards at our door. "The religious leaders want to speak with you," they said.

"What have we done?" I asked. They did not answer.

"Just follow us," the tall one said.

Soon we stood before the Pharisees and the council. Our son was there in the synagogue, too. "Is this your son?" they demanded. "Was he born blind? If so, how can he now see?" They threw questions at us without giving us a chance to answer.

I knew where this was going. If I told them Jesus had healed him, they would ban my wife, myself, and our family from the synagogue. I decided to tell the truth and lie all at the same time. "We know this is our son and that he was born blind, but we do not know how he was made to see or who healed him." I knew it was Jesus, but I could not bring myself to say it. "He is of age, ask him." I pointed to our son. "He can tell you who healed him."

They realized there was no point in pursuing the matter with us any further. They knew we were aware of the ban on referring to Jesus as the Messiah or the Son of God or even a healer. With a wave of his hand, the Pharisee in charge told us to go. For days afterward, I regretted not telling the truth about who had healed our son. I wished I hadn't been afraid of standing firm on the truth. After Jesus' death, we all became followers of the Way.

July 18 *John 9:24–34*

The Beggar Questioned Again

My father was upset and my mother in tears. Why were they doing this to us? It was a time for celebration, not incrimination. After interviewing and dismissing my parents, they led me down to where the council sat. As I stood before them, the leader spoke, "God should get the glory for healing you, not this man Jesus, because we know He is a sinner."

I looked at him incredulously and replied, "I don't know whether He is a sinner, but this much I do know: I was blind and now I can see."

"What did He do? How did He heal you?" another Pharisee asked.

"Listen," I said, "I already told you once. Didn't you hear me? Why do you want me to say it again? Perhaps you want to become His disciples, too?" I smiled at the thought of these self-righteous hypocrites becoming disciples of Jesus.

As expected, my words infuriated them, and they began to curse me. "You are His disciple, but we are disciples of Moses. We know God spoke to Moses, but we don't even know where this man comes from," the spokesman spat out.

"Well, isn't that strange," I replied. "We know that God doesn't listen to sinners, but He listens to those who worship Him and do His will." I boldly continued, "Ever since the world began, no one has been able to open the eyes of someone born blind. If this man were not from God, He couldn't have done it."

One of them shouted at me, "You were born a total sinner," referring to my blindness as the result of some gross sin committed by me or my parents, "and yet you are trying to teach us?" They sneered in anger and fury. Then they stood up and physically grabbed me by the coat and pulled me to the door of the synagogue, muttering curses under their breath. Throwing me out into the street, the leader said, "You are banned from this place and are never to come here again." He slammed the door. I sat there bewildered for a few minutes, then I got up and went to the temple to offer a sacrifice of thanksgiving.

July 19 *John 9:35–41*

Jesus and Spiritual Blindness

All my life I had imagined what things looked like. In fact, I had all these ideas about how things would appear. Now that I could see, I had to laugh at most of my mental images. I had heard the noise at the temple steps, the bantering, buying and selling, but I never imagined what it might look like. I could only afford the doves for an offering, so I purchased two and took them to the priests. They had seen me begging and were surprised I now had my sight. I told them Jesus had healed me. They became quiet and completed the ritual sacrifice. I left the temple courtyard and walked down the steps.

On my way home, someone came up to me and asked, "Do you believe in the Son of man?"

I looked at Him. What a loving, peaceful countenance He had. "Who is He, sir? I want to believe in Him," I said, sensing He was acquainted with my benefactor.

"You have seen Him," the man said, "and He is speaking to you."

"Yes, Lord, I believe!" I cried. Here He was standing in front of me, Jesus, my Lord and Healer! Overwhelmed with gratitude, I fell to my knees and worshipped Him. In my heart I knew He was more than just a prophet. He must be the Son of man and Son of God. He took my hand, and I stood before Him. By this time a crowd had gathered around us.

He spoke to all of us. "I entered the world to render judgment, to give sight to the blind and to show those who think they see that they are really blind." Not far away stood some of the Pharisees who had thrown me out of the synagogue earlier. Jesus looked in their direction. On His face was compassion and longing. In His heart was redemption and forgiveness.

"Are You trying to tell us we are blind?" one of them shouted with disdain in his voice.

"If you were blind, you would not be guilty, but you are guilty because you claim to be able to see," Jesus answered.

I knew I'd rather have physical blindness than spiritual blindness. Thanks to Jesus I could see from within and without.

July 20   *John 10:1-10*

The Sheep

The crowd remained while Jesus continued to speak. I wanted to see my parents after the rough treatment they had received from the Pharisees, but I also wanted to hear Jesus. Down the street near the temple came a shepherd leading about twenty sheep. "Anyone who sneaks over the wall of the sheepfold instead of using the gate must be a thief and robber," Jesus said. The bleating of the sheep caused the crowd to turn and look in the direction of the shepherd who was leading them. "The one who enters the gate is the shepherd. The gatekeeper opens the gate, and the sheep hear his voice and recognize it. He calls his sheep by name and leads them out of the fold and walks ahead of them, calling. They follow because they know his voice." As the shepherd came closer, we could hear him calling to his sheep, and they kept close to him. "They will not follow a stranger because they do not know his voice," Jesus continued.

Someone in the crowd said, "We don't know what You are driving at. What point are You making?" Others chimed in.

"I tell you the truth," He said, "I am the gate for the sheep. All who have come before Me were thieves and robbers, and the true sheep did not listen to them. Yes! I am the gate. Those who come through Me will be saved. They will come and go freely and will find good pastures. The thief's purpose is to steal, kill, and destroy, but My purpose is to give them a rich and satisfying life."

The shepherd had stopped to listen while the sheep gathered close to him. The people were paying close attention to what Jesus was trying to explain to them. I thought to myself how all my life I had felt like an outcast, abandoned by God because of some terrible sin. I had felt like a lost sheep that no one cared about. Then Jesus came and found me. He scooped me up in His arms, made me whole, and made me feel secure and important, accepted of God. He gave me back my life. I left the crowd and headed home to celebrate with my family.

July 21   *John 10:11-21*

The Good Shepherd

I was surprised how much this man knew about herding sheep. I knew all the shepherds in the area and had never seen Him on the fields with a flock or at the shearing pens. Caring for sheep had been my life. It was a solitary life, but I had learned to play the flute and spent the days entertaining my flock. I asked someone close by who the preacher was. "Jesus of Nazareth," came the answer.

Jesus continued to speak, "I am the Good Shepherd. The Good Shepherd sacrifices His life for the sheep." I remembered chasing a wolf from my flock with my rod once. "A hired hand will run when he sees a wolf coming. He will abandon the sheep because they do not belong to him, and he isn't their shepherd. Then the wolf attacks the sheep and scatters them. The hired hand runs because he is only working for the money and doesn't really care about the sheep."

Just a few days ago a hired man had run from a pack of wolves and left the flock at their mercy. The owner of the sheep was furious and fired him.

"I am the Good Shepherd. I know My sheep, and they know Me, just like My Father and I know each other."

Who is His Father? I wondered.

"I will sacrifice My life for My sheep. I have sheep not of this fold. I must bring them also. They will listen to My voice. There will be one flock and one shepherd."

One flock and one shepherd? How will he do that? I wondered.

"The Father loves Me," He said. "I sacrifice My life so I can take it back again. No one can take My life from Me. I lay it down voluntarily, for I have the authority to lay it down when I want to and take it up again. For this is what My Father has commanded."

"Who is His Father?" I asked the people nearby.

"He claims that God is His Father," one of them replied.

"God?" I said in surprise. Everyone started to argue. Some said He was demon possessed and out of His mind, while others countered that someone who was demon possessed could not heal a blind man. I didn't know much about Him, but I wanted to find out more. One thing for certain, He knew all about sheep.

July 22   John 10:40–42

Back to Galilee

My brother Andrew and I had gone home after the Feast of Booths, and then returned to Jerusalem to conduct business for our father and rejoin Jesus. We were with Him when He healed the blind man. We had been in the crowd when He spoke about being the Good Shepherd. We had heard the division among the people concerning Him and worried about the malice the priests and rulers were openly manifesting toward Him. I suggested it might be time to return to Galilee, but I knew He would not go unless He was ready.

We stayed with friends that night. After breakfast the next morning, Jesus announced He was ready to go home to Galilee. Andrew and I glanced at each other and smiled. Expressing thanks to our gracious hosts, we left the city by way of the Kedron Valley and the Mount of Olives. Jesus paused at the crest of the hill just before the road descended into Bethany and on to Jericho. He stood there and looked at the city while tears trickled down His cheeks. I put my hand on His shoulder.

Finally, He turned northward, and we continued our journey. We traveled through many of the towns we had visited before. A man in Bethel asked Jesus to heal his wife. In Sychar, everyone wanted us to stay with them. Jesus accepted the invitation of the woman He had met at the well. She was a different person now; married and happy and very grateful to Jesus. Jesus spent a day healing the sick who came to Him. The next day we arrived in Capernuam. News spread quickly that Jesus was back. Before we finished breakfast, a crowd had already gathered outside our door. Things were back to normal! We spent the rest of the autumn days traveling around Galilee. Wherever we went the crowds gathered—many for healing, many to hear the words of encouragement Jesus offered. Jesus spoke of His death again and warned us to spend time in prayer. The days went by, and the time for the Feast of Dedication drew near. That meant going back to Jerusalem.

July 23 *Luke 9:51–56*

The Journey to Jerusalem and the Samaritans

Jesus seemed more somber than ever as we headed for the city once again. My brother John asked me why Jesus seemed so stressed and distant. A crowd of part-time disciples and others followed us. Since there was such a crowd with us, Jesus asked John and me to make arrangements for accommodations.

We entered a Samaritan village named Dothan and asked if we could lodge there for the night. "How many are coming?" the innkeeper asked.

"About a hundred or more," I answered.

"Where are you headed?" the innkeeper queried.

"Jerusalem," John answered.

Just as Jesus arrived, the innkeeper flew into a rage. "I will not have a bunch of Jews staying at my inn on their way to worship at a temple not recognized by God Himself." I felt the anger burn in my chest and face as he ranted on about us being blasphemers. "Get out of our village," he shouted.

Other bystanders took up the innkeeper's chant. "Get out, blasphemers!"

John and I were furious. In the distance I could see Mount Carmel by the sea, and I remembered Elijah. "Lord," I shouted above the din, "should we call down fire from heaven to burn them up? These Samaritans are the blasphemers," I muttered under my breath.

Jesus looked at me with great sadness on His face. "What are you saying? You want to destroy these people just because they do not want us to stay for the night?"

I realized how crazy my thoughts were and what I was capable of in a fit of anger. Jesus said, "Let's move on to the next village."

We went to Sychar and received a warm welcome. The people were only too happy to provide shelter for everyone and charged us nothing. "We want to repay you for all that you have done for us," they said. I learned a valuable lesson that day about turning the other cheek.

July 24   *Luke 9:57–62*

Tests of Discipleship

The people of Sychar were very gracious hosts. After a good night's rest and a delicious breakfast, we headed south. As we walked, a man from Sychar came to Jesus and asked if he could be a disciple. Evidently he had asked Judas for an interview with the Lord, and Judas had brought him to Jesus. "I will follow You wherever You go," the man said in all earnestness.

Jesus replied, "Foxes have dens to live in, and birds have nests, but the Son of man has no place to lay His head." I noticed Jesus seemed to be speaking more to Judas than to the man asking to be a disciple. I looked at my brother Peter. He had noticed too. Jesus stopped, looked at one of the part-time disciples, and said to him, "Come, follow Me and be a full-time disciple."

The man said, "Lord, I will, but first let me go home and be with my father until he dies and the funeral is over."

Jesus said to him, "Let the spiritually dead bury their own dead. Your duty is to go and preach about the kingdom of God."

This man had been with us off and on for a long time, but he refused to make a commitment because of his elderly father. In reality, he wanted to be sure he got his share of his dad's inheritance at his death.

Someone else said, "Lord, I will follow You but first let me go say goodbye to my family." I knew this man too. He was controlled by his parents who refused to let him live his own life. Whenever he was with us for more than a week, they would send a servant to tell him his family needed him right now. Even though we encouraged him to stay, he would always go.

Jesus looked at the crowd and said, "Anyone who puts his hand to the plow and then looks back is not worthy of the kingdom."

I looked at Peter, and he nodded. Our families were not happy when we told them about our plans to become full-time disciples. But Peter and I are so glad we made the decision to follow Jesus.

July 25   *Luke 10:1–12*

Mission of the Seventy-Two

After leaving Sychar we traveled to Mount Gerizim, then to a small village to the east near the Herodian fortress of Alexandria. After everyone had eaten lunch from food purchased at local vendor stands, Jesus called us together. He chose seventy-two of these disciples who were not part of the twelve and told them He wanted them to go to the towns and villages He planned to visit. He teamed them up two by two and told each team where He wanted them to go. I couldn't help but remember the good times Thaddeus and I had together on our missionary journey.

Before the group parted, Jesus gave them some last instructions. "The harvest is great, but the laborers are few, so pray to the Lord of the harvest to send more workers into the fields. Now go, and remember I am sending you out as lambs among wolves. Don't take any money with you, not even a traveler's bag or an extra pair of sandals. Don't stop to greet people on the road—you are on a mission. Whenever you enter someone's house, say, 'May God's peace be on this house.' If those who live there are peaceful, the blessing will stand. If they are not, the blessing will return to you. Don't move around from house to house, but stay in one place, eating and drinking what they provide. Don't hesitate to accept hospitality because those who work deserve their pay. If you enter a town and it accepts you, eat whatever is set before you. Heal the sick and tell them the kingdom of God is near. If a town refuses to welcome you, go out into the street and say, 'We wipe even the dust of your town from our feet to show you that we abandon you to your fate. And know this, the kingdom of God is near.' Truthfully, even a wicked city like Sodom will be better off than such a town on judgment day."

I looked into the faces of the men who had been chosen for this important mission. They all had personal problems and issues, but they were honest at heart and committed to Christ. They all wanted to advance the kingdom. These were the ones who would pave the way for the establishment of the kingdom of God.

July 26   Luke 10:13–16

A Lament for Cities Rejecting the Gospel

Tears formed in His eyes. I noticed and mouthed "What's wrong?" to Thaddeus, standing beside me in front of Jesus. He shook his head and shrugged. "What sorrow awaits you Chorazin and Bethsaida!" He burst into sobs as though He had gotten news that someone very dear to Him had died.

Thaddeaus leaned over and whispered to me, "James, do you remember how those cities rejected us and especially Jesus? They called us wandering heretics and told us to go home." I remembered.

Jesus continued, "For if the miracles I did in You had been done in Tyre and Sidon, their people would have repented of their sins long ago, clothing themselves in burlap and throwing ashes on their heads to show their remorse." Peter, James, and John went to His side and tried to comfort Him but the tears continued to flow. "Yes, Tyre and Sidon will be better off than you in the judgment day," He continued. "And you, people of Capernaum, will you be honored in heaven? No, you will go down to the place of the dead." He paused to catch His breath. Then He turned to all of us with red eyes and a tear-stained face and said, "Anyone who rejects you also rejects Me. And anyone who rejects Me is rejecting God who sent Me."

I couldn't help but wonder why the rest of us did not feel the same emotion over lost people as He did. I just figured it was their own fault and they would suffer the consequences of their own poor choices. After He regained His composure Jesus called all of us close to Him. We realized how important this mission was. He asked the twelve of us to divide into our original teams of two to meet with three teams of two or six of the new missionaries and share our experiences with them. Thad and I found three teams and told them our stories. They were encouraged. Then Jesus called the men together, blessed them with the Holy Spirit and they were on their way. We prayed for their success.

July 27 *Luke 10:17–24*

The Seventy-Two Return

While the seventy-two were away, Jesus and the twelve of us worked with the local people in Sychar and the nearby villages. The crowd that had followed us from Galilee returned home. It was during this time that Jesus spoke to us about the kingdom. He tried to help us understand that the kingdom was within us, put there by the Holy Spirit.

In a few weeks the seventy-two returned, transformed by their experiences. We gathered together while each group shared their stories—some funny, some sad, but all spoke of God's power at work in the lives of people. I nudged my brother John. He smiled. Their stories were similar to our missionary stories. They told about healings, sharing the good news, and driving out demons in Jesus' name.

After they had finished, Jesus said, "I saw Satan fall from heaven like lightning." It was as though He was seeing something we could not. He paused and looked heavenward, raising His hands. Then He turned to us. "I have given you authority over all the power of the enemy; you can walk among snakes and scorpions, crushing them. Nothing will injure you. Don't rejoice because evil spirits obey you. Rejoice because your names are written in the book of life in heaven."

Suddenly His face came alive with joy and the presence of the Holy Spirit, and He said, "O Father, Lord of heaven and earth, thank You for hiding these things from those who think themselves wise and clever and revealing them to the childlike. Yes, Father, it pleased You to do it this way."

After His prayer, He spoke to all of us. "My Father has entrusted everything to Me. No one understands the Son but the Father, and no one knows the Father but the Son and those to whom the Son choses to reveal Him." Then He led us away from the village and said, "Blessed are your eyes, that you have seen what you have seen. Many prophets and kings longed to see and hear what you have seen, but were unable."

What a day it had been!

July 28 *Mark 10:1; Matthew 19:1, 2*

East of Jordan

The following day Jesus announced we were going to the area just east of the Jordan River. Many of the seventy-two missionaries returned to their families and occupations, but a number continued to accompany us. As we traveled east and southward, the people from around Judea heard we were coming. When we came to the towns and villages visited by the seventy-two, we received a warm welcome. Large crowds formed. Everyone wanted to be with Jesus.

Perhaps He will announce His plans for the kingdom, I thought. Many came from Jerusalem bringing their sick loved ones. The Pharisees came, too, hoping to turn the people away from Jesus. Every day the people came to hear the words of life. It was wonderful to see how much the people loved Jesus. We couldn't have been in a better place for reaching the people. Merchants and caravans traveling north to south and back stopped and listened to Jesus' words. Some of my publican friends came and listened to the words of the Lord. They wanted to know what it was like being with Jesus all the time and how I got so lucky to become one of His disciples. "He found me and called me to follow Him," I replied. It truly had been a fantastic journey for the past three years.

I asked my friend Simon the Zealot when he thought Jesus would make His announcement about the kingdom. He shrugged and said, "I don't know, but now would be the perfect time." I agreed. The crowds seemed to get larger every day. Hawkers from Jerusalem, seeing an opportunity to serve food and make money, came and set up shop. Those days east of the Jordan were wonderful days. We were busy from morning to night caring for the people. The days were long but very rewarding as many were helped.

July 29   *Luke 10:25–37*

The Good Samaritan

A particularly large crowd gathered this afternoon east of the Jordan. Jesus spoke to the people from a small knoll. It reminded me of the time Jesus had spoken to the multitude from the mountaintop in Galilee and then fed them with the loaves and fishes. Part way through Jesus' discourse, a young lawyer associated with a group of Pharisees stood up to ask a question, or should I say test Him. "Teacher, what should I do to inherit eternal life?" he asked.

Everyone turned to see who had spoken, before turning their attention back to Jesus. "What does the law of Moses say?" Jesus asked in response. "How do you read it?"

"You must love God with all your heart, soul, mind, and strength, and your neighbor as yourself," the lawyer replied.

"Correct," Jesus responded. "Do this and you will live."

Seeking to justify his disregard for certain people, the lawyer asked, "Who is my neighbor?"

Jesus shared a parable with the crowd. A Jewish man traveling from Jerusalem to Jericho was attacked by bandits. They stripped him, beat him, and left him for dead beside the road. A priest came by, saw the man, and crossed to the other side of the road. A Levite traveling the road went over and looked at the victim, but continued on his way. A despised Samaritan came next. Seeing the beaten and bruised man, he had compassion on him. He soothed his wounds with olive oil and wine and then bandaged them. Putting the man on his own donkey, he brought him to an inn where he took care of him. The next day he handed the innkeeper two silver coins and asked him to care for the man. He assured the innkeeper that if the bill ran higher he would pay when he returned.

"Now," Jesus asked, "who was the neighbor to the bandit victim?"

"The one who showed him mercy," the lawyer replied.

Jesus agreed. "Yes. Now go and do the same."

The crowd fell silent as they thought about what Jesus had said. Some people had tears in their eyes while the Pharisees displayed signs of disgust. Jesus continued speaking to the people, but I kept thinking about the story. As a zealot, it really affected me.

July 30   Matthew 19:1-12; Mark 10:2-12

The Divorce Question

A few days later a number of Pharisees and Sadducees joined the large crowd. Because the two groups did not see eye to eye on many religious topics, they usually avoided one another, so it was strange to see them together. Toward evening one of the Pharisees called out while Jesus was speaking, "Rabbi, should a man be allowed to divorce his wife?"

Jesus turned toward the questioner with a question of His own. "What did Moses say in the law about divorce?"

"Well, he permitted it," they replied. "A man can give his wife a written notice of divorce and send her away."

"This is an obvious trap," I said to my brother Peter. "They are trying to get Him to discredit Moses and the law."

Jesus responded, "Moses wrote this commandment only as a concession to your hard hearts." Moving closer to where they stood, He continued, "God made male and female during Creation. That is God's ideal. This explains why a man leaves his father and mother and is joined to his wife, and the two are united as one. Since they are no longer two but one, let no one split apart what God has joined together." He stood there and looked at them, not with anger or malice but compassion.

They could not look at Him, so they turned and left. It was getting late, and the crowd began to disperse. Some people in a nearby village invited us to stay with them for the night.

As we walked to our host's home, I mulled over Jesus' comments above divorce. We had been taught you could divorce your wife for any reason, even if you didn't like her looks. When we were settled in the house, I asked Him, "Can a couple ever be divorced for any reason?"

He replied, "If a man or woman divorces their spouse and remarries, they commit adultery unless their spouse has committed adultery."

As I thought about what Jesus had said, I remarked, "It is better not even to get married."

Jesus responded, "Some chose to remain single—those whom God helps. Some are born eunuchs, some are made eunuchs. Some chose not to marry for the kingdom's sake. Let anyone accept this who can." This discussion with Jesus made the subject of divorce a lot more serious than I had once thought.

July 31   *Luke 10:38–42*

Jesus Visits Mary and Martha

I live in a small village just north of Jerusalem. My sister Martha and I own a small business in Bethany, our home town. Our brother Lazarus is a carpenter. Years ago he became acquainted with Joseph and Jesus, carpenters from Nazareth when they brought wood products to sell in the city. We became good friends, and they often stayed overnight in our home. As time passed, I realized Jesus was more than just an ordinary man.

When we heard He was east of the Jordan, the three of us went to hear Him speak. Pushing through the crowd after He finished His message, we urged Him to come visit us. Thanking us for the invitation, He assured us He would stop in on His way to the Feast of Dedication.

It was mid-afternoon the day He and the disciples arrived. The first thing Martha asked was if they had eaten anything. "Not since breakfast," Peter answered. Martha set about to make a meal. Lazarus poured everyone a drink of water. I sat as close to Jesus as I could. I loved to hear Him speak. He began to talk about the kingdom and the importance of being part of it. As the afternoon wore on, I vaguely heard Martha in the kitchen grumbling to Lazarus about all the work she had to do with no help.

Finally, she came into the living room where we were seated and said in an angry voice, "Lord, doesn't it seem a little unfair to You that my sister just sits here while I do all the work?" My face turned red. I was so embarrassed! Then she said, "Tell her to come and help me!" I felt like running away as I waited for Jesus to order me into the kitchen.

Instead He spoke to Martha. "My dear Martha! You are worried and upset about all these details. There is only one thing to be concerned about. Your sister has discovered it, and it will not be taken from her." I looked at Jesus and He smiled. Martha sat down beside me while Jesus finished His talk. Then, at Jesus' suggestion, we all went to the kitchen and finished preparing the meal. Dinner was wonderful, but Jesus' words of life were even better.

August 1   *John 10:22–33*

To the Feast of Dedication

It was winter now, and the nights were getting colder. Our friends at Bethany prepared us a nourishing breakfast and sent us on our way. We traveled south, up the winding road to the crest of the hill that led down into the city. Everyone was getting ready for the Feast of Dedication. You could sense the excitement and amiable spirit in the air. We were in the temple walking near the area known as Solomon's colonnade when some Pharisees and Levites surrounded us and asked Jesus, "How long are You going to keep us in suspense? If You are the Messiah, tell us plainly."

Jesus looked for a long time at the man who asked the question and finally replied, "I have already told you, and you won't believe Me." They stood glaring at Him. Then He smiled ever so slightly, "The proof is in the work I do in My Father's name. You don't believe Me because you are not My sheep." A few of them scoffed. "My sheep listen to My voice. I know them, and they follow Me. For My Father has given them to Me, and He is more powerful than anyone else. No one can snatch them from the Father's hand. The Father and I are one."

It was easy to see that they were agitated. I noticed some even picked up stones and held them up as if threatening to kill Him. I called to my brother Andrew, and we moved in front of the Lord. But He stepped around us and confronted the angry men face to face, saying, "At My Father's direction I have done many good works. For which one are you going to stone Me?"

The leader came close to Jesus with a stone as big as his fist clutched in his hand. "We are stoning You, not for any good work, but for blasphemy. You, a mere man, claim to be God!" he yelled into Jesus' face.

Fearlessly, the Lord stood His ground and looked the man in the eyes with that penetrating look that reaches deep into one's very soul. The man backed up a step or two. I admired Jesus' courage. He seemed so at peace in the safety of His Father's care.

August 2   *John 10:34–42*

Jesus Reasons With the Pharisees

Jesus seemed fearless as He stood before the angry Pharisees. He spoke in calm, clear tones, "It is written in your own Scriptures, and you know the Scriptures cannot be altered, that God said to certain leaders of the people: 'I say, you are gods!' Therefore if these people who were called gods received God's message, why do you call it blasphemy when I say I am the Son of God?"

His argument was a good one. If God calls the leaders of Israel 'gods' because they stand before the people on His behalf, why are these people ready to stone Him when He calls Himself God's Son? He paused to give them a chance to speak, but they were silent. So He continued, "After all, the Father set Me apart and sent Me into the world." He raised His hands and pointed to Himself. "Don't believe in Me unless I carry out My Father's work. If I do His works, then believe in the evidence of the miraculous works I have done, even if you don't believe Me. Then you will know and understand the Father is in Me and I am in the Father."

The Pharisees were livid. In their fury they called upon the temple guards to arrest Him for blasphemy. The guards arrived, but when they saw it was Jesus whom the Pharisees wanted arrested, they stopped for they remembered His words to the people that had touched their hearts. "This man is no criminal; He is from God," they announced. The Pharisees shouted at the guards, calling them Samaritan dogs for refusing to obey their orders.

"Peter, let's leave while they are arguing," Jesus said. We slipped away with the other disciples. Jesus led us through the city, out the gate across the Kidron, and to the crest of the hill. We stood and looked out over the city for a few moments, then Jesus turned and went to where John had baptized Him.

It didn't take long before a large crowd was gathered. The people said to each other, "John did not perform any miracles, but everything he said about this man has come true." And many of the people who came to us at the Jordan believed in Jesus.

August 3   Luke 11:1-13

Ministry by the Jordan in Perea

We awoke to a beautiful day. The sun was just beginning to peak over the hills. Jesus was already up praying at a spot not far from our camp. We could hear Him crying out to His Father, something about a cross He would soon have to bear. His prayer was passionate, and we felt drawn to join Him and kneel down beside Him. When He finished, I said, "Lord, teach us to pray, just as John taught his disciples to pray."

"This is how you should pray," He replied. "Our Father in heaven, may Your name be kept holy. May Your kingdom come soon and Your will be done here on earth as it is in heaven. Give us each day the food we need, and forgive us our sins as we forgive those who sin against us. Don't let us yield to temptation, but deliver us from evil."

He then emphasized the importance of persevering in prayer by telling a story. He looked at me, "Thomas, suppose you went to the home of a friend at midnight to borrow three loaves of bread. You tell him that another friend has arrived for a visit and you have nothing to feed him. Calling out from his bed, he says, 'Don't bother me. The door is locked for the night, and my family and I are all in bed. I can't help you.' But if you kept knocking long enough, he would get up and give you whatever you needed because of your shameless persistence. And so I tell you, keep on asking and you will receive what you ask for. Keep on seeking and you will find. Keep on knocking and the door will be opened to you. For everyone who asks, receives. Everyone who seeks, finds, and to everyone who knocks, the door will be opened."

Jesus let the words sink in before continuing. "Some of you are fathers. If your daughter asks for a fish, do you give her a snake instead? If your son asks for an egg, do you give him a scorpion? Of course not! So if you, who are sinful, know how to give good gifts to your children, how much more will the Father give the Holy Spirit, the best gift of all, to those who ask Him."

Jesus' discussion on prayer is just what I needed to hear. You see, I often doubt whether or not God loves me and if He is listening to my prayers.

August 4 *Luke 11:33–36*

The Inner Light

People were already beginning to gather as Jesus finished teaching us how to pray. We were grateful to have been able to spend that time alone with Jesus. I think the other disciples were as happy as I was to receive guidance from Jesus as to how to pray to God. Sometimes I didn't know what to pray about. God seemed so much more approachable after Jesus compared Him to a loving earthly father. I had an amazing dad who would do anything for me.

Jesus started the day's discourse with the people by talking about light within. "No one lights a lamp in a house and then puts it under a basket. Instead a lamp is placed on a stand where its light can be seen by all who enter the house. Your eye is a lamp that provides light for your body. When your eye is good, your whole body is filled with light. When it is bad, your whole body is filled with darkness. Make sure," He continued, "that the light you think you have is not actually darkness. If you are filled with light and have no dark corners, then your whole life will be radiant, as though a floodlight were filling you with light."

I could relate to what Jesus was saying because of some of the problems I struggled with in my own life. Ever since I was just a boy I had an enormous curiosity about the opposite sex. I knew it was wrong, but I laughed along with everyone else at dirty jokes. Once I got caught peeking around the door of the bathhouse while my sister was taking a bath. I will never forget the loud shrill, "Philip, what are you doing?" when I got caught red-handed. And I will never forget the spanking, either! Ever since, I have struggled with keeping my eyes filled with light and not darkness. Being with Jesus and watching His example has made a big difference for me. It can be so easy for darkness to creep in. A lingering look or a lustful thought is all the foothold Satan needs to cause a person to fall. My goal is to be like Jesus every day. As the psalmist wrote, "The Lord is my light and my salvation, whom shall I fear?"

August 5 *Luke 11:37–44*

Dinner With a Pharisee

I arrived as Jesus was talking about inner light. When He finished His discourse, I maneuvered closer and invited Him and His disciples to my place for dinner. I lived in Jericho, only five miles away. This dinner was actually set up by the Sanhedrin because the Pharisees and teachers of the law wanted to test Him with questions. Being a Pharisee and living close to where Jesus was teaching, my place was the perfect location. Jesus graciously accepted. He requested a few minutes to attend to some people needing healing, but soon we were on our way, arriving at my home in just over an hour.

When we arrived at my home, I stopped to ceremonially wash my hands as all good Jews must, but Jesus did not. He and His disciples walked in and took their places at the table. I was shocked. *A teacher of the people disregarding Jewish tradition!* I thought.

As we ate He spoke, "You Pharisees are so careful to clean the outside of the cup and dish, but inside you are filthy, full of greed and wickedness."

We all knew He was referring to religious appearance. Still, I thought it rude of Him to speak to us as He did. His face became animated as He continued. "Fools! Didn't God make the inside as well as the outside? So clean the inside by giving gifts to the poor, and you will be clean all over."

I could see the anger on the faces of the other Pharisees. Even His disciples seemed surprised at His comments.

"What sorrow awaits you," He continued, "for you are careful to tithe even the tiniest income from your herb garden, but you ignore justice and the love of God." His tone softened. "You should tithe, yes, but do not neglect the more important things. What sorrow awaits you because you love to sit in seats of honor at the synagogue and receive everyone's greetings as you walk in the marketplace. You are like hidden graves in a field. People walk over them not knowing all the hidden corruption they are stepping on."

At first I was offended at His accusations, but something within me made me admit that what He said was true. Yes, we looked good on the outside, but inside, most of us had big problems.

August 6   Luke 11:45–54

Experts on the Law Speak Out

I had been invited to a dinner to ask Jesus some legal questions, which I definitely intended to do. You could feel the tension in the air. I didn't like the way this itinerant rabbi was speaking to the elders, so I decided to put Him in His place. "Teacher," I said, "You have insulted us with your comments."

"Yes, I know," Jesus answered. "What sorrow awaits you, teachers of religious law, for you crush people with impossible religious demands, and you never lift a finger to ease their burdens. What sorrow awaits you, for you build monuments to the prophets whom your own ancestors killed long ago. But in fact, you stand as witnesses to agree with what your ancestors did. They killed the prophets, and you join in their crime by building the monuments. This is what God in His wisdom said about you, 'I will send prophets and apostles to them but they will kill some and persecute the others.' As a result, this generation will be held responsible for the murder of all God's prophets from the creation of the world, from the murder of Abel to the murder of Zechariah, who was killed between the altar and the sanctuary. Yes, it will certainly be charged to this generation."

I couldn't believe He would charge us with the deaths of all the prophets. Why? Again He spoke, "What sorrow awaits you experts in religious law, for you remove the key to knowledge from the people. You don't enter the kingdom yourselves and you prevent others from entering."

Abruptly, He stood and prepared to leave. My colleagues and I were upset because He never gave us a chance to speak. I started to ply Him with questions as He headed for the door. He turned to me and said, "If you are an honest seeker of truth, meet with me at the Jordan."

Some of the Pharisees openly showed their hostility and tried to provoke Him, but He kept walking.

At the door, He thanked the host for inviting Him and the disciples. I had to admit, I liked His boldness. Sometime soon I would go to the Jordan, for I desired to know the truth.

August 7   Luke 12:1–3

The Yeast of the Pharisees

Leaving the home of the Pharisee, we made our way back to the Jordan. Many people were still there waiting for us to return. When the word got around that Jesus was back, the people came in droves. Everyone wanted to see Jesus. In fact, the crowd grew so large we were afraid people might step on each other. There must have been thousands milling about. Jesus looked out at the people, then turned to us, His disciples, and said, "Beware of the yeast of the Pharisees; watch out for their hypocrisy." I saw some of those who had been at the Pharisee's home to which we had been invited standing together in the crowd.

Then Jesus turned to the crowd and spoke. "The time is coming when everything that is covered up will be revealed and all that is secret will be made known to all. Whatever you have spoken in the dark will be heard in the light."

I began to think about some of the gossip I had spread and some of the things I'd said about others. The last thing I wanted was for anyone else to know. I felt ashamed and embarassed as I remembered telling my brother John what an impulsive loudmouth Peter was. Behind his back, I had criticized Thomas for his lack of faith. A number of times I had criticized Judas because he seemed to think himself better than the rest of us. I had even criticizing Jesus for inviting Matthew to become a disciple. No, I would never want these people to know my inner thoughts or the things I had said. I felt really bad and wished I could take back what I had said.

Jesus continued, "And what you have whispered behind closed doors will be shouted from the housetops for all to hear."

Later that evening, after the crowds had dispersed and the twelve of us were sitting around a fire with Jesus by the river's edge, I asked everyone to forgive me for the unkind remarks I had made. Tears flowed freely. I really wanted to be forgiven and have a change of heart. More than anything else, I wanted to be like Jesus. The others put their arms around me and forgave me.

August 8   Luke 12:4–12

Don't Be Afraid

The next day the crowds were back. About midmorning Jesus stood up to speak. The people immediately quieted down. They were eager to hear what He had to say.

"Dear friends, don't be afraid of those who want to kill your body. They cannot harm you further after that. I will tell you whom to fear—fear God who has the power to take your life and throw you into hell. Yes, He is the one to fear." He was saying that men can only affect what happens to us here on earth, but God controls eternal circumstances.

Then He said, "I ask you, what is the price of five sparrows? Two copper coins? Yet God takes notice of each one of them. Don't forget, the very hairs of your head are numbered."

How can I be that important to God? I wondered.

"Don't be afraid; you are of more value to Him than a whole flock of sparrows," Jesus exclaimed. "I tell you the truth, everyone who acknowledges Me publicly here on earth, the Son of man will also acknowledge in the presence of God's angels. But anyone who denies Me here on earth will be denied before God's angels. Anyone who speaks against the Son of man can be forgiven, but anyone who blasphemes the Holy Spirit will not be forgiven."

Jesus once said that blasphemy against the Holy Spirit was unforgivable in this world and in the world to come. He said it because the Pharisees were accusing Him of casting out demons by the power of Satan. Attributing to Satan the work of the Holy Spirit is blasphemy against God's Spirit. I found Jesus' next statement very encouraging.

"When you are brought to trial before rulers and authorities in the synagogues, don't worry about how to defend yourself or what to say, for the Holy Spirit will teach you at that time what needs to be said."

Deep down, I know that someday we will all be called upon to give a defense of our faith and what we believe. It doesn't matter what happens to me as long as I stand up as His witness.

August 9   *Luke 12:13–21*

The Story About the Rich Fool

My brother and I were friends growing up, but we grew apart when I married and he remained single. It didn't help matters that my wife openly criticized him for decisions he had made. The time came when he refused to come to our home. Now, it was no secret that our father liked him better than me, so it was no surprise that Dad chose my brother as executor of the estate. After Dad passed away, I asked my brother for my share. I was shocked when he said he would on condition that I divorce my wife. I refused to comply with that demand, so he refused to divide the property and possessions.

I had come to believe Jesus was the Messiah, and I respected what He said. One day while listening to Jesus I saw that my brother was in the crowd. When Jesus paused in His talk, I shouted, "Teacher, please tell my brother to divide our father's estate with me."

Jesus looked right at me and said, "Friend, who made me a judge over you to decide such things as that?" Then He said, "Guard against every kind of greed. Life is not measured by how much you own." That was not what I had expected to hear from Him.

He continued with a story I have not been able to forget. "A rich man had a good farm that produced good crops. One day he said to himself, 'What should I do? I don't have room to store everything.

I know, I will tear down my barns and build bigger ones. Then I will have room to store all my goods. I'll sit back and say, "My friend, you have enough stored for years to come. Now, take it easy, eat, drink, and be merry." ' God said to him, 'You fool, you will die this very night. Then who will get everything you have worked so hard for?'"

Jesus concluded His story by saying, "A person is a fool to store up earthly wealth and disregard his relationship with God." He looked right at me, and I recognized that I had been greedy and self-serving. What He said was true. I decided right then and there to forget about the inheritance. I didn't want to be like the rich fool in Jesus' story. Instead, I determined to cultivate a rich relationship with God like Jesus talked about.

August 10   Luke 12:22–31

Jesus Warns Against Worry

I admit it; I am a worrier. I come across as being in control and self-assured, but underneath the surface I worry a lot. When Jesus brought the subject up by the river that day, I took notice. The thing that I was worrying about the most at the time was where this kingdom thing was going. When was He planning to announce the new kingdom to overthrow the Romans? As I was worrying about the timing of things, He looked right at me and said, "Don't worry about earthly things. Instead, make sure you have a strong relationship with God. I am telling you not to worry about everyday life, whether you have enough food to eat or clothes to wear. Life is more than food and the body more than clothes. Look at the ravens. They don't plant or harvest or store food in barns, but God feeds them. You are far more valuable than any birds." It was true. The purse I carried always had enough money for our needs and even a little extra.

He continued. "Can worry add time to your life? If worrying can't do that small thing, it can't help with the larger issues. Look at the lilies and how they grow. They don't make clothes, yet Solomon in all his glory was not dressed as beautifully as these." He pointed to some lilies close by. "If God cares so wonderfully for flowers that are here today and burned up tomorrow, He will certainly care for you. Why is your faith so weak? Don't worry about what to eat or drink. It is a waste of time. God knows your needs. Seek the kingdom first and all else will be added to you. Your needs will be met."

I wanted to ask about His plans for the kingdom, but I kept my mouth shut. Then He said, as if reading my mind, "Don't worry, little flock, it is your Father's pleasure to give you the kingdom. Sell your possessions and give the money to the poor. Store up treasure in heaven, because the purses of heaven never get old and worn. Your treasure will be safe. No moth can destroy it or thief steal it. For where your treasure is, there will the desires of your heart be also." I knew He was right, but He needed to understand how important the kingdom of Israel was to me.

August 11   *Luke 12:35–38*

Waiting for the Lord's Return

It was midday and the sun was hot. Jesus invited everyone in the crowd to take a break from sitting and listening to His words. We stood up, moving about, and restored circulation to our arms and legs. Most of the people had come prepared with a lunch. Since we disciples were all hungry, we ate our bread, cheese, and figs. Water from the river was a cool and refreshing drink. Everyone rested after the meal.

About an hour later, Jesus stood up to speak again. The people roused, refreshed and ready to listen again. "Be dressed for service, and keep your lamps burning as if you were waiting for your master to return from a wedding feast. Then you will be ready to open the door and let him in the moment he knocks. Every servant who is ready and waiting for his return will be rewarded."

I remembered the servants at home. When Dad, Andrew, and I went fishing, they were always ready with our lunch and whatever else they thought we might need as we worked. We usually fished at night, so when morning came, we tied up the boats and walked to the house. The servants were awake and ready to greet us. They always had warm herb tea and food prepared with a big fire in the fireplace. It didn't matter when we returned—three, four, or five in the morning—they were always ready. We were sure they were the best servants in all Israel.

Jesus continued, "I tell you the truth, the master will seat them, put on an apron, and serve them as they sit and eat." I thought back to one morning after a good catch that we decided to reward our servants by serving them. We came in the door, washed up, and tried to get the servants to sit and drink while we served them. However, they could not bring themselves to let us serve them, no matter what we said. So we finally let them serve us.

Jesus continued, "The master may come in the middle of the night or just before dawn, but whenever he comes, he will reward the servants who are ready."

I vowed to be the best servant I could be to my Master, the Lord. I wanted to be ready whenever He needed me.

August 12   *Luke 12:39–48*

Faithful Until Jesus Comes

As I studied the crowd, it was easy to see that everyone was caught up in what Jesus was saying. One man shouted out, "If I served my servants, they would be so shocked they would faint. I'd have to revive them to get my meal!" Everyone laughed, including Jesus.

"Think about it this way," Jesus continued. "If a homeowner knew exactly when a thief was coming, he would not permit the thief to break into his home. Likewise, you must be ready all the time for the

Son of man will come when least expected."

I wondered if this illustration was intended just for us, His disciples, or for everyone. So I asked, "Lord, is what you are saying for us or all the people?" He kept on with His sermon without answering my question.

"A faithful servant," He said, "is one to whom the master can give the responsibility of managing the other household servants and feeding them."

The reason I asked Jesus if the householder illustration was for us or all the people was to find out if perhaps He thought we were not being diligent enough in our work.

"If the master returns and finds the servant has done a good job, there will be a reward. I tell you the truth, the master will put that servant in charge of all he owns. But what if that servant begins to think, my master is away and won't be back for awhile, so he starts beating his fellow servants, partying, and getting drunk. When the master returns unexpectedly and unannounced, he will cut that servant in pieces and banish him with the unfaithful."

I remembered a servant we had once who was like that, and we had to let him go. But what did Jesus mean about the Son of man coming when least expected?

"A servant who knows what the master wants but does not carry out his instructions will be punished severely. Someone who does something wrong but does not know any better will be punished lightly. When someone has been given much, much will be required. Of someone who is entrusted with much, even more will be required."

I knew in my heart I wanted to do my best for my Lord. To be His faithful servant is my daily goal.

August 13 *Luke 12:49–53*

Jesus Warns of Division

Late that afternoon as some of the people were preparing to go home, Jesus caught everyone's attention when He suddenly cried out, "I have come to set the world on fire, and I wish it were already burning." Then He really shocked everyone, especially us disciples. "I have a terrible baptism of suffering ahead of Me, and I am under a heavy burden until it is accomplished."

His face was contorted as though He was already suffering just thinking about it. It was as though in a brief moment He had taken on a new personality—one I had not seen before. The crowd stood still. They stared at Him, not sure what was going to happen next. He raised His arm and pointed at the crowd. "Do you think I have come to bring peace to the earth?" No one moved or said a word. "No!" He shouted. "I have come to divide people against each other."

What a strange remark to make, I thought. *Usually a leader wants to unite people under one banner for one cause. Now He is telling us He has not come to unite but to divide people against each other.*

"From now on families will be split apart." He continued, "If there are five in one house, three will be in favor of Me and two against, or two in favor and three against. A father will be divided against his son and the son against his father. Mother against daughter and daughter against mother. Mother-in-law against daughter-in-law and daughter-in-law against mother-in-law."

As I thought of my own experience, I understood what Jesus meant. When I had told my father I planned to be Jesus' disciple, he had been furious. "Nathanael," he yelled, "I'm sure Jesus is a good man, maybe even a prophet, but you must finish school. Don't waste your time wandering around with some Nazarene preacher." I tried to reason with him, but he wouldn't listen. He is still very upset with me and won't speak to me when I go home. All he says is, "I lost my son to some itinerant preacher with big ideas." I don't regret making the decision to follow Jesus, but I pray often for my dad and wish things were different.

August 14   Luke 12:54–59

The Coming Crisis

Jesus' tone softened considerably, but He was still very serious as He continued to speak to the people. "When you see clouds form in the west, you say, 'Here comes a shower.'"

Working as a fisherman with my brother James, we were well acquainted with the signs by which we could predict the weather. We watched the sky carefully in order to determine how to plan our day. Clouds in the west coming from the great sea always meant rain. Sometimes you welcomed it, sometimes you didn't.

Jesus looked at us and said with a smile, "You are right. When the south wind blows in from the south over the hot desert, you say, 'Today will be a scorcher,' and it is." Then He looked out at the crowd, focusing especially on a group of religious leaders who were pointing at Him and laughing. "Fools!" He cried out at them. "You know how to interpret the weather by the signs of the earth and sky, but you don't know how to interpret the present times."

The attention of the crowd was riveted on Jesus. "And why can't you decide for yourselves what is right? When you are on your way to court with your accuser, try to settle the matter before you arrive at court. Otherwise the accuser may drag you before the judge. And the judge may hand you over to an officer who will throw you into prison. If that happens, you won't be free again until you have paid the very last penny."

After Jesus finished speaking, He headed over to join us. The people gathered up their things and left. It had been a good day. It had also been a long day, and Jesus looked tired. A few of the Pharisees remained; they seemed to be arguing among themselves. A family approached Jesus with their sick little boy and asked if He would heal their son. Immediately He lovingly touched the lad and smiled as the family left rejoicing. I wanted to ask Him about the suffering He had spoken of earlier, but I held my peace. I didn't want to think about anything happening to Him. He was as close to me as my brother James—I loved Him as a brother.

August 15   *Luke 13:1–9*

Jesus Calls the People to Repent

It happened midmorning in Jerusalem. I was standing near the temple steps when suddenly a dozen Roman soldiers appeared with their captain. They sent temple guards into the courtyard to arrest six Galilean zealots offering sacrifices. The temple guards brought them out. The captain read their crimes of treason from a document signed by Pilate. They were executed right there on the temple steps. Their bodies were then thrown on a cart and taken away. I stood in shock at what I had just witnessed. Deciding Jesus must know about this, I headed out right away. Since I had the use of a donkey, I arrived midafternoon while Jesus was speaking to the people. I whispered to Him that Pilate had just murdered some Galilleans.

"Do you think these Galileans were worse sinners than all the other people from Galilee?" Jesus asked. "Is that why they suffered?" The thought had crossed my mind, but I shrugged my shoulders to indicate I didn't know. Jesus answered His own question. "Not at all!" He said with emphasis. "What about those eighteen people who died when the tower of Siloam fell on them? Were they the worst sinners in Jerusalem? You will perish too unless you repent of your sins and turn to God."

I remembered that event. The Romans had hired some Jews to help build an aqueduct. Many people thought the falling of the tower was God's retribution upon them for helping Rome. In fact, the Pharisees were spreading that rumor around. Jesus looked out at the crowd, "I tell you again, unless you repent, you will perish too." His words burned deep into my consciousness.

Then Jesus launched into a story about a man who planted a fig tree. Even though he cared for it for three years, it produced nothing, so he told the gardener to cut it down. The gardener pleaded for one more year. "I will give it extra special care. I'll fertilize and nurture it. Then, if there is no fruit, you can cut it down," the gardener said.

I had the feeling Jesus was speaking directly to me. Just then, Simon called to me, "Judas, there is a family here who needs a few coins for food."

August 16   *Luke 13:10–17*

The Crippled Woman

I knew most everyone in Bethel since I'd lived there all my life. My late husband was a flamboyant figure, always trying something new and different. One of his ventures was the healing arts in which he would call upon the spirits of good health to heal people. I warned him against it, but he assured me it was perfectly fine. Some of his patients appeared to get well, but I did not believe it was because of his practices.

One day I lifted a large basket of grapes and injured my back. Determined to heal me with his incantations, he invoked one of the spirits of health against my will. Instead of being healed, I felt something seize up in my lower back, and I was immediately unable to stand up straight. That was eighteen years ago. You can only imagine how difficult life has been being bent over, but it helped me grow closer to God and rely on Him. Each Sabbath I attended the synagogue.

One Sabbath Jesus was in town, and He was speaking at the synagogue. At the close of the service, He approached me and said, "Dear woman, you are healed of your sickness." As soon as He laid His hand on me, whatever had bound my spine was released, and I stood up straight! When I looked in His eyes, I saw love and compassion. I was overwhelmed with joy. Tears trickled down my cheeks as I knelt and took Jesus' hands in mine. I thanked Him and praised God for His power.

The leader of the synagogue was a hardliner for obeying the Sabbath traditions, so he verbally accosted me, which was also an attack on Jesus. "There are six days in the week for work. Come on one of those days to be healed and not on the Sabbath."

Jesus stepped in and said, "You hypocrite! Each of you works on the Sabbath. Don't you untie your donkeys from the stall and lead them to water?" Then, placing His hand on my shoulder, He said, "This dear woman, a daughter of Abraham, has been held in bondage by Satan for eighteen years. Isn't it right that she should be released, even on the Sabbath?"

The synagogue leader, furious for being chastised in front of the people, stormed out with his attendants. Everyone else in the synagogue celebrated my healing and God's wonderful mercies.

August 17 *Luke 13:18-21*

About the Kingdom

No matter where we went, the religious leaders watched our every move. It seemed each time Jesus spoke there was someone in the crowd who tried to turn the people against Him. On the other hand, the people were hungry for the truth, and they gladly gathered to hear His words. The day after Jesus healed the crippled woman in the synagogue we went to the marketplace, and soon a group had formed around Jesus. "Tell us about the kingdom of God—we want to know the truth," a man stated, expressing the desire we all had.

Jesus paused a moment before speaking. "What is the kingdom of God like? How can I illustrate it?" He asked. This was His favorite topic, and I never tired of hearing Him speak about it. Stepping down from the bench on which He had been standing, Jesus walked over to a man selling a wide variety of spices and seeds. He spoke with the merchant briefly, then took a handful of mustard seed, which He brought to me. "Peter, would you and the other disciples please hand a seed to everyone."

When everyone held a seed, Jesus continued, "The kingdom is like a tiny mustard seed that a man planted in his garden. It grew and became very big, providing the birds with a place to build their nests. Take this seed home and plant it as a reminder of the kingdom." I watched the people put their seeds in safekeeping, intending to plant them.

Then Jesus asked, "What is the kingdom of God like?" Again He stepped down from the bench and walked over to the vendors. A woman was selling tiny grains of dried yeast. He spoke with her and took a handful of the yeast grains and asked us to distribute these also. Then He spoke, "The kingdom is like the yeast a woman uses in making bread. Even though she puts only a pinch of yeast in three measures of flour, it permeates the whole dough and makes many loaves of good bread." The people nodded in agreement. God had big, far-reaching plans for Israel.

August 18 *Luke 13:22–30*

Entering the Kingdom

After leaving Bethel, Jesus tried to reach as many of the towns and villages the seventy-two had worked in as possible. In almost each one the people gladly welcomed Jesus. We traveled the coastal towns of Judea and Perea. Jesus made it clear our ultimate destination was Jerusalem. In Hebron, Jesus spoke near the town square, encouraging the people to repent and be saved. Someone in the crowd asked Him, "Lord, will only a few be saved?"

He replied, "Work hard to enter the narrow door to God's kingdom, for many will try to enter but will fail." Across the street from where Jesus was speaking stood an old building with a very narrow door. It must have dated back to the time of David and the kings. An old man sat on a chair nearby. Jesus crossed the street and spoke briefly to the man, who listened then nodded. Jesus opened the narrow door but had to turn sideways to enter. The entire crowd watched His every move. Jesus spoke to the old man once again. The man smiled, nodded, and then went inside and locked the door.

The Lord turned to the crowd and spoke, "When the Master has locked the door, it will be too late. You will stand outside, pleading and knocking, 'Lord, open the door for us.'" At that moment, the old man opened a small window in the center of the door, and Jesus continued, "The Master will reply, 'I don't know you or where you came from.' Then you will say, 'But we ate and drank with You, and You taught in our streets.' And He will reply, 'I tell you I don't know you or where you came from. Get away from Me all you who do evil!' There will be great distress when you see Abraham, Isaac, Jacob, and all the prophets in the kingdom but are not allowed in the kingdom. People will come from all over the world to take their places in the kingdom of God."

Jesus thanked the man and went back to the crowd. "And note this, some who seem least important now will be the greatest then, and some who are great now will be least then."

I thought to myself, *Surely I will be among the greatest because I was Jesus' first follower.*

August 19 *Luke 13:31–35*

Jesus Grieves Over Jerusalem

Leaving Hebron, we traveled to the fortress town of Herodian. Jesus was teaching near the synagogue when some Pharisees came out of the building to listen to His words. I watched as they talked among themselves while the Lord spoke. One of them appeared to be very concerned about something.

Making his way forward, he asked to speak. Jesus acknowledged him, and the man said, "Get away from here if You want to live because Herod Antipas wants to kill You."

Jesus replied, "Go tell that fox I will keep on casting out demons and healing people today and tomorrow, and the third day I will accomplish my purpose." As He spoke, I saw a look of determination and what even seemed like defiance in His eyes. It was as though He was saying, "Let that despot of a ruler try to interfere with the work of God—it will never happen." He continued on, "Yes, today and tomorrow and the next day I must proceed on my way. It wouldn't be right for a prophet of God to be killed anywhere except in Jerusalem."

He paused and looked at the Pharisees. It almost sounded like a warning to them. The crowd watched the Pharisee who had spoken, expecting him to respond to what Jesus had said. Instead, he turned and walked back to the others without a word. Then Jesus turned to the crowd and cried out, "O Jerusalem, Jerusalem, the city that kills the prophets and stones God's messengers!" Tears flowed down His cheeks as He continued to speak, "How often I have wanted to gather your children as a hen protects her chicks beneath her wings."

The Pharisees and synagogue leader turned their backs and strode purposely toward the building. Jesus raised his voice. It almost seemed as if His words were directed chiefly at them. "But you would not let Me!" He shouted. "Now look, your house is abandoned, and you will never see Me again until you say, 'Blessings on the one who comes in the name of the Lord.'" They had reached the door, stepped inside, and closed the door.

What does He mean? I wondered.

August 20   Luke 14:1- 6

Healing the Man With Swollen Limbs

I'm a second cousin to one of the most influential Pharisees in Bethlehem, actually, in most of Judea. When Jesus arrived in town on the day of preparation, my cousin decided to have a feast. He planned to host a dinner after the synagogue services on Sabbath, so he wrote up a guest list of relatives, friends, and visitors with the object of making an impression.

I have a disability affecting my limbs. My arms and legs swell, causing severe pain and making it impossible for me to work. My cousin takes care of me, but at the same time he lets me know that I am indebted to him for his kindness, and he freely uses me as an example of his generosity. I think he really has a good heart, but he desperately wants to look good in front of the other Pharisees.

The guests were invited, the meal prepared, and Sabbath came. Jesus was invited to speak at the synagogue that Sabbath. He focused mainly on God's love for His people. I was blessed and encouraged. After the service, the guests, including Jesus, made their way to my cousin's home where they waited for the host to arrive. When my cousin entered with the ruler of the synagogue and some experts in Jewish law, Jesus asked a question, "Is it permitted in the law to heal people on the Sabbath day or not?" No one spoke. No one had ever been healed in our town on the Sabbath before. My cousin, a stickler for Jewish tradition, hung his head while the experts in law talked quietly with each other.

While everyone was talking, Jesus came over to me, smiled, reached out His hand, and touched me. Instantly, I felt something happen inside my body that I cannot explain. My arms and legs were no longer swollen, and the pain was gone. I felt wonderful! I was overwhelmed! "Thank You, Lord!" was all I could say, again and again.

"You can go if you like," He said. It was like being set free. As I started walking away, I heard Him ask the Pharisees and other guests, "If your son or a cow falls into a pit, don't you rush out to rescue him?" Everyone was silent.

I smiled, walking, running, skipping with excitement. I was free to live my own life now, and it would be as a follower of Jesus.

August 21 *Luke 14:7–14*

Jesus Teaches Humility

We stood in awe as the healed man left, praising God. Finally, the host moved to seat himself, and the guests rushed to sit in the most prestigious seats. Jesus didn't move, and we took our cue from Him. Pushing and arguing erupted as guests tried to sit as close to the host as possible. We watched until everyone was seated. Now only places at the foot of the table remained. The other guests looked at us, puzzled. Why had we not clamored for the best seats, too? Jesus took the very lowest place at the foot of the table, facing the host, and we sat around Him.

Jesus seized upon the opportunity to instruct them in the ways of His Father, saying, "When you are invited to a wedding feast, don't sit in the seat of honor. What if someone more distinguished than you has also been invited?" Some of the guests hung their heads, knowing that Jesus should be seated beside the host. "The person in charge will come to you and say, 'Give your seat to this person more distinguished than you.' Then you will be embarrassed and have to take whatever seat is left at the foot of the table. Instead, take the lowest seat at the foot of the table. Then when your host sees you, he will come and say, 'Friend, we have a better place for you,' and you will be honored in front of all the other guests. Those who exalt themselves will be humbled, and those who humble themselves will be exalted."

Our host was not a hard man like the Pharisees we had encountered in Jerusalem. I could tell Jesus' words made an impression on him. He stood, made his way to the foot of the table, and seated himself beside Jesus, thus making the Lord the most important person. I saw him lean near Jesus and say, "Lord, please forgive me for being so rude." Jesus smiled at him.

As the servants brought the food, I heard the Lord encourage our host not to invite just friends and neighbors but to invite the poor, crippled, lame, and blind because in the resurrection of the righteous God would reward him for inviting those who could not repay with their own invitation. Our host wasn't the only one to take Jesus' message to heart; I too learned from His words.

August 22   *Luke 14:14–24*

Parable of the Great Feast

Jesus' words really touched my heart. When the host stood up and seated himself beside the Lord, placing the rest of us in the lesser seats at the table, I began to feel ashamed. *What must God think of our behavior*, I wondered, *acting like children scrambling for the biggest and best?* I tried to imagine what it would be like in the kingdom, with God right there in our midst. "What a blessing it will be to attend a banquet in the kingdom of God!" I burst out loudly.

Conversations stopped as everyone looked at me. I didn't like being the center of attention, but thankfully, Jesus stood up and spoke, taking the spotlight off me. He told a story about a man who prepared a great banquet, sending out invitations to friends and neighbors asking them to come. When the feast was ready, he sent his servants to tell the invited guests to come. But everyone had an excuse for not being able to attend. One had just been married, one needed to try out a new pair of oxen, one wanted to inspect a field he had just purchased. So they all begged to be excused. When the servants returned and reported to the master of the banquet what the guests had said, he was furious. "Go into the alleys and back streets. Invite everyone you see—the poor, the blind, the lame." His servants did what he requested. When the master saw there were still empty chairs, he sent the servants out again to look for more people. "Go into the country and check the hedges where the poor people are huddled. Urge them all to come, everyone and anyone who is willing," he cried. "I want my house to be filled with people, even the ones no one else wants to associate with. Those people who received the invitation and made excuses will never taste a morsel of my banquet."

After the story, Jesus sat down. We all looked at each other in shocked silence. If this was a story about the kingdom, how could God invite just anyone to come in? Even those suffering the displeasure of God with some disease? I thought the kingdom was just for us Jews, the chosen people, but Jesus made it sound as though the kingdom was for everyone, no matter who they were.

August 23   *Luke 14:25–30*

Cost of Discipleship (Part 1)

A large crowd had gathered outside the Pharisee's home, all of them waiting to see Jesus. After dinner, we thanked our host for a wonderful meal and made our way toward the center of town. Some people from Bethlehem came to Jesus and asked to become disciples. Jesus stopped, turned, and faced the crowd, saying, "If you want to become My disciple, you may come into conflict with everyone else. You may have to stand against father, mother, wife and children, and brothers and sisters. Yes, in fact, you may even lose your own life. Unless you are prepared to face these issues, you cannot be My disciple. What it comes down to is this: if you are not willing to carry your own cross and follow Me, you cannot be My disciple."

Most of the people knew how controversial a figure Jesus had become. It wasn't uncommon for families to be divided because of Him. I am glad Jesus warned the people about the cost of discipleship. I knew firsthand how divisive being a follower of Christ could be. The last time I had been at home, my dad told me he had disowned me and that I was no longer his son. I had feared this would happen, but I knew I was doing the right thing.

"Whatever you do," Jesus said, "sit down and count the cost of discipleship before you decide. Who would ever begin construction on a building without calculating the cost to make sure there would be enough money to finish it. Otherwise, all you might complete is the foundation before running out of money and then everyone would laugh at you."

I remembered back to when my brother decided to build a fishing boat. He spent all his money on the hull and couldn't afford a mast or sail. We had to row everywhere we went. Needless to say, I was not impressed. We were the laughing stock of the fishing grounds.

Jesus continued, "People would say, 'There is the person who started a building and couldn't finish it.'"

My brother and I had spent hours discussing becoming full-time disciples. How would we support our families? What if He wasn't the Messiah? I'm convinced we made the right decision.

August 24 *Luke 14:31–35*

Cost of Discipleship (Part 2)

I didn't want to be in the Roman army or even be a soldier at all. I wanted to be home with my family. Augustus required that all young men of a certain age be conscripted, and unfortunately that included me. I would rather be in Palestine than fighting some battle in North Africa or quelling riots in the North. Before being assigned to Bethlehem, I was stationed in Jerusalem, where I encountered a young Jewish rabbi named Jesus. What He said impressed me.

I heard He was in Bethlehem, so I searched Him out. I didn't understand what He meant by taking up one's cross and following Him. Who would want to carry a cross, and why was this a requirement for discipleship? I listened as He told about a king going off to war.

"What king would go off to war," Jesus said, "without first sitting down with his counselors to discuss whether his army of ten thousand could defeat the twenty thousand soldiers marching against him."

I thought about the stories old timers told of foolish generals who led their armies into death traps simply because they had not taken the time to calculate the odds and take factors such as timing, surprise, terrain, weather, armor, etc. into consideration. It came down to poor leadership.

Jesus continued, "If he decides he cannot win the battle, he will send a delegation while the opponent's army is far away and try to arrange for a peaceful settlement." I understood the part about the builder and the king, but then He said, "You cannot become my disciple unless you give up everything for Me."

Endure suffering, give up my worldly possessions, all for discipleship? Is that what He expects?

Then He looked right at me as though reading my mind. "Salt is good for seasoning, but if it loses its flavor, how do you make it salty? It isn't good for the soil or the manure pile; it has to be thrown away. Everyone with ears should hear and understand."

I would rather be His disciple than a soldier, but the cost is so great. Yet I do not want to become flavorless salt. There are no other military men in His group of disciples. I just don't know what to do.

August 25   Luke 15:1–7

Parable of the Lost Sheep

In the morning we left Bethlehem to travel east toward Jamnia. A large crowd followed us to the edge of town. While in Bethlehem I had become acquainted with some of the city tax collectors. They wanted to know how I, a tax collector, had become a disciple of Jesus. I told them what I told everyone who asked that question, "He invited me to come and follow Him. He wants you to follow Him, too." I introduced Jesus to my new friends. He smiled and greeted them warmly.

Off to the left we heard a group of Pharisees from Jerusalem complaining bitterly. "How can a teacher of the people show acceptance toward tax collectors whom God has rejected. He even has one for a disciple, and He has dined in their homes!"

Several shepherds who had been watching their sheep on a nearby hillside came to see why there was a crowd. One was holding a lamb. There was a rise where the shepherd stood by the road, so Jesus went to him and asked to hold the lamb. "Let me tell you a story," He announced. "If a man has a hundred sheep and one goes missing, what will he do?" He turned toward the shepherds.

"We would leave the ninety-nine in the wilderness and search for the one lost sheep," they replied.

"I would search for it until I found it," said the shepherd who owned the lamb. Jesus handed the lamb back to him.

Everyone was listening, even the Pharisees from Jerusalem. Jesus turned to the crowd and said, "And when he has found it, he will joyfully carry it home on his shoulders. And then he will call his friends and neighbors to celebrate with him. 'Come,' he'll say. 'Let's have a party! My sheep was lost, but I have found it.'" The shepherds smiled and nodded in agreement.

Then Jesus came to me, put His arm around me and said. "In the same way, there is more joy in heaven over one lost sinner who repents and returns to God than over ninety-nine righteous people who have not strayed away."

Tears trickled down my cheeks as I stood there, remembering how good and kind and patient and forgiving Jesus had been to me. If ever there had been a lost lamb, it was me. I thank God He found me.

August 26   *Luke 15:8–10*

Parable of the Lost Coins

I thought my world would end when my husband handed me a certificate of divorce. "Why?" I cried. He said he'd fallen out of love with me. I could not believe what he was telling me. "Have you found another woman?" I asked. "Perhaps," was all he would say. I was utterly devastated. Never in my life could I have imagined after thirty years of marriage and three children, he would just walk out on me. I tried to reason with him, but his mind was made up. He told me while he packed his things that I could have the house and that he was moving far away and I would probably never see him again. With that, he left. I wept for days. My children tried to console me, but I was convinced I was a terrible person and an even worse wife. I felt so lost and alone. I prayed for God to take my life. But as time passed, I slowly began to heal.

This morning my son invited me to come with him to hear Jesus. I had heard Him speak near the temple at one of the festivals a few years before. At the time, I was still very distraught and could not concentrate on anything. I could relate to the story of the lost sheep. I felt like the lamb Jesus held in His arms. I still wore my wedding coins that every Palestinian woman received as a wedding gift.

At that moment Jesus looked at me. Then He approached me and asked if I would come with Him. I followed Him to the front of the crowd. "Suppose a woman has ten silver coins," He said, pointing to mine, "but then loses one." He put His arm around my shoulder. I felt safe and comforted. "Won't she light a lamp and sweep the entire house until she finds it?" He asked. "And when she finds it, won't she call her neighbors and friends to celebrate, saying, 'Rejoice with me because I have found my lost coin.'" Everyone in the crowd nodded, knowing how important those coins were. "Likewise," Jesus continued, "in the same way, there is joy in the presence of God and the angels over one sinner who repents." Jesus squeezed my shoulder as though He knew my pain. I smiled for the first time in four years. God still loved me. I was the cast off coin that now was found.

August 27   *Luke 15:11–32*

Parable of the Lost Son

We religious leaders stood off to the side away from the rabble. I listened halfheartedly while He spoke, but my ears perked up when He began telling a story about two sons of an elderly father who were different as day and night. The story could have easily been about my boys. Evidently, the younger of the two, a rebel at heart, asked for his share of the estate even before the old man died. If my kid did that to me, I'd give him a thrashing, but this dad agreed to divide the wealth. The boy packed up his stuff and moved to a distant city, blowing all his money on wild living. Just as his money ran out, a famine came to the land, and he found himself starving.

Serves him right, I thought.

Jesus continued speaking. A local farmer gave him a job feeding pigs. He was so hungry he was ready to eat pig food, but no one gave him permission. One day, surrounded by the pigs, he came to his senses. "Even the servants at Dad's house have plenty to eat while I am dying of hunger. I'll go home and say to my dad, 'I have sinned against you and heaven. Please make me a servant. I am not worthy to be called your son.'" The father saw him coming home and ran to meet him. He embraced him and ordered the servants to get a robe, ring, and sandals for him. "Kill the calf we have been fattening for a celebration. My son who was dead is alive! The boy who was lost has been found!" Friends and neighbors were invited, and the party began.

Tears filled my eyes as I thought about the love of the father. According to Jesus' story, the older son came from the fields and asked a servant, "Why the feast?" The servant told him that his younger brother had come home and they were celebrating his return. The older brother was furious and refused to go in even though his dad begged him.

"All these years I have been faithful. When did you give me a party? Yet, this son of yours squanders his money and you welcome him with a feast."

The father said, "Son, all I have is yours, but we had to celebrate this day because your brother whom we thought was dead is alive." Jesus stopped talking.

We waited. *Did the brother go in to the feast?* I wondered. I couldn't get the story out of my mind. Years later I realized He was waiting for me to finish it by my acceptance of others.

August 28   Luke 16:1–9

The Shrewd Manager (Part 1)

It was too late in the afternoon to travel after Jesus finished speaking with the people, so we returned to Bethlehem to stay in the inn where Jesus had been born. He and His parents had traveled to Bethlehem to visit when He was young and had stayed in the inn. It had changed owners, but it looked pretty much the same. In the stable we saw the stone feeding trough and the stalls where animals were still kept.

Early the next morning we made our way out of the city. It took us all day to get to the coastal port town where we were headed, but it was a beautiful day, so we enjoyed the walk. We took lodging in a place close to the water. After breakfast we found the marketplace where people gathered. Jesus started the day by telling us a story. A few people stopped to listen. "There was a rich man who hired a manager to handle his affairs."

More people joined the group. "He heard one day that the manager was wasting his money so he called him in and asked him, 'What is this I hear about you? Make me a final report because I am going to fire you.'"

The crowd grew larger; everyone loved a story. Jesus continued, "The manager thought, 'Now what? My boss has fired me. I can't dig ditches, and I am too proud to beg.' The solution, he reasoned, was to make a lot of friends who would care for him when he was unemployed. So he called in all the debtors and reduced what they owed to a manageable sum. For example, one man owed 800 gallons of olive oil, so the manager reduced it to 400. Another man owed a thousand bushels of wheat, so the manager reduced the debt to 800 bushels. When the rich man found out what the manager had done, he had to admire the rascal for being so shrewd. The children of the world seem wiser than the children of light. Here is the lesson," Jesus said, "Use your worldly resources to benefit others and make friends. Then, when your earthly resources are gone, you will be welcomed into an eternal home."

What can I do? I wondered. *I am just a penniless former tax collector-turned-disciple with no resources.* Then I thought of all my publican friends who had money. They could give to the poor, and my job would be to convince them.

August 29   Luke 16:10–18

The Shrewd Manager (Part 2)

By the time Jesus finished with the story of the manager, a large crowd had gathered. People brought sick loved ones, mothers came with children to be blessed, and, of course, there was the ever present religious establishment. After a brief intermission, Jesus continued to teach. "If you are faithful in small things, you will be faithful in bigger ones. If you are dishonest in little things, you will not be honest in larger responsibilities. And if you are untrustworthy about worldly wealth, who will trust you with the true riches of heaven?"

He looked at me and paused. I wondered if He knew I had been helping myself to the purse. The pause seemed awfully long to me, and I felt uncomfortable under His searching gaze. Finally He spoke, "If you are not faithful with other people's things, why should you be trusted with things of your own?" Again He looked at me, and said, "No one can serve two masters, for you will hate one and love the other; you will be devoted to one and despise the other." Another look my direction and His next words convinced me that He knew of my deception. "You cannot serve both God and money."

He might as well have shouted out my name. A group of Pharisees were close to me. They loved their money and began to scoff. He stepped down from the bench and walked toward us. Addressing the Pharisees, He said, "You like to appear righteous in public, but God knows your hearts." He looked at me again. I noticed Him wiping tears from His eye as He said, "What the world honors is detestable in the sight of God." I hung my head.

He walked back to the front of the crowd. "The law of Moses was your guide until John the Baptist came and began proclaiming the good news about God's kingdom, and now everyone is eager to get into the kingdom, but the law hasn't lost its force. It is easier for heaven and earth to disappear than the smallest point in God's law to be overturned. Like the adultery commandment. A man who divorces his wife and marries another woman commits adultery, and anyone who marries a woman divorced from her husband commits adultery."

I heard people murmuring against Him because divorce was common. I felt like He was just picking on everyone, including me for how I was handling our money.

August 30 *Luke 16:19–31*

The Rich Man and the Beggar

The people in and around Jamnia did not want Jesus to leave. One by one we visited the towns the seventy-two had worked in. They had prepared the way for Jesus to be welcomed. We traveled south to Raphia and then worked our way north on the Great Trunk Road passing through Gaza, Ashkelon, Azotus, Joppa, and Antipatris, and finally up to Capernaum to spend time with our families. Before leaving Jamnia, Jesus had told a story about a rich man and a poor beggar named Lazarus. The rich man dressed in purple (only the very rich could afford garments dyed in purple) and fine linens and lived each day in luxury.

At his gate lay a poor diseased beggar covered with sores. As he lay there, he longed for scraps from the rich man's table. The dogs would come and lick his open sores. Finally, the poor man died and was carried by angels to be with Abraham. The rich man also died, and his soul was taken to the place of the dead. From there he saw poor Lazarus with Abraham in the far distance. Suffering and in great torment, he called to Abraham to have pity. "Send Lazarus here to dip his finger in water to cool my tongue. I'm in anguish here in these flames." Abraham said, "Son, in your lifetime you had everything you wanted. Lazarus had nothing. Now the tables are turned with you in anguish and Lazarus being comforted. Besides, there is a great chasm separating us, and we cannot reach each other."

The rich man begged Abraham to send Lazarus to his father's home to warn his five brothers not to end up where he was. Abraham replied, "Moses and the prophets warned them. Your brothers can read what they wrote." The rich man replied, "No, father Abraham, if someone is sent to them from the dead, they will listen, repent, and turn to God." Abraham said, "If they won't listen to Moses and the prophets, they will not listen to someone from the dead."

The Pharisees had been furious because they knew the story was about them. Jesus called to me, "Peter, gather the others. We are leaving." Within the hour, we were on our way to the coastal cities in the south. I realized there would be no place in the kingdom for the Pharisees if they refused to listen.

August 31 *Luke 17:1–10*

Forgiveness, Faith, and Service

There was time to relax with family and friends in between visiting small villages around the lake with Jesus. One night at Peter's home after only a few weeks in Capernaum, He told us it was time to go back to Jerusalem. Knowing how much the Pharisees wanted to kill Him, I said anxiously, "Lord, it is dangerous to go there."

He simply replied, "It is God's plan." Then, changing the subject, He said, "There will always be temptations to sin, but what sorrow awaits those who do the tempting. It would be better to have a millstone tied around your neck and be thrown into the sea than be guilty of causing one of these little ones to fall into sin. So watch yourselves!" He gestured to Peter's grandkids and their friends.

He continued, "If someone sins, rebuke that person. If he repents, forgive. Even if that person wrongs you seven times in one day, and each time repents and asks forgiveness, you must forgive."

I couldn't believe what I was hearing—seven times in a day! I said impulsively, "Lord, show us how to increase our faith!"

"If you had faith the size of a mustard seed, you could say to this mulberry tree," He said, pointing to the tree outside the window, "be uprooted and thrown into the sea, and it would obey you." I wanted my faith to grow like that. "When a servant comes from the field after plowing or sheep shearing, does the master say, 'Come eat with me?' No, he says, 'Prepare my meal. Put on your apron and serve me while I eat, then you can eat later.' Does the master thank the servant for doing what he was told to do? Of course not. In the same way, when you obey Me you should say, 'We are simply doing our duty.'"

For a long time I pondered what Jesus said about how serving the Lord is a privilege, not something required of us. I realized we didn't appreciate the opportunity given us to spend each day with Him.

A few days later we headed south toward Samaria. John, my brother, started complaining about the Samaritans, recounting their earlier rebuff of Jesus. I turned to him and reminded him it was our privilege to be with Jesus no matter where He led us.

September 1   *Luke 17:11*

Ten Lepers

People expected lepers to be invisible. Out of sight, out of mind. We, the afflicted, tried to avoid civilization except when we needed to beg for food and money. Eking out an existence, we waited until the disease would end our miserable lives. For us, there were no racial, cultural, or other distinctions. We were all the same—lepers.

Begging beside the road near the Galilean/Samaritan border, my friends and I heard a rumor that Jesus was going to pass our way. We had heard other lepers had been healed by Him, so we decided to ask Him for healing. What did we have to lose? All He could say was no. We stood at the outskirts of a small village asking people for help. So as not to frighten them, we stood back a distance from our dirty baskets. Someone put a loaf of bread in mine just as we heard a shout, "Jesus is coming!"

We saw Him and His companions headed our direction. We shouted, "Jesus, Master, have mercy on us!"

Without hesitation, He called back, "Go show yourselves to the priests."

It took us a minute to realize that His response could mean only one thing—healing! As we turned toward the road that led to Jerusalem, suddenly the miraculous happened. I felt something permeate my body with sudden, vibrant, healing virtue. The other men felt it too. We looked at each other, clean and leperless, hardly able to believe the miracle. We jumped and shouted, praising God as we comprehended our good fortune.

Half a mile down the road, I stopped still. None of us had thanked Jesus! I ran back, feeling even more gratitude when I considered that we Samaritans were usually treated with contempt by the Jews. Falling at His feet, I shouted, "Praise God!" Looked up into His face, I thanked Him for healing me.

Jesus turned to those with Him and asked, "Didn't I heal ten lepers? Where are the other nine? Has no one returned to give God glory but this foreigner?" Then Jesus took my arm and said, "Stand up, and go your way because your faith has healed you." With a big smile, He thanked me for coming back.

September 2 *John 11:1-6*

Lazarus (Part 1)

We continued on through Samaria, visiting some of the small villages we had missed before. The people joyfully welcomed us. The healed lepers had been like trumpeters announcing our arrival. They told everyone they met what Jesus had done for them. Most of the time Jesus had warned healed people to remain quiet, but He hadn't given that injunction recently.

Near Ephraim a messenger found us and went straight to Jesus. He knelt in front of the Lord and cried out, "Lord, Mary and Martha, the sisters of Lazarus, sent me to find You because Your dear friend is dying and needs Your help. I saw him myself, and he is very ill."

I expected Jesus to excuse Himself and immediately follow the messenger to Bethany, but instead He turned to the crowd and said, "Lazarus' sickness will not end in death. No, this happened for the glory of God so that the Son of Man will receive glory from this." Jesus turned to the messenger and sent him back to Bethany with the message, "Lazarus' sickness will not end in death."

Then He went back to His conversation as if nothing was wrong. I was confused. Jesus' best friend was dying, but the Lord said he wouldn't die. And how strange that his illness came to him so God could be honored. Finding my brother John, I asked him if he knew why Jesus had not gone with the messenger. He felt as bewildered as I. We stayed in that village for two more days while Jesus continued to teach the people and minister to their needs, apparently oblivious to the urgent request of the friends He loved.

It was a mystery to all of us. We talked about it whenever He wasn't near. Why? I expected the messenger to return with the news that Lazarus was dead. Why did Jesus seem so indifferent? On other occasions when people needed immediate attention, Jesus left whatever He was doing and hurried to help them, but here, He was leaving His good friend to languish and suffer. I just didn't get it. When I finally asked Him why He didn't go, He simply said, "I am doing God's will. Lazarus will be okay."

September 3   John 11:7-16

Lazarus (Part 2)

On the morning of the third day after the messenger had delivered his message about Lazarus, Jesus said to us, "Let's go back to Judea." He didn't say anything about going to Lazarus, just Judea, which implied Jerusalem. There was so much hostility toward Him there that I objected, "Rabbi, the last time we were in Judea the people tried to stone You, and now You want to go back there?" I was beginning to question His mental integrity. There was the weird way He had dealt with Lazarus being sick and now talking about going back to Judea. *What is He thinking?* I wondered. *Maybe He's under too much stress and is burning out.*

Jesus spoke, "There are twelve hours of daylight every day. During the day people can walk safely. They can see because they have the light of this world. But at night there is danger of stumbling because they have no light. Our friend Lazarus has fallen asleep, but now I will go and wake him up."

"Lord, if he is sleeping, he will get better. Let's avoid Judea, let him rest and get well."

He looked at us and said, "Lazarus is dead."

Dead? He had told the messenger to tell Mary and Martha that Lazarus was not going to die. I knew Jesus had the power to raise Lazarus because He had raised other people back to life, but why didn't He tell us Lazarus was going to die right from the start or that He was going to let him die and raise him up?

He asked us to come close, and He spoke softly, "And for your sakes, I am glad I was not there, for now you will really believe. Let us go to him."

The last two days we had talked among ourselves as to our concerns regarding Jesus' behavior. Now Philip leaned over to me and whispered, "Thomas, what did Jesus mean about walking in the light and dark?"

There were so many confusing thoughts running though my head. Releasing a long sigh, I said to the others. "Well, let's go too, and die with Him."

Going back to Judea seemed crazy, but in our hearts we knew that wherever He led us we would never turn our backs on Him.

September 4   John 11:17-27

Lazarus (Part 3)

When the messenger returned with the good news our brother would not die, we were ecstatic. Both Mary and I rushed to his bedside and told Lazarus that Jesus said he would not die. He offered a faint smile and answered, "I feel like I'm dying." Those were the last words He uttered.

Later that evening he slipped into unconsciousness and died about midnight. We were devastated.

"How could this be?" we asked each other. "Jesus promised he would not die."

I felt all kinds of emotions. I had to admit I even felt angry that Jesus hadn't come and healed our dear brother. And yet, I knew He loved Lazarus and had to believe He knew what He was doing. He wouldn't make a promise and break it.

Lazarus was prepared for burial and placed in the tomb the next day. We wept—our hearts were broken. Many people came to console us. Four days after our brother had been buried, I heard that Jesus had finally arrived. I hurried out of Bethany to meet Him.

The first words out of my mouth were, "Lord, if only You had been here my brother would not have died." Tears ran down my face. The words had come with indignation and reprimand. What I really meant was, "Why did You break Your promise and let my brother die?" But when I saw the compassion in His eyes, I knew He felt and understood my pain. He reached out and took my hand, squeezing it gently. I softened and said, "But even now I know God will give You whatever You ask."

Jesus looked at me and said, "Your brother will rise again."

"Yes," I answered, "he will rise when everyone else does at the last day."

He replied gently, "I am the resurrection and the life. Anyone who believes in Me will live though they may die. Do you believe this, Martha?"

"Yes, Lord," I replied, "I have always believed You are the Messiah, the Son of God, who has come into the world from God." I felt much better after talking with Him. There was such peace and comfort in His presence. He asked to see Mary. I told Him I would call her. I headed back into town with a hope in my heart that I would see my brother again before the last day.

September 5   **John 11:28-37**

Lazarus (Part 4)

I had been so deep in my own grief I hadn't even noticed that Martha had been gone until she came and whispered in my ear that Jesus was nearby and wanted to see me. I jumped to my feet and hurried with Martha to where He was waiting just outside Bethany. The spot was close to where we had buried Lazarus. The mourners in the house followed me, thinking I was going to the tomb to weep.

When I saw Jesus, I fell at His feet and sobbed. "Lord," I wept, "if only You had been here my brother would not have died." I looked up at Him through my tears and saw that He was deeply troubled. He looked at me with great compassion. Then His eyes went to the mourners who had followed me. A look of anger or frustration seemed to creep over Him as He listened to the loud wailing. "Where have you put him?" He asked bluntly.

I said to Him, "Lord, come and see." The whole group followed us as we walked to the tomb. Suddenly, Jesus burst into tears. Putting His hands up to His face, He let the tears flow. I put my hand on His shoulder and wept with Him. Someone said, "See how much He loved His friend, Lazarus." I couldn't help but wonder, *If He loved my brother so much, why didn't He come and heal Lazarus when we called for Him? And why did He tell the messenger that Lazarus would not die?* There were so many unanswered questions and so many emotions—sorrow, anger, hurt, pain, frustration—going around inside me. I wished Jesus and I could have gone somewhere at that moment so I could sit at His feet like so many times before. I knew He could answer my questions and calm my emotions. I heard a man say, "This man Jesus healed a blind man. Couldn't He have kept Lazarus from dying?"

We were all like that blind man, unable to see the Messiah for who He is. Later, I realized the resurrection and life was standing right there with us, and no one seemed to recognize that He had the power to raise my brother to life. We were so caught up in our own grief.

September 6   John 11:38–44

Jesus Raises Lazarus

The last memory I had was of feeling so horrible that I was sure I was dying. Now I was alive! After all of the excitement died down, Mary and Martha told me the whole story.

Mary confirmed that they had wrapped my body in burial cloth and laid me in the tomb where they expected me to remain until the resurrection. Jesus appeared agitated as He stood before the tomb; some even thought He was angry.

Martha said He stood there for some time, waiting until the people quieted down and the mourners stopped their wailing. Then He commanded the stone be rolled away. Martha protested. "Lord, Lazarus has been dead four days. The smell will be terrible."

Looking at her patiently, He said kindly, "Didn't I tell you that you would see God's glory if you only believed?" She said she suddenly remembered the hopeful feeling she had felt after her conversation with Jesus earlier.

Four of the disciples rolled the stone away from the tomb entrance. Then Jesus looked up to heaven and said, "Father, thank You for hearing Me. You always hear Me, but for the sake of all the people standing here, I will say it out loud so they will hear and believe that You sent Me." Then Jesus paused, looked at the tomb entrance and shouted, "Lazarus, come out!"

At the sound of Jesus' voice, I became fully conscious. I remember lying there in the dark trying to figure out why I was wrapped in cloth so tight that I could barely move. I scooted off the cold stone slab I was lying on. I then managed to loosen a few of the cloths that bound me. At that moment I realized where I was and that the illness must have taken my life. *It must be the last day*, I concluded. *The resurrection! I can see my parents and other family again!*

I walked awkwardly, still partially bound, to the door of the tomb. There were my sisters and Jesus and a host of shocked people staring at me. Jesus told them to unwrap me. My sisters ran and embraced me. What a reunion! It was then I found out it was not the last day, but it was wonderful to be alive and well. I made my way to Jesus, fell on my knees and thanked Him for restoring my life.

September 7 — John 11:45–52

Council Decides That Jesus Must Die

Lazarus and his sisters were very good friends of mine, and I felt such loss at his death. I also felt distress for his sisters, having to make it in life without their brother. But then, an amazing turn of events! Jesus raised Lazarus from the dead! The people who witnessed the event were overwhelmed, myself included. It was truly a miracle only God could have done.

As you can imagine, the news spread like wildfire! Nothing could have given Jesus more public exposure than this. In retrospect, I could see that Lazarus' resurrection was part of a plan to bring Jesus' name before the thousands attending the Passover in Jerusalem. When I came into the city, I was notified that a council meeting of the Sanhedrin had been called. When I arrived, I was told they had a quorum and to go home. I found out later both Joseph of Arimathea and I had been banned. They purposely excluded anyone who was sympathetic toward Jesus.

Apparently, some people who witnessed the resurrection went directly to the leaders and reported what Jesus had done. Hence the reason for the meeting. After the meeting someone came and told me what went on. The main question that was posed to the group was "What are we going to do with this man who performs so many miracles?"

"If we allow Him to continue," someone said, "everyone will believe in Him."

"Then the Romans will destroy our temple and our nation."

Apparently at this point, Caiaphas, the high priest that year, stood up and said, "How can you be so stupid? Why should the whole nation be destroyed? Let this one man die for the people."

That comment threw the council into quite a discussion about what the people might do if anything happened to Jesus. Considering the events that took place a short time later on Golgotha, it was plain to see that Caiaphas did not utter those prophetic words of his own volition. He prophesied not only for Israel but for all the children of God scattered around the world.

When I was told these things, I thanked God that He is in charge of the affairs of men and His will prevails. Even, greater than that, I thank God for Jesus and that the world might be saved through Him.

September 8 — John 11:53–57

Withdrawal to Ephraim

The situation went from bad to worse. After the meeting of the high council, the religious leaders publicly ordered that anyone who saw Jesus must report to them immediately so they could arrest Him. Both Joseph and I continued to be excluded from meetings held by the Sanhedrin because they knew we would stand up on His behalf. However, we had a few friends who reported to us what transpired in those meetings. The most distressing news was that the council was plotting Jesus' death. Joseph and

I made sure Jesus was aware of these reports. As a result, Jesus and the disciples went to a place not far away, a small village called Ephraim. This, of course, ended His public ministry in Jerusalem.

As the pilgrims poured into the city in preparation for the Passover, people kept asking about Jesus, wondering if He would come. There were pilgrims from all over the country and many from distant places. I made my way to the temple and found a large crowd standing near the steps discussing the order the priests had made regarding the arrest of Jesus. They questioned what crime He had committed and why they wanted to arrest Him. It didn't make any sense to them. A few of the local people with whom I was acquainted asked if I knew where Jesus was and if He was planning to attend the Passover in spite of the decree from the Sanhedrin. I told them I could not give them any answers as to where He was or if He would attend.

Many of the people gathered at the temple had heard that Jesus would be there. They had come, some from a great distance, with their sick loved ones who were in need of healing. Mothers were there because they simply wanted Him to bless their children. As I turned to leave, I heard a man comment, "This is wrong. We have a right to know why Jesus is being arrested."

I felt the same anger and frustration they did. *How can a man be charged and arrested for no crime?* I wondered. I prayed God would bring about justice and that He would care for my Friend.

September 9 *Luke 17:20–25*

The Pharisees Question Jesus About the Kingdom

The Passover was drawing near, and more people than usual crowded the streets of Jerusalem in hopes of seeing Jesus. When they heard an order had been given to arrest Jesus, many were furious. There was an outcry that the order be lifted in light of the fact that the Pharisees had no official charge against Him. They had no choice but to rescind the order.

The next day Nicodemus sent a messenger to tell us the arrest order had been lifted and that we could safely return to Jerusalem. That very day we journeyed to the city. As we traveled we were confronted by a group of Pharisees. "When will this kingdom You talk about come?" they demanded.

Jesus replied, "The kingdom of God cannot be detected by visible signs. You won't be able to say, 'here it is' or 'there it is' because it is already among you." I thought the kingdom was our nation, the future glory of Israel. When Jesus saw the look of surprise on our faces, He turned to us, His disciples, and said, "The day is coming when you will long to see the day when the Son of man returns, but you won't see it. The people will say, 'Look, there is the Son of man' or 'here He is,' but don't go out and follow them. For as the lightning flashes and lights up the sky from one end to the other, so it will be when the Son of man comes again."

He paused as if deep in thought. "But first the Son of man must suffer terribly and be rejected by this generation," He said as He turned and looked at the Pharisees who were daily plotting His death.

I knew about false christs and false prophets who were everywhere, but what did He mean by this suffering and rejection? The people seemed to love Him. The Pharisees had to rescind their arrest order because the people demanded it. Would the Romans cause Him to suffer? What did He mean by the sky lighting up when He returns? I had so many questions. When and where did the nation of Israel fit into all of this? Our spiritual leaders had promised us the Messiah would restore Israel. It seemed like everything Jesus said and did was contrary to our dreams of national greatness.

September 10 *Luke 17:26–37*

The Kingdom of God

I asked Peter for answers, but he seemed as perplexed as I. Jesus was talking about a kingdom that we had never imagined. He continued, "When the Son of man returns, it will be like it was in the days of Noah. In those days people enjoyed banquets and parties and weddings right up to the time Noah entered the ark and the flood came and destroyed them all. In the same way, the world will be just like it was during the time of Lot. People went about their daily business, eating and drinking, buying and selling, farming and building, until the very morning Lot left Sodom. Suddenly fire and burning sulfur rained out of the sky from heaven and destroyed them all. Yes, it will be business as usual right up to the day when the Son of man is revealed."

"He must be talking about the last day and the resurrection and the final judgment," I said aloud. Peter nodded in agreement.

Jesus continued, "On that day you must not worry about personal possessions. Don't go down from the deck of your house to pack or come home from the field to get anything. Remember what happened to Lot's wife. If you cling to your life, you will lose it, but if you let your life go, you will save it."

I realized that He was telling us to trust God to provide for our needs. We were not to trust in ourselves.

"On that night," Jesus continued, "two people will be sleeping in one bed. One will be taken and the other one left. Two women will be grinding flour at the mill. One will be taken and the other one left."

"When will this happen?" I blurted out.

Jesus replied, "As the gathering of vultures shows there is a carcass nearby, so these signs indicate the end is near."

Then it came clear to me. In the illustrations Jesus used about Lot and Noah, only a few were saved and many were lost. In the end, one will be saved over here and another saved over there. I certainly wanted to be one of those who obeyed God and was saved.

September 11   Luke 18:1–8

Parable of the Persistent Widow

Because of the animosity of the religious leaders, we stayed in the Mount of Olives near the Garden of Gethsemane. It was quiet and peaceful there, and many other travelers to Jerusalem camped there as well. One morning after we had risen and eaten a breakfast of figs, cheese, and bread, Jesus called us near and told us a story about faith and prayer.

"There was a judge in a certain city," He began, "who neither feared God or cared about people." *Sounds just like my twin brother*, I thought to myself. He was a blasphemous reprobate if there ever was one. A magistrate in Bethsaida, he had acquired the position by dishonest means. Jesus continued, "A widow of the city came to him repeatedly, saying, 'Give me justice in this dispute with my enemy.' The judge ignored her for a long time, but finally admitted to himself, 'I don't fear God or care about people, but that woman is driving me crazy. I am going to see that she gets justice because she is wearing me out with her constant requests.'"

Why would anyone ever remain in a position of responsibility toward the people they served if they didn't care? I had asked my brother that very question and his answer was, "For the money, Thomas, for the money." I was sure Jesus' condemnation and warning to the residents and leaders of Bethsaida was in a large part because of my brother's unscrupulous practices.

Jesus continued with His story. "Learn a lesson from this unjust judge. Even he rendered a just decision in the end."

Yes, I thought, *but only after he was in danger of losing his mind over the importunateness of the poor widow who only sought justice.*

"So," Jesus concluded, "don't you think God will surely give justice to His chosen people who cry out to Him day and night? Will He keep putting them off? I tell you, He will grant justice to them quickly! But when the Son of man returns, how many will He find on earth who have faith?"

So then, faith, I mused, *must come from persistent communion with God.*

September 12   Luke 18:9–14

Two Men Who Prayed

I seemed to be buried beneath a pile of guilt, no matter how I rationalized my line of work. I would be the first to admit there were honest and dishonest publicans, but I always tried to treat everyone fairly. Still, there was this stigma that surrounded me, and everyone categorized us as sinners similar to prostitutes and criminals. This guilt drove me crazy even though I went to the temple every day to pray. This particular day, I walked up the temple steps and saw the Nazarene preacher. I knew His disciple Matthew, and talking with him always made me feel better. As I passed by, I heard Jesus say something about a Pharisee and a tax collector going to the temple to pray. I stopped and listened. He called him a 'despised tax collector.'

Jesus said, "The Pharisee stood by himself and prayed this prayer: 'I thank You, God, that I am not a sinner like everyone else. I don't cheat or commit adultery. I am not like this tax collector.'" The Galilean used gestures to emphasize the attitude of the Pharisee. "'I fast twice a week, and I give You a tenth of my income.'" He paused and glanced over at a group of Pharisees. They didn't like having their hypocrisy pointed out in public, although everyone knew they were guilty. Jesus had the guts to tell them they were hypocrites. Then Jesus talked about the publican—me.

"The tax collector stood at a distance and didn't dare lift his eyes to heaven as he prayed." I knew that feeling. He continued, "Instead, he beat his chest in sorrow saying, 'O God, be merciful to me, a sinner, for I am a great sinner.' I tell you the truth, this sinner and not the Pharisee returned home justified before God. Those who exalt themselves will be humbled, and those who humble themselves will be exalted."

I never forgot Jesus' words. I could be a publican and do an honest day's work without feeling guilty no matter what anyone else thought because God accepted my honest prayers.

September 13 *Luke 18:15-17; Matthew 19:13-15; Mark 10:13-16*

Jesus Blesses the Children

We had come to the Passover from Galilee. Ten of us parents had traveled together looking for Jesus to bless our children. We were told He could be found near the temple steps. He wasn't there, but a man had heard one of His disciples say they were going to Bethany. Apparently the Pharisees were angry because He had implied they were a bunch of hypocrites. So we made our way to Bethany and gratefully found Him at the home of three siblings named Mary, Martha, and Lazarus. He was speaking to a group of people in their courtyard. I noticed that the crowd included some Pharisees. I can't remember what He was talking about, but I waited for a pause in His discourse.

When He reached for a skin of water, I said to my friends, "Let's go!" We brought our children up to where He was, and I asked if He would bless them.

Immediately one of the disciples stepped between me and the Lord and said with irritation, "What do you mean by interrupting Jesus with all these children? Can't you see He is busy with more important things? Take them out of here and bring them back some other time."

Several other disciples stepped in and began to escort us away, when Jesus stopped them. "Don't send these children away! Don't stop them! Let them come to Me." Then He stood and picked up my little girl with one arm and invited us to come back to where He was seated. Turning to His disciples, He said, "Don't you know that the kingdom of God belongs to those who are like these children?"

It was easy to see the annoyance of the Pharisees at Jesus' actions. Some of the other "religious people" were upset at being upstaged on account of some little kids. As the crowd began to leave, Jesus said,

"I tell you the truth—anyone who does not receive the kingdom of God like a child will never enter it."

He spent the rest of the day talking to us parents and blessing our children. Our kids had the time of their lives playing games with Him and listening to His stories. And we parents determined to be children of God.

September 14   *Matthew 19:16-24; Mark 10:17-25; Luke 18:18-25*

The Rich Young Ruler

For the most part I felt good about being who I was. I had money, lots of it, and was set for life. When Jesus told the story about the Pharisee and publican at the temple steps, I liked His view of divine justice. If ever there were hypocrites, the Pharisees fit the bill. I admired His courage to tell the truth no matter whose toes He stepped on. I followed Him to Bethany and watched as He blessed the children. Deep inside me something changed. I wanted that blessing, too, just to have the assurance that I was justified in God's eyes. He said goodbye to the children and their parents and was about to leave for Jerusalem when I approached Him.

"Good teacher, what must I do to inherit eternal life?"

Jesus looked at me and asked, "Why do you call Me good? Only God is truly good." I expected something different, like His hand on my head and a blessing because of my good record. Then He said, "To answer your question, you know the commandments—you must not murder, commit adultery, steal, or lie, and you must honor your parents."

My spirit was charged because I had done all these things since I was little, and I told Him so with a big smile on my face. Jesus stood silent for a moment as He looked at me with love and an intensity in His eyes. "There is only one thing you have not done. Go and sell all your possessions and give the money to the poor so you will have treasure in heaven. Then come and follow Me."

Those words hit me like a sledgehammer. *Give away all my money? Become penniless like the rest of the disciples?* I thought. *I can't do it. He is asking too much.*

I saw tears in His eyes as I walked away, and I heard Him say to the people, "It is hard for the rich to enter the kingdom. In fact, it is easier for a camel to go through the eye of a needle than for a rich person to enter the kingdom of God."

I immersed myself in my business enterprises and tried not to think about what Jesus had called me to do.

September 15   Matthew 19:25; Mark 10:26–31; Luke 18:26–30

The Rewards of Discipleship

I was shocked at what Jesus had just said. "Then who in the world can be saved?" I asked in astonishment. We had always been taught the rich people were certain candidates for heaven because the Lord loved them and was very obviously blessing them.

Jesus looked at me and said, "Humanly speaking, it is impossible for anyone to be saved, but with God, all things are possible."

Then my brother Peter spoke up and said, "Lord, we have given up everything to follow You. What will we get?" It was true. We had all made sacrifices to follow Jesus. Making ends meet was a challenge for some of us. Being gone from home caused tension in some of our homes. Even though Jesus sent us home often to be with our families, it was true that we were away much of the time.

Jesus responded to Peter's question. "Yes, when the world is made new and the Son of man sits on His glorious throne, you who have been My followers will sit on twelve thrones judging the tribes of Israel. I assure you that everyone who has given up houses, or brothers, sisters, mother, father, children, or even property for My sake and the good news, will receive in return a hundred times as many houses, brothers, sisters, mothers, children, and property, along with persecution."

I knew of homes and families divided because of the gospel. I didn't understand exactly what Jesus meant about receiving all those things a hundred fold. And what did He mean by persecution? Perhaps, He was talking about persecution like what Philip was experiencing at the hand of his father. I was convinced that no sacrifice was too great for the sake of discipleship with Jesus and the good of the kingdom. Jesus concluded His remarks with this statement, "And in the world to come that person will have eternal life. Those who seem great now will be least important then and those who appear least now will be great then."

All that mattered to me was to have my family by my side in the world to come and enjoy eternal life with God.

September 16   Matthew 20:1–16

The Vineyard Workers

Jesus told us a story that brought the whole idea of the kingdom and rewards and sacrifice into perspective. "The kingdom of heaven," He said, "is like a landowner who gets up early in the morning to go to the labor pool and hire workers for his vineyard. He selected a few men, agreed upon a wage for the day, and sent them out to work. At nine o'clock he was passing through the marketplace and saw people standing around, so he hired them, telling them he would pay them what was right. At noon and again at three in the afternoon he hired more laborers because they had no work, and he wanted to get the job done. At five o'clock he passed the marketplace and asked a group of people standing around why they hadn't been working. "No one has hired us," they responded. So the landlord hired them to join the others in the vineyard.

"That evening at six, he gave orders to his foreman to call the laborers in and pay them, beginning with those hired at five. Those who only worked for one hour were shocked to receive a full day's wage. The ones who were hired at six in the morning were excited to think of what they would be paid. When they received the same as everyone else, they protested, 'These people only worked one hour, but you paid them as much as you have paid us, and we have worked all day in the scorching heat.'

"The owner answered them, 'Friends, I didn't treat you unfairly. I paid you what we agreed upon. Take your money and be satisfied. I wanted to pay these last workers the same as I paid you. Can't I do whatever I please with money that belongs to me? Should you be upset because I show generosity and kindness to others?' So those who are last shall be first and those who are first will be last."

That story made me angry. I had always been taught, "You earn what you get, and you get what you earn." My brother James and I talked about it late into the night. Were we, Jesus' first disciples going to get the same treatment as those who became disciples last? What kind of a kingdom is this anyway? We agreed it was our right to be seated on Jesus' right and left hand in the new kingdom.

September 17   *Matthew 20:17-19; Mark 10:32-34; Luke 18:31-34*

Jesus Again Predicts His Death

After Jesus finished telling the story about the vineyard owner, we headed out. There were a number of the seventy disciples, my mother, and a few of the other women with us. Jesus called the twelve of us aside from the others. When we were alone, Jesus began to describe everything that would happen to Him in Jerusalem.

"Listen," He said, "soon we are going to Jerusalem where all the predictions of the ancient prophets concerning the Son of man will come true. He will be betrayed to the leading priests and the leaders of religious law." It seemed like He paused and looked at Judas. Maybe Judas had some inside knowledge or instructions from Jesus. We were all distressed to hear that He would be betrayed. Who would do that to Him? Would it be the Romans? "They will sentence Him to die," He continued.

"Die?" I said under my breath, while thinking. *What is He saying? That He will be killed? He must be mistaken. The people would never allow that to happen. Besides, if anyone tried to harm Him, they would have to deal with the twelve of us before they did anything to Him. What will become of the kingdom He has been talking about? And what will become of us if anything happens to Jesus? He must be mistaken—it just doesn't make any sense.*

He continued to speak, "Then they will hand Him over to the Romans to be treated shamefully, mocked, spit on, flogged with a whip, and crucified."

"No!" I gasped softly, "this can't be true!"

Jesus concluded, "But on the third day, He will be raised from the dead."

I asked my brother John, "Do you understand what He is talking about? I sure don't. I think He must be speaking in parables again."

The rest of the group joined us, and we traveled on to Jericho.

September 18 *Matthew 20:20-23; Mark 10:35-40*

The Ambition of James and John

The more James and I talked about our rightful places in the kingdom, the more convinced we were that someone needed to speak to Jesus on our behalf. And who was better qualified to do so than our mother? At first she was reluctant to go along with our plan, but love for her sons won her over. We were proud of our mother because she was good-hearted and had a kind, gentle spirit. If anyone could present our request to Jesus in the most convincing way, it would be her. The cue for her to approach Him would be at the next stop for food, water, and rest.

Not far from Jericho, we came to a group of roadside vendors where we bought some fruit and bread for dinner. Mother timidly approached Jesus with the two of us at her side. She knelt down before Him respectfully to ask for a favor. Jesus looked at her and smiled. "What is your request?" I glanced at the other disciples. They were watching everything.

"In your kingdom," Mother said, "please let my two sons, James and John..." She paused and looked up at me.

"Go on," I whispered.

"Please let my sons sit in places of honor next to You—one on Your right and one on Your left."

I could feel the anger and animosity of the disciples behind me without even turning around. Jesus put down his lunch and looked at us. Then He said, "You don't know what you are asking. Are you really able to drink from the bitter cup of suffering I am about to drink from?"

"Oh, yes!" I replied. "We are able."

Jesus paused a long moment, His eyes drifting away as though He was seeing things we could not. Then He focused at us, first at James and then at me, "You will indeed drink from My bitter cup," He said with emphasis on the word bitter, "but I have no right to say who will sit on My right or left. My Father has reserved those places for the ones He has chosen."

I looked at James, then turned to Jesus and thanked Him for hearing our request. He nodded. We helped Mother to her feet and turned to face the others.

September 19 *Matthew 20:24-28; Mark 10:41-45*

Jesus Speaks About Serving Others

Needless to say, the other ten disciples were not happy with us. Matthew spoke first. "What gives you the right to make such a request?" His voice was filled with sarcasm. The others added their voices of indignation to his.

Judas approached me—hostility was written all over his face. He got in my face, grabbed my coat with a clenched fist, and said, "If there is a high position to be had in this kingdom, you can be sure I will have it because I am much more qualified than an uneducated, ignorant fisherman like you." He didn't let go of me until Jesus called us together. I was glad to get out of Judas' grasp. I suppose Jesus allowed the chiding from the others to go on as long as He did so they could vent their feelings and help us realize how miserably our little scheme had failed.

Jesus spoke to us with deep conviction. It was vital that we be clear on what He was about to say. "You know the rulers of this world lord it over their people," He began, "and officials flaunt their authority over those under them. But among you it *will* be different. Whoever wants to be a leader among you must be a servant, and whoever wants to be first among you must be your slave."

The spirit Jesus was referring to was the complete opposite to what we had just exhibited. I looked at my brother at the same time he looked at me. I saw how greedy and selfish I really was. We both hung our heads in shame.

Jesus continued, "For even the Son of man came not to be served but to serve others and to give His life as a ransom for many." That last sentence tore into my soul and made me realize I had a lot of growing to do.

When Jesus finished speaking, I turned to the other disciples and said, "James and I are sorry for what we did, and we ask for your forgiveness." There were tears in my eyes as I thought about what Jesus had said. They all forgave us except Judas—he turned his back and walked away.

September 20 *Luke 18:35-43*

Healing of the Blind Beggar

No one paid much attention to me. I was just a blind beggar—I was of little value to anyone. Twenty years earlier, in the prime of life, an illness took my eyesight, and since then I have had to beg to provide for me and my family.

The people of Jericho were good to me. One kind lady would bring bread and fruit each day. Others put a few coins in my cup. Early one morning after my wife brought me to the gate, I heard the footsteps of many people leaving the city. "Where is everyone going?" I asked, but no one answered. With my stick I started down the road leading out of the city. Before long I heard the noise of a crowd approaching. "What is happening?" I shouted.

"Jesus, the Nazarene, is going by," someone said.

Jesus! He had restored the sight of my friend from Jerusalem. I believed He was the promised Messiah. "Jesus, Son of David, have mercy on me!" I shouted with all my might. Some didn't like the idea of my calling Him "Son of David" since that was a Messianic title, so they yelled at me to shut my mouth. I yelled all the louder because I believed what I was saying—I didn't care what they thought.

Jesus heard me so He stopped and asked that I be brought to Him. When I stood before Him, He said, "What do you want Me to do for you?" I could hardly believe I was standing in front of the only person in the world who could give me what I wanted.

"Lord," I cried, "I want to see!"

Without hesitation He responded, "All right, receive your sight—your faith has healed you."

My eyes were instantly opened. For a moment I stood there in stunned silence, hardly able to believe it. The first face I saw was His smiling face. I fell at His feet and thanked Him for healing me. Then I jumped to my feet and danced around, hugging everyone and praising God. The crowd was as surprised as me, and they joined me in praising the God of heaven for making the blind to see.

September 21   *Luke 19:1-10; Mark 10:46-52*

Zaccheaus

I had been the brunt of more jokes than you could imagine and had endured the ridicule that goes with being short. You see, I wasn't just short—I was super short. I tried to increase my stature, but nothing worked. Most of the people in Jericho hated my guts because I was the chief tax collector in the region. Working for the Romans, I was allowed to charge people whatever I wanted over and above what the government required as long as I didn't start a rebellion. The mansion I lived in and the tailored clothes I wore were thanks to the high taxes I charged. I managed most of the tax stations in the area, including Jerusalem, and I took a cut from each one. It was a lonely existence with no friends, except for a few fellow publicans.

Three years ago I heard John the Baptist speak at the Jordan about honest tax collecting. "Don't cheat people," he had said. I couldn't shake the conviction, so I started cutting back on my take. It blew me away when I learned Jesus had invited Matthew to be a disciple.

One ordinary day as I was standing at my station word came that Jesus was in town. *I have to see Him*, I thought. I told my assistant to take over, and I ran to the main street. I couldn't get to Him or even see Him through all the people. Down the street was a sycamore tree, so I ran ahead of the crowd and climbed up to get a ringside seat. Jesus came right beneath me, stopped, and looked up. He smiled and said, "Zacchaeus, come down. I want to be a guest at your house today."

I couldn't climb down fast enough. I was thrilled! People in the crowd started to grumble. Out loud I said, "Lord, I will share my wealth with the poor and restore fourfold to those I have cheated."

Jesus turned to the crowd and said, "Salvation has come to this house today, for this man has shown himself to be a true son of Abraham. I have come to seek and save the lost."

Jesus and I had the best visit. I became His follower and carried out my promises. Having to sell the mansion was such a small price to pay for my new Friend and peace of mind.

September 22   *Luke 19:11–27*

The Nobleman's Servants

My family couldn't believe I was able to see! "Who healed you?" they asked.

"Jesus the Messiah," I replied.

My wife said, "Why don't you tell your friends, the two blind beggars at the other gate? Maybe Jesus will heal them too."

Walking down main street, I found Jesus with Zacchaeus, the tax collector, heading to the publican's house. That did not sit well with the Pharisees. Before entering the home, Jesus turned and told the crowd a story about the kingdom. Many of the people, including me, believed Jesus the Messiah was about to start the new kingdom.

"A nobleman was called to a distant country to be crowned king. He divided ten pounds of silver among his servants, telling each one to invest it and make money while he was gone. His people hated him and sent a delegation telling those in charge not to make him king. He was crowned anyway, traveled home, and called his servants to account. The first increased his investment tenfold. 'Great!' exclaimed the king. 'You have been faithful in little, I will put you in charge of ten cities. The next servant made five times as much and became governor of five cities. The third servant said he hid the silver and kept it safe. 'I was afraid,' he said, 'because you are a hard man, taking what isn't yours and harvesting where you didn't plant.'

"The king was furious. 'Why didn't you invest it in the bank and at least earn interest?' The king ordered the pound be taken and given to the one who earned ten. They protested, 'But master, he already has ten pounds.' The king said, 'Those who work hard and earn more will be given more, but those who do nothing, even the little they have will be taken away. And now, about those who do not want Me to be king, bring them in and execute them in front of Me.'"

Jesus paused to look at those who complained about Zacchaeus. I pondered that story for a long time. I needed to use the gift of sight to help others and advance the kingdom. For now, I will tell my friends what Jesus did for me.

September 23   Matthew 20:29–33

Bartimeaus' Friends

I hurried to the western gate to find my friends. As I looked at them sitting beside the road, I thought to myself, *That was me just yesterday*. I called their names, and they greeted me warmly. When I embraced them they said, "Where is your walking stick?"

"I threw it away," I answered.

"Whatever for?" Jonas asked.

"Because I can see!" I shouted. They were astonished.

"I can't believe it," Thomas said.

"It's true!" I replied.

"Who made you well?" they asked.

"Jesus," I said, "and He will heal you too. In fact, He is coming this way en route to Jerusalem."

They wanted to hear all about my healing, so I told them the amazing story. When we heard a crowd coming toward us, I told them to say what I had said, so they began shouting at the top of their lungs. "Lord, Son of David, have mercy on us!"

I shouted with them, "Son of David, please be merciful to us."

Two of the city's religious leaders told us to shut our mouths. "Do you realize you are calling this man David's son, the Messiah?"

"Yes!" I answered. "We believe that's who He is." They were furious, but we continued shouting. "Jesus, Son of David, have mercy on us."

Jesus stopped and called out, "What do you want Me to do for you?"

I took my friends by the hand and led them to the Lord. When we stood before Him, I said to them, "Tell Him what you want."

"Lord," they cried, "we want to see."

They knelt before Him, their faces turned upward. I saw His eyes fill with compassion. He looked at me with a smile, then touched their eyes, and instantly they could see. They jumped to their feet shouting praises to God.

"We can see! We can see! Thank You, thank You, Jesus!" they shouted. We hugged and danced, laughed and cried. Never had there been three happier ex-blind beggars than the three of us! The crowd joined in praising God. Later, I wondered why He had just spoken to make me see but had touched my friends' eyes. It didn't matter, we were blind but now we could see!

September 24   *Luke 7:36–44a*

Simon the Pharisee (Part 1)

    I heard Jesus was coming from Jericho to Bethany, so I decided to hold a feast in His honor in appreciation for healing me of leprosy. I made arrangements to have prominent people attend. Martha would naturally cater my feast. And Lazarus would be an added attraction since he had just been raised from the dead. I sent word to Jesus inviting Him to the feast.

    When He arrived, everything was ready for dinner to begin. My servant showed Him and His disciples to their seats. Everything was going according to plan until Mary, Martha's immoral sister, entered uninvited through the back door. She knelt at Jesus' feet. I tried to get her attention, but she ignored me. I did not want her there because some people believed I was the one responsible for her immorality. Then, to make matters worse, she took out an expensive alabaster box of pure nard, broke it open, and began pouring it on His feet. The scent of the spikenard permeated the room, and if people didn't notice her before, they couldn't miss the scene now with the fragrance drawing everyone's attention to Jesus and Mary.

    I watched her kneeling there weeping and kissing Jesus' feet in what appeared to be some kind of anointing ceremony. I thought to myself, *This man cannot be a prophet, because if He were, He would not allow this sinful woman to touch Him.*

    No sooner had the thought formed in my mind and Jesus turned toward me and said, "Simon, I have something to tell you."

    "Go ahead," I replied.

    "A man loaned money to two people. He gave five hundred pieces of silver to one and fifty pieces of silver to the other. Neither of them could repay the loans so he forgave them both, canceling their debts. Who do you suppose appreciated and loved him more after that?"

    I replied, "The one who owed the greater debt."

    "You're right," Jesus said. Then He gestured to Mary, still at His feet. "Look at this woman kneeling at my feet."

    I looked and nodded. I was sure He would tell me what a great sinner she was and that I should call one of my servants to have her removed. He glanced around to be sure no one was listening to our conversation. Then He continued to speak but He did not say anything I had expected to hear.

September 25   *Luke 7:44b—50*

Simon the Pharisee (Part 2)

    I leaned toward Him as He spoke. "When I entered your home, you didn't offer Me water to wash the dust off My feet."

    I knew I hadn't been a very hospitable host, but I hadn't wanted to appear too accommodating toward Him because of the controversy surrounding Him. I didn't want my friends to think I was one of His disciples. I had a reputation to uphold.

Again, pointing to the woman, He continued, "But she has washed my feet with her tears and wiped them with her hair." He continued in hushed tones so only He and I knew what was being talked about. I appreciated that He didn't put me down in front of everyone else. "You didn't greet Me with a kiss, but she has not stopped kissing my feet. You neglected the courtesy of olive oil to anoint My head, but she has anointed My feet with rare perfume."

At first I felt angry and defensive, but I quickly realized Jesus was not saying these things to make me feel bad about being a terrible host. He was genuinely concerned about my whole attitude. I saw compassion and love in His eyes. He paused, and we both looked at Mary. She looked at Jesus and smiled through her tears and tangled hair. She even had a smile for me, which was much more than I was prepared to offer her. For the first time in my life, I began to see myself for the person I really was—a hypocrite.

Then Jesus said, "I tell you, her sins, and they are many, have been forgiven, and because of her gratitude, she has shown Me much love. But a person who is forgiven little shows only little love."

I saw immediately where I fit into the story He told about the debtors. Then Jesus stood up, and in front of everyone, He took Mary's hand, helped her to her feet, and said to her, "Your sins are forgiven."

My friends at the table said to each other, "Who does this man think He is forgiving sins?"

Again Jesus spoke to Mary, "Your faith has saved you—go in peace."

That experience changed my life. I am so glad Jesus is able to forgive the sins of all sinners, both great and small.

September 26   *Matthew 26:6-13; Mark 14:3-9*

Mary at Simon's Feast

I knew it would be risky, but I had to do it. I hadn't been in Simon's house since he took advantage of me and ruined my reputation. Life became unbearable for me after I was targeted as "one of those" women. I thought it was strange that no one ever blamed Simon for what he did.

I moved to Magdala with relatives after the incident, but they soon disowned me. I decided if I was going to be labeled immoral, I might as well be immoral. I hated my life as a prostitute, but I was able to earn money.

When Martha found out, she and Lazarus made me come home. I was grateful they still loved me. No one else wanted to have anything to do with me. Except Jesus. Just days ago when He visited our home, He told me He would soon be killed by the priests and religious leaders in Jerusalem. The news of His impending death broke my heart. I vowed the next time He came to Bethany I would anoint Him before He died. Hearing He would be at Simon's feast, I decided to go even though I knew Simon would never invite me.

I slipped in the back door and offered to help Martha with the meal. She sent me to the banquet room with a bowl of fruit. Simon was surprised to see me, but Jesus smiled. Setting down the fruit, I opened the nard and poured some on Jesus' head, then His feet. Simon tried to get my attention, but I ignored him. As I thought about all the good things Jesus had done for me, the reality that He was about to die overwhelmed me, and tears poured down my cheeks.

A disciple sitting close by said, "What a waste of good money. This perfume could have been sold for a high price, and the money given to the poor."

I was embarrassed and was about to sneak out when Jesus spoke in my defense. "Stop criticizing this woman for doing a good thing. You will always have the poor, but you will not always have Me. She has done this to prepare Me for burial, and wherever the gospel is preached throughout the world, this woman's deed will be remembered." I sighed in relief and smiled at Jesus through the tears. Then He publicly announced that my sins were forgiven. I was set free!

September 27 *John 12:1–8*

Judas at Simon's Feast

It was six days before the Passover. This was Jesus' last chance to announce His Messiahship and establish the new kingdom. He needed the support of the priests and Pharisees, but He kept pushing them away. Attending Simon's feast was the smartest thing He'd done in a long time. Simon had connections. He knew Caiaphas personally; I hoped this was a turning point.

Personally, I was sick and tired of waiting for Him to make His move. There were a lot of leading officials attending the feast. Jesus was the guest of honor, and Simon was seated right next to Him—this was perfect.

I was seated on the other side of Simon, so I saw her first. This immoral, worthless prostitute, Mary, came in, uninvited, and knelt at Jesus' feet. She pulled a twelve-ounce bottle of spiknard out of an alabaster container, broke it open, and anointed Jesus' head with it, then His feet.

Is she crazy? I thought to myself. *Who would waste a costly twelve-ounce bottle on Jesus?* I looked at Simon, and he looked at me. I whispered, "Get rid of her." He leaned over and tried to get her attention, but she ignored him. He looked back at me and shrugged. *Why is Jesus allowing this woman to do this to Him? She is wrecking everything.*

By now everyone could smell the fragrance. I had to say something. "That perfume is worth a year's wages," I said with indignation, giving Mary a hateful look. "It should have been sold and the money given to the poor," I continued.

"Since when have you been concerned about the poor, Judas? You seem to take good care of yourself," John said, but I ignored his comment.

Then Jesus spoke up. "Leave her alone," He said, rising to His feet. He looked directly at me. "She did this in preparation for My burial. You will always have the poor among you, but you will not always have Me."

Then He turned to this woman and forgave her sins. That was the last straw. I was furious. I glared at Him, got up, and walked out. He had just blown His last chance. I would have to take matters into my own hands.

September 28   *Matthew 26:1–5; Mark 14:1, 2;*
Luke 22:1, 2; John 12:10, 11

The Plot to Kill Jesus

The Passover was only two days away, and all of us knew something had to be done about Jesus of Nazareth. As high priest I called an emergency meeting of the Sanhedrin to discuss the best way to deal with this troublemaker without upsetting the people—we certainly didn't want a riot on our hands. I personally made sure that none of Jesus' sympathizers were present, like those traitors Nicodemus and Joseph of Aramathea. The last thing we needed was for them to come to His rescue again.

I told those present that this Jesus was about to ruin the nation. Rumors were circulating everywhere that He was soon to establish a kingdom of His own. He would draw many, if not all the people, to Himself, and we would certainly be excluded. I figured that the Romans would then send an army to destroy the entire nation. He had to be put to death and soon. The Sanhedrin was in favor of killing Him, but how? We had very little time.

"How can we put Him on trial, condemn Him, and kill Him in two days?" someone asked.

One member suggested we hire an assassin to murder Him. "Too risky," I replied. "If he is caught, he will implicate us. We need a good solid plan that will condemn Him so that we can arrest Him, place Him on trial, and sentence Him to death."

We talked long into the night, but the longer we talked the more frustrated everyone became. Every suggestion the council made seemed good, but none was problem free. In the midst of our discussion, someone brought up Lazarus' resurrection.

"Do you really think He resurrected him?" I asked. "Personally, I believe it was trickery," I said with a sneer.

"I was there," one of the members said in objection. "He'd been dead for four days."

"Well then," I replied, "if Lazarus is the cause of His great popularity, we will put him to death as well." That suggestion did not go over very well. Since we couldn't come up with a perfect plan, we decided to adjourn and go home, but before we could leave there was a knock at the chamber door.

September 29   *Matthew 26:14–16; Mark 14:10, 11;*
Luke 22:3–6

Judas Meets With the Priests

I left Simon's feast furious. *How dare He reprimand me in front of everyone?* I thought. In addition to my frustration of Him speaking to me in that way, I was also mad that He refused to move forward with plans for establishing His kingdom. As I mulled everything over, I decided that I had to come up with some plan that would force Him to declare Himself as Messiah and King of Israel while giving me credit for making it happen. There had to be a way to do it.

I rented a room in the city from a relative because all the other lodging was taken. I needed a place to think and devise a plot. I heard the priests were meeting with the Sanhedrin each evening until very late. The rumor was that they were plotting how to get rid of Jesus. Well, I didn't want to get rid of Jesus, but perhaps I could scratch their back, and without them knowing it, they would scratch my back. If my scheme worked, I figured I could make a little profit and get a little glory. I decided to go to where they were meeting that night under the cover of darkness.

Just after midnight I knocked on the chamber door. Caiaphas opened it, smiled and invited me in. "What can we do for you?" he asked.

"I have come to make you an offer," I said with a smile, "if you are interested that is."

"What sort of offer, Judas?"

"I will betray Jesus into your hands for a small fee. I will take care of all the details; you just make sure you do your part."

Caiaphas laughed, "Of course we are interested. Doesn't it bother you just a little to sell out your Friend?"

"He's not my Friend," I snapped. "I want thirty pieces of silver."

Everyone on the Sanhedrin agreed to my proposal, and we signed the agreement. The deal was a good one because now all I had to do was figure out a way to betray Him and turn Him over to them. I knew He would never allow Himself to be arrested. My little plan would force Him to declare Himself as king, and I would be a rich hero. I just had to come up with a failproof plan. I admired my shrewd plan. Everyone would know I was someone to be reckoned with once I pulled this off.

September 30 *Matthew 21:1-7; Mark 11:1-7;*
Luke 19:28-35; John 12:14

Disciples Sent for a Donkey

From Simon's feast we made our way up the Mount of Olives toward Jerusalem. On the way we would pass through Bethphage, a small village on the outskirts of the city, but before we reached the village, Jesus sent my brother Andrew and I into the village to fetch a donkey with a colt that had never been ridden. "Untie them and bring them to Me. If anyone asks you what you are doing, just say, 'The Lord needs them.' The owner will let you take them."

On the way to the village I said to Andrew, "I think I remember reading a prophecy in Isaiah, something about 'your King is coming to you; He is humble, riding on a donkey.'"

"And doesn't Zechariah say something about 'riding on a donkey's colt'?" Andrew asked in response. We stopped and looked at each other in excitement.

"Is He going to announce Himself as king?" I asked in wonder. Anciently, newly crowned king's always rode into Jerusalem on a colt that had never been ridden before. With renewed energy we turned down main street and there, halfway down the street, we saw a donkey with a colt. The owner and some of his friends were standing close by. Without a word we began to untie both donkey and colt.

"Hey! What are you doing?" the owner asked.

I told him exactly what the Lord had told us to say. "The Lord has need of them."

The owner looked closely at me, then said, "Okay, you may take them."

We headed back to where Jesus was waiting with the other disciples and the crowd that had followed us from Bethany. On the way we talked about what this could mean for the kingdom. It was Passover. Thousands of people would be in the city. The resurrection of Lazarus had spread like wildfire. Jesus was about to ride into Jerusalem on a colt, the signal of a king taking office. Everything seemed perfect! When we reached Jesus with the animals, Andrew and I tore off our coats and placed them on the colt's back. Then we bowed before Him, extolling Him as King of kings. Without hesitation, He mounted the colt, and we moved toward the city.

October 1 *Matthew 21:8-11; Mark 11:8-10;*
Luke 19:36-44; John 12:12-13, 15-19

Jesus Comes to the City

When Peter and I placed our coats on the colt's back, others spread theirs on the ground. Some people cut branches off the trees and spread them on the road. Jesus was in the center of the procession with people shouting, "Praise God for the Son of David! Blessings on the One who comes in the name of the Lord! Praise God in the highest heaven!" I recognized that as a quote from one of the Messianic psalms.

The news that Jesus was entering Jerusalem swept through the city, and the people came out to meet Him. Some cut palm branches as they came. Many were singing another Messianic psalm, "Hail to the King of Israel!" It was like a dream come true—Jesus was about to be anointed king!

As we entered the city through the north gate, people asked, "Who is this?"

The crowds replied, "It is Jesus, the prophet from Nazareth in Galilee."

The Pharisees in the crowd were more than a little upset at the praises being shouted in honor of Jesus, and one of them finally shouted, "Teacher, rebuke Your followers for shouting these Messianic praises. Tell them to stop."

The crowd came to a standstill when Jesus did. Everyone became silent and looked at Jesus who said, "If the people remain quiet, the stones along the road would burst into cheers."

As we approached the city, I noticed that Jesus had tears in His eyes. When we reached the temple, He burst into wrenching sobs. Everyone stared at Him in shocked silence. He spoke through the tears, "Oh, how I wish all of you would understand the way to peace. Now it is too late, and peace is hidden from your eyes. Soon your enemies will build ramparts against your city and encircle you, closing you in. They will crush you to the ground and your children with you. Your enemies will not leave a single stone in place because you neglected salvation." When He finished speaking, the crowd began to disperse.

This was not the way things were supposed to happen, I thought as I watched people walk away with heads down.

October 2   Mark 11:11

Jesus Looks Around the Temple and Returns to Bethany

Everyone thought the day would end in a great celebration, but it faded into a big disappointment. People left the procession and went about their business. Meanwhile, I noticed that Judas had returned to the group.

"Where have you been?" I asked when he was within earshot.

"Taking care of business," he replied irritably.

Jesus composed Himself, got off the colt, and walked toward the temple steps. It was late in the afternoon, and those selling sacrificial animals were gathering up their things for the day. Jesus watched them. I could tell that some of the money changers remembered Him from three years earlier when He had driven them away because a number of them avoided His searching eyes. He walked inside the temple courtyard. A great sorrow seemed to hang over Him as He watched the services being conducted. He stood there in silence for a bit before turning and telling us that we would return to Bethany for the night.

It was dusk when we reached the home of Mary, Martha, and Lazarus. They were always so happy to have us visit. Mary greeted everyone warmly, except Judas. It seemed like she was afraid of him. Martha set about preparing supper since we were all very hungry. Lazarus recounted the day's events to his sisters while they prepared the meal.

When there was a break in the conversation, I asked the question on everyone's mind. "Lord, why were You so upset when we were leading the procession down the Mount of Olives? Was it because of something we did? Or was it something the Pharisees said?"

He paused a long time before replying. "No, Matthew, it had nothing to do with you. It had to do with lost opportunities—a rejection of the plan of salvation. Eternal issues are at stake. People are either saved or lost forever based on how they respond to the invitation to be part of the kingdom. I came to try to help them understand how to be part of God's kingdom. I came to tell them that I am the way, the truth, and the life. I wept because My heart is broken. So many have rejected My message and refused to accept the gift of God. I wept because I must let them reap the consequences of their decision."

October 3   *Matthew 21:18, 19; Mark 11:12-14*

The Withered Fig Tree

The next morning Jesus woke us early. I washed my face with cold water but was still half asleep when Jesus asked me to write a note of appreciation for the hospitality we had been shown. Mary got up to say goodbye as we headed out toward Jerusalem. The air was cool, and the sun still well below the horizon, but the clouds showed signs of a bright new day.

As we neared Bethphage, Jesus saw a fig tree about a hundred feet off the main road. "Let's check it out," He said. Even though it wasn't time for figs to be ripe, the tree was in full leaf. Since the fruit of a fig tree appears before the leaves open, this tree gave promise of ripened fruit. But its appearance was deceptive for even though we checked every branch, we found no figs. We were hungry and disappointed.

Jesus stood back and said to the tree, "May you never bear fruit again." Immediately the tree began to wither. The leaves curled and started turning brown.

"Lord, how could this tree die so quickly?" I asked.

He answered, "If you have faith, Peter, and do not doubt, you can do things like this and much more. You can even say to this mountain, 'May you be lifted up and thrown into the sea,' and it will happen. You can pray for anything, and if you have faith, you will receive it."

We continued toward the city. The early morning sun reflected off the temple dome. I thought about what Jesus had said regarding faith and wondered why so many of the things I asked for I never received. I remembered Him saying the same thing about having faith the size of a mustard seed and moving mountains. I believed and I had faith. Why didn't I get what I wanted? I also wondered why Jesus had cursed that tree and killed it? He was always performing acts of restoration. It wasn't like Him to destroy anything. It was a disappointment not to find ripe figs, but the foliage made good shade, and the tree was nice to look at. Jesus must have had some reason. I concluded I had lots to learn, but my faith in Him was strong.

October 4   *Matthew 21:12-17; Mark 11:15-19; Luke 19:43-48*

Temple Cleansed Again

I came to the temple early, hoping to find Jesus, but all I saw were the merchants and money changers getting ready for business. This time of year was very profitable for them. Most people disliked the fact that they were located right in front of the temple courtyard entrance, but there didn't seem to be anything to be done about it. The noise was deafening. Sometimes you could not even hear what the priest was saying. I had not come to sacrifice this day. I had come seeking help for my leg. My knee was so arthritic I could hardly walk. I sat down on a step to take the weight off my leg.

Just then I heard someone shout, "There's Jesus!" Looking over, I saw Him grab a moneychanger's table and upend it. He turned over other tables—coins scattering everywhere. Instead of trying to stop

Him, the money changers ran away as fast as they could go. One fat seller of turtle doves tripped over his robe and tumbled head over heels. The rest of us stared in amazement as Jesus unlatched animal and bird cages, setting the creatures free.

While He was chasing out the merchants, He announced, "The Scripture says 'My house will be called a house of prayer,' but you have made it a den of thieves!" When everything was quiet again, He called those of us who wanted to see Him to come close. When He asked me what I needed, I told Him about my knee. With two words—"Be healed"—the pain vanished! What amazing relief! Others were healed, too, and together we praised God. Even the children sang praises to Him.

Down the street I saw the merchants complaining to the Pharisees. When they arrived to hear all the praises, especially of the children, they confronted Jesus, "Don't You hear what these children are saying."

His reply was, "Haven't you read the Scriptures? 'You have taught children and infants to give You praise.'"

It was easy to see they wanted to get rid of Him but were afraid of what the people might say. I continued to praise Him in front of them. They looked at me with disdain.

October 5 *Mark 11:20, 21, 27-33; Luke 20:1-8*

Pharisees Challenge Jesus' Authority

We spent the rest of the day at the temple while Jesus taught the people and healed the sick. Slowly the money changers and sellers crept back to retrieve their things, but they dared not resume their trade. What a wonderful day! Everyone was at peace, and the temple was quiet. In the evening we headed back to Bethany. I recounted the whole story of the day's events, including the fat merchant tripping as he tried to scurry away.

The next morning we once again rose early to return to the city. As we passed Bethphage, I called Jesus' attention to the withered fig tree with its blasted branches and dropping leaves. With deep sadness, Jesus told us it was like the Jewish nation. Specially favored of God, it professed allegiance to Him but in reality yielded nothing but leaves. I wanted to ask Jesus to explain this further, but we were approaching the temple, and I could see that the Pharisees, lawyers, and leading priests were waiting for us, along with some of the merchants. They were upset about yesterday's events. "By what and whose authority are You doing all these things?" the leader of the group demanded.

The air was full of tension and hostility. Jesus had upset their economy and interfered in their world. He waited a few moments while the tension mounted. Finally He spoke, "Let me ask you a question first. Did John's authority to baptize come from heaven or was it merely of human origin?"

They stood silent for a long time before the spokesman called them into a huddle where they talked it over. "If we say it was from heaven," one of them conjectured, "He will ask why we did not believe John. But on the other hand, if we say it was merely human, the people will stone us because they are convinced John was a prophet."

The multitude waited with intense interest. The only response the priests could give was "We do not know." This indecision compromised their authority in the eyes of the people.

"Then I won't answer your question either," Jesus stated. The whole group of confronters turned and angrily walked away. I marveled at Jesus' answers. He was definitely the wisest person I had ever known.

October 6 *Matthew 21:28–32*

The Two Sons

The delegation of religious leaders had not gone very far when Jesus called out, "But what do you think about this?" They stopped and turned to face Him. Jesus continued, "A man had two sons. One day he told his oldest boy to go out and work in the vineyard for the day. The boy complained that he had other things to do and, besides, it was just too hot. He said to his father, 'No, I won't go.' The father was very disappointed and told him how rude and disrespectful he was. The son went into town to meet some of his friends, but he began to think about how badly he had treated his father. He headed back home, changed his clothes, and went to work. Meanwhile, the father had gone to his younger son and told him to go work in the vineyard. 'Sure, Dad, I'll go,' he said. But the day passed, and he did not go to work. Which of the two obeyed his father?"

I thought the leaders would have been hesitant to answer, considering the trick question Jesus had just asked them. But one of them answered immediately, "The first one."

Then Jesus explained the meaning of His story. "I assure you that corrupt tax collectors and prostitutes will get into the kingdom of God before you do. For John the Baptist came and showed you the way to life, and you didn't believe him, while tax collectors and prostitutes did."

The religious leaders stood in stony silence. Jesus continued, "And even when you saw their changed lives, you refused to turn from your sins and believe John." The priests were in a hard place before the people. I thought it served them right, but as I looked at Jesus, I was amazed to see tears in His eyes. I realized it wasn't His purpose to humiliate them; He really cared about them and was trying to wake them up to their real condition. I understood from Jesus' story that although the Pharisees professed obedience, they were really disobedient like the second son.

I want to be obedient to God and serve Him because of His amazing love for me while I was still a tax collector.

October 7   *Matthew 21:33; Mark 12:1–12; Luke 20:9–19*

Story of the Evil Farmers

Jesus moved right into another story, this one was a parable about a man who planted a vineyard. My mind drifted back to visiting my grandfather Philip's grape farm. According to Jesus' story, the man leased the vineyard to tenant farmers and moved to another country for several years. The owner had gone to great lengths to make the vineyard productive, including building a wall around it to keep out animals. He dug a pit in which to press the grapes and built a tower for the watchmen. When the time for harvest came, he sent his servants to collect his share of the income. The tenants attacked the servant, beat him up, and sent him back to the owner empty-handed.

Shocked at such audacity from men he had trusted with his property, the owner sent another servant whom they insulted and beat even more cruelly. Astonished by what the farmers had done to the servants, he sent a third, but this servant died from the wounds the tenants inflicted.

Finally, he said to himself, "I will send my only son; surely they will respect this child I cherish." When those evil farmers saw the son of the owner coming, they said, "Here comes the heir. If we kill him, the estate will be ours." So they murdered him and threw his body on the hard ground outside of the vineyard.

"What do you suppose the owner will do to those farmers?" Jesus asked.

The delegation spoke up, "He will put those farmers to death and rent the vineyard to someone who will pay him." They had unknowingly pronounced their own judgment.

Jesus looked at them and asked, "Haven't you read the Scriptures? 'The stone the builders rejected has become the cornerstone. This is the Lord's doing, and it is wonderful to see.' Truthfully, the kingdom of God will be taken from you and given to a nation that produces proper fruit. All who stumble on that stone will be broken but upon whom it falls will be crushed."

I saw it dawn on the Pharisees that the parable was about them. They were the wicked farmers. Their faces were so full of anger and hatred I thought they might try to kill Jesus on the spot.

October 8   *Matthew 22:1–10*

The Wedding Banquet

Even though the Pharisees hated Jesus, they seemed inexplicably drawn to Him. They would storm off, shaking their fists, but they always seemed to come back. The next story He told illustrated the kingdom of heaven.

"A king held a wedding banquet for his son. When the banquet was ready, he sent his servants to notify the guests it was time to come. They all had an excuse for not coming, so he sent other servants with the same invitation, 'Come to the banquet.' The invited guests ignored the king's servants and went their own way."

I saw the delegation move a little closer to Jesus, caught up in the story. "The servants pleaded, 'Please come! The food has been prepared, the bulls and fatted cattle have been killed, and all is ready. Please, for the king's sake, come and honor his son.' One went to his farm, ignoring the servants' pleading; another went about his business; others beat the servants of the king and killed them. The king was furious and sent an army to destroy the murderers and burn their town."

I watched some of the Pharisees nod in agreement. "Serves them right," a man shouted.

Jesus continued. "The king gathered his household servants and said, 'The wedding is ready, but the guests I have invited are not worthy of the honor.'" Jesus stood tall, spread His arms, and shouted, "'Now go out wherever there are people; it doesn't matter who you find. Search the streets and the hovels, including the marketplace and the farms. Invite them all to come to my banquet. There must be guests for the most important day of my son's life. We will take everyone—good, bad, black, white, rich or poor—anyone who is willing.' So the king's servants went out to the streets and all the places where people were gathered, inviting them to come to the king's great feast. Everyone was invited; not one person was left out. Soon the banquet hall was filled with guests."

The delegation talked among themselves, then one of them asked me sarcastically, "Is this another story about us, Nicodemus?"

Another of my colleagues raised his voice, "What do you make of this tale?" Before I had a chance to respond, Jesus spoke again.

October 9 *Matthew 22:11-14*

The Wedding Garment

Everyone quieted down as Jesus continued the story. "The king walked among the guests who were enjoying the food and entertainment provided for the wedding. Suddenly, he saw a man standing at the food table who was not wearing a wedding garment."

It is customary in Jewish culture for all wedding guests to wear a garment provided in honor of the groom and bride. To refuse the garment would be an insult to both the host and the groom. Either the host would think that the guest was arrogant and felt he did not need the clothes graciously provided or, even worse, was openly scorning the host and the groom. It was a serious offense.

Jesus' story continued, "The host said to the guest, 'Friend, how is it you are here without the required wedding clothes?' The guest hung his head and had nothing to say. He had no excuse."

I remembered a wedding feast I attended where a similar situation had occurred. The guest, however, was Greek and had somehow been overlooked. Clothes were brought to him, which he gladly received and quickly put on.

Jesus spoke, "The host called a servant and asked, 'Was this man offered no wedding garment?' The servant looked at the man and replied, 'Yes, sir, he was offered a garment, but he said he wanted the people to see the new set of clothes he had purchased yesterday.' The host looked at the guest without sympathy. 'Is this true?' the king shouted. The man stood there, very embarrassed. The king ordered his servants to take this ungrateful guest, bind his hands and feet, and throw him into outer darkness where there is weeping and gnashing of teeth. The guest quickly offered to put on the garment, but the king would not listen. 'You had ample opportunity, but your pride kept you bound.' The servants threw the man out of the banquet hall."

Then Jesus looked at the delegation of religious leaders and said, "For many are called, but few are chosen."

My Pharisee friends knew he had spoken of them again. They walked away murmuring against Him. They expected me to follow, but I waved them on. I wanted to be near Jesus.

October 10   *Matthew 22:15-22; Mark 12:15-17; Luke 20:20-26*

Taxes to Caesar

My colleagues knew I was sympathetic toward Jesus, which is why they had begun holding Sanhedrin Council meetings at unscheduled times and not notifying me of the proceedings. Although not invited, I figured the delegation had gone back to the council chamber to concoct some scheme to entrap Jesus. When I had a chance to speak with Jesus, I told Him that I was certain the religious leaders were planning to trick Him into saying something the governor could arrest Him for. I stayed with Jesus while He healed those who came to Him.

I spoke with some of the disciples about my concern for His life. They were worried too. Late in the afternoon some young lawyers, disciples of the Pharisees, and several government aids from Herod's court came to Jesus. First, they tried to flatter Him. "Teacher," one of them said, "we know You speak and teach what is right and are not influenced by what other people think. In fact, You teach the way of God truthfully. Now, tell us, is it right for us to pay taxes to Caesar?"

The trap was clever, but it was obvious to me. If Jesus said "No," they would report Him to Pilate. If He said "Yes," they would condemn Him before the people as a supporter of Rome. Jesus glanced over at me, saw the anxiety written all over my face and nodded before turning to His questioners. "You hypocrites," He said. "Why are you trying to trap Me?" By this time a large crowd had gathered. Jesus said, "Show me a coin." They fumbled in their pockets, found a coin, and handed it to Jesus. "Whose picture and title are stamped on it?" He asked.

"Caesar's," they replied.

"Then give to Caesar what belongs to him and to God what belongs to Him."

The delegation stood there looking dumbfounded at the unexpected answer Jesus had just given. It was easy to see that they were embarrassed. The crowd was amazed at His answer and commented on His wisdom.

October 11   *Matthew 22:23–33; Mark 12:27; Luke 20:27–40*

The Resurrection Question

It was becoming obvious that the Sanhedrin had recruited everyone they could think of to try to trap Jesus: the Pharisees, the Herodians, the lawyers, and now the Sadducees, who were famous for their notions regarding the resurrection. A Sadducee spokesman stepped up to Jesus and said, "Teacher, Moses said if a man dies and has no children, his brother should marry the widow and have a child to carry on the brother's name."

I leaned over to Peter, my brother, and asked, "Aren't these the people who don't believe in a resurrection of the dead?" He nodded an affirmative.

The Sadducee paused but Jesus said nothing, so he continued, "Well, suppose that there were seven brothers. The oldest married and died without children. The second married his brother's widow, but he also died without children. The third then married her and died as well. In fact, all seven brothers married her and died without producing an heir. Then the woman finally passed away also."

The story was rather ridiculous, so the people smiled and shook their heads. The Sadducee spokesman cleared his throat, stood up tall, and asked the inevitable trick question: "So tell us, whose wife will she be in the resurrection since all seven brothers were married to her?"

Jesus replied, "The problem here is simple. You don't know the Scriptures or the power of God. When the dead rise, they will neither marry nor be given in marriage. In this respect they will be like the angels in heaven. Regarding the resurrection," Jesus continued, "as to whether or not there will be one, have you never read the Scriptures and studied these things? Years after Abraham, Isaac, and Jacob had died, God Himself said, 'I am the God of Abraham, Isaac, and Jacob.'"

I said loudly to Peter so everyone, including the Sadducees, could hear, "That's found in the second book of Moses, I believe." The crowd laughed while the Sadducees scowled.

"So," Jesus continued, "He is the God of the living, not the dead." Once again the crowd was impressed with Jesus' answers while the Sadducees, looking embarrassed, turned and left the temple.

October 12   *Matthew 22:34–40; Mark 12:28–34; Luke 20:39, 40*

Greatest Commandment

The Pharisees recruited me to entrap the Galilean teacher. They flattered me with platitudes, boasting I was the best lawyer of religious law in Jerusalem. If anyone could silence this Jesus, it would be me, they said. I had arrived at the temple early in the day and watched as He cleared out the money changers. Then I saw people come to Him to be healed and encouraged. I heard His response to the Pharisees' questions about His authority and listened to each of His stories. I was impressed with His answer to the Herodians regarding taxes and the Sadducees about the resurrection. I began to see Him as more than just a man.

I honestly wanted to know the truth, so dismissing the question the Pharisees told me to ask, I asked one I had been thinking about a lot lately. "Teacher," I called out, "of all the commandments, which is most important?"

"The most important is this one," Jesus replied, fixing His eye on me. "Hear, O Israel, the Lord our God is the one and only God." I recognized the passage from Deuteronomy. "You must love the Lord your God with all your heart, with all your soul, with all your mind, and with all your strength. The second is equally important. You must love your neighbor as yourself. No other commandment is greater than these," He concluded.

It dawned on me He had just summarized the Ten Commandments into love for God and love for man. I was convinced He was a prophet and perhaps even more. "Well done, Teacher, You have spoken the truth by saying there is only one God," I replied. "And I know it is important to love God with all my heart, understanding, and strength and to love my neighbor as myself. This is more important than to offer all the burnt offerings and sacrifices required by the law." Those words came from deep within me.

The Pharisee standing beside me jabbed me in the ribs, "What are you saying, you fool?"

"The truth," I told him.

Jesus smiled and said, "You are not far from the kingdom of God, my friend!"

That was the end of my religious law career with the Sanhedrin, and the beginning of a new life in Jesus Christ, who has never failed me.

October 13   *Matthew 22:41-46; Mark 12:35-37; Luke 20:41-44*

Jesus Questions the Pharisees

It was midafternoon. Jesus looked tired, but the Pharisees kept plying Him with questions and accusations. He stood His ground and answered them all. Then Jesus went on the offensive and asked the group of Pharisees that surrounded Him a question. "What do you think about the Messiah? Whose Son is He?"

They all answered in unison, "The Son of David."

The crowd nodded in agreement. Everyone listened carefully to hear what Jesus would say next. Creating a bit of suspense, He knew just how to reach the crowd and make them hang on every word. He posed another question, "If the Messiah is the Son of David, why does David, speaking under the inspiration of the Holy Spirit, call the Messiah, 'my Lord'?" Jesus paused and let the words sink in.

I leaned over to my brother James and asked him why David had called Him "my Lord" when He wasn't even born yet? James gave me a blank look and shrugged his shoulders, indicating he had no idea. Then he turned back to listen to Jesus, who immediately quoted from the book of Psalms. "'The Lord said to my Lord, sit in the place of honor at My right hand until I humble Your enemies beneath Your feet.'" Everyone knew Jesus had quoted a Messianic psalm.

I watched the Pharisees talk with each other about the question. One of the Pharisees whispered to the others, "This is a question designed to make us admit that the Messiah is greater than David and existed before him. Most of the people in this crowd are beginning to believe that this man is the Messiah."

Jesus continued, "Since David called the Messiah 'my Lord,' how can the Messiah be his Son?"

No one in the group of Pharisees, including the lawyers and priests, could or would answer Him. And no one dared ask Him anymore questions. The people began to talk, asking, "Why can't these teachers answer Him?" Embarrassed, the Pharisees decided it was time to go.

It was true. "Everything Jesus has told us about who He is proves true," I said to my brother. He grinned and nodded.

October 14　　　　　　　　　　　　　　　　　Matthew 23:1-7; Mark 12:38-40; Luke 20:45-47

Jesus Warns the Crowd About the Religious Leaders

My colleagues on the Sanhedrin left, but I wanted to stay and listen to this teacher from Galilee. I pretended to leave but slipped back, trying to be inconspicuous at the edge of the crowd. I had never heard this Jesus speak before today. Nicodemus knew I was open-minded and had tried to get me to accompany him to hear Jesus speak, but I always refused. Now I wish I had gone.

Jesus said to the crowd and those beside Him, who I assumed were His disciples, "The teachers of the law and the Pharisees are the official interpreters of the law of Moses. So you must practice and obey whatever they tell you, but don't follow their example because they do not practice what they teach."

"Explain yourself, Teacher," I called out.

His eyes found me in the crowd. "You crush people with impossible religious demands and never help the people by lifting a finger to ease the burden."

"That is part of the law," I protested.

"No," He shot back, "that is the teaching of men, traditions added to Moses' law." He walked through the crowd toward me. I was beginning to wish I had gone with the others. "Everything you do is for show like extra wide prayer boxes attached to your arms and robes with long tassels. You love to sit at the head of banquet tables and in seats of honor in the synagogues. You love to receive the respectful greetings in the marketplace when you walk among the people, and you relish in being called rabbi." Now He was standing right in front of me. I tried to protest, but there was nothing to contradict. Everything He said was true. I tried to avoid looking in His eyes, but He was so close I could not help myself. I saw no spite or vindictiveness; instead I saw tears. "You shamelessly cheat widows out of property and then pretend to be pious by praying long prayers in public. Because of this, your punishment will be severe."

Conviction griped me and all I could do was mutter, "You speak the truth, Teacher."

As I turned and made a hasty exit, I heard the Galilean say, "There is a Pharisee with a heart for the truth."

October 15 *Matthew 23:8–12*

The Humble Will be Exalted

I was conflicted. I wanted to leave, but I also wanted to stay and hear more. I finally decided to head toward the council room. As I made my way through the crowd, I met a group of fellow Pharisees. When they saw me, one of them said, "We must find something to condemn Him with today."

"But He is telling the truth," I replied. "I listened to Him, and He spoke directly to me."

"Have you been swept away with His lies too?" another one of them asked sarcastically. "You are no better off than the rabble!"

I'm afraid I responded with some animosity in my voice. "He has answered all our questions today, and not one of us can answer His questions."

"Well, Caiaphas said we must find something to condemn Him for today or it will be too late," Jonas replied with finality.

I shook my head, shrugged, and said resignedly, "Let's go then."

As we neared the edge of the crowd, He began to speak, "Don't let anyone call you rabbi, for you have only one teacher."

Yes, I thought to myself, *God is our teacher*. That is what they told us at the rabbinical school in the temple, and it is what I taught my students.

"And all of you are equals as brothers and sisters," He said.

Then why do we distain the Galileans and Samaritans? I wondered. *We Judeans don't even treat each other as equals.*

I saw Him looking at me again. "Don't address anyone here on earth as your spiritual father, for only God in heaven is your spiritual Father." Then He unloaded a powerful statement that rocked me to the soles of my feet. "Don't let anyone call you teacher, for you have only one teacher, the Messiah."

He paused to let what He said sink in. As I listened, I became more and more convinced that He wasn't just a man. I looked at my friends, but they were discussing how to twist His words. How could I be so convicted and they so indifferent?

"The greatest among you must be your servant," Jesus cried out. "Those who exalt themselves will be humbled, and those who humble themselves will be exalted." My heart responded to His words. I wanted to be humble like Him. I was tired of all the pretense. Now that I had heard Him for myself, I was convinced that He had the words of life, and I wanted to hear more.

October 16   *Matthew 23:13–36*

Woes Upon the Pharisees

Jesus looked at all of us huddled together at the edge of the crowd. Somehow He could speak words of warning with compassion. "What sorrow awaits you religious leaders because of your hypocrisy. You shut the door to heaven in people's faces and will not go in or let others go in. You cross land and sea to make one convert, and then turn that person into twice the child of hell as you are."

My Pharisee friends scowled. He exposed the hypocrisy of swearing by the temple gold instead of the temple itself. "You say only swearing by the gifts on the altar and not the altar itself is binding. When you swear by the temple, you are swearing by God who lives in it, and when you swear by heaven, you are swearing to God and His throne and everything there."

He reprimanded us regarding tithing for the smallest things but leaving out the important things like justice, mercy, and faith. "Blind guides," He said, "you strain your water to remove a gnat, but you swallow a camel. You wash your ritual cups on the outside, but the inside is full of greed and indulgence. Clean up the inside, and then the outside will be clean, too. You whitewash the tombs but inside are dead people's remains. Outwardly you look like good religious leaders, but inside there is hypocrisy and lawlessness."

He chastised us leaders for taking care of the prophets' tombs and declaring we would never have joined our ancestors in killing the prophets. Then Jesus said, "Go ahead and finish the work your ancestors started." I knew my fellow Pharisees wanted Him dead. "Sons of snakes, you vipers, how will you escape the judgments of hell?" Things were heating up, and I could tell how angry they were. "I send you prophets and wise men, and you kill some, whip and flog others, and chase them from city to city. But you will be held responsible for killing all the prophets, from Abel to Zechariah. Judgment will fall on this generation."

By now they were shaking their fists and shouting at Him. I was embarrassed to be associated with them. I knew there had to be hope for someone like me. I prayed, *Father in heaven, forgive me; save me in Your kingdom.* At that moment, I felt peace—I knew my prayer had been heard.

October 17   *Mark 12:41–44; Luke 21:1–4*

The Widow's Mite

The Pharisees were stirring the people up against Jesus, claiming He was condemning this generation to hell. Now the people started to argue with each other. It was impossible for Jesus to say more, so He led His disciples into the temple away from the noisy crowd. I watched them go over to where the collection box stood.

Besides coming to the temple to hear Jesus, I also wanted to give an offering. The line was long, and most of the people looked rich. I went to the back and stood behind a very wealthy man holding a large sack of coins in one hand and a gold bar in the other. He turned and scowled at me in my patched dress and moved closer to the person in front of him. I clutched my two small coins, waiting my turn. The rich made a big display of putting their offering in the box. They stood in front of the collection and emptied their sacks of coins, trying to outdo each other with the clanging. Others had servants stand nearby handing them bags of coins.

I felt very conspicuous standing there with my measly two coins. The smallest coins minted, they were hardly worth putting in the box, but it was truly a sacrifice to give them. As I neared the collection box, I seriously considered stepping out of line and coming another day when it wasn't so crowded. What would Jesus think of my tiny offering? The man in front of me stepped up to the box and emptied his sack with great display. He held up his gold bar for all to see, then dropped it in the box. It was my turn. I stepped forward and quickly threw in my coins. I heard some people laugh, and I felt embarrassed.

Jesus stood up and said, "This widow has given more today than anyone else." Then He came to where I stood. Tears ran down my cheeks as He placed His hand on my shoulder. "Everyone else has given from their surplus, but she, poor as she is, gave all she had, even what she had to live on."

The rich man in front of me slipped out, and no one else dared make a big display of their offering. I felt very comforted by Jesus' words.

October 18   *Matthew 23:37–39*

Jesus Grieves Over Jerusalem Again

We left the temple treasury and exited the city. By now it was early evening as we made our way up the Mount of Olives toward Bethany. What a day full of conflict! My brother Andrew asked, "Do you think Jesus will ever acquire the support of the priests and Pharisees?"

I shook my head. "No. I don't believe they want reconciliation. They just want to trap Him with something He might say, which is what they tried to do all day. I personally think they want to kill Him."

My brother looked at me incredulously, "How will they do that when He is so popular with the people? Peter, you can't be serious! It will never happen."

I smiled and said, "Andrew, you know how fickle people are. They can be very supportive one minute and completely against you the next. Don't you remember what happened in Nazareth? He was the honored guest in the synagogue one minute, and the next He was being dragged to His death."

"I do remember," he replied. "Maybe you are right."

We were near the top of the mount when Jesus stopped and looked down at the city. The setting sun bathed the temple in a golden wash of color. The sky was ablaze with reds and oranges and purples. It was a magnificent evening. Jesus spoke, "O Jerusalem, Jerusalem, the city that kills the prophets and stones

God's messengers." He paused, and then spoke again with deep pathos. It was as though He was seeing things we could not see. "How often I wanted to gather your children together as a hen protects her chicks beneath her wings, but you wouldn't let Me. And now, look, your house is abandoned and desolate."

Tears streamed down His face. I asked if He was okay, but He didn't respond. He just stared straight ahead at something else. Finally He spoke again, "I tell you this; you will never see Me again until you say, 'Blessings on the One who comes in the name of the Lord.'"

Without another word He turned, and we walked in silence toward Bethany. "I feel like I've heard that psalm recently." I said.

"You have. The people shouted it again and again when Jesus rode the donkey into Jerusalem."

Of course, it had been when the people really believed Jesus was the Messiah, the Savior.

October 19   *John 12:20–28a*

The Greeks (Part 1)

We had traveled from Corinth to Jerusalem for the Passover. But my friend Achaicus and I had not come just to celebrate the Passover. We wanted to meet with Jesus of whom we had heard so much. There were so many conflicting reports about Him. Some said He was a great deceiver. Others claimed He was the Messiah. We knew He was associated with a disciple named Philip, so we decided to speak with him first. We thought it might be easier to obtain an interview if we spoke to someone with a Greek name. We found Jesus and the disciples near the temple. Locating Philip, we made our request known. "Sir," we said, "we want to see Jesus."

He asked us to wait while he went and conversed with another disciple. He soon returned and introduced us to another man named Andrew. I told him I was Stephanus from Corinth and had come to Jerusalem with my friend Achaicus. He nodded and gestured for us to follow him.

Standing in front of Jesus, I introduced myself and my friend and told Him where we lived. I told him my family and many others in Corinth believed He was the Messiah because of all the miracles He had performed and the prophecies of Daniel that foretold His coming. Then I fell to my knees and begged Him to come to Corinth where the people were anxious to meet the Messiah, the Son of God. I looked up into His face and saw a battle raging inside Him.

In anguish, He cried out, "Now the time has come for the Son of man to enter into His glory. Truly, unless a kernel of wheat falls into the ground and dies, it remains alone. But its death will produce many new kernels—a harvest of new lives. All who love their lives in this world will lose them, but those who give up their lives will keep them forever. If you want to be My disciples, you must follow Me and be where I am. The Father will honor those who serve Me."

He took my arm and helped me to my feet. I stood before Him. "My soul is troubled. Shall I pray, 'Father, keep Me from this hour'? But this is the very reason I came. Father, bring glory to Your name." I could tell He was in deep distress.

October 20   John 12:28b–36

The Greeks (Part 2)

Without warning, thunder crashed around us. But the sky was clear? Then a voice, like that of an angel or God Himself, vibrated around us. "I have already brought glory to My name, and I will do it again."

The people were terrified! Some said, "It thundered, but why?" and others said, "An angel spoke to Him."

Jesus stood before the crowd and declared, "The voice was for your benefit, not Mine." He looked directly at me and continued, "The time for judging this world has come, when Satan, the ruler of this world will be cast out."

"What does He mean?" I asked Achaicus. He shrugged.

Then Jesus said something that began to put things into perspective. He raised His arms and extended them slightly above His head with fingers stretched out as I had seen those who had been crucified do. Then He said, "When I am lifted up from the earth, I will draw everyone to Me."

"Him? Crucified? On what grounds?" I queried. "He is telling us He will be crucified!"

We stood in stunned silence. "The people will never allow it," Achaicus finally replied.

A Pharisee called out, "We understand from Scripture that the Messiah will live forever. How can you say the Son of man will die? Who is this Son of man anyway?"

It upset me that this hypocrite would speak so contemptuously to the Son of God. Jesus replied, "My light for you will shine just a little longer. Walk in the light while you can so the darkness will not overtake you."

"So I suppose You are the light to guide the rest of us, You ignorant Galilean," the Pharisee muttered under his breath.

Jesus kept speaking, "Those who walk in darkness cannot see where they are going." He raised His arms above His head and shouted, "Put your trust in the light while there is still time. Then you will become children of the light."

The Pharisee stormed off, furious. I heard a few people begin to complain about Him. I turned to my friend and said, "Let's go." I thanked Jesus for speaking with us and told Him I understood. He smiled and we headed back to Greece.

October 21   John 12:37–43

The Jew's Unbelief

We decided to walk from Jerusalem to the coastal city of Joppa, a distance of about forty miles. It gave Achaicus and I time to talk about the events of the past few days. I could not understand why the people refused to believe on Jesus after all the miracles He had performed.

"If Jesus had performed as many miracles in Corinth as He has in Jerusalem, everyone in the city would believe on Him," I said to my friend.

He looked at me and replied, "That is exactly what the prophet Isaiah predicted, 'Lord, who has believed our message? To whom has the Lord revealed His powerful arm?'"

I responded to his quote from the prophet, "But the people could not believe because they were blind."

My friend nodded and continued to recite Isaiah. "The Lord has blinded their eyes and hardened their hearts—so that their eyes cannot see and their hearts cannot understand…"

I joined in for the last phrase, "…and they cannot turn to Me and have Me heal them." We stopped beside the road and thought about what Isaiah had written. Finally, I broke the silence, "Isaiah was referring to Jesus in that prophecy, wasn't he?"

Achaicus answered, "Yes. Isaiah had it right. He described those people perfectly."

"He was shown the future and spoke of the Messiah's glory." I remembered what the prophet had said about the suffering servant. "He was despised and rejected, a man of sorrows acquainted with grief," I repeated quickly.

"He was pierced, beaten and whipped so we could be whole," Achaicus continued.

"Unjustly condemned, He was led away, although He had done no wrong," I added.

It all came together for us very clearly. We knelt beside the road and thanked God for opening our eyes so that we could see. "There must be others whose eyes are open. They can't all be blind," I said.

"Perhaps even some of the Jewish leaders believe in Him but are afraid to admit it," Achaicus said encouragingly.

"I'm sure there must be," I replied. He nodded, and we continued our journey back to Greece. We would miss the Passover, but we had met the Passover Lamb.

October 22 *John 12:44–50*

Jesus Concludes His Message to the People

The Pharisees had done a good job of turning the people in the crowd against Jesus by condemning Him as a blasphemer. I overheard one of them say, "This man thinks He is the Son of God and wants us to bow down and worship Him."

Jesus raised His hand and cried out to the crowd. "If you trust Me, you are not only trusting Me but also God who sent Me." The crowd quieted down, hushed by the Pharisees who hoped to catch Jesus saying something they could condemn Him for. "For when you see Me, you are seeing the One who sent Me," Jesus continued. "I have come as a light to shine in this dark world so that all who put their trust in Me will no longer remain in the dark."

The leader of the Pharisees cried out, "We are children of Abraham. How can You say we are in the dark?"

Jesus continued speaking without acknowledging him, "I will not judge those who hear Me but do not obey Me, for I have come to save the world and not condemn it. But all who reject Me and My message will be judged on the day of judgment by the truth I have spoken."

"God judges Gentiles, not Jews! We are sons of Abraham," someone in the crowd shouted. A chorus of cheers followed that remark.

Jesus waited for the crowd to quiet down before He resumed speaking. "I don't speak on My own authority," He cried out. "The Father who sent Me has commanded Me what to say and how to say it."

A man shouted, "Are you claiming God as Your Father?" This caused a huge stir.

"Blasphemer," several Pharisees shouted with clenched fists raised in the air.

Jesus had to really shout to be heard above the noise. "And I know His commands lead to eternal life, so I say whatever the Father tells Me to say."

This was more than the crowd would tolerate. Some began to look for stones.

"We need to get Him out of here," I said to Peter. He agreed, so we took Jesus by the arms. He allowed us to lead Him away while the angry crowd shouted epitaphs and accused Him of blasphemy. We left the city and headed toward the Mount of Olives. Those in the crowd who believed in Jesus followed us.

October 23 *Matthew 24:1-3; Mark 13:1-4; Luke 21:5-7*

A Question About the Temple's Destruction

As we were leaving the temple area, the afternoon sun lit it up so beautifully that I called everyone's attention to the craftsmanship and beauty of that magnificent building. That was when Jesus stopped, turned to all of us, and said something so shocking, so frightening, I could not believe it.

He spread His arms out toward the temple and the buildings around it and said, "Look at all these buildings. I tell you the truth; every one of them will be completely demolished. Not one stone will be left standing on another."

It was as if He'd hit me in the chest with a hammer. The others looked as shocked as I was. Without a word of explanation He turned and walked toward the city gate. "Did you hear what He said?" I asked John.

"Yes! Whatever does it mean?" he asked.

I shook my head, shrugged, and followed Jesus in silence. We crossed the Kidron Valley, passed the Garden of Gethsemane, and climbed up the Mount of Olives to a grassy knoll. I caught my brother's eye and motioned for him to come over to where James, John, and I were standing. "We have to ask Him what He meant about the destruction of the temple," I said. "He can't just leave us hanging without an explanation." I agreed to be the spokesman.

We approached Jesus and asked to speak with Him privately. By the look on His face, I'm sure He knew what we wanted to talk about. Once we were alone, I said, "Tell us when all these things are going to happen—the destruction of the temple and all these things You spoke of? What signs can we look for that will help us realize these things are about to be fulfilled?"

He paused, smiled, and invited everyone to come close, including the eighty or so who had followed us up the mount. We made ourselves comfortable in the warm afternoon sun. I looked down at the temple dome and tried to picture the destruction of God's house, but I could not begin to imagine how it could actually happen or why God would ever allow His temple to be destroyed.

October 24   *Matthew 24:4–13; Mark 13:5–13; Luke 21:8–19*

Signs of Christ's Coming (Part 1)

"Don't let anyone mislead you," Jesus began. Then He warned about false messiahs. I had seen false christs before. They seemed to show up regularly. He spoke of wars, large and small, and famines and earthquakes occurring in unusual places. "These events are only the beginnings of what is still to come." He spoke of persecution and being arrested and even killed. "The world will hate you for being My followers," He said.

"I have seen that hatred in the eyes of the Roman soldiers," I whispered to my brother James.

He nodded and whispered, "They hate us just for being Jews. And I've seen that hatred in the eyes of the Pharisees too."

Jesus spoke of false prophets deceiving many people and sin everywhere, with love growing cold and hard. But He promised that those who endured to the end would be saved. He talked about a time of great persecution when we would be dragged into synagogues and prisons, called to stand trial before governors and even kings, giving us the opportunity to tell about our Lord.

What would I say standing in front of Pilate or Herod? I wondered.

Then, as though reading my mind, He answered my question. "Don't worry in advance about what you will say for I will give you the wisdom to speak the right words so that none of your opponents will be able to reply or refute you." He warned us that family members would betray us, even parents, brothers, sisters, and close relatives. "Some of you will be killed, and everyone will hate you because you are My followers, but not a hair of your head will perish," He said seriously.

I was confused. If He said we would be killed, how could not a hair of our head perish? Perhaps it was a reference to what He said earlier about living forever and eternal life.

"By standing firm," He assured us, "you will win your souls."

I thought about my family and who I could trust if persecution became severe. I thought of Matthew and wondered whom he could trust because some of his family were Roman sympathizers. I knew one thing for certain. When persecution came, my only hope would be to trust completely in Jesus.

October 25   *Matthew 24:14–31; Mark 13:14–27; Luke 21:20–28*

Signs of Christ's Coming (Part 2)

Jesus told us that the gospel message He had been sharing with us would be preached throughout the entire world and then the end would come. As a small boy, I would go with my dad to the ports near Athens where the ships docked and listen to the stories the sailors told of mysterious places. *How will the gospel ever go to these places*, I wondered, *when none of us can speak a foreign language?*

Next He spoke of Daniel and the desolation and abomination standing in the Most Holy Place. *He must be referring to the desecration of the temple*, I thought. *I remember hearing about Antiochus, the Assyrian, sacrificing a pig on the temple altar, but Jesus is referring to the holy place inside the temple.*

Then He told us, "When you see Jerusalem surrounded by Roman armies, know that destruction is eminent. Those in the city must get out along with those in Judea. Everyone must run and hide in the hills. It will be especially hard for pregnant women and nursing mothers. Pray that this does not take place in the winter or on the Sabbath. If you are in your house, don't pack; if you are in the field, don't go back into the city for anything."

He spoke of disaster, killings, torture and captivity, and Jerusalem being trampled down. I wondered what would happen to my Jewish relatives living in Greece. Jesus told us that as time went on things would get so bad that unless those days were shortened, no one would survive. I wondered what calamity could endanger the entire world. He warned us again about false christs; then he told us there would be signs in the sun, moon, and stars. The sun would be darkened, the moon would give no light, and the stars would fall from the sky. I remembered the prophet Joel had said exactly the same thing as Jesus about the sun and moon.

Then Jesus told us of His coming again in glory, as visible as lightning flashing across the whole sky. He said He would return with angels and a trumpet blast and then gather His chosen ones from all over the world. "Look up when you see these things, because your salvation is very near."

October 26   *Matthew 24:32–51; Mark 13:28–36; Luke 21:29–37*

Stories About Remaining Faithful and Alert

As a boy I lived in a house with a huge fig tree in the front yard. I loved that tree because I could climb halfway to the stars, build a tree house in its branches, or tie ropes to it and make a swing. Plus, it produced the best figs ever. At harvest time, my dad would say, "Nathanael, you are small and a good climber. You pick as many near the top as you can." The top of the tree was where the fruit grew best, and I made sure I ate my fill.

When Jesus told us His coming was like a fig tree budding, I knew what He was talking about. When a fig tree buds and the flowers bloom, it won't be long until harvest. Jesus said that within our generation Jerusalem would be surrounded by armies and destroyed. He told us that no one but the Father knows the day or the hour of His return. Things on earth would be as bad as when Noah lived on earth and the flood came and swept them away. Just as in Noah's day, when some were saved and others lost, there will be two men working in a field, one saved and the other lost. Of two women grinding at a mill, one will be saved and one lost. I thought about the flood where so many were lost and only eight were saved.

"Be alert and watchful," Jesus warned us. "If a man knows when a burglar will raid his house, he'll be ready for him. Be watchful at all times because the Son of man will come when least expected."

He then told a story about a servant who was told that he would be rewarded if he was faithful and managed his master's household well in his absence. However, if he abused his responsibility or abused his fellow servants, got drunk and partied, saying to himself, "My master won't be back for a while, I will do as I please," he would lose his role as leader and be thrown out with the hypocrites where there will be weeping and gnashing of teeth.

As I listened to Jesus' words, I determined to be a faithful servant and do the work God had called me to do. I believed the others were making that same commitment in their hearts.

October 27   Matthew 25:1–13

The Story of the Ten Virgins

I watched a bridal procession wind its way through the east gate of the city, the bride and her attendants all dressed in white. Young virgins threw flower petals before the bride, and musicians announced their coming. It brought back memories of my own wedding, although it had not been as extravagant. Someone called Jesus' attention to the event, so He paused to watch. The party entered a large banquet hall where the festivities would last as long as the food and wine held out.

As soon as the procession passed, Jesus began another story. "The kingdom of heaven is like a wedding," He said. "There were ten bridesmaids who went out to meet the groom. Five were foolish and five were wise. The foolish had oil in their lamps, but the wise had also brought extra oil with them. The wedding party was delayed, and all the girls fell asleep. At midnight a loud cry roused them. 'Look! The bridegroom is coming! Come out and welcome him' was the proclamation. The girls discovered their lamps were empty and the fires extinguished. The wise girls filled their lamps with the extra oil they had brought. The foolish girls begged to borrow some, but the wise virgins had no extra and suggested that they purchase some. The foolish virgins hurried off to wake up a vendor, but by the time they returned with oil in their lamps, the bridegroom had come and gone. The wise girls had entered into the feast and the door was locked. The five foolish girls rushed to the banquet hall and cried, 'Lord, Lord, open up and let us in.' He called out from within, 'I'm sorry but I do not know any of you.'"

Thoughts of an experience my wife and I had when invited to a wedding flashed into my mind. We had arrived late. Forced to wait outside the banquet hall so as not to disturb the ceremony, we begged and pleaded—we even tried to bribe the doorman. Unfortunately, we had missed the wedding.

Finishing His illustration, Jesus said, "You must keep watch because you do not know the day or the hour of My return." He caught my eye as if to say, "Matthew, this is one wedding you don't want to be late for!" I smiled and determined to keep a constant watch for His return.

October 28 *Matthew 25:14–30*

The Story of the Talents

For those of us with children who had followed Jesus to the Mount of Olives, it was time to head back to the city. Just then Jesus began another story about a rich man going on a long trip. I just couldn't pull myself away, so I stopped to listen to one more story.

"A rich man called his servants together and gave them each a portion of his money to care for while he was gone. Knowing their capabilities, he gave the first servant five bags of silver, the second man two bags, and the third one bag. He told them to take good care of it and be wise. The man with five sacks invested his portion and earned five more. The man with two doubled his silver, but the man with one sack buried his in the ground."

Jesus continued, "The master returned and called the servants to give an account. The first servant boasted that he had doubled his master's investment. The second servant showed that he had done the same. 'Well done,' said the rich man. 'Let's celebrate! You both deserve to be given greater responsibility.' Then the man who had been given one sack revealed the same sack he had been given; now worn, dirty, and muddy. 'I knew you were a shrewd man and hate to lose money because you harvest where you do not plant and reap where you do not sow. Therefore, I buried it. Here it is, all of it.' The master was furious. 'If you knew I was shrewd, why didn't you invest the money like your peers and at least I could have gotten interest?' Then he ordered the bag be taken and given to the man with ten."

Jesus paused, and then spoke. "To those who use well what they are given, more abundance will be given, but those who do nothing with what little they have, it will be taken away. Now the master said, 'Throw this servant out where there is sorrow and much regret.'"

As my wife and children and I walked back to the city in the evening shadows, I continued to ponder the story. The message was clear. I'd invested in myself to the exclusion of everyone else. But I did not want to end up like the unproductive servant. I would change before it was too late.

October 29   Matthew 25:31–46

The Sheep and the Goats Story

Jesus had told stories about bridesmaids and servants, but now He was talking about His return with angels in glory and sitting upon a throne. What really caught my attention was His comparing the nations at His coming with sheep and goats. I had spent many years herding sheep and goats, so my ears perked up as He began to talk about these two very different groups of animals.

The evening air was getting cool, but I sat down to hear what He would say. He said that when He comes, all people from all nations will be gathered together in His presence, and He will separate the people like a shepherd separates sheep from goats.

Many times I had done exactly that, the sheep on the right hand and the goats on the left.

Jesus said, "The King will cry out, 'Come you blessed of My Father, inherit the kingdom prepared for you from the creation of the world. When I was hungry and naked and in prison, you took care of Me.' The people ask, 'When did we see You in need?' 'When you did these things for someone on My behalf, you did it for Me,' He answered.

"Then He turned to the goats on His left and said, 'Away with you, cursed ones. You will be cast into the eternal fire prepared for the devil and his angels. I was hungry and naked and in prison, but you didn't care enough to help Me.' 'When did we see You in that condition?' they ask. 'When you refused to help the least of My brothers and sisters, you refused to help Me,'."

I pondered the rewards. They appeared to be based on a relationship to the Shepherd and helping others. Just like I always help any animal in need, I am responsible to help any human being in need also. I left the mount viewing people and my relationship to Jesus in an altogether different way. Up until now, I had ignored the ever-present beggars at the city gate. But now I noticed that they were people with families and faces and needs. I dug deep into my pockets and gave away all the money I had. It felt good to be a brother sheep.

October 30   Matthew 26:17-19; Mark 14:12-16; Luke 22:7-13

Preparation for the Passover

The people returned to their lodging after Jesus told the story of the sheep and goats. We walked to the place in the Garden of Gethsemane where we stayed on the nights we didn't go to Bethany. Philip and Nathanael built a fire, and we ate a meal of fruit, bread, and cheese. Everyone except Jesus went to bed. He went to His favorite place to pray. James, John, and I talked for awhile about the events of the day and tried to figure out what Jesus meant regarding the destruction of Jerusalem and His coming in glory.

The next day, the first day of the feast of unleavened bread, was beautiful. This day was the day the Passover lamb was sacrificed and the Passover meal eaten. After breakfast, Jesus asked John and I to go into the city and make preparations for the Passover meal so we could celebrate the occasion together.

"Where do You want us to prepare it?" I asked Him.

He said, "As soon as you enter the city, a man carrying a pitcher of water will meet you. Follow him. At the house he enters, say to the owner, 'The Teacher asks, "Where is the guestroom where I can eat the Passover meal with My disciples?"' He will take you upstairs to a large room already set up, and that is where you should prepare our meal."

We headed out across the Kidron Valley and through the city gate. Sure enough, the first person we saw was a man carrying a pitcher of water. We followed him into a large house with a beautiful courtyard. I said to John, "How did Jesus know all this would happen?"

John replied, "He is the Son of God."

"Of course," I agreed. The man with the pitcher asked us whom we wished to see. "The owner," I replied. The owner, a distinguished, well-groomed man appeared. I repeated Jesus' words, and he smiled and invited us to follow him upstairs. The room was spacious with a table large enough for our group. Everything necessary for the Passover was there, just as Jesus had said. Even the basins and towels were in place. We set the table for thirteen guests, thanked the owner, and went back to the garden, reporting to Jesus everything, including the meal, was ready. He smiled and thanked us.

October 31   Luke 22:24–30

Who Will Be the Greatest?

We spent the rest of the day celebrating the great festival in which God had delivered His people from Egypt with a powerful hand. The killing of the Passover lamb affected Jesus deeply. I noticed tears flowing down His cheeks as the lamb was slain. He began to breathe heavily and turned away from the spectacle. When I asked Him if He was alright, He nodded. Then suddenly, like a lightening bolt, John the Baptist's words came to my mind. "Behold the Lamb of God, slain from the foundation of the world." Him? Jesus? The Lamb? How could He die and still fulfill the Messianic expectations we'd been taught all our lives?

After the ceremony and ritual of the day, Jesus led us toward the upper room. Judas, lagging behind, brought up the subject nobody really wanted to discuss. "Do you think He will declare Himself Messiah? If He does, I am best qualified to be second in command."

This started everyone jockeying for top position. By the time we reached the upper room, tempers were hot. Jesus was already seated, and Judas made a grab for the seat to His right. I took the seat to His left, casting daggers at Judas. The tension was oppressive.

Jesus spoke, "The kings and great men of the world lord it over the people they rule, yet they are called friends of the people. But with you, it should be different. Those who are great should become the servant. Who is more important, the one who sits at the table or the one who serves?" No one spoke. "The one who sits at the table, of course," He said, answering His own question. "But not here," He continued, "for I am among you as one who serves. You have stayed with Me in My time of trial. Just as My Father granted Me a kingdom, I grant you the right to eat and drink at My table with Me in My kingdom, and you will sit on thrones judging the twelve tribes of Israel."

Everyone sat in stony silence, still angry even after what Jesus said. We had asked the owner for a servant to wash the guests' feet, but no one came. Something inside me said, *John, you do it*. But my pride would not let me. "Let Judas do it," I muttered under my breath.

November 1   *John 13:13*

The Upper Room Scene

It had always been beyond my comprehension that my Commander, Beloved Lord, Creator of the universe, would become a human being. When He first made the announcement to all of us assembled before the throne of the Father, we could not believe what we were hearing. The Supreme Being, God Himself, become a man? Second in command, I, Gabriel, knelt before the Lord and begged to be permitted to go in His place. I told Him that He was needed in heaven. But the real reason was that I did not want Him to have to endure what the rescue mission would involve. He told us that the mission would ultimately end in His death on a cross. Other angels also offered themselves in His place. He smiled and thanked us for our love toward Him, but He told us only the Creator, not the created, could die on behalf of the human race.

Now that the time has come, I'm not sure I can stand watching Him bear the weight of all that is before Him. But whether we like it or not, the battle is raging, and we are intimately involved. Satan is present in the upper room, making sure Judas fulfills his role. Jesus lovingly looked at each of His disciples around the table. He had faithfully taught them what they needed to know so that they could stand on their own against the enemy once He was gone. I knew He would love and support them to the very end.

I watched as Satan whispered lies to Judas. It was hard to watch my former heavenly friend, once the champion of love to God and unfallen worlds, now my enemy and foe, at work deceiving all who would listen. I made my way to Jesus' side and reminded Him that all of heaven was behind Him. *The Father has given You complete authority over everything. Don't forget You have come from God, and You will most certainly return to God.* He smiled. I could tell by the expression on His face that my message had brought Him much needed encouragement.

November 2   *John 13:4–10*

Jesus Washes the Disciples' Feet

All of us were fuming. We were angry with Judas for bringing up a controversial subject and then grabbing the seat of honor at Jesus' right side. The tension in the room was heavy. Jaws were set, and no one moved to do what everyone knew needed to be done. Suddenly Jesus did the unexpected. He stood and looked at us as if He was examining our souls. I felt ashamed, embarrassed, and very uncomfortable. Then He took off His robe, wrapped a towel around His waist, and poured water into a basin. We stared in disbelief. No one expected Him, of all people, to do the work of a servant and wash our feet!

He began with Philip, then Thomas and Matthew. I watched the expression on each face. Mostly I saw embarrassment and shame, knowing that they should be doing for Him what He was doing for them. I began to think of all the times Jesus had come to my rescue when my impulsive nature got me into trouble. I recalled all of His kindnesses to me personally: the healing of my mother-in-law, paying the temple tax, going fishing when He needed to rest, helping my wife with kitchen chores. Now He was about to wash my feet when I should be washing His. After He dried Matthew's feet, He turned and knelt before me.

"Lord," I cried, "are You going to wash my feet?" At the same time, I pulled away from Him.

He looked up at me and replied, "You don't understand what I am doing, but someday you will."

"No, Lord," I protested impulsively, "You will never wash my feet!"

"Unless I wash you, Peter, you won't belong to Me."

When I realized my resistance would separate me from Him, I cried out, "Lord, then wash my hands and head along with my feet." Tears trickled down my cheeks as I thought about life without Jesus.

He took my feet in His hands and said, "One who has bathed does not need to wash except his feet to be clean. You are clean, but that isn't true for everyone here." He sighed deeply, dried my feet, and moved to Nathanael.

I knew at that moment that there was nothing more important in my life than Jesus.

November 3 *John 13:11*

Jesus Washes Judas' Feet

The reason I brought up the subject of who would occupy the place next to Christ in the kingdom was to force the Lord's hand in front of the other disciples. He knew I was most qualified to lead the rest, especially since most were ignorant fishermen. They knew, too, that I was by far the best choice, and this seemed like the perfect opportunity for Jesus to resolve the problem. But instead of appointing me and setting the record straight, He just sat there.

I began to realize that things were not going according to my plan when He began to talk about servanthood and how we should serve one another. I started to wonder if He was any smarter than the rest of them. As I watched Him washing feet like a servant, I sincerely wondered if this whole kingdom thing was just a farce. When did a king ever wash His subject's feet? The strange part of all this foot washing was that the attitude in the room began to change from anger and bitterness to humility and submission.

Finally it was my turn. At first I resented Him, but then I looked into those piercing eyes that seemed to read the thoughts and even motives of my inner soul. He took my left foot and washed it.

Then the right foot. I saw His tears fall into the basin. Suddenly an overwhelming desire to confess what I had done and seek forgiveness came over me. He knelt, drying my feet with the towel. His eyes appeared to plead with me to repent of my actions. I came so close to confessing the betrayal plot, but another power seemed to grip me and plant thoughts in my mind: *There is nothing to be gained here. Look at Him—broken, weeping, washing feet. He must be forced to acknowledge the kingly authority that is His. The betrayal plot will do just that!* I steeled myself against any notion to confess and was more committed than ever to follow through with the betrayal plot.

November 4   *John 13:12–20*

Jesus Explains the Footwashing

Everyone sat in silence as Jesus put away the basin and towel. Then, putting on His robe, He took His place at the table. He looked around at each one of us and said, "Do you have any idea why I washed your feet?"

I knew He was doing the work of a servant, which I should have done, but beyond that, I didn't have a clue. Then He said, "You call me 'Teacher' and 'Lord,' and you are right in doing so because that is what I am. Since I, your Teacher and Lord, became a servant and washed your feet, shouldn't you be willing to wash each other's feet? I have given you an example to follow—do as I have done to you."

I never forgot what Jesus did that day and the words He spoke. In my future missionary travels, when situations arose where people refused to stoop to menial work or fill the role of a servant, I remembered what Jesus had done for me.

Jesus continued, "To be honest with you, a slave is not greater than his master, nor is a messenger more important than the one who sends the message. Now that you know these things, God will bless you if you do them," He added, a big smile spreading across His face.

Then He became serious as He looked around the room. "What happens here tonight will fulfill what the Scripture says, 'The one who eats bread with Me has turned against Me.'"

Turned against Him? What could He mean? Who would do such a thing? I looked carefully around the table at each of my fellow disciples. Each of them sat motionless, seeming as puzzled as I felt. The only movement I saw was that of Judas putting down the bread he was eating.

Jesus went on, "I am telling you this now so that when it happens you will believe I am the Messiah. I tell you the truth, anyone who welcomes My messenger, welcomes Me. Anyone who welcomes Me also welcomes the Father who sent Me."

When Jesus had finished speaking, we looked at each other. Who would turn against Him, I kept wondering. Someone in the room was a betrayer, but who?

November 5 *Matthew 26:20; Mark 14:17; Luke 22:14–16*

Jesus Eats the Passover Meal With His Disciples

The Passover meal was on the table ready to be eaten. Jesus bowed His head and invited us to pray with Him as He asked God's blessing upon the Passover meal. We then ate the food and recited the story of the deliverance of our ancestors from Egyptian bondage. Every aspect of the meal was a reminder of God's saving power as shown in the story of the Exodus. My kids always played an important part in the service. Tonight was the first time I had celebrated the Passover away from my family. Jesus had asked us to spend this Passover with Him, emphasizing how important it was that we celebrate this once at His table.

"I have been very eager to eat this Passover meal with you before My suffering begins."

I nudged my friend Philip, "What does He mean by suffering?"

"Nathanael, I don't know any more than you, but it bothers me when He talks like that."

We listened as Jesus continued, "I promise you, I will not eat this meal again until its meaning is fulfilled in the kingdom of God."

Every Jew is required by the law to celebrate the festivals, so why is He saying He won't eat it again? And what could He mean about its significance being fulfilled in the kingdom of God? Does He mean He will soon establish His kingdom? But if He establishes His kingdom, why is He talking about suffering? My mind whirled with questions. It seemed so confusing. Turning again to Philip I said, "I don't understand what He is talking about."

He smiled and answered, "Don't worry about it, Nathanael. There's lots of things we have questions about, but either He explains them to us eventually or, as time passes, we come to understand." I nodded.

The other disciples seemed confused too. I could see them whispering to each other. The only one not saying anything or talking to someone was Judas—he just sat at the table with his head down. I didn't think much about it because he'd always been a loner.

Jesus stopped speaking, and I couldn't tell if He was listening to the discussions or preoccupied with some other important issue. I wished I could read His thoughts.

November 6   *Matthew 26:21–29; Mark 14:18–25;*
                                                                                                Luke 22:17–23; John 13:21–30

The Lord's Supper

I wondered if some of the other disciples already suspected me. Then without warning, Jesus just blurted it out, "I tell you the truth, one of you will betray Me."

The room went silent until, beginning with Peter, one by one they started asking, "Am I the one, Lord?"

I knew I had to ask like everyone else, but before I had a chance to speak, Jesus said, "One of you, in fact the one who has just eaten from this bowl, will betray me." Because they had been talking, no one had noticed that I had just dipped my bread in the bowl. "The Son of man must die," He continued, "as the Scripture declared long ago, but how terrible it will be for the one who betrays Him. It would have been better for that man if he had never been born."

When Jesus finished speaking, I turned to Him and quietly asked, "Rabbi, am I the one?"

His eyes became very sad as He looked into my soul with that piercing gaze. Again I had an overwhelming urge to confess. He spoke, "You have said it."

He then took some bread, broke it, and handed pieces to us. "Take and eat, for this is My body." He asked God's blessing on the cup; then He passed it around, saying, "Each of you drink from it, for this is My blood that confirms the covenant between God and His people. It is poured out as a sacrifice to forgive the sins of many."

As I wavered, I heard a voice in my head tell me I could not be forgiven because I had gone too far.

Again Jesus vowed never to drink of the fruit of the vine again until His Father's kingdom was established. Peter was determined to know who the betrayer was, so he motioned for John to ask. "Who is the betrayer?"

"It is the one I give the dipped bread to." Someone to my right asked me to pass the dates, so what Jesus said didn't register right away. He handed me the bread, I ate it, and then I realized everyone knew. They stared. Jesus turned to me and said, "Hurry and do what you are going to do."

Few of them understood what was happening. They thought Jesus wanted me to pay the Passover fee or help the poor since I was the treasurer. I got up and walked out of the room, very relieved to be away from them. I went to look for the priests—I had a job to do.

November 7   *Matthew 26:30–35; Mark 14:26–31;*
                                                                                                 Luke 22:31–38; John 13:31–38

Jesus Predicts Peter's Denial

As soon as Judas left, Jesus spoke these words, "The time has come for the Son of man to be glorified. The Father is glorified, too, because of the Son's glory. Children, I will be with you only a little longer. Just as I told the Jews," Jesus continued, "you will search for Me, but you cannot come where I am going. Here is a new commandment: love each other as I have loved you. Your love for each other will prove to the world that you are My disciples."

Where was He planning to go where we could not come? I didn't like the idea of Him leaving us. He began to sing a hymn, and we joined in. After the hymn, we headed for the Garden of Gethsemane.

As we walked Peter asked the question on everyone's mind, "Lord, where are You going?"

Jesus replied, "You can't go with me now but you will follow Me later."

"But why can't I go now?" Peter asked. "I am ready to die for You."

Jesus stopped. We gathered close to Him. "All of you will desert Me just as the Scripture says: 'God will strike the Shepherd, and the sheep will suffer.' After I am raised from the dead, I will go ahead of you to Galilee and meet you there."

"Lord, even if everyone else deserts you, I never will," Peter said.

Earnestly Jesus said, "Peter, this very night before the rooster crows twice, you will deny Me three times, saying you never knew Me."

"No!" Peter declared emphatically. "Even if I have to die with You, I will never deny You." The rest of us vowed the same.

Then Jesus said, "All that the prophets wrote about Me is about to be fulfilled." We continued on to Gethsemane. Was He about to form an army to establish the kingdom? But He said He was going where we couldn't come, and what about death and resurrection? I didn't understand it, but I trusted Him.

November 8   *John 14:1-14*

Jesus Is the Way to the Father

We crossed the Brook Kidron and made our way up the gentle slope to where we had spent many nights together. It was almost like a home away from home. Each of us had our favorite spot in the Garden of Gethsemane. Because of the Passover, there were lots of campers around us. They were mostly poor people who could not afford a room in the city's inns. With a fire burning, we gathered around Jesus, and He spoke to us. He told us not to be afraid but to trust God. He told us He was going away to prepare a place for us. There would be many rooms in His Father's house and when everything was ready He would come and get us and we would always be with Him. I really liked the sound of that! Then He said, "You know where I am going and how to get there."

Thomas looked at Him and said, "No, Lord, we don't know where You are going."

Jesus replied, "I am the way, the truth, and the life, and it is through Me you get to the Father. If you really knew Me, you'd know the Father, but now that you have seen Me you have seen the Father."

I said, "Lord, show us the Father, and we will be satisfied."

Jesus sighed deeply and shook His head slowly. "Philip, I have been with you all this time and you still don't know who I am?" He told us He and the Father worked hand in hand. Everything we had seen Jesus do the Father would do also. "I am in the Father, and the Father is in Me. Don't you believe this? The words I say are not My own, but My Father who lives in Me and works through Me. So at least believe because of what you have seen Me do." He reminded us that His followers, the believers, would do the same work He had done.

My mind went back to the time we were sent out two by two and were given the power to heal and even cast out demons. He said He would go to the Father and give us anything we asked for. I wondered if He was planning to send us on another mission, only farther away. "All you do through Me will bring glory to the Father. Just ask Me, and I will give you whatever you need to bring glory to the Father."

November 9   John 14:15–31

Jesus Promises to Send the Holy Spirit

Up until now, life hadn't been complicated. Jesus taught us, healed people, fed large crowds, talked about the kingdom, and cast out demons. Now He talked about death and going away to the Father. It seemed like life had suddenly become very complex. He talked about sending us an Advocate, a Comforter. Why? He was our Advocate!

"If you love Me, obey My commandments," He said. He told us the Comforter would be the Holy Spirit whom the world did not know but we knew because He lived in us. Jesus promised not to abandon us like orphans, but then He talked about being raised to life. He told us we would understand more clearly after His resurrection. I wasn't sure if I understood anything at this point and time. I still had questions about the kingdom and Israel. I spoke up and said, "Lord, are You only going to reveal Yourself to us and not the world at large?"

His response was that all who loved Him would obey Him and He, along with the Father, would abide in them. He told us that He didn't need to be a king—the people who loved Him would come to Him as He was. Then He told us the Advocate would come, this Holy Spirit, and be our teacher as well as remind us of everything Jesus had taught us. He told us He would give us the gift of peace of mind and heart so we did not need to be afraid. He promised He would come back for us, but none of us wanted Him to go anywhere in the first place. Then He said, "If you really loved Me, you would be happy to know I am going to the Father. I am trying to tell you these things now so that when they happen, you will believe."

He looked down the path toward the city and told us the ruler of the world was about to come but no matter what, He would remain faithful to the Father for the sake of the entire world. There seemed to be so much to learn and understand, but He seemed to have so little time to tell us. He didn't seem His usual self. There was something unnatural about Him tonight.

November 10   *John 15:1–17*

Jesus Teaches About the Vine and the Branches

It was getting late, but there was an urgency in Jesus' words and what He was sharing with us from His heart. On this night, He spoke of Himself as the grapevine and the Father as the gardener. He cuts off the branches that bear nothing. Those who do produce fruit are pruned so they will be even more fruitful.

When I was a kid, I worked in my neighbor's vineyard for a single coin each day in the hot sun. Jesus told us we had been pruned and purified by the message He had given us. I was glad to hear I was a fruitful branch. I remember one year in that vineyard when the pruners had missed an active row of vines. The branches produced small, unattractive grapes that nobody wanted. Jesus reminded us that in order to be fruitful we had to remain in Him and He in us. A branch cannot produce fruit severed from the vine, and in the same way, we are fruitless apart from Him. "Apart from Me, you can do nothing," He said.

Any branch that does not draw life from the vine dies and is cut off because it withers and dies. These branches are thrown into heaps and set on fire because they are lifeless. My vineyard job included throwing the dead branches in a heap and burning them.

As fruitful branches we can ask Jesus for whatever we want, and it will be given. The world will see we are Jesus' disciples, and thus, we will bring glory to God. If we remain in Him, we will be obedient to His commandments and be filled with love for Him and each other. As a result, we will experience great joy. "There is no greater love than one lays down His life for a friend," He said. As a former zealot, I had seen many lay down their lives for friends. "You are not slaves but friends. I've told you what the Father told me. I have chosen you," He said. "Go and produce lasting fruit, and the Father will give you whatever you ask for to accomplish the work. My commandment to you is to love each other."

I am now a zealot with a mission of staying connected to Jesus, being fruitful and glorifying Him.

November 11   *John 15:18–16:4*

The Hatred of the World

We huddled around the fire while Jesus spoke. It was late, and I wondered why we couldn't save these instructions for the next day. I love His teachings, but it is hard to concentrate and listen so late at night.

"If the world hates you," He said, "remember that it hated Me first." As disciples of Jesus, His enemies became our enemies. He reminded us of something He'd said earlier, "A slave isn't greater than his master. So if they persecute Me, they'll persecute you too. If they listened to Me, they'll listen to you. They have a vendetta against you because of Me, simply because they rejected the One who sent Me." He made it clear that it was God the Father they were rejecting, not us.

"If I hadn't backed up my claims about Myself and My Father with miracles, they would not be guilty, but since they saw everything I did to prove I was not some crazy person when I claimed to be the Messiah, they are guilty. They still hate Me and My Father. It's a fulfillment of Scripture, 'They hate Me for no reason.'" That was true. There didn't seem to be any logical reason for the hatred shown to Jesus.

"I promise to send you an advocate, the Spirit of Truth. He will come from the Father and testify about Me," He continued, "but all of you must testify about Me because you've been with Me from the start." Jesus said He wanted us to know these things so our faith would remain strong and we wouldn't fall away. "The time will come when you will be expelled from the synagogues and those who kill you will think they are doing God a service." When we were persecuted, He wanted us to remember that He'd warned us about all we were going through in advance. It sounded to me like really hard times ahead, but I knew that whatever we might face in the future, He would be with us.

November 12 *John 16:5–15*

The Holy Spirit

"He just said it again," I whispered to Philip.

"What are you talking about, Nathanael?" he asked with some irritation in his voice.

"He's talking about going away," I responded. "When He talks about going away where we cannot come, I worry, because I don't want to be left here alone without Him."

Jesus looked at me. "I'm going to the One who sent Me, but no one has asked Me where I am going. Instead you are upset because I told you I am going away," He said. "The truth of the matter is this: if I don't go the Advocate will not come. When I go, I will send Him to you. You won't be alone. He will convict the world of sin and God's righteousness and the coming judgment. The world needs to know about these things because the world's sin is simply that they do not believe in Me. They need to know righteousness is available to them. The world needs to be convicted of the coming judgment because the ruler of this world has already been judged. I've spoken to the world and done My work. Now it is the Advocate's job to convict the world of these things. You are the ones through whom the Advocate will speak."

He paused, lowered His voice, and bowed His head. Then He looked up at us as if He were searching each of our souls. "There is so much I want to tell you," He said, "but if I did you would be overwhelmed. But when the Spirit of truth comes, He will guide you into all truth."

I assumed the Spirit of truth was the same person as the Advocate. This Spirit of truth would not give us His own opinion but only the things He heard. *Who will be His source?* I wondered. Jesus answered my unspoken question. The Spirit of truth would reveal the future and bring glory to Jesus by sharing with us what the Lord had shared with Him. All the resources of the Father belong to Jesus who would communicate through the Spirit of truth these blessings to us. All the blessings of heaven would be ours. Having the assurance that Jesus and the Father and the Advocate would all be with us made me feel better. We would not be left alone. Heaven would be with us.

November 13   John 16:16–33

Jesus Explains About Going Away

I was contemplating who this Spirit of truth might be and just how we would relate to Him when Jesus made a statement that got everyone talking. "In a little while, you won't see Me anymore, but a little while after that, you will see Me again."

"What does He mean by that?" my brother Andrew asked.

I didn't have a clue.

"And what does this 'little while' mean?" John queried as though I had all the answers.

I shrugged my shoulders. I was just about to ask Jesus to explain Himself when He did just that.

"I suppose you are confused about not seeing Me, then in a little while seeing Me." Everyone nodded. He told us we would soon be very sad over things that were about to happen to Him. Then He added, "But the world will rejoice." He told us our sadness would turn to joy, like a woman giving birth, suffering through labor but when the baby comes, the pain is forgotten as she focuses on her newborn. "Likewise, you will have sorrow now, but don't give up, in a little while you will rejoice."

It sounded to me like He knew exactly what was about to happen with Him and with us. How could He read the future so well? He then reminded us that no one could steal away our joy.

"At that time you won't need to ask Me for a thing, because you can ask the Father in My name and He will give you whatever you need. I know this is something new to you," He continued, "asking in My name, but if you do, you will receive and will have great joy. Sometimes the things I tell you seem confusing, but don't worry, the Father loves you dearly because you love Me. It is true, I've come to this world from the Father and will soon return to Him."

We affirmed that we believed He came from God—we understood that much. He said, "Do you really believe? The time is here when all of you will scatter and leave Me alone. But I'm not alone, because the Father is with Me. Take heart, in this world you may have many trials, but remember, I have overcome the world so you can have peace."

Under my breath I said, "The others may abandon You, but I won't. You will see that You can count on me."

November 14   *John 17:1–5*

Jesus Prays for Himself

For a few minutes everyone sat around the fire reflecting on what Jesus had been sharing. It seemed like He was really anxious to give us all this information. I thought about His last statement. "Here on earth you will have many trials and sorrows, but take heart because I have overcome the world." Those words comforted me, because He was telling us that whatever the world might tempt us with, afflict us with, or try to overcome us with, Jesus would guide us through because He had overcome the world. His voice suddenly interrupted our reflections as He looked heavenward and began to pray. "Father, the hour has come," He cried. "Glorify Your Son so He can give glory back to You."

I've thought about those words often. Jesus' whole purpose in life was to give glory to His Father. *Is the purpose of heaven*, I wondered, *to glorify the Father?*

Jesus continued praying, "You have given Me, Your Son, authority over everyone. I give eternal life to each person the Father gives Me."

If He has authority over everyone, then eternal life is available to all people, I thought. That was a concept far from the exclusive teachings of the scribes and Pharisees.

Next He told us what we needed to do to obtain eternal life. "This is the way to have eternal life: to know You, the only true God and Jesus Christ, the One You sent to earth."

"It is that simple?" I asked out loud, "To know the Father and You?"

He smiled and nodded. *Then what is the purpose of the many rules and requirements?* I wondered.

He continued to pray. "I brought glory to You here on earth by completing the work You gave Me to do. Now, Father, bring Me into the glory we shared before the world began."

If eternal life was in knowing and having a relationship with Jesus, then I could be certain that I had eternal life. That was very good news! I need all the good news I can get because I, more than all the others, struggle with doubt.

November 15   *John 17:6–19*

Jesus Prays for the Disciples

"I have revealed You to the ones You gave me from this world," I heard Jesus pray. He was saying that we, the disciples, had always belonged to God so were like a gift from the Father. Everything Jesus had He received from the Father. We had kept Jesus' word and He affirmed that we had accepted His call and fully believed the message from the Father. It was true—we believed that Jesus was the Son of the living God sent from the Father. His prayer was not for the world but for us, His disciples, because we belong to God. "Whoever belongs to You, Father, belongs to Me and the result is glory to God."

He prayed about departing this world, and He mentioned that we would stay here while He would go to the Father. He prayed for our protection and that we would be unified as the Father and Son were. While He was here, He had protected us by the power of His name and not one strayed except the one bent on destruction as the Scriptures foretold. I think He was referring to the one He spoke about earlier who would betray Him. I was having a hard time wrapping my mind around any of us actually doing that.

He said that His message was calculated to bring joy to us. I didn't feel very joyful at the moment, knowing that He would be leaving us, but I clung to His promise. His prayer continued, "I have given them Your word, and they do not belong to the world just as I don't belong to the world. And as a result, the world hates them as it hates Me. But please, Father," He pleaded, "I'm not asking You to take them out of the world. Just keep them safe from the evil one. They are no more a part of the world than I am." I knew how the world could be harsh and cold, stripping one of godliness. It was the truth as seen in Jesus that transformed me, Thaddeus the loser, into a disciple.

"Make them pure and holy by teaching them Your word of truth," He cried. We watched Him pray with great intensity, sweat poured off His face. "Just as You sent Me into the world," He cried out, "I'm sending them into the world. I give Myself, Father, as a holy sacrifice for them so they can be made holy by Your truth."

Whatever did He mean by a "holy sacrifice"? I pondered.

November 16   John 17:20–26

Jesus Prays for Future Believers

Wiping the sweat from His face, Jesus continued to pray. "I am not only praying for these disciples but for all the disciples they will make—the people who will believe their message." It sounded more and more to me like we were the ones assigned to take Jesus' place after He went back to the Father. Our job would be to take His message to the world. *How is that going to work when we are not allowed to have anything to do with the Gentiles?* I wondered.

Jesus prayed that we would be unified in purpose like He and the Father were one in purpose. Father, Son, and disciples all together, united for the purpose of spreading the message of truth to the world so the whole world would believe Jesus was sent by God.

He raised His hands heavenward. "I have given them the glory You gave Me, so they may be one as We are one." His prayer emphasized the importance of unity. "If I am in them and You are in Me, there will be such perfect unity that the world will have to take notice."

I thought about our little group and all the differences between us. How would we ever have that perfect unity He was praying for? I guessed we would have to ask Him to help us with that.

Passionately He prayed, "The world will know that You sent Me and that You love them as much as You love Me." Tears streamed down His cheeks, "Father, I absolutely must have these true believers with Me wherever I am. I want them to see the glory I had, the glory You gave Me because You loved Me so much before the world began. O righteous Father, the world does not know You, but I do and so do these disciples You have sent to Me. I have revealed You to them, and I will reveal more of You to them. They will feel and experience the same love You have for Me, because We will be in them."

As I watched and listened to His prayer, I was drawn to Him. Seeing His tears and the intensity of His love and concern for us brought tears to my eyes. I, Peter, did not understand everything He said, but I knew one thing—He was truly the center of my life, my Alpha and Omega.

November 17   *Matthew 26:36-46; Mark 14:32-42; Luke 22:40-46*

Gethsemane

Jesus finished praying, stood, and looked at us seated around the fire. I stood up, too, and stretched my arms and legs, but my eyes were fixed on Jesus. He seemed to be overtaken by powerful emotions. I couldn't tell what it was, but it was totally uncharacteristic of Him. It was as though something or someone was draining the life out of Him.

"Peter, James, and John, come with Me. I need you to join Me in private." We followed Him to His favorite place of prayer, a quiet area surrounded by olive trees. I had never seen anyone so full of anguish. "I must pray. My soul is crushed with grief to the point of death," He stammered. I couldn't understand what could be the cause of His great despair. The three of us tried to comfort Him, but to no avail. "Stay here and keep watch with Me."

He walked about a stone's throw away from us, fell to His knees, and groaned as though in great agony. With His face to the ground, He prayed. "My Father, if it is possible, let this cup pass from Me. Everything is possible for You. This cup of suffering, let it be taken away; yet, may Your will be done, not Mine."

I was overwhelmed with sadness as I watched Him. I felt full of fear for Him. It seemed as though He was dying. I prayed along with James and John for His safety. The last thing I remembered was looking over at Him lying on the ground clutching the grass, pleading with His Father. I don't know how long I slept, but I woke to Him tapping my shoulder. He was bent over me. "Peter, are you asleep? Couldn't you stay awake and watch with Me?"

I looked up into His face, which was filled with pain and horror. James and John awakened. I said to Him, "Lord, are You okay?" I felt ashamed that I had fallen asleep and embarrassed at what I said. It was pretty obvious that He was anything but okay.

"Keep watch and pray so you will not give into temptation. The Spirit is willing, but the flesh is weak."

I wanted to help Him, but I didn't know what to do. He left us and went back to His place of prayer, repeating His pleadings. I looked at James and John and said, "We have to pray for Him." The others nodded.

November 18   *Luke 22:40–46; Mark 14:41a*

His Prayer for Deliverance

Again He lay face down on the ground and cried out, "Father, if it is at all possible, please take this cup of suffering away from Me." We watched helplessly as He writhed on the ground. It was as though some unseen force was torturing Him. Momentarily, He looked in our direction. His face was contorted and glistened with sweat.

We prayed for some time, but then it was as if we had been drugged and this stupor overwhelmed us. I tried desperately to focus on Jesus and the agony He was going through, but I kept nodding off. I'd force myself into consciousness, but soon I would be asleep again. Before long the three of us were sound asleep.

What I remember next of that night in Gethsemane was Jesus shaking us awake. "Wake up," He kept saying. "The hour is almost here."

"What hour?" I asked stupidly in a daze of dreams. I looked at His face and hardly recognized Him.

Peter woke, saw the blood on His face, and asked, "Lord, what happened to You?" He reached for his sword, thinking that someone had attacked Him.

"Please, can't you pray with Me?" Jesus begged. Sympathy in suffering is something we all long for and it truly was our desire to be there for Him. We watched as He stumbled back to His place of prayer. He lifted His arms to heaven and cried, "Oh, Father, please help Me. I am alone."

We tried our best to stay awake, but we kept slipping into a stupor. At one point I felt certain I saw light and the presence of an angel from heaven, but I was so drowsy that I wasn't sure what was happening.

When Jesus awoke us the third time, He said that the time was at hand. I slowly stood up, very embarrassed that I had let Him down.

November 19   *Matthew 26:46–50; Mark 14:42–45;*
                                                                                                  Luke 22:47–48; John 18:1–9

The Betrayal

The three of us were wide awake now. In the distance, through the trees, we could see torches and hear voices. We watched and listened as the crowd approached.

"Let's be going," Jesus said. "My betrayer is here."

We walked to where the other disciples slept. In the distance we could see Judas approaching with a battalion of armed men carrying swords and clubs and torches. By now the others were awake, eyes wide open in surprise. I stared at Judas. "Is he the betrayer?" I asked half out loud. I couldn't believe it, but then I remembered some of the things Jesus had said in the Upper Room, and the puzzle started to fit together. I burned with anger when he stepped up to Jesus and greeted Him with a kiss as though all was well.

"Rabbi," he exclaimed. I wanted to punch him, but Jesus was speaking.

"Judas, would you betray the Son of man with a kiss?"

I learned later that this was the signal he had prearranged with the priests, telling them to arrest the one he greeted with a kiss. Without answering, Judas melted back into the mob. I was furious. Jesus put His hand on my shoulder to calm me. I glared at the traitor, wanting to call fire and brimstone down on his head.

Jesus stepped toward the crowd. "Whom are you looking for?" He asked.

"Jesus, the Nazarene," they replied.

"I am He."

As soon as the mob moved forward to arrest Jesus, a legion of angels flashed their brightness and power, knocking every man in the crowd backwards to the ground. Momentarily stunned, they quickly got back on their feet.

Giving them a chance to think about what they were doing, Jesus asked again, "Whom are you looking for?"

Again they replied, weakly this time, unsure of what might happen, "Jesus, the Nazarene."

"I have already told you that I am He," Jesus replied. "Since you are looking for Me, let these other ones go." He turned and pointed to us.

I didn't want to go. I wanted to stay and fight, and I wanted Judas to be my first victim.

November 20 *Matthew 26:51–56; Mark 14:46–52;*
Luke 22:49–53; John 18:10, 11

Jesus Arrested

The crowd surged forward, grabbing Jesus' arms. As one of them tied His hands behind His back, I cried out, "Jesus, we brought the swords. Should we fight?" I pulled my own sword from its sheath and slashed at one of them, trying to split open his head; however, I merely cut off his ear. He screamed, letting go of Jesus' arm and grabbing the side of his head. Everything seemed to stop momentarily as blood poured from the man's head and the crowd watched in disbelief.

Then Jesus spoke, "Enough of this! Peter, put your sword back in its sheath. Should I not drink from the cup of suffering My Father has given Me?" Releasing His hands, He bent down to retrieve the severed ear. He then re-attached it to the head of the man whom I had tried to kill. The man was named Malchus, a servant of the high priest. Everyone witnessed the miracle, but no one said a word. I looked closely at the man's ear. It was completely healed—only some blood remained. The Lord spoke, "Peter, don't you realize those who use the sword will die by the sword. If I wanted to, I could ask My Father to send twelve legions of angels to protect us. He would send them instantly, but then how would the

Scriptures be fulfilled that describe what must happen now? Shall I not drink from the cup the Father has given Me?"

Then He turned to the mob, "Am I some dangerous revolutionary that you come to arrest Me with swords and clubs? Why didn't you arrest Me in the temple where I taught every day? But this is your moment, the time when the power of darkness reigns. The words of the prophets in Scripture are being fulfilled."

At that moment the priest shouted, "Arrest them all!" The soldiers moved toward us. They grabbed Jesus and tied His hands.

I shouted, "Run for your lives!" A soldier grabbed at Philip, stripping off his outer garment. My last glimpse of Jesus was Him standing there alone, His face toward us as we ran away, deserting Him. I watched from a distance as they led Him back to the city.

November 21 *John 18:12–24*

The Trial at Annas' House

The others had taken Peter's advice and run for their lives. Now he and I watched as they led Him away. "How could He have allowed this to happen, Peter?"

"Didn't you hear what He said?" Peter replied. "He could have asked for legions of angels to set Him free, but then how would Scripture be fulfilled? Let's follow them. I want to know what becomes of Him."

They first took Him to Annas' house, Caiaphas' father-in-law. Both the high priest and his father-in-law had homes built in one common courtyard. I shuddered as I thought about what Caiaphas had told my father in reference to Jesus: "It is better that one man should die for the people." I sought entrance at the courtyard gate. The girl recognized me as a relative of Caiaphas so allowed me to come in. I spoke with her so she would allow Peter in.

"Aren't you one of Jesus' disciples?" she asked him.

I was shocked to hear his answer, "No, I am not!" I looked at him, but he put his head down. The soldiers and some of the servants had built a fire because it was cold.

I moved as close as possible so that I could see and hear what was going on inside Annas' house. Annas questioned Him, "What are You teaching the people?"

Jesus replied, "Everyone knows what I teach because I teach regularly in the synagogue and the temple where the people gather. I have not spoken in secret. Why are you asking Me this question? Ask those who heard Me, for they know what I said."

The high priest was very upset with Jesus' answer because it made him look stupid. He threw down the judge's gavel and walked out across the courtyard to his own place. One of the temple guards slapped Jesus across the face with the back of his hand. "Is that how You answer the high priest?" he demanded.

A trickle of blood flowed from Jesus' lip as He replied, "If I said anything wrong, you must prove it. But if I have spoken the truth, why are you beating Me?"

The guard gave no answer. Annas had Jesus' hands rebound and sent Him to Caiaphas. I stood near the door and witnessed all that had just happened when Jesus walked past me. I hoped my presence buoyed His spirits.

November 22 *Matthew 26:69–75; Mark 14:66–72;*
Luke 22:54–62; John 18:25–27

Peter Denies Jesus

From my vantage point, I could see John just inside Annas' house. Once in awhile I could see Jesus standing with His hands bound. Some of those near me noticed that I was very interested in what was taking place. When the temple guard struck Jesus in the face, I blurted out, "Hey, you can't beat an uncondemned man!" My fists were clenched and the veins bulged out on my neck and forehead. I was angry. Suddenly I became aware of everyone watching me. The servant girl from the gate was speaking to others and pointing at me. One of the men who had been with the mob arresting Jesus came up to me and said, "You must be one of His disciples. Your accent is Galilean."

Would they put me on trial, too, just for being a disciple? Everyone was staring at me, so I cried out, "I do not know the Man, and I swear an oath I have had nothing to do with Him!"

I removed myself from the group and hung back in the shadows, trying to avoid the stares and questioning glances. About an hour passed before the man whose ear I had cut off approached me and said, "You were there in the garden! It was you who tried to kill me!"

The others chimed in, "Then you are His disciple!"

Afraid, tired, and emotionally spent, I called a curse down on my head if I knew the man, Jesus. At that instant the rooster crowed. I looked toward Annas' house just in time to see them leading Jesus down the steps. He looked directly at me. His words flooded into my head: "Before the rooster crows tomorrow morning, you will deny Me three times." The look of betrayal and sadness on His face devastated me. I ran from the courtyard to the garden and fell down on my knees at the exact location where Jesus had struggled and wept bitterly just hours before. I pleaded with God to forgive me. How could I have denied Him when He needed my support? I remained there for hours, pouring out my heart, praying for Jesus, and searching my own soul.

November 23   *Matthew 26:57-68; Mark 14:53-65;*
Luke 22:63-65

Trial at Caiaphas' House

As the guard led Jesus down the steps, He stopped and looked at Peter, who suddenly raced across the courtyard and out the gate. At the time I thought he was going to look for the others—I found out the true story later.

A guard pushed Jesus from behind. "Get moving," he shouted.

I followed them to Caiaphas' house on the other side of the yard. Gathered there were the leading priests, teachers of religious law, and other leaders. The temple guard who had hit Jesus at Annas' house swore at Him and pushed Him up the steps, causing Him to fall. Once inside, Caiaphas called the meeting of the Sanhedrin to order. The officials sat at a table with Jesus standing before them. A group of witnesses stood to one side. They needed evidence from credible people to condemn Jesus to death.

When Caiaphas saw me standing by the door, he appeared upset that I was there, but he said nothing. He charged Jesus with violation of Jewish law and insurrection against Rome. The witnesses were called forward, but no two stories were the same. In fact, they all contradicted each other. At last, two witnesses agreed that Jesus had said He would destroy the temple made with human hands and in three days build another made without human hands, but even they had trouble agreeing on all of the details of their story.

Finally, in frustration, Caiaphas stood up and asked Jesus, "Aren't You going to answer these charges?" He said nothing. Caiaphas, fearful he might lose the trial, shouted in Jesus' face, "Are You the Messiah, the Son of the living God?"

Jesus looked at him. "I am," He replied. "In the future, you will see Me seated at God's right hand, coming in the clouds of heaven."

Caiaphas tore his high priestly robe to pieces as he yelled in a loud, shrill voice, "You've heard His blasphemy! What is your verdict?"

"Guilty!" they cried in unison. "He deserves to die."

Then, like a mob of crazy men, they spit on Him and slapped His face. Next they blindfolded Him and punched His face with their fists. "Prophesy!" they shouted. "Who hit You?"

I could no longer stand to watch the abuse. I remembered He had said something to us about suffering at the hands of evil men. I prayed He would have the strength to endure.

November 24   *Matthew 27:1, 2; Mark 15:1; Luke 22:66–71*

Jesus Condemned

The sun was turning the sky a slight red on the eastern horizon. It looked as though it would be a beautiful day. Inside Caiaphas' house, the entire high council planned their strategy. They knew Pilate's stamp of approval must be on whatever death sentence they sought and that Jesus had to be convicted of treason. I wondered why Nicodemus was not here, although I had heard he was sympathetic to Jesus. I walked near the stair railing and watched as the guards placed a black cloth sack over Jesus' head, punched Him in the face, saying, "If You are a prophet, tell us who punched You."

Then one of them cried out, "If You are the Messiah, why doesn't God deliver You from us?" I recognized the man. He had slapped Jesus at Annas' house. Right at that moment, he raised the cane he held in his hand and brought it down as hard as he could on Jesus' back.

I winced and turned away in distress, unable to watch. Caiaphas suddenly emerged from the room, and I hurried to him. As a kinsman, I entreated him to stop the abuse. "Why are they mistreating the prisoner and punishing Him before He has been condemned by Pilate?" I asked.

His eyes narrowed. "What are you doing here?" his voice full of annoyed anger. "Don't you have a family to be with?"

Pointing to Jesus, I said, "He is my family, my friend and my God."

Caiaphas spat, "Zebedee raised fools who believe in false messiahs. He deserves to die, and He will die!" With disdain, he spun around and walked back into the meeting.

Listening carefully, I could overhear their discussion. They were counting heavily on Pilate's weak, vacillating character to help them accomplish their purpose. It was true. Pilate had condemned many a man without a proper trial. Soon the council appeared, and Caiaphas ordered the soldiers to take the prisoner to Pilate. He was lying on the ground, His face bloody. A soldier reached down, grabbing the rope that bound His hands, and pulled Him to His feet. I wanted to do something, but there was nothing I could do. I felt completely helpless—my emotions gave way to tears.

November 25   *Matthew 27:3–10*

Judas Returns the Betrayal Money

On the way to Pilate's judgment hall, Caiaphas and a few other members of the Sanhedrin stopped at the temple to confer with the priests on duty about the Passover. I waited at the temple steps with the others, feeling helpless. Jesus stood there, hands tied behind His back, erect and alert. He looked like a king, very noble. Just beyond where Jesus stood, I saw a familiar figure come into view.

"Judas," I called, but either he did not hear me or chose to ignore me. I noticed a money sack in his hand, so I decided to follow him. He walked up the steps and through the temple gate to the priest's quarters. He turned and looked around for a moment before entering. I was certain he hadn't seen me, but I noticed he looked very distraught. I moved near the open doorway. Judas' back was toward me. He took the money bag, opened it, and forcefully flung the coins at the feet of the priests. "I have sinned," he cried, "for I have betrayed an innocent Man."

Caiaphas sneered, "What do we care about what you have done? If you feel guilty about betraying Jesus, it's your problem, not ours." Judas rushed out of the room and was gone before I could say anything. I couldn't help but feel sorry for him, remembering Jesus' words—"It would have been better if he had never been born."

The priests gathered up the coins. "It wouldn't be right to put this money in the temple treasury since it was payment for murder," I heard Annas say. After some discussion, they decided to use it to buy the potter's field to use as a cemetery for foreigners. It became known as the "Field of Blood." A verse the prophet Jeremiah had written flashed into my mind: "They took thirty pieces of silver, the price the children of Israel paid for Him, and purchased the potter's field." It dawned on me that prophecy was being fulfilled right before my eyes!

Caiaphas gave his instructions to the priests concerning the Passover before leaving. Spotting me as he exited the room, he approached and spat out angrily, "I thought I told you to go home to your family!" Then he strode back to where Jesus and the others stood. I followed, pondering Jeremiah's prophecy.

November 26   John 18:28–31; Luke 23:1, 2

Jesus Before Pilate

I was fast asleep when a servant woke me and said, "The leading Jews are outside." Annoyed at being awakened so early, I wondered what on earth could be so important. "They want you to sign an execution warrant for the man named Jesus."

Fully awake now, I asked, "Isn't He the miracle worker?"

The servant replied, "Yes, Sir, I believe He is."

"Tell them to bring Him inside to the judgment hall for trial while I get dressed," I instructed.

"They won't enter a Gentile's place," he replied, "because of the Passover and being defiled."

Frustrated with their stupid regulations, I dressed and went out on the balcony above where they stood with the prisoner. I had given into their demands before and signed death decrees without a trial of the accused, but not today. They were going to have to prove Jesus was a criminal. "What is your charge against this Man?" I shouted.

"We would not have brought Him to you if He wasn't a criminal," they shouted back sarcastically. "This man has been leading our people astray, telling them not to pay taxes to Rome and claiming to be the Messiah."

I looked at the prisoner. He did not look like a criminal deserving of death. In fact, He had the bearing and noble look of a king. A strong conviction came to me that this Man was innocent. As I stared at Him, He looked up at me. I was taken aback because it felt like I was the one on trial. Again the conviction of His innocence surged through me. I had to find a way to release Him. "If you think He is a criminal then take Him away and judge Him by your own law," I told them.

"Only the Romans are permitted to execute someone," they replied impatiently. I could see they expected me to sign His death decree without a trial. There had to be a way out of this. I decided to speak with Him and perhaps find a way out of having to condemn Him. I was determined to prove Jesus' innocence.

November 27 *Matthew 27:11-14; Mark 15:2-5;*
Luke 23:3-6; John 18:33-38a

Jesus' Interview With Pilate

I went back into the judgment hall, away from the noisy crowd, and told a guard to bring the prisoner to me. Soon He was standing before me, bruised and bloody but with great dignity. I asked Him, "Are You the King of the Jews?"

He replied, "You have said it."

The Jews in the courtyard kept yelling accusations at Him, so I asked, "Aren't You going to answer them?" He stood with His head down and said nothing. I couldn't believe it—most prisoners facing a death penalty fight for their lives. I asked Him again, "Are you the Jew's king?"

He looked at me. "Is this your own question or are you asking because someone told you about Me?"

What kind of answer is that, I wondered. *Does He expect me to believe in Him?* "Am I a Jew?" I retorted. "Your own people bought You to me for trial. Why? What have You done to deserve death?"

For a moment, it seemed the divinity of the gods flashed through Him, and He stood there as King above all kings. He answered, "My kingdom is not an earthly kingdom. If it were, My followers would fight."

Instantly, that overwhelming conviction swept over me again that He was all He was being accused of. "So You are a king," I said, realizing I was being drawn to Him, wanting the peace and noble bearing He displayed.

He responded, "You say I am a king. Actually, I was born and came into this world to testify to the truth. All who love the truth recognize that what I say is the truth."

"What is truth?" I asked, wanting to hear more. Suddenly the crowd started yelling for me to give them a verdict. Without waiting for His answer, I went out to them. "I find nothing wrong with Him," I shouted at them. They were enraged and began accusing Him of causing riots with His teachings from Galilee to Jerusalem. "Is He a Galilean?" I asked.

"Yes," they chorused.

"Then He is in Herod's jurisdiction, and I will send Him there." They weren't happy about my decision, but they had to comply. This was my way out! By placing the responsibility on Herod, I would be guiltless. I ordered a platoon of soldiers to escort Him to Herod.

November 28 *Luke 23:6–12*

Jesus Appears Before Herod Antipas

I was delighted Pilate thought to involve me in this case. In one way I really wanted to meet Him, but in another way I was scared because some said He was John the Baptist raised from the dead. I dreaded a reincarnated John appearing before me to enact revenge for something my wife had orchestrated. Besides, I was anxious to see if He really could perform miracles as was rumored.

When they brought Him in, I expected to see a battered and broken man. But instead, even though beaten and bloodied, He stood tall and erect, appearing almost victorious. He seemed at peace even though He was about to be condemned to death. I asked Him what charges were being brought against Him, but He wouldn't answer me. The Jews accused Him of many crimes. I asked if He wanted to respond to their accusations. He remained silent. I asked Him if He was John resurrected. Not a word. I was not used to being ignored. I reminded Him I could possibly secure His release. He showed no emotion—He just looked straight ahead as though I did not exist. I told Him if He would perform a miracle I would secure His release. Silence. I called for the sick to be brought in and commanded Him to perform a miracle. He looked at them in pity but did nothing. In anger I cursed Him and accused Him of being a fake.

My soldiers mocked Him by bowing down to the "King of the Jews." They slapped His face, shoved Him on the floor, and ordered Him to show respect. Then the whole crowd mobbed Him, beating, kicking, and spitting. If it hadn't been for the guards that brought Him, the mob would have killed Him. I ordered Him to His feet, but He could not get up. Soldiers had to help Him.

I put one of my royal robes on Him, bowed, and said, "Take Him back to Pilate."

Even with blood streaming down His face, He still looked kingly. His eyes pierced my soul, and I shuddered involuntarily. I hoped I would never see Him again.

November 29 *Luke 23:13–18*

Jesus Before Pilate Again

Herod sent a note thanking me for including him in the trial and inviting my wife and me to come to the palace for dinner at our convenience. Herod and I had been enemies for awhile, but maybe he wanted to mend the rift. In another note carrying his official seal, he declared that he had no reason to believe Jesus was a criminal. I had hoped Herod would condemn Him, relieving me of the responsibility of His death. I was convinced the priests wanted Jesus dead because they were jealous of the influence He had with the people. I had to do something to save Him.

"You brought this Man to me, accusing Him of leading a revolt. I have examined Him thoroughly on this point, even in your presence, and I must conclude legally that He is innocent." I could tell by the looks on their faces that was not the verdict they wanted to hear. "Herod came to the same conclusion," I continued. "Nothing this Man has done, according to Roman law, warrants the death penalty."

"Since when did you become a sticker on supporting Roman law?" the high priest spat.

My track record was poor. I had condemned men to death without a trial before, and they were intent on pointing that out now in their favor.

"I have decided to have Him flogged and released," I told them, trying to restore my authority as governor.

The whole crowd was unhappy with my decision and cried out with one voice. "Kill Him! We want Him crucified!" Then they began to chant, "Crucify Him! Crucify Him!" Their chanting was deafening. I tried to restore order, but they would not be quieted. There was only one thing they wanted—Jesus on a cross. I looked at Him standing there in the royal robe Herod had placed on Him. Blood was clotted on His face, and although He looked weaker, He was still dignified. Again a conviction came over me along with a voice within that said, *This is the Son of God—do not condemn Him*. I was caught in a really tough situation. The crowd was about to riot, and it was my job as governor to keep peace with the Jews. But I didn't want to send Him away to be crucified. I had to come up with something fast.

November 30 *Matthew 27:15–18; Mark 15:6–11;*
Luke 23:18, 19; John 18:39, 40

Barabbas or Jesus

Feeling as though I was on trial and about to be condemned, it suddenly occurred to me that I did have an escape route! The Jews had a custom of asking for the release of one prisoner during Passover. I conferred with the captain of the guard at the praetorium.

"Who is the worst prisoner you have?" I asked.

"Barabbas, by far," he answered. "He is being held for crimes against the state, insurrection, murder. He will kill anyone who gets in his way, Jews included."

"Send him to me under heavy guard with chains," I commanded. Soon Barabbas stood before me, hard, cold, angry—hatred was written all over his face. What a contrast between his demeanor and that of Jesus. Leading the two of them before the crowd, I reminded them of the Passover custom. "Who shall I release to you? Barabbas, the murderer, or Jesus, who is called the Messiah?"

It was an easy choice for any reasonable person. Barabbas shouted epitaphs at the people, spitting over the balcony railing on the crowd below. He cursed everyone in sight. Even the soldiers hated him. Jesus stood in silence, saying nothing, holding his head high, surrounded with an aura of peace.

I wanted what He had, but this was no time to find out how to get it. I saw the priests and Jewish leaders speaking to the people, telling them to condemn Jesus and ask for Barabbas' release. I knew their motive for wanting Jesus put to death was purely out of envy, but this was a no-brainer. Surely reason would prevail and they would put their prejudice aside and choose to release Jesus instead of Barabbas. I shouted out to the crowd a second time, "Which of these two do you want me to release to you?"

The Jewish elders had worked the people into a frenzy, and there was no reasoning with them. The crowd shouted back, "Release Barabbas!"

The murderer! This can't be happening, I thought. *They are behaving like demon-possessed people.*

"Barabbas, Barabbas, give us Barabbas!" they chanted. A mob environment prevailed. I knew there was little hope of saving Jesus.

December 1 *Matthew 27:19*

Pilate's Wife

Early to bed and early to rise works best for me, contrary to my husband, Pilate. He likes to burn the midnight oil, claiming the late night hours are when he gets most of his work done. The night of Jesus' arrest and trial I had the worst nightmare of my life. I awoke in the morning with a start. Looking around the bedroom, I saw Pilate was gone. He never got up early unless there was some kind of emergency to deal with.

I lay in bed trying to shake an uneasy feeling, when memories of the dream came flooding over me. Every detail came vividly to mind. I saw the man Jesus arrested and tried at both Annas' and Caiaphas' homes. I heard them accuse Him of blasphemy. The way they treated Him was despicable. I wondered why they hated Him so much because in my dream I also saw the amazing miracles He had performed. I heard the sermons He gave and His messages spoke to my heart. They brought Him to my husband to be condemned, but he sent Him to Herod. Herod sent Him back to Pilate. I watched Pilate try to pacify the Jews by letting them choose a prisoner for release and heard the mob demand Jesus be crucified. Pilate handed Him over to them. The soldiers abused Him and then led Him away to be crucified. I watched Him die and be placed in a tomb. Then, miraculously, I watched Him come out of the tomb and ascend to heaven.

Next in my dream, I saw this same Jesus coming down from the heavens seated on a majestic throne with a rainbow above, surrounded by thousands of angels. Pilate's tomb opened and he emerged terrified as he looked into the sky, shielding his face from the brightness. Herod came out of his tomb and they both cried to be hidden from the light. I saw Annas and Caiaphas looking up too and screaming in terror. "It was true! We are lost!"

I awoke with such a start. As I lay there remembering my dream, I quickly wrote a message to Pilate and instructed my personal servant to be sure it was delivered to him immediately. He must be warned before he makes the worst mistake of his life.

December 2   *Matthew 27:22-26; Mark 15:12-15;*
                                                       Luke 23:20-25; John 19:1-16

Pilate Orders Jesus' Crucifixion

As I stood there watching the crowd become more insane and determined to kill Jesus, my wife's personal servant delivered a message, which I read immediately. "Leave that innocent Man alone. I suffered through a terrible nightmare because of Him last night." Again I was seized by an overwhelming conviction to release Jesus in spite of the Jews. They were still chanting for Barabbas. I saw the crowd had grown. Some were weeping. Others wanted to know why Jesus was on trial but were quickly silenced. I stepped to the railing and raised my arms. "Crucify Him, Crucify Him!" they screamed. I could see they were ready to riot, which was the last thing I needed. I knew things had gone beyond recovery, but I must try.

I ordered Jesus to be flogged with lead tips on the leather, hoping to satisfy the mob. Soldiers stripped off His outer garment and hit him with the whip. He cried out in pain. After the beating, I told the mob He had been punished for His crimes and should be released. Like demons they screamed, "Crucify Him!"

"Take Him yourselves and crucify Him, because I find no fault in Him. He is not guilty," I screamed back at them.

The Jewish leaders yelled, "He is guilty by our law for claiming to be the Son of God!"

That thought terrified me. I had Jesus brought back into the courtroom and asked, "Where are You from?" He said nothing. "Don't You know I have the power to crucify You?"

He spoke, "You have no power over Me were it not allowed from above. He who released Me to you has the greater sin."

I went back to the crowd and appealed for His release. "If you release Him, you are no friend of Caesar!" they cried.

I brought Jesus out, sat on the seat of judgment, and said, "See, here is your King."

"We have no king but Caesar. Let His blood be on us and our children."

I released Barabbas to them, called for a basin of water, and washed my hands of all guilt. Then, defeated by the mob, I turned Jesus over to the soldiers to be crucified. Not a day goes by that I don't think about that trial and my part in it. Killing myself seems like the only way to escape this constant guilt.

December 3   *Matthew 27:27-31; Mark 15:16-20*

Soldiers Abuse Jesus

My men didn't respect any Jew because of the hypocrisy they had seen and the loss of friends or family to the zealots. One of my men knew that the prisoner, Jesus, had made Simon the Zealot a disciple. I reminded them that we had not had any trouble from Simon ever since he had joined Jesus. "Besides," I told them, "there is something different about this prisoner."

As centurion and captain of the guard assigned to protect Pilate, I had witnessed many trials, overseen many executions, and encountered many prisoners, but none like this One. I escorted Jesus to the praetorian headquarters and told them to prepare the prisoner for execution by crucifixion. This meant securing the beams of the cross and gathering the nails and tools to dig the hole to secure the cross. I needed to see Pilate to obtain the execution document, which had to be signed and sealed by him. I also wanted to know what to write above the head of the prisoner. Pilate was in a foul mood, so getting what I needed took much longer than expected.

Finally, frustrated, I returned to the headquarters and heard laughing and insults. Hidden from view behind the door, I saw the majority of the regiment was there. They had stripped the prisoner, put a scarlet robe on Him and woven a band of thorns for his head. In His hand was a swamp reed. They knelt before Him and tauntingly mocked Him, saying, "Hail, King of the Jews." I saw one soldier spit on Him, grab the reed from His hand, and beat Him on the head with it, calling Him a zealot-lover. Someone said, "Let's crucify Him. He deserves to die."

I entered the room and demanded to know what was going on. There was sudden silence. They knew I was angry and would deal with them later. I ordered them to remove the thorns and reed and to dress Him in His own clothes. I asked for a basin and washed the blood from His face, but the wounds in His head continued to bleed. He gave me an appreciative look that I will never forget. I lifted the cross, placed it on His back, and we headed out into the street toward Golgotha.

December 4 *Matthew 27:5, 32-34; Mark 15:21-24;*
Luke 23:26-31; John 19:17

Simon and the Road to Golgotha

I was standing with my two sons, Alexander and Rafus, not far from the judgment hall where Jesus had been tried. My sons were friends of Jesus and the disciples; they had traveled with the group a few times. I lived in Cyrene some distance away and had decided to come visit my boys and offer sacrifices in the city. Thaddeus, a close friend of Rafus, informed us Jesus had been arrested early that morning.

When I saw Jesus, I could not believe how severely they had beaten Him. He stumbled and fell. One of the soldiers started to beat Him again. I shouted at him, "Have you no compassion? Can't you see He is unable to carry that heavy cross?"

The soldier approached, grabbed my arm, and yelled into my face, "Then you carry His cross!"

At first, I resisted because if I carried the cross I could not celebrate the Passover according to Jewish tradition. But I could see that the weight of the heavy cross was crushing the life out of Him, and I felt compelled to help Him. I bent down and lifted the heavy beam off His bloodied and broken body. Soldiers lifted Him up and forced Him to walk in front of me. I couldn't understand it, because according to my boys, He had done nothing but good for these people. Some wept and others at least looked sympathetic. A large crowd followed behind us. Some grief-stricken women close behind us wept for Him. At one point, Jesus stopped, turned to them, and told them not to weep for Him but for themselves and their children. He predicted that in the days ahead the childless would be the fortunate ones.

"People will beg the mountains to fall on them and the hills to bury them," He said to them. "If they do these things when the tree is green, what will happen when it is dry?"

A soldier pushed Him and shouted, "Move on, Jew!" We passed through the city gate. Suddenly Jesus stopped. Beside the road under a large oak tree, lay the body of Judas. The crowd became silent. Even the Jewish leaders stopped speaking. We finally reached Golgotha, the place of the skull. The centurion offered Jesus a pain killer, but He refused it. I threw the cross on the ground.

Jesus turned to me and said, "Thank you for bearing My cross."

All I could say was, "It was an honor, Lord."

December 5

Matthew 27:35–44; Mark 15:24–32; Luke 23:32–38; John 19:18, 23, 24

Jesus Placed on the Cross

The soldiers stripped off His outer garments, leaving Him standing naked except for a loincloth. I stood nearby as His executioners pushed Him down on the rough-hewn wood. Stretching out His arms on the crossbeam, they drove large iron spikes into His hands. He groaned in pain, wrenching away from the hammer and nails. One of the soldiers reached into his bag and produced the crown of thorns and jammed it down on His head. The wounds on His scalp were torn open, and blood poured down His face. As the nails were driven into His feet, blood splattered the soldier. I stood helpless, wanting to stop this madness.

Jesus lay on the cross in a state of semi-consciousness. A soldier posted the inscription Pilate had made, "Jesus of Nazareth, King of the Jews," above His head. The five of them then lifted the cross and dropped it into the hole. The jarring effect tore the flesh where the nails had been driven, causing Him to cry out in pain. I turned away, unable to endure His suffering. Tears streamed down my face, mingling with His blood still on my cheek from the cross.

It seemed the entire crowd was insane, bereft of compassion or feeling. The soldiers at the foot of the cross argued and gambled for His garment. Nearby, priests and religious leaders insulted and mocked Him. They shouted, "He saved others, but He can't save Himself. Let this Messiah come down off the cross, so we can believe in Him."

The people joined in, "Ha, look at You now! You were going to destroy the temple and rebuild it in three days. Save Yourself; come down from the cross."

Even the thieves on either side of Him yelled insults. In the midst of the insults and the intense suffering, He clearly and unmistakably said, "Father, forgive them because they do not know what they are doing."

My mouth dropped open! How could He forgive them for all they had done to Him? That clinched it for me. I knew He was sent from God if He could forgive like that. At that moment, I became His follower.

December 6   *Luke 23:39–43*

The Repentant Thief

My companion and I joined up with Barabbas, the revolutionary, and got caught breaking into the Roman armory. "The Boss," as we called him, assured us it would be easy to overpower the two soldiers guarding the entrance. There were fifteen of us and two of them. As it turned out, there were only three of us who showed up. I balked. Barabbas offered us two years' wages to help him pull it off. We agreed. Overpowering the guards was easy enough, but we soon discovered a whole platoon of soldiers stationed inside. We were tried for our crimes and given the death sentence. I was so angry when the crowd chose to release Barabbas instead of Jesus. The jerk looked at us and laughed when they removed his chains. "I'll see you in hell," my condemned compatriot shouted.

They led us to the praetorian headquarters to prepare us for crucifixion. I watched them heap abuses on Jesus. This Jesus was different than anyone I'd ever seen before. He was calm and at peace, no sign of vindictiveness shadowed His countenance. On the way to Golgotha, I saw Him stumble and fall under the weight of His cross. Never once did I see Him retaliate or even cast a hateful glance at His tormentors. I finally said, "Hey, leave Him alone! Can't you see He is half dead?"

A soldier's fist shot out and landed on my jaw, knocking me down. "Don't tell us what to do," he shouted into my ear.

Once to Golgotha they put us on crosses and hoisted us up for the world to see. People, soldiers, even the priests railed at Him with insults and curses. My friend and I flanked Him, one on either side. At first we mocked Him, saying, "If You're really the Messiah, get us down from these crosses. Save us and Yourself."

Then with clarity, I remembered the words of a Messianic psalm I'd been taught as a child about His hands and feet being pierced. A conviction of His kingship overcame me, and I shouted at my friend. "Don't you fear God? We deserve to die for our sins, but this Man has done nothing wrong." Looking at Jesus I said, "Lord, please, remember me when You come into Your kingdom."

He turned to me and promised I would be with Him in paradise. For the first time in my life, I was at peace.

December 7   *John 19:19–22*

Contention Over the Inscription

The guilt I felt for condemning Jesus Christ to death by crucifixion gnawed at me. I had never felt this way about other accused men. Without a doubt Jesus was innocent and did not deserve to die. I rehearsed the scenes of the morning over and over in my mind, trying to think of what I could have done differently.

After the trial my wife confronted me and asked what I had done with the Galilean. I told her the Pharisees and religious leader made me crucify Him. "Didn't you receive my message?" she shouted at me.

"Yes, but they were going to riot, so I didn't have a choice. I tried everything I could think of to save Him."

"You are a marked man because God will judge you far more severely than you judged Him." Then she told me what she had seen in her dream.

I was terrified. How could I have allowed everything to get so out of control? I was ready to go to Golgotha and order Him to be released when the Jewish leaders arrived. They complained about the inscription I had written to be placed above His head on the cross. The place where Jesus was crucified was near the city. Everyone passing by on their way to Jerusalem would see the crucifixion. I had written the inscription in Hebrew, Latin, and Greek. I can't tell you why I wrote it in three languages. All other inscriptions were written in Greek only, but I had felt impressed to add the other two languages.

The priests wanted me to take the sign down and replace it. "You have to change it from saying 'King of the Jews' to 'He said I am King of the Jews.'"

I loathed these worthless hypocrites. They should have been on that cross instead of Jesus. "Why should I change it?" I asked.

"Because He is not our king—we want nothing to do with Him," they answered.

I looked at them in disgust and spoke with indignation. I resolved they would not order me around again. "No," I said flatly, "what I have written, I have written. The inscription will remain exactly as it is."

They left disgruntled, but they knew better than to push the issue further. Since then, not a day goes by that I do not regret allowing the execution of the Son of God.

December 8   *John 19:23–27; Psalm 22*

The Mother of Jesus

I stood near the cross—numb, exhausted, angry, and overwhelmed with grief. "How can this be happening?" I kept asking myself again and again. "Why is God, Yahweh, permitting ungodly men to abuse and crucify His Son, my Son?"

Destined to be King over all of Israel, He now hung on a cross with a crown of thorns and an inscription above His head, "The King of the Jews." After all the good He had done, where was the justice in this? John, faithful to the end, stood beside me trying to shield me from the horrible scene. My sister, Mary the wife of Clopas, and Mary Magdalene all stood close to support me. I watched through a steady stream of tears as the four soldiers who had brought Him to this place of crucifixion gambled for His clothing. Hardened as they were to human suffering, they had no knowledge of the One they were crucifying.

As intense as His physical pain was, I saw another kind of pain only a mother can see. Pain deep down beneath the surface in the depths of her child's soul. I could see He was struggling with issues and powers of darkness that none of us standing at the foot of the cross understood.

Standing there watching Him suffer, Yahweh, in His mercy, brought a passage to mind. It was one that I had taught Jesus to memorize as a boy. Written by the psalmist, it was a description of the events taking place before us. It was about Him and His suffering, yes, but also about so much more. "All the ends of the earth shall remember and turn to the Lord. And all the families of the nations shall worship before You." Thousands would discover salvation through Him. So all of this was part of God's plan to save mankind. It didn't make it any easier watching my Son die, but it did help to know there was a purpose to it.

He looked at me, eyes swollen nearly shut from the beatings. "Dear woman," He cried out, "here is your son." Then He said to John, "Here is your mother." We understood.

I felt John's arm around my shoulder as he whispered, "You are part of my family now." He wanted to take me away from this madness, but he also knew I needed to be there. My boy still needed to have His mother close by.

December 9 *Matthew 27:45–53; Mark 15:33–38;*
Luke 23:44–46; John 19:28–37

Jesus Dies on the Cross

I stood by the cross with Mary, the mother of Jesus. Around us were numerous other women from Galilee. I wondered what each was thinking as they gazed upon the One they had cared for during His ministry. The One whom we had placed our hopes and dreams in, believing He would deliver Israel. *What now?* I wondered. *Where do we go from here?*

It was about three o'clock in the afternoon. Darkness had covered the area for the last three hours. Through the dark cloud, I heard Jesus cry, "I'm thirsty." One of the soldiers soaked a sponge on a stick with some wine and held it up for Him. When Jesus tasted it, He refused it and gave an agonized call, "*Eloi, Eloi, lama sabachthani?*" which means "My God, My God, why have You abandoned Me?"

One of the priests, misunderstanding His words, shouted, "He is calling for Elijah to save Him."

The soldier holding the sponge said, "Let's see if this Elijah will come to take Him down."

Suddenly, Jesus cried out, "Father, into Your hands I commit My spirit." Then, with all the strength left in Him, He said, "It is finished!" His whole body shook, His head fell toward His chest, and He was gone. The darkness, now thicker around the cross, made it difficult to see.

How we had hoped He would come down from the cross at the last moment and destroy His enemies. Suddenly a great earthquake knocked us all to the ground. The earth heaved like sea waves. The rock making up the skull for which Golgotha was named split in two, causing the crosses to lurch forward. Everyone was terrified. A messenger came running, shouting, "The veil in the temple has been torn from top to bottom!"

A cry of dismay escaped Caiaphas' lips, "Who committed such a sacrilege?"

"It was torn by an unseen hand."

Caiaphas muttered, "Impossible." He and the other priests ran down to the city

December 10   *Matthew 27:54–56; Mark 15:39–41;*
Luke 23:47–49; John 19:1–37

The Roman Soldiers

In all my life, I had never participated in an execution like the one for Jesus the Nazarene. I thought the world would end when He took His last breath. Right from the very beginning I knew there was something different about Him. All during the trial, the beating, the abuse by the soldiers He never once retaliated. He had a peace, a confidence, something I couldn't quite define, but I truly admired. Even when nailed to the cross, He submitted peacefully. The soldiers were amazed because most criminals had to be wrestled down, swearing and calling down curses on us as we drove in the nails.

A strange darkness descended at noon like a black fog, almost like a warning that we were crucifying an innocent man. The priests had gone to Pilate and asked that the legs of the condemned be broken to hasten death because they didn't want them on the cross after sundown. The governor wrote the order, which was brought to me at three o'clock, just when Jesus cried out, "It is finished!"

An earthquake knocked everyone to the ground, and the crosses tilted forward as the rock was split. We were all terrified. A messenger arrived with the news the temple veil had been torn. The priests and most of the people left, but a group of His followers remained on the scene. I ordered the soldiers to break the legs of the two thieves but to leave Jesus alone because He was already dead. The two thieves screamed when the hammers snapped their lower legs and they were no longer able to raise themselves up to breathe. They soon died of suffocation.

When one of the soldiers pierced Jesus' side to be sure He was dead, blood and water flowed out. Amazed, I uttered the only thing I could think of as I recounted the events of the day. "Truly, this was the Son of God." I fell to my knees in fear as I thought of the role I had played in His death. I then found one of His disciples who was still near the cross and asked him to tell me more about Jesus. Although still a centurion, I wanted to become a follower of Jesus Christ.

December 11   *Matthew 27:57-61; Mark 15:42-47;*
Luke 23:50-56; John 19:38-42

The Burial

"You are a member of the council, Joseph," Nicodemus urged. "If anyone has influence with Pilate, it is you." Up until now I had been a secret follower of Jesus, but I agreed to go to Pilate and request the body of Jesus if my friend Nicodemus would go with me. We knew all this needed to be done quickly because the Sabbath was only a few hours away.

I could tell Pilate was angry and filled with remorse for ordering Jesus' death. "Now, what do you Jews want?" he sneered.

"I would like to ask permission to bury Jesus the Nazarene in my tomb," I responded.

"Is He dead already?" he asked in amazement.

"Yes," I said, "He died at three o'clock."

"I don't believe you," he said incredulously. He called for the Roman officer in charge.

"He is dead," the soldier confirmed.

Pilate turned to me and told me I had his permission to take the body. We thanked the governor and purchased seventy-five pounds of myrrh and spices at the marketplace. We also purchased a long, linen burial cloth and made our way to Golgotha. What a relief to find two soldiers there along with a few of the women who followed Jesus. The soldiers helped us take the body off the cross. With the help of the women, we prepared the spices and covered His body with the mixture according to Jewish custom and wrapped Him in the linen cloth.

I had purchased a new tomb near a garden close to Golgotha. We took His body there and placed Him on the stone slab. With tearful goodbyes we left the burial chamber. Nicodemus and I needed the help of the soldiers to roll the stone in place across the entrance. I offered to pay them, but they refused. "He was a good man," they exclaimed and left.

It was nearly Sabbath. Mary Magdalene and the other Mary wanted to stay by the tomb. As Nicodemus and I were leaving, Mary Magdalene remembered some other ointment and spices that we needed to anoint Him with. On the way home, I thought about Jesus and wished I could have been with Him every day like Peter or John. Nevertheless, I was grateful to be His disciple.

December 12   *Matthew 27:62-66*

The Guard at the Tomb

It was the day following the crucifixion of Jesus—the Jew's Sabbath. I had spent most of the night awake, contemplating Friday's events. I didn't know of anyone who had come back from the dead, but there were lots of rumors floating around that Jesus would rise again. If this Jesus came back from the dead, what would He do to those who had crucified Him? I just hoped He'd know that I had asked for forgiveness and was working on becoming a believer.

From my vantage point on the steps outside the palace, the sunrise was gorgeous. It looked like another beautiful spring day. It was at that moment that I noticed a group of people coming up the street. As they neared, I could see it was a delegation of leading priests and Pharisees. They came through the gate demanding to see Pilate. The governor was not a morning person, so they had to wait until he appeared on the balcony.

"Sir," they began, "when the deceiver was still alive, He said, 'After three days I will rise from the grave.' So we request that you seal the tomb until the third day to prevent His disciples from coming and stealing His body and then telling everyone He was raised from the dead. If that happens we will be worse off than we were at first."

Pilate was loathe to do anything for these Jewish scoundrels, but I looked at him and knew what he was thinking before he spoke. He was fearful that what they said might be true, so he ordered us to stand guard at the tomb. The Pharisees followed us to the tomb and watched as we carried out Pilate's order to seal it. I then set a guard of thirty men to protect the seal of Rome. Satisfied, the Pharisees and priests left.

As I sat with my men, one of them approached me and asked. "Do you think this Jesus will really come back to life?"

"I honestly don't know, but one thing is certain. His disciples will not steal His body!"

He nodded in agreement.

December 13 *Matthew 28:1–4*

The Angel Rolls Away the Stone

Saturday evening Pilate called me in and asked for a report from the tomb. I reported that all had been quiet. I then returned to the tomb to spend the night with my men. The conversation throughout the night had focused mostly on family and work when one of the men changed the subject near daybreak. "Do you believe this Jesus will really rise on the third day?"

"Perhaps He will," I remarked. "Look at all the strange things that happened on Friday—darkness in the middle of the day, the earthquake right when He died, the Jewish temple curtain torn."

"Those are just Jewish stories," one of the soldiers retorted.

"That earthquake when He died was no fable," I shot back.

"I was talking about the temple curtain," he said in a somewhat more subdued voice.

I continued, "There's other unexplained stuff, too. Like one of the soldiers who went to arrest Jesus told me some bright being knocked everyone down in the Garden of Gethsemane. What chance do we have against a divine being?" I asked. The words were no sooner out of my mouth than another earthquake struck and all of us were knocked to the ground by its force.

One of the men cried out in terror, "He is going to get revenge for what we did to Him!"

Then, like a lightning bolt, an angel appeared—tall, towering over us, his face shining like lightning and his clothes as white as snow. We were dumbfounded, shaking with fear, wondering what he would do. At the tomb, he rolled the massive stone away with one hand. Then he mounted it and sat down. All of us fainted, crashing to the ground. When I awoke, I raced back to the city. Jesus was alive; I had to tell Pilate.

December 14 *Matthew 28:1, 5-7; Mark 16:1-11; Luke 24:1-11; John 20:1, 2*

Mary at the Tomb

In the semidarkness of early morning Mary, the mother of James, Salome, and I gathered up the spices we had purchased after sunset and headed for the tomb to anoint Jesus' body. On the way, an earthquake shook the ground. I screamed and grabbed for Salome to keep from falling, knocking the spice container out of her hand. We all ended up in a heap before the shaking stopped. As we gathered up the spices, Roman soldiers ran past us toward Jerusalem, looking as though they'd seen a ghost. Having retrieved all the spices, we continued toward the tomb.

"Who is going to roll the stone away?" I asked.

"We should have asked the soldiers," Salome said, "but they're long gone."

We passed Golgotha with its three crosses still standing eerily in the early morning light. Arriving at the tomb, we had mixed feelings at seeing the stone rolled away. Cautiously we approached the entrance and peered inside. As our eyes adjusted to the darkness, we could see the tomb was empty. "They have taken Him and put Him somewhere else," I announced. "I must tell the others!" I turned around and ran toward Jerusalem, leaving the other women at the tomb.

Most of the disciples were in the upper room where they had celebrated the Passover with Jesus. Peter unbolted the door when I knocked. "Jesus' body is gone. They have taken Him out of the tomb, and I don't know where they have put Him," I cried, tears streaming down my cheeks.

Peter didn't believe me because he knew soldiers had been stationed at the tomb to guard it. After delivering my message, I turned around and ran back to the garden. Peter and John ran ahead of me. My heart pounded as I tried to understand what was happening. My Lord had been crucified on Friday and laid to rest in the tomb, and now His body was missing. The grief was almost too much to bear.

December 15 *Luke 24:12; John 20:3-10*

The Disciples at the Tomb

Mary rushed into the Upper Room and told us that Jesus' body was missing. I jumped up and rushed out the door with John at my heels. John outran me and arrived at the tomb first, both of us out of breath. Sure enough, the stone had been rolled away. John peered inside but didn't go in. I wanted a closer look, so I bent down and entered the burial chamber.

John cautioned me, "You will defile yourself."

I told him I couldn't be more defiled than I already was, remembering how I had denied Jesus. Once inside, John followed me in. My eyes adjusted to the low light, and I saw the linen cloth that Jesus had been wrapped in neatly folded and lying on the stone slab. We stared at it in silence, remembering now that He had told us He would rise on the third day. We had been so wrapped up in a military takeover of Rome and Israel once again becoming a great nation that we had missed the purpose of His mission.

The women arrived, and together we rejoiced the tomb was empty. The women confirmed that two angels had met them in the tomb and told them that Jesus was alive! But where was He? Had He gone back to heaven?

"Where are the other disciples?" I asked one of the women. "Why didn't they come?"

"They are afraid of the Jews and scared that they may be arrested," she answered.

In some ways I wished they would arrest and crucify me for denying my Lord. Ever since Thursday night, remorse, guilt, and fear had overwhelmed me. What would He say to me? Would He even speak to me? Maybe He would forgive me like He had forgiven the woman caught in adultery. But then, my sin was so much greater. Hadn't He said, "Whoever denies me, I will deny before My Father and all the angels in heaven." Would He forgive me for what I had done? These thoughts and questions plagued me day and night. I thought I should just go home to my family in Galilee. I stopped at the Upper Room and announced to the other disciples that it was true—Jesus was raised; the tomb was empty. Everyone rejoiced but me. I was afraid I had lost my Friend.

December 16   *John 20:11-18; Matthew 28:8-10*

Mary Magdalene Meets Jesus

After telling Peter and John that the tomb was empty and Jesus' body was missing, I returned to the tomb. I didn't know where else to go. I felt so emotionally drained. When I arrived at the tomb, I couldn't hold back the tears. I stood by the doorway weeping, wondering where they might have taken Him. I looked inside the tomb again, thinking we might somehow have missed seeing Him lying where He had been placed on Friday. The stone slab was bare except for the carefully folded linen. If someone had taken His body, why would they pause to fold the linen cloth? Questions like this popped into my head with no apparent answers. Why would anyone steal a corpse in the first place? Nothing made any sense at all.

Then suddenly two angels appeared, one at the head of the stone and the other at the foot. "Dear woman, why are you crying?" the one asked.

"Because they have taken away my Lord, and I don't know where they have put Him," I replied tearfully. I turned to leave and saw someone standing there. I couldn't make out who it was because my eyes were so clouded with tears.

"Dear woman, why are you crying?" the Man asked. The voice sounded somewhat familiar.

It must be the gardener, I told myself. "Sir," I cried, "if you have taken Him away, please tell me where you have put Him, and I will go get Him."

Then He spoke my name, "Mary."

It was Jesus! "Rabbi!" I cried out, falling to my knees at His feet, which bore the nail prints from the crucifixion!

"Don't cling to Me, for I haven't ascended to My Father yet. But go find My brothers and tell them I am ascending to My Father and your Father, to My God and your God."

I couldn't believe it! Jesus was alive! I had to tell the others as Jesus commanded! I had the best news in the world to share.

December 17   *Matthew 28:11-15*

The Soldiers Meet With the Priests

I was scared. How was I going to face Pilate with the report that a dead man we had been commanded to guard had escaped? I and the entire guard ended up in Caiaphas' courtyard. A few of his servants built a fire in the pit we had gathered around earlier.

"What are we going to tell him?" one of the soldiers asked.

"The truth," I replied. Even if it cost me my life, I was determined to tell the high priest the truth.

A servant appeared and asked, "What can I do for you?"

"I must see the high priest now," I requested with urgency in my voice.

Caiaphas appeared a few minutes later. I told him everything that had occurred. Shaken, he called for a meeting of the high council. As centurion in charge of the guard, I was invited to be there. After hearing my story, they offered us a large bribe to tell a lie. I told them I wanted nothing to do with it.

Caiaphas pulled me aside and said, "You must tell people that Jesus' disciples came during the night while you were sleeping and stole His body. If the governor hears of it, we will stand up for you so you won't get into trouble for sleeping. Besides Pilate doesn't want this resurrection story to get around either."

I stood there thinking. Something was wrong with this picture. I was a Gentile who was standing up for the truth while this man, supposedly a man of God, was promoting deception and lies. I told him I wanted no part of his deception and if asked, I would tell the truth, but my soldiers would have to decide for themselves what they wanted to do.

The council convinced them to spread the lie and take the money. They did their work well because most people believed their story. Pilate heard that His disciples had stolen Jesus' body, but he didn't believe twelve unarmed men could overpower a guard of Roman soldiers. He called me in and asked for the truth. I told him exactly what took place.

"Just as He promised," Pilate said. "He said He would rise from the grave and He has." Pilate thanked me for being honest with him. I left the governor's house feeling sorry for him but more determined than ever to know more about this man named Jesus.

December 18   Mark 16:12; Luke 24:13–24

The Road to Emmaus (Part 1)

My friend, Asher, and I were on our way home to Emmaus, a small town seven miles from Jerusalem. We had been part-time followers of Jesus, in the sense that we spent as much time with Him as family responsibilities and work would allow. We had seen many miracles and heard many parables, and we believed He was indeed the Messiah. The last thing we expected was for Him to submit to a Roman cross.

"I don't understand why He allowed the Romans to crucify Him," I said to my friend. "Why did He subject Himself to them when all along we believed He would force them to be our slaves?"

"None of it makes any sense to me, Cleopas. And now His body is gone."

The weekend's events were just too much for us to understand. A stranger who had been following behind asked if He could join us so He wouldn't have to travel alone. We readily invited Him to walk with us.

"It appeared as if you were discussing something of great importance."

"You must be the only person in all of Jerusalem who hasn't heard all the things that have happened these past few days," I replied.

"What things?" He asked.

I was flabbergasted that anyone could have been in the city and not heard, but I proceeded to tell Him of all that had happened to Jesus of Nazareth. "He was a prophet, a mighty teacher from God." We continued to tell Him how the religious leaders had condemned Him and handed Him over to be crucified.

"We hoped that He would be the Messiah to deliver Israel," I said with anger and disappointment in my voice. "Some of the women went to the tomb early this morning and found that His body was missing. They said they saw two angels who told them Jesus was alive. Some of the disciples went out to see for themselves, and it was true, His body was not in the tomb. Gone, just like the women had said. We just don't know if He is alive or if His body has been stolen."

The stranger shook His head back and forth, a look of disappointment on His face.

December 19   Luke 24:25–34; Mark 16:13

The Road to Emmaus (Part 2)

After a long pause, the stranger spoke in slow deliberate tones.

"You foolish people!" There was something familiar about His voice. "You find it so hard to believe all that the prophets wrote in Scripture. Wasn't it clearly predicted that the Messiah would have to suffer all these things before entering into His glory?" He asked. Then He took us through the writings of Moses and the prophets, repeating from memory passage after passage. We asked many questions, especially in regards to what we had been taught by the Pharisees regarding the Messiah's role as conqueror of Israel's enemies. He carefully explained the Scriptures. I wondered how this stranger could know so much.

By the time we reached Emmaus it was getting late. We turned in toward the city, but the stranger continued on the road, which led to the coast. I called out to Him, "Sir, please stay the night with us. It is getting late and will soon be too dark to travel."

He came to my home along with Asher. My wife was happy to invite both of them to join us for the meal she had prepared. Taking the bread, He blessed it, broke it, and gave it to us. I had this strange deja vu of Jesus on the mountain with the loaves and fishes.

"Oh!" both Asher and I said in unison as we recognized Jesus! Instantly, He disappeared! We sat and stared at the spot where He had been sitting. Asher was first to speak. "Cleopas, didn't your heart burn within you as He explained the Scriptures to us?"

"Yes," I replied. Within the hour we were on our way back to Jerusalem to share the good news. When we arrived at the Upper Room, we found the disciples and other followers of Jesus gathered together. "Jesus traveled with us to Emmaus today," we announced excitedly. "He opened our eyes to the Scriptures. Now we understand. He has risen!"

Everyone shouted, "Hallelujah!"

December 20   *Luke 24:35–43; John 20:19–23*

Jesus Appears to the Disciples

While we listened to Cleopas tell of the encounter with Jesus on the road, Thomas announced that He did not believe Jesus had risen. "I don't know if there is an empty tomb," he declared.

"Well, why don't you go to where He was buried and see for yourself?" my brother James suggested.

"Alright, I will," and he was out the door and gone. After Peter had bolted the door behind Thomas, Cleopas continued telling us how they had recognized Jesus when He broke the bread. We still weren't totally convinced. Then suddenly we saw Jesus standing there in front of us!

"Peace to you," He said. Everyone was terrified because we thought He might be a ghost since the door was bolted shut. It certainly looked like Jesus.

"How did You get in?" I stammered. "Are You really the Lord?"

"Why are you frightened?" He asked as He showed us the wounds in His hands and feet and side. "Look at My hands and feet," He said, walking to where I stood. Seeing we were skeptical, He said, "Touch Me and see for yourself; it is really Me." He held out His hand to me, and I touched Him. "Why are you so full of doubt?" He asked. "Ghosts don't have bodies, but I am here in the flesh."

Dumbfounded would be a good word to describe us. "Do you have anything to eat?" He asked. Peter found a piece of broiled fish. He ate it while we watched. We were finally convinced, but it was such a shock to see Him alive after all He had been through. Everyone was excited and happy.

"Come close to Me," He said. We gathered around Him. "As the Father has sent Me, so I am sending you," He told us. Then He breathed on us and said, "Receive the Holy Spirit. If you forgive anyone's sins, they are forgiven, but if you do not forgive them, they are not forgiven."

No one spoke at first, then Peter shouted, "He is alive!" and the whole place erupted into a celebration of Jesus' resurrection.

December 21   Luke 24:44–49

Jesus Gives Specific Instructions

What a celebration! The grief and tension that had gripped us over the weekend evaporated. Jesus was here with us and that was all that seemed to matter. We were safe. No one could touch us with Jesus in our midst. We laughed and cried and shouted praises to God. My brother James asked Jesus what He experienced after death. "Nothing," He replied. "I was asleep."

Then Jesus raised His hands and asked for a chance to speak. "When I was with you before, I tried to tell you everything written about Me in the Law of Moses, the prophets, and the psalms. I told you that all these things must be fulfilled, but you did not fully understand." He quoted passages of Scripture and our minds were opened to understand what had before seemed obscure.

Cleopus said, "These are the same things He shared with us on the road to Emmaus."

When He recited the psalms, I remembered Him saying some of these words on the cross: "My God, My God, why have You forsaken Me?" The writings of the psalms and Isaiah were most impressive. I said to Him, "Lord, we had no idea the Scriptures had so much to say about Your life and death!"

He answered, "Yes, it was written long ago that the Messiah would suffer many things and that He would die and rise from the dead on the third day."

The Pharisees had taught us falsehoods about the Messiah's mission and work, but now the truth was revealed. As Jesus mentioned these Scriptures, I had recollections of Him quoting them to us and trying to teach us the truth. I realized we had been so determined that He should follow our hopes and dreams that we had completely missed the larger picture. His death was God's way of bringing salvation to the whole world.

Jesus continued, "It was also written that this message will be proclaimed in the authority of My name to all the nations, beginning in Jerusalem. There is forgiveness of sins for everyone who repents. This is where you come in. Because you are witnesses of all these things, you can spread this message far and wide."

The kingdom was far more than just Israel. It was to be worldwide, and we were to be the messengers!

December 22   *Mark 16:14; John 20:24–29*

Thomas

Eight days after the others had seen Jesus, or at least claimed they had, we were all together in the same room where we had celebrated the Passover before Jesus was arrested. Even though I had seen the empty tomb for myself and heard many testimonies from people who maintained that they had seen Jesus or even touched Him, I was skeptical. When I returned from checking out the tomb last week and everyone told me Jesus had been there, I refused to believe. They related how He had shown them His scars and that He had eaten some fish. I told them I would not believe unless I saw the nail prints in His hands and put my fingers in them and placed my hand on the wound in His side. My stubbornness may have been the result of self-pity.

Why hadn't the Lord come to the group while I was there? Why would He show Himself to all the others and not me? I wondered.

Although they hadn't bothered us yet, we were still concerned about the Jewish leaders hunting us down, so we kept the doors bolted. Suddenly, as the others said He had come before, Jesus was in the room and standing next to me. "Peace be to you," He said.

I was overwhelmed. It was Him! He turned to me and said, "Thomas, put your hand here," pointing to His side. Then He held up both hands and said, "Look at My hands." They were both scared. He took my hand and pushed it into the wound on His side and said, "Don't be faithless anymore. Believe."

I felt ashamed. I fell to my knees exclaiming, "My Lord and my God."

Jesus said, "You believe because you have seen Me, but blessed are those who believe having never seen Me." I deserved the rebuke and knew He was disappointed in my faithlessness. Then I felt a hand on my shoulder. I looked up—it was Jesus. He helped me to my feet, put His hands on my shoulders and smiled. "God has great plans for you, my brother. Be faithful, and He will accomplish much through you." We embraced. I felt loved and forgiven.

December 23   *John 21:1–3*

Jesus Appears to Seven Disciples at Galilee

After Jesus appeared to us the second time, we remembered that He had told us to meet Him in Galilee. We gathered our things, paid the caretaker for the use of the room and headed north. It felt good to be going home. The Passover and all that had happened with Jesus had taken a toll on each of us. We talked about the future and what it might hold. We had a role to play in God's kingdom, only in a way we had not expected.

We took our time traveling, recounting events we experienced with Jesus in our company. James mentioned the little children Jesus had healed in this town. A miracle performed in another village stood out in Andrew's mind. Philip was especially touched by a sermon preached here. We decided to travel through Samaria as Jesus would have and made a stop in Sychar. The people welcomed us warmly. Everyone wanted to know about Jesus, and we shared everything that had happened during that Passover weekend.

It was a joyous homecoming in Galilee, and we were happy to spend time with our families. A few days later, seven of us disciples met at Peter's place to discuss the future and speculate on when Jesus would appear to us again. Finally, Peter stood up and announced, "I'm going fishing."

The rest of us said, "We want to come too."

"Let's go then!" Peter said.

It was evening when we arrived at the dock, the usual time for fishing. Peter rigged the boat and we were off. The moon was full and again we reminisced about all the good times we'd had with Jesus. I talked about the night the storm came down on us with such fury and Jesus calmed the waters in an instant by saying, "Peace, be still." Peter recalled the night Jesus came to us walking on the water and we all thought He was a ghost.

"Do you think He will walk out to meet us again?" Thomas asked.

John remembered the time shortly after meeting Jesus that we made the biggest catch of our lives. We spent the night fishing but caught nothing but seaweed and a float from someone else's net. However, it felt good to talk and reminisce about the good times we'd had with Jesus.

December 24 *John 21:4–7a*

Miracle of the Fish

The sky was showing signs of a new day as light peeked over the Geneseret hills. The others had all fallen asleep, but my brother James, Peter, and myself, seasoned fishermen, were used to staying awake all night. We had lit candles to try to attract the fish into our net but caught nothing. Now with the approaching daylight, we knew that catching anything would be impossible. Slowly the other men began to awaken. Peter was frustrated at not having caught any fish, not even a couple for a meal. Heading back to the dock, I noticed someone standing on the shore waving to us.

"Who's that?" I asked, pointing to the lone figure.

The Man called out, "Fellows, have you caught any fish?"

"Not a thing," we replied.

"Throw your net on the right-hand side of the boat, and you'll catch some," He shouted.

Peter gave us a look that said that's crazy, but he hauled in the net, cleaned out the weeds, rigged it for the right side, and threw it in. Suddenly, the boat lurched sharply to the right. We pulled up the sides of the net but couldn't haul it in. Fish! All we could do was secure the net and head for the dock.

The net was full of large fish. *Where did they come from?* I wondered. *How could there be so many fish at the wrong time of day and on the wrong side of the boat?*

It didn't make any sense. Then I remembered a night just like this one. After spending the whole night fishing and not catching anything, Jesus had suggested we let down the nets once more in deep water. To be polite, we had done as He suggested and nearly sank the boat with all the fish. "Peter, it's the Lord!" I exclaimed. "Remember three years ago?" We took a better look at the Man on the shore. Sure enough, it was Jesus, waiting there for us.

December 25 *John 21:7b–14*

Peter Jumps in the Water and Heads for Shore

When John recognized that it was Jesus on the shore, I jumped in the water. The others in the boat held tight to the net and rowed for the dock while I veered off to where Jesus was. As much as I wanted to be with Jesus, the memories of betraying Him and the denial pushed into my head. What would He say to me in private with no one around? Would He tell me I had ruined our friendship and that He no longer needed me as a disciple? The others were busy hauling the net onto shore and taking care of the fish.

I reached the shoreline and saw that Jesus was bent over a fire cooking a few fish on the coals. He looked up at me and grinned, which made me feel better. The others were finishing up securing the boat and the fish when Jesus turned their direction and said, "Bring some of the fish you just caught."

I headed over to the boat. Glancing over the catch, I noticed all the fish were large. Top quality fish like this would bring a great price at the market. John was counting them, so I waited until he had finished to pick up a couple. "One hundred and fifty-three," he announced.

"A miracle just like when He called us to become fishers of men," I said. He nodded and we exchanged smiles. We made our way over to the fire, and I handed the fish to the Lord. He cut them open, gutted each one, and lay them flat on the iron grill. Then, along with some bread, He passed out the fish He had already broiled. Hungry after the night on the lake, we gratefully accepted His hospitality. He asked a blessing on it and on us. "Enjoy your breakfast!" He said. There was no question, it was the Lord!

This was the third time we had seen Him since the resurrection, and it just felt so wonderful to be in His presence. We ate breakfast in silence, probably thinking about the times He had fed the thousands with a few loaves and fishes. Paramount on my mind, however, was my constant worry about where I stood with Him. I wished He would yell at me or confront me. Something, anything—I just wanted it out in the open. I didn't know what to say to Him, so I made some lame comment about how good the food tasted.

December 26   *John 21:15-19*

Jesus Challenges Peter

After breakfast we sat around the fire, each caught up in his own thoughts. Jesus looked at me a couple of times. I couldn't help but wonder what He was thinking. The silence made me feel uncomfortable. I looked at the fish we had caught and knew it was a miracle, so I turned to Him and thanked Him for the catch. He smiled and nodded, then He looked at me and I at Him. We looked into each other's eyes for at least a minute. I began to feel very uncomfortable, but I couldn't look away.

Finally He spoke, "Simon, son of John, do you love Me more than these?" gesturing toward the other disciples.

My response sprang up from beneath a lot of pent up emotion. "Yes, Lord! You know I love You," I replied with earnestness, allowing the guilt from that night of denial to wash away.

I was about to apologize, but He spoke before I had a chance. "Then feed My lambs," He said.

I nodded and said, "Yes, Lord, I will."

Then He asked the same question again, "Simon, son of John, do you love Me?" He emphasized the word "love."

"Yes, Lord," I replied, emphasizing the affirmative, "You know I love You."

Jesus said, "Then take care of My sheep."

Then He asked the same question again, a third time. "Simon, son of John, do you love Me?" by now the others were wondering where this conversation was headed.

I thought about the night I denied Him and the look on His face. Tears trickled down my cheeks into my beard. I said, "Lord, You know everything, so You know I love You." Three times I had denied Him. Three times I affirmed my love for Him, but it hurt that He asked if I loved Him.

Then He told me my future in a few brief sentences. "When you were young, you dressed yourself, did what you pleased and went where you chose. When you are old, others will dress you, stretch out your arms and take you where you do not want to go." I knew what He meant. If they crucified Him, they wouldn't hesitate to crucify me. Then He spoke the same words in the same place He'd spoken them three years earlier, "Follow Me."

That's what I wanted to hear—He wanted me back!

December 27   *John 21:20-23*

Question About John

The affirmation I received from Jesus restored my peace of mind. Just to know that He wanted me to follow Him was what I really wanted to hear. The lesson of not depending on my own strength but always depending on Jesus was a lesson I learned the hard way.

As I reflected on being forgiven, my eye caught John off to my right, and I remembered the discussion we had had on the lake as we had fished. It was concerning all the events that had taken place leading up to the crucifixion. We couldn't understand how Judas, who had been a part of us for three years, could betray the Lord. Looking back, we recalled all the times Jesus had tried to reach him and bring him to confession, but to no avail. I specifically remembered John asking Jesus who would betray Him and the look on Judas' face. Already one of the twelve was dead, but of course, that was his own doing because of his false thinking.

Looking at John, I knew he had been at the trial and crucifixion. If anyone was at risk, it would be him because everyone knew he was a friend of Jesus. Would he be the next disciple to die, arrested, and put on trial as Jesus was, then crucified? I pointed at John and asked, "Lord, what about him?" John hung his head, not sure he wanted to hear what the future held for him.

Jesus paused then looked at John and then at me. "If I want him to remain alive until I return, what is that to you?" He asked. It was a deserved rebuke. Then He repeated the invitation, "As for you, follow Me." I understood His words to say, "Peter, mind your own business; you need to focus on keeping yourself on track."

Because of my question and Jesus' answer, the rumor began to go around that John would never die and that he would remain alive until the Lord's return. That isn't what Jesus said at all. I reminded those who asked me about the conversation that it doesn't matter if we live or die in this world. What matters most is that we receive His gift of eternal life when Jesus does come again.

December 28 *Matthew 28:16–20; Mark 16:16–18; Acts 1:6–8*

The Great Commission

For a period of forty days after the Passover, Jesus met with us from time to time. He proved to us that He was alive and talked to us about the kingdom. Jesus never told us this kingdom would be about Israel; instead, it would include all nations.

The eleven of us and many of His other disciples arranged to meet Him on top of Mount Olives because He needed to tell everyone something very important. There was an air of expectation as Jesus began to speak. He reminded us not to leave Jerusalem until the Father sent the gift of the Holy Spirit. He said, "John baptized with water, but you will be baptized with the Holy Spirit."

Some who were present asked if the time had come for Him to free and restore Israel. He replied, "The Father alone has the authority to set these dates and times; they are not for you to know." Jesus continued, "You will receive the power of the Holy Spirit and be My witnesses, telling everyone about Me everywhere, in Jerusalem, throughout Judea, Samaria, and to the ends of the earth. Anyone who believes and is baptized will be saved."

He told us we would cast out demons in His name and many miraculous signs would accompany those who believed. We would speak in new languages. God would protect us from poisonous snakes and from angry people who might try to poison us. "Creatures or people will not be able to harm you. You will place your hands on the sick, and they will be healed." Then He called us to come closer to Him. He told us all authority had been given to Him in heaven and on earth and that we were to go and make disciples of all nations, baptizing them in the name of the Father, Son, and Holy Spirit, teaching them all the commands He had given us and that we could be sure that He would be with us to the end of the age. I wondered how we were to go to the Gentiles when we were not to associate with them or enter their homes, but before I had a chance to ask the question, something happened that will remain etched in my memory forever.

December 29 *Mark 16:19; Luke 24:50–52; Acts 1:9–11*

Jesus Ascends

Jesus had just given us the commission of taking the gospel to the whole world and assured us that He would always be with us when He began to rise heavenward. Lifting His hands to heaven, He blessed us and asked His Father to protect us and care for us. I could see the nail prints in His hands, and I remembered the day soldiers had driven the nails into them. I remembered how He had cried out in pain when they slammed the cross down into the hole dug for it. I had watched when the jolt of the cross tore the flesh of His palms. I remembered having my arm around His mother and turning her away from the awful scene. If only all those priests, rulers, and soldiers responsible for the crucifixion could see Him now! They would be prostrate on the ground, begging for forgiveness.

We watched as He ascended higher and higher until a cloud received Him. Straining to see Him, I realized the cloud was the only one in the sky and it was not made of firmament but consisted of thousands and thousands of angels greeting Him and singing praises.

Suddenly I became aware of two white-robed men standing beside us! I wanted so much to go with Jesus and be with Him forever, and I had a feeling that they wanted to be with Him every bit as much as I did, but they had been sent to comfort us. I imagined that more than anything they wanted to be part of that great gathering of heavenly beings welcoming Jesus and escorting Him home. The cloud became smaller and smaller until it disappeared from our vision.

Our hearts were heavy because the One we had come to love, the One we had grown to depend on was gone. When would we see Him again? Would it be soon? How would we be able to carry on without Him to guide us and counsel us? All these thoughts and questions were running around in my head when one of the angels spoke, "Men of Galilee, why are you standing here gazing into heaven? Jesus has been taken from you into heaven for now, but someday He will return from heaven in the same way you saw Him go."

As soon as they had spoken these words, they were gone like lightning bolts to join the others. My heart thrilled knowing that He would come back. I would see Him again.

December 30   *Mark 16:19; Psalm 24:1–10*

Jesus Received Into Heaven

After leaving the disciples and joining the other angels escorting our Lord and King to heaven, we sang songs we had written just for this occasion. When we approached the city, a million angelic voices greeted us with the psalm David wrote: "The earth is the Lord's and everything in it. The world and all its people belong to Him."

We answered with, "For He laid the earth's foundation on the seas and built it on the ocean depth."

"Who may climb the mountain of the Lord?" they sang. "Who may stand in His holy place?"

We echoed back, "Only those whose hands and hearts are pure; who do not worship idols and never tell lies."

The city was alive with the entire angelic host of heaven welcoming the King of glory. Those in the city responded with, "They will receive the Lord's blessing and have a right relationship with God their Savior."

We cried out in song, "Such people may seek You and worship in Your presence, O God of Jacob."

Then the Father Himself rose above the city gate, seated on His magnificent throne with the rainbow around it. We cried, "Open up ancient gates, open up ancient doors and let the King of glory enter."

"Who is this King of glory?" they cried out in unison.

"The Lord, strong and mighty, the Lord invincible in battle," we shouted. "Open up ancient gates, open up ancient doors and let the King of glory enter," we repeated.

They responded with, "Who is this King of glory?"

It wasn't because they didn't know it was Jesus. They wanted to hear His name and continue singing praises to Him. "The Lord," we cried out.

Every angel in heaven joined voices, "He is the King of glory."

The gates swung open and we entered the city. We watched as Father and Son embraced. Again we shouted praises to His name, "You are the King of glory," and all heaven knelt in worship of the Father, Son, and Holy Spirit. Then Jesus was seated at the right hand of the Father's throne. Our King and our God had come home! Words cannot describe the joy in our hearts. I couldn't help but wonder what the celebration would be like when Jesus would return with all those from earth who love Him as we do.

December 31   *Mark 16:20; Luke 24:52, 53;*
John 20:30, 31; John 21:24, 25

The Work Begins

After Jesus' ascension we returned to Jerusalem filled with assurance and joy. We spent our days in the temple worshipping Him and sharing the good news of salvation with all who would listen. We preached and taught the good news of Jesus everywhere, beginning in Jerusalem, Judea, and Samaria. The priests warned us to stop, but we could not. They sent temple guards to arrest us. They beat us and threw us in jail, but we told them it is better to obey God than men.

We didn't always understand God's ways, for James was beheaded by Herod while Peter was rescued from prison by an angel. But we trusted in His providence, for He promised to always be with us. One day in response to Peter's preaching three thousand people became followers of Jesus and were baptized. This meant more arrests and more suffering, but we counted it a privilege to suffer for our Lord. Some of us stayed in the region and preached the good news. Others traveled to distant places. Paul and Barnabus along with Silas, Timothy, and John Mark traveled to the cities of the Gentiles, telling the story of Jesus to all who would listen.

The new church grew rapidly, and people started calling us Christians. Persecution came to those in Asia and Rome. Many were killed in the Coliseum, torn apart by wild animals. The Jews had Paul arrested and sent to Rome for trial by the emperor. He was condemned and beheaded. Peter was crucified upside down because he felt unworthy to be put to death in the same way Jesus died.

I was arrested and thrown in a vat of boiling oil. God preserved my life and caused a great fear to fall on the hearts of those who wanted me dead. They finally banished me to an island called Patmos. Here I have received visions of wonderful things, terrible things. I have written a gospel and some letters to churches in Asia. If all the things Jesus had done were written down, there would not be a book large enough to contain them all. We thought He would return in our lifetime, but we know that He will come and every eye will see Him. He will call those of us who sleep out of our graves to be reunited with Him. And everyone who accepts Him as their Savior will live forever with Him. Even so, come Lord Jesus!

We invite you to view the complete
selection of titles we publish at:

www.TEACHServices.com

Scan with your mobile
device to go directly
to our website.

Please write or email us your praises, reactions, or
thoughts about this or any other book we publish at:

P.O. Box 954
Ringgold, GA 30736

info@TEACHServices.com

TEACH Services, Inc., titles may be purchased in bulk for
educational, business, fund-raising, or sales promotional use.
For information, please e-mail:

BulkSales@TEACHServices.com

Finally, if you are interested in seeing
your own book in print, please contact us at

publishing@TEACHServices.com

We would be happy to review your manuscript for free.

www.ingramcontent.com/pod-product-compliance
Lightning Source LLC
Chambersburg PA
CBHW082113230426
43671CB00015B/2682